Igba Boyi

A Study of the Igbo Apprenticeship
Scheme in Onitsha Markets

Adonis & Abbey Publishers Ltd

Office: United Kingdom:

24 Old Queen Street,
London SW1H 9HP
Tel: 0845 873 0262

Office: Nigeria:

Plot 2560, Hassan Musa Katsina Street, Asokoro, Abuja, Nigeria
Tel: 234 7058078841, 234 8052213212
www.adonis-abbey.com
E-mail: info@adonis-abbey.com

British Library Cataloguing-in-Publication Data
A catalogue record for this book is available from the British Library

ISBN: 9781913976194

Igba Boyi
A Study of the Igbo Apprenticeship Scheme in Onitsha Markets

Nkemdili Au. Nnonyelu
Ezimma K. Nnabuife
Chinedu Onyeizugbe
Rosemary Anazodo
Blessing Onyima

ADONIS & ABBEY
PUBLISHERS LTD

Table of Contents

List of Tables

List of Figures

Acknowledgement

I t is with a profound sense of responsibility and affection that we express our immeasurable gratitude to Dr. Obiora Okonkwo, Chairman and Founder, Pro-Value Humanity Foundation, and the Board of Trustees, for sponsoring this study on *Igba Boyi*: A Study of the Igbo Apprenticeship Scheme in Onitsha Markets.

There is no doubt that Dr. Obiora Okonkwo is very passionate about rekindling the spirit of Igbo enterprise and getting our youths off the street.

We are equally grateful to the Vice-Chancellor, Nnamdi Azikiwe University, Prof. Charles Okechukwu Esimone, FAS, whose invaluable support was quite apposite to the completion of this project. The new Director, UNIZIK Business School, Prof. Emma Okoye has given the research team very huge support. We thank you.

We need to place on record the exceptional assistance received from the market leaders, current and past presidents of Anambra State Markets Amalgamated Traders Association (ASMATA), Onitsha Market Amalgamated Traders Association (OMATA), and their executive members. The leadership of the Onitsha Chamber of Commerce supported the study a great deal and also participated in the in-depth interviews and focus group discussions as critical stakeholders.

They were all present during the flag off of the study and contributed in no small measure to the success of the study. The fact that we had seamless, unhindered execution of the study for several months is an eloquent testimony to their uncommon support.

Our thanks also go to Pastor Chioma Okeke, who served as the Secretary of the Research Team, and Adoniram Muvukor, ICT Officer of the Emeka Anyaoku Institute for International Studies and Diplomacy, who worked tirelessly throughout the research.

We note with gratitude the contributions of different resource persons, Prof. Uzoma Okoye, Dr. Okey Anazonwu, Ogochukwu Onyima, and the fifty research Assistants.

They were simply diligent and wonderful.

About the Authors

Principal Investigator

Prof. Nkemdili Au. Nnonyelu (au.nnonyelu@unizik.edu.ng/aunnonyelu @yahoo.co.uk) is a Professor of Industrial Relations in the Department of Sociology, Nnamdi Azikiwe University, Awka. He holds a B.Sc Sociology, M.Sc Industrial Sociology, and Ph.D. Industrial Relations in the Department of Sociology/Anthropology, University of Nigeria, Nsukka. He is a widely published, and widely travelled scholar. He has been at various times, Head of Department of Sociology, Dean of the Faculty of Social Sciences, Director, Continuing Education Programme, Director, UNIZIK Business School, and is currently Director, Emeka Anyaoku Institute for International Studies and Diplomacy. He was a former member of the Governing Council of Nnamdi Azikiwe University for two terms.

Outside the University, he has served as Chairman, Anambra State Housing Development Corporation, Special Adviser to the Governor on Ecology and Environment, Transition Chairman, Awka South Local Government Area, and Honourable Commissioner for Education in 2003. He is currently the National President of the Nigerian Anthropological and Sociological Practitioners Association. He is a Fellow of the Nigerian Anthropological and Sociological Practitioners Association; Fellow Chartered Institute of Management Consultants, and a member of the British Sociological Association (BSA), American Sociological Association (ASA), and Association of Black Sociologists in America. Prof. Nkemdili Au. Nnonyelu is a Papal Knight of the Order of St. Sylvester, and 1st Vice Grand President, Awka Grand Commandery of the Knights of St. John International. He is happily married to Nkiru Nnonyelu and the marriage is blessed with children.

Co-Principal Investigators

Prof. Ezimma Nnabuife (ke.nnabuife@unizik.edu.ng /ezimmannabuife @gmail.com) is a Professor of Management. She holds a Ph.D. and MBA degrees in Management and BA in Hotel and Restaurant Management from Washington State University, Pullman, USA. She has published most of her works in the area of industrial democracy, organizational behaviour, and different areas of entrepreneurship in journals, books, and book chapters. Prof EzimmaNnabuife is a Fellow, Nigerian Institute of Management Sciences, Fellow, Institute of Strategic Management and Member, Nigerian Academy of Management. She has served as Head, Department of Business Administration, Dean, Faculty of Management Sciences, and External Examiner to many universities. She has supervised many Post Graduate works and has served as Director of different Units within the University. She is a current member of the University Governing Council. She has also served as both member and Chairman of different Accreditation teams. She has won both academic honours and prizes for exceptional performance. Outside UNIZIK, Awka, Prof Ezimma Nnabuife has served in different capacities like pioneer Vice-Chancellor, University of Akpajo, Akpajo, a private University in Rivers State, and Member, Governing Council of Chukwuemeka Odumegwu Ojukwu University (COOU), Igbariam (2015-2021). Prof. Nnabuife is a Third Degree Knight of St. Mulumba and the current Deputy National Representative (DNR) of Inner Wheel Nigeria. She was happily married to Prof. E. L. C. Nnabuife of blessed memory and the marriage is blessed with children.

Dr. Chinedu Uzochukwu Onyeizugbe (cu.onyeizugbe@unizik.edu.n g /edu_phd@yahoo.com) is a Reader in the Department of Business Administration, Nnamdi Azikiwe University, Awka, Anambra State, Nigeria. He holds a Ph.D. degree in Business Management and his area of interest is in General Management/Production and Operations Management.Dr. Chinedu has authored and co-authored books and published many articles in reputable national and international journals. He is officially recognised as one of the Top 100 Scholars at Nnamdi Azikiwe University. He is a full member of, Nigerian Institute of Management, British Academy of Management, Academy of Management Nigeria, and Fellow, Institute of Management Consultants. He is also a Knight of St. Christopher (KSC) is married to Margret Onyeizugbe and the marriage is blessed with five children.

Dr. Rosemary Anazodo (ro.anazodo@unizik.edu.ng / rosyzodos6 4@yahoo.com)is a Senior Lecturer in the Department of Public Administration, Nnamdi Azikiwe University, Awka. She graduated from the University of Nigeria, Nsukka, and Nnamdi Azikiwe University, Awka respectively. Dr. Anazodo is a Fellow at, Nigeria Institute of Public Administration; Fellow Nigerian Institute of Human Resources Management; Member Nigerian Institute of Management, and Co-editor Arabian Journals. She has published most of her works in many reputable international journals in the areas of Human Resources Management, Project Management, and Civil Service. She served as acting Head of the Department of Public Administration in 2015. Dr. Anazodo currently serves as a Senior Special Assistant to Anambra State Governor on Industry, Trade and Commerce, and Secretary-General, Anambra State Markets Amalgamated Traders Association (ASMATA).

She is a Lady Knight of St. John International. She is happily married to Sir Franklin Anazodo and the marriage is blessed with children.

Dr. Blessing Nonye Onyima (bn.onyima@unizik.edu.ng /nonyelin20 03@yahoo.com) is an Anthropologist in the Department of Sociology/Anthropology at Nnamdi Azikiwe University, Awka since 2012. She holds a Ph.D., MA in Medical Anthropology, and BA in Cultural Anthropology all from the University of Ibadan, Ibadan, Nigeria. Her published journal articles and book chapters are focused on ethnographies with themes on '*culture, health, gender, environment and conflict studies.*' She is a Fellow of the African Humanities Program (AHP/ACLS); laureate of American Political Science Association (APSA) Workshop Grant 2013; Association of Commonwealth Universities (ACU) Early Career grant 2014, Tertiary Education Trust Fund (TETFUND) grant 2014; African Humanities Program research residency in Rhodes University South Africa, member of the American Anthropological Association (AAA), and currently a co-principal investigator in the International Science Council sponsored grant for the Leading Integrated Research Agenda for Africa (LIRA, 2030).She is happily married to Mr. Chukwuma Okoli.

Executive Summary

Introduction and Background

The entrepreneurial dexterity and ingenuity embedded in the cultural ethos of the Igbo which has produced many successful Igbo entrepreneurs started receiving research attention most recently. The Igbo who have been described as naturally industrious and enterprising have survived through difficult terrains of very challenging economic situations. An instance being the leveling treatment meted on the Igbo after the Nigerian-Biafran Civil war of 1967-1970 when twenty pounds was given to every Igbo irrespective of the amount held in a bank account ab initio. The treatment which ordinarily, would have resulted to melancholy and resignation, after all the Igbo was just coming out of a war that decimated over three million children, women and men as soldiers, rather, ignited the spirit for which Igbo have always been known – the spirit of hard work, adventure, resilience among others. To the Igbo, *"mberede ka eji ama dike", "ntiadighiezuike ma iheonataagwughi".*

Entrepreneurship, which invokes words and phrases like creativity, change, innovation, investment of resources, risk taking, wealth creation has been the watch word for the Igbo and truly explains the nature and character of *Ndi Igbo*. They are found in all parts of Nigeria and the world at large, doing what they know best; harnessing everything entrepreneurially, making profit and creating wealth for themselves and their immediate environment, host community as well as growing the economy.

Behind the success so far recorded in the Igbo entrepreneurial venture is *Igba Boyi* which has been described as the largest business incubator model in the world. The *Igba Boyi* scheme is as old as the Igbo race itself continually nurturing the spirit of hard work and service of *"onye fee eze, ezeeruoya"*. Igba Boyi is believed by the Igbo as the way to prepare the ones to take over the successful Igbo entrepreneurism. *Igba Boyi*, an apprenticeship method aligned to the Igbo, involves some type of informal vocational education of mentoring a younger one, the mentee, under the tutelage of the *Oga*, the master and the mentor, over a specified period of time, to learn the skills and secrets of a trade or a craft, with the hope of graduating one day to start his own business venture.

Ndi Oga who first went back to their business domains and witnessed the wonton destruction and ruins stayed back in the same spirit of resilience to rebuild from the devastation. They soon came back to the villages, sought for and took *Umu Boyi*, who were mostly kin-related in the spirit of *"akulue uno"*, to help them in their already thriving businesses. The *Umu Boyi*, were soon freed after obediently, diligently and honestly serving *Ndi Oga*, who have ended up replicating themselves, pro-genetically, in them, to start their own business. This practice became regenerative and has continued to form the bases for the success behind the Igbo entrepreneurial venture.

Most recently however, it was noticed that due to greed, quest for materialism, dishonesty, lack of patience to learn, the effect of social media, get rich quick syndrome (*ego mbute; igbuozu; ibutike*) all pointing to the loss of value, and what may be regarded as stigma associated with *Igba Boyi* as servitude among other reasons, the need has arisen to interrogate and investigate the existing *Igba Boyi* model with a view to recommending a better model that will re-ignite the spirit of service, hard work and resilience devoid of the feeling of exploitation which is part of the reason many young persons now shun the *Igba Boyi* scheme. This was done under the topic; Re-Invigorating Igbo Entrepreneurial Behaviour Through Enhanced Apprenticeship Scheme: A Study of Onitsha Markets, Anambra State, Nigeria. Altogether, twelve objectives, research questions and hypotheses guided the study.

Concepts and Methods

The concepts of Igbo entrepreneurship, and the *Igba Boyi* scheme of apprenticeship dominate this research space. Entrepreneurship which has been generally seen as a process that involves creativity and innovation through risk taking with the aim of making profit that leads to wealth creation and its antecedents, is not different from Igbo entrepreneurship. However, the Igbo have been seen for decades as naturally entrepreneurial through their uncommon display of hard work, resilience, adventure, among other attributes, and this predates European colonialism in Africa. Such entrepreneurial prowess of Igbo entrepreneurship has to a large extent, and over years, been contributing to the general wellbeing of the Igbo through wealth creation and employment in Nigeria and Africa. It has however, been established that *Igba Boyi*, a unique apprenticeship prototype peculiar to the Igbo has been the secret of the successes recorded over time in Igbo entrepreneurship and this has been established by numerous scientific researches. The *Igba Boyi* apprenticeship scheme has been in the decline for which reason and others this research was undertaken.

A concurrent mixed method of triangulation involving both qualitative and quantitative modes was adopted in the study. Systematic purposive sampling and snowball techniques were used to select study sites and participants with In-depth Interviews (IDI), Key Informant Interviews (KII) and Focus Group Discussions (FGD) employed as the major qualitative tools. Altogether 35 *Ndi Oga, Ndi Madam* and *Umu Boyi* aged between 30 and 72 were engaged in the In-depth Interview. Key informants/Stakeholders Interviews (KII) were conducted with 18 identified key personalities that have held various top positions in the Onitsha Markets, with their consent and preferred venues. They include experienced retired traders, owners of industries (both defunct and functional), and business owners *Ndi Oga* (masters), and market union leaders. Focused Group Interview (FGI) was conducted with 68 males and 12 females selected form all the markets at their various locations.

For the qualitative method, the study adopted a survey research design and judgmental sampling was used to select five (5) markets in the Onitsha metropolis in the order of time of the creation of the markets from four Local Government Areas. The markets covered were, Main Market, Ochanja Market, Bridge Head Market, Spare Parts Market, Nkpor and Building Materials Markets, Ogidi/Ogbunike. A research team comprising of the Principal Investigator (PI) and the Co-Principal Investigators (Co-PIs), research assistants, and interviewers for data collection visited all the markets.

The sample size determined for the study applying the Fisher (1998) formular, was 2,401 split into 1201 for *Ndi Oga* and *Ndi Madam* and 1200 for *Umu Boyi*, purposively. Two sets of questionnaire were designed, one for *Ndi Oga*/*Ndi Madam* and the other for *Umu Boyi* respectively.

Open Data Kit (ODK) soft copies of questionnaire were distributed through 50 Research Assistants pre-trained on the use of ODK application/software who constantly searched for the GIS coordinates before submitting collected data online. Two sets of questionnaire were designed and used for "*Ndi Oga*" (Masters) "*Umu Boyi*" (Apprentices). Systematic sampling and Cluster sampling were used in the distribution of the copies of questionnaire. The field research of data collection lasted for three months.

For the analysis of data, quantitative methods of descriptive and inferential statistics were adopted. Specifically, Chi Square, Pearson Product Moment Correlation, and Analysis of Variance (ANOVA) were employed in testing the twelve hypotheses formulated for the study. Thematic method of analysis was employed for the qualitative data.

Results

Out of the twelve null hypotheses formulated for the study, only three were rejected and nine accepted. The study hypotheses results reveal that

- Socio-cultural characteristics generally relate to entrepreneurial success;
- *Ndi Oga* who served as *Umu Boyi* are more likely to succeed than *Ndi Oga* who did not go through the apprenticeship scheme;

- The type of business *Ọga* is dealing in and the length of stay of the *Nwa Boyi* are positively related;
- *Ndi Ọga* with higher levels of education are more likely to achieve business success than those with lower levels of education;
- Older apprentices are not more likely to be in a non-kin-related apprenticeship than younger apprentices;
- Younger *Ndi Oga* are not more likely to hire female apprentices than older *Ndi Oga.*
- Availability of adult education contributes to entrepreneurship and apprenticeship skills development among traders in Onitsha Market;
- There is relationship between *Igba Boyi*, Employment and Wealth Creation
- There is a relationship between the acquisition of basic skills and values by *Umu Boyi* and entrepreneurial success;
- The emergence of sales girls will not likely displace the *Igba Boyi* scheme among *Ndị Igbo* in Onitsha markets;
- There is a relationship between the decline in *Igba Boyi* among Igbo youths and loss of family values and
- The government does not interfere in the relationship between *Ndi Ọga* and *Umu Boyi.*

Conclusion and Recommendations

There is definitely obvious decline in *Igba Boyi* scheme of *Ndị Igbo* majorly due to the drastic fall in Igbo cultural values that have ab initio, formed the bedrock for child rearing in Igbo families and this and other issues associated with the scheme like increased quest for materialism, get rich quick syndrome, lack of patience to learn requisite skills, influence of social media, partly, the derogatory way *Igba Boyi* is regarded among others, have caused the observed shift in narrative. There is therefore need to reinvigorate the Igbo entrepreneurship through these measures:

- The *Igba Boyi* scheme should be reconfigured and known as "*Nkwado Ogaranya*" by institutionalizing it through teaching in institutions of higher learning and enculturation in communities, families, churches, seminars among other methods for the younger generation to realize that it is their future, that is being prepared for sustainable empowerment and development.

- By training the younger generation on the concept of "*Apprentice-preneurship*" which is a form of mutual business relationship where the *Oga*, the mentor and trainer gains from the apprentice,
- "*Nwanaakwadoibaogaranya*" through the various assistance rendered to the *Oga* and his family and, the apprentice in turn gains from the *Oga* by learning the necessary skills and secrets of a trade or craft. By so doing *Igba Boyi* will no more be regarded as servitude or slavery but the period of service needed for the preparation of the *Nwa Boyi* for creation of wealth and greatness.
- The Igbo Entrepreneurial Incubation Scheme (IEIS) which is explained by the two former concepts; *Nkwado Ogaranya* and *Apprenticepreneurship*, should be seen as a special incubation period of preparation when the necessary sacrifice and discipline must be made to prepare the younger apprentice for future greatness and this is amply buttressed by the "no pain no gain" cliché.
- Families need to revert to the ancient ways of raising children and those were the times when honesty, diligence, discipline, hard work among others, were seriously considered as basics.

The above two areas are where the family institution, communities and higher institutions are required to play serious roles in the required paradigm shift arising from the study.

Policy Issues

The government that is responsible for policy formulation and implementation is expected to get involved in moderating the relationship between *Ndi Oga* and *Umu Boyi* in a tripartite form that will be made up of the family, the community and the government. Policies should be formulated in the following areas:

- Government's involvement is recommended in formulating the guidelines for regulating and implementing a more formal agreement whose terms can be enforced.
- The government also needs to assist in the provision of the seed capital for start-ups in the form of grants and soft loans as the case may be.
- It is also the prerogative of the government to provide an enabling and peaceful environment devoid of insecurity as well as provide necessary infrastructural facilities for businesses to thrive.

- Provision of Adult Education facilities especially near the markets will help both *Umu Boyi* and *Ndi Oga* to further their knowledge in relevant issues concerning their trade or crafts.
- Creation of a Ministry of Apprenticepreneurship in all the five Eastern states in Nigeria.

Section One

Introduction

Section One

Introduction

1.1 Introduction

Igbo apprenticeship that, over time, has become emblematic as the fountain of the legendary Igbo entrepreneurship is recently receiving some attention in the literature (Adeola, 2021; Ekesịobi & Dimnwobi, 2021; Nnonyelu & Onyeizugbe, 2020; Agu & Nwachukwu, 2020; Iwara, 2020; Igwe, Newberry, Amoncar, White & Madichie, 2018; Madichie, Nkamnebe & Idemobi, 2010). Hitherto, studies on global entrepreneurship have concentrated on the exploits of western entrepreneurs. These studies were given theoretical traction and impetus by the work of McLelland (1962) who enthused about the intersection between western cultural values and possession of high need for achievement (n-arch) as the explanatory variable responsible for the growth, development, and entrepreneurship in western societies.

Such a mindset conceals the unique features of African entrepreneurial behaviour that requires more penetrating insights and studies. This current study seeks to change the thrust of the conversation by focusing on a comprehensive and expansive study of the Igbo Apprenticeship model, popularly known as *Igba Boyi*. The *Igba Boyi* model, although largely neglected, was correctly described by (Neurwith, 2017, as cited in Adeola, 2021) as the largest business incubator in the world. For the outstanding dexterity of the Igbo in business, commerce, and innovation, some refer to them as the Jews of Africa, while others call them the Chinese or Japanese of Africa (Adeola, 2021).

Indeed, there is no part of Nigeria, or even Africa, that you visit without being confronted by the visible signs of Igbo businesses (Mbaegbu & Ekianabor, 2018; Olakunle, Iseolorunkanmi & Segun, 2016). In an incisive presentation, Adeola (2021) observes that the Igbo entrepreneurial orientation distinguishes them from other ethnic groups in Nigeria given the uncommon attributes and qualities that they bring to business transactions. This led Kate Meagher (2009) to see the Igbo as naturally enterprising and industrious, evident in their commercial prowess across the country. The Igbo are not only adventurous, but also have an uncanny ability to adapt to changing environments, and this is critical to Igbo entrepreneurial behaviour.

Epistemologically, the concept of entrepreneurship evolved from the word entrepreneur which refers to one who organizes, manages, and assumes the risk of a business or enterprise (Merriam-Webster, 2021). Nwachukwu (1990) identifies an entrepreneur as one with the ability to form a business, nurture it to fruition and profitability. Entrepreneurship arises from and is sustained by a society's social and economic environment (Igwe et al, 2018; Ratten, 2014).

Nnonyelu & Onyeizugbe (2020) contend that entrepreneurship involves pathfinding or trailblazing, the ability to be innovative in creating resources that serve the society, while some other scholars present entrepreneurship as the process through which individuals embrace life-changing opportunities and challenges, through ingenious methods, satisfying needs in the process even amidst the attendant risks (Madichie, Gbadamosi & Rwelamila, 2021; Ndoro, Louw & Kangale, 2019).

Given the deluge of attention paid to western entrepreneurship (World Economic Forum, 2016) it is necessary as we have earlier indicated, to focus on African, particularly Igbo entrepreneurship. What are the major characteristics or features of Igbo entrepreneurial behaviour? What are its significant markers? How did it develop and what is the defining trajectory of Igbo entrepreneurial behaviour?

Igbo entrepreneurial behaviour has a long history that predates european colonialism of Africa. In the past, the Igbo were mainly agriculturists, fishermen, craftsmen, and traders who had many trading relationships outside Igboland (Afigbo, 1981; Isichei, 1977; Basden, 1966). With the abolition and end of the slave trade, most Igbo men and women became actively involved in the lucrative palm oil trade (Dike, 1956) which Iwara (2021) observed, led to the massive growth of the Igbo economy. It is important to remember that the eastern part of Nigeria, the geographical location of the Igbo, accounted for more than 70 percent of the global trade in palm oil during colonial rule and the early part of Nigerian independence, before the discovery of oil. During that period, the Igbo had traversed the length and breadth of the country plying their trade, and selling their wares, while facing like other ethnic groups, environmental and other socio-economic challenges of the new Nigerian State (Nnoli, 1978).

This hostile environment escalated soon after independence, and more tragically after the January, 15th 1966 coup. Oyewunmi, Oyewunmi & Moses (2021) rightly captured the collective ethnic feeling in this way;
The overriding insecurity of the Igbo was reflected in their sentiments that resources were asymmetrically distributed and indicative of being denied their just proportion in the arrangement. These circumstances, deliberate or otherwise, had the overarching effect of justifying the agitation to separate from Nigeria and marked the beginning of the conflict of ideologies, struggle for identity, and the cutthroat battle for power and resource control. A cocktail of these conflicts and struggles culminated in the Nigerian Civil War of 1967 – 1970 (p.16).

The combined effects of the war of almost three years left Old Eastern Nigeria, and some parts of the Mid-Western Region with substantial Igbo presence completely devastated and in ruins. At the end of physical hostilities in 1970, villagers could hardly recognize their homesteads. In almost all Igbo communities, there were no habitable structures as all had been razed to the ground (Anueyiagu, 2020). Entire livelihoods were destroyed, teenagers as young as thirteen were conscripted into the battlefront in defense of their motherland (Anueyiagu, 2020). The Nigerian Federal Government in apparent abandonment of its post-war policy of Reconciliation, Rehabilitation, and Reconstruction, declared that all Igbo (those who had money in their bank accounts) shall only be entitled to 20 pounds. As insufferable as this was, the Igbo leveraged on their communal cultural ethos of "Igwebuike" (Kanu, 2020; Kanụ, 2019) (strength in unity) and "*Ọnye aghana nwanne ya*" (be your brother's keeper) to respond to this starvation strategy. It is this cultural attribute that is implicated in the activation of Igbo entrepreneurship that was witnessed at the end of the Civil War in 1970.

The Igbo, faced with hostile governmental policy, leveraged communal solidarity, and cohesion, the sense of brotherhood and oneness to assist each other. As necessity is the mother of invention, rather than continue to bemoan their individual and collective fate and misery, the Igbo rose like one man, carrying their destiny in their hands. In no time, they started getting back to their pre-war cities and villages outside Igboland where they had domiciled, while many moved back to big Igbo commercial cities like Onitsha and Aba (also in total ruins). The Igbo unarguably became Nigeria's most mobile ethnic group (Madichie et al, 2018; Kilani & Iheanacho, 2016). The people's ingenuity came to the fore through the traditional apprenticeship system which had given many Igbo people a head start in business before the war. There was a major occupational shift where commercial activities, typically referred to as buying and selling in Nigeria, became a center of interest among many Igbo. In a short time, communities that were in total damnation started having a cohort of new millionaires, in their hundreds and thousands.

The events and aftermath of the Nigerian Civil War reinforce the belief among scholars that Igbo ecological resilience is high (Igwe & Ochinanwata, 2021) as it would have been infeasible to survive, let alone achieve tremendous business success. The transformation witnessed in Onitsha, the destroyed Igbo commercial nerve center was phenomenal. A city that was in ruins in 1970, almost leveled to the ground had become a bustling city with the ubiquitous presence of shops all over. Onitsha, rightly seen by Madichie & Nkamnebe (2010) as a "melting pot of an entrepreneurial enclave" immediately started playing host to millions of traders from across Nigeria and Sub-Saharan Africa.

With the largest market in West Africa, Onitsha is easily the epitome of Igbo entrepreneurship, a rendezvous for commerce, a conclave of Igbo business cognoscenti, the hub of Igbo apprenticeship. It was and still is, the training ground for several Igbo entrepreneurs. These progenitors of the Igbo entrepreneurial spirit and mindset inadvertently became the ambassadors of the Apprenticeship scheme in Igboland. It is not surprising, therefore, that Adeola (2021, p.6) argued that the "success of the Post-war Igbo enterprise development was not premised on the availability of capital, or funds, as that was non-existent, but on the visible Igbo spirit of enterprise". The successes recorded over the years seen in the number of businesses and even many large organizations owned by the Igbo may be the reason for the recent disquisition (Ekesịobi & Dimnwobi, 2021; Igwe et al, 2020; Iwara, 2020).

Sixty years after the Nigerian Civil War, the hostility of the environment has not abated but may have changed complexion, unraveling new dynamics. Cries of marginalization, inequality and social injustice pervade the air, Youth unemployment skyrockets, deepening poverty, and rising crime wave and general insecurity. The socio-economic environment in Nigeria is still fraught, a medley of challenges including but not limited to cost of doing business, dilapidated infrastructure, epileptic power supply, terrible roads, constant harassment of informal sector traders left at the mercy of government, sometimes phony officials at the grassroots level and policy inconsistency (Nnonyelu, 2018). It is within this context that Igbo entrepreneurship is located. Indeed, "putting entrepreneurship in the context of its historiography and socio-economic environment helps us understand how situational factors inform both the nature and characteristic of entrepreneurial activities and behaviour" (Igwe, Madichie & Amoncar, 2020, p.166).

A major plank of Igbo entrepreneurship is its embeddedness in the cultural matrix of the people. Igwe et al (2020) in their study sought to explore Igbo ethnic entrepreneurship from three main lenses namely cultural and Family factors, influencing Igbo business enterprise; the process of Transgenerational family business transfer; and how intrageneric succession and conflicts are managed (p.172). It is safe to canvas that the Igbo apprenticeship model resonates largely due to its contiguity with the cultural milieu that embodies it (Iwara, 2021; Adeola, 2021; Iwara, Amaechi & Netshandama, 2019). Therefore, the distinct character or traits of communities are implicated in the entrepreneurial behaviour of ethnic groups (Igwe, Madichie & Amoncar, 2020). It must however be noted, that the cultural domain is not a static, immovable ensemble, but undergoes changes, and these have a profound impact on the nature of social relationships, including the apprenticeship institution.

The International Labour Organisation (ILO) defines apprenticeship as a systematic long-term training taking place substantially within an undertaking or under an independent craftsman, governed by a written contract of apprenticeship and subject to established standards. However, the definition given by ILO does not take into consideration the pervasive informality that exists here in the practice of *Igba Boyi* in Igboland. Singleton (1989, p.6) somehow mirrors Igbo apprenticeship when he notes that "apprenticeship takes place in situations where a novice learns from someone more expert".

Amongst the Igbo an Apprentice is seen in different guises. On the one hand are those that are described as *Umu Boyi* – who are young persons, usually from early teenage years to young adulthood (12 – 30 years), who have been engaged by an older person (**Ọga**) who possesses specialized knowledge, to undergo training for a specific number of years (3 – 10 years), after which the new graduand is free from the restrictions of the apprenticeship, and is helped financially to set up his own business. The ***Ọga*** (master) plays dual roles in the context of Igbo apprenticeship (*ịgba bọyị*). He stands in loco-parentis, coach, teacher, and mentor. Nnonyelu et al (2020) therefore argue that the process of *igba boyi* may commence and be consummated verbally through oral Symbolic gestures supported by traditional and cultural ethos, not strictly through written agreements or legal contracts (Olulu & Udeorah, 2018).

Olulu & Udeorah (2020) observe that the Nigerian Labour Act expects the apprentice to be of the right age, and not forced into accepting conditions of apprenticeship. This stands in contradistinction to what obtains at the customary milieu that is largely unregulated and left to the whims and caprices of the master **(Ọga)**. There is no doubt that the current Nigerian Labour Law is somewhat vacuous, alienated from the cultural orientation of the people. This explains the sharp criticism the law elicited from Amucheazi & Orji (2009). This is supported by Oregun & Nafiu (2014) who see apprenticeship as a usually informal and unstructured training program. *Nwa Bọyị* also goes with co-residency, living in the household of the *Ọga* and performing all manner of domestic and household chores. Performing these tasks, which is the defining feature of *Igba Bọyị* is not only obligatory for the *Nwa Bọyị*, but inseparable. This, he does daily before proceeding to the market, or workshop to learn the trade, or new skill.

There are, on the other hand, still within the domain of apprenticeship, those who pay to learn a trade (*Ịmụ Ahịa*), under the tutelage of a master, who usually do not live with the masters **(Ọga),** far removed from the menial domestic tasks, and enjoy shorter period of training. It is therefore incorrect to lump them together (*Igba Bọyị* and *Ịmụ Ahịa*) or to use them interchangeably as Oyewunmi et al (2021) have done. This may obfuscate the clear distinctive features that separate them. This study unpacks the different types and features of *Igba Bọyị* in Igbo land. *Ọdịbọ* stands on its own, conveys and embodies the attributes of servility, and usually does not have rights as *Nwa Bọyị*, or *ọnye na amụ ahịa* (one who pays to learn a trade). On the whole, however, the "*Igba Bọyị* model is of great significance to the Igbo as it serves as a source of seamless creation of Entrepreneurs and Enterprises, and provision of much-needed capital for startups" (Nkamnebe & Ezemba, 2021, p.30). It is important to ascertain the cost of settlement, or freeing *Nwa Bọyị* from the apprenticeship, as this study would reveal.

Lancy (2012) captured the duality of apprenticeship when he observed that: It is a formal contractual relationship between a master and a novice for a specific duration which is designed to serve two ends: to provide cheap labour by the apprentice and fees to support the master's enterprise, and to allow the apprentice to learn and receive certification from the master (p.113 – 114).

The master who is not only a repertoire of knowledge and wielder of authority accepts the aspirant learner (trader, craftsperson) into his abode for training and learning (Lancy, 2012). With time these novices are transformed into experts in various fields (Dennen, 2004). In this way, entrepreneurial traits like effective negotiation, risk-taking, saving culture, thrift, concept innovation, and investment strategies are learned (Adeola, 2021).

Learning of requisite skills is central to apprenticeship. How is this learning conducted? It will be interesting to look at issues of pedagogy that may affect the training or duration of the programme. The centrality of apprenticeship in the lives of generations of Igbo entrepreneurs, the importance of what is learned, and how it is delivered have persuaded Adeola (2021), Agu & Nwachukwu (2020), and Iwara (2020) to aptly dub Igbo apprenticeship as the "Igbo Traditional Business School", while some others refer to it as Igbo University or alternative education.

Several writers have demonstrated this unique feature of *Igba Boyi* in presenting the intersection between apprenticeship and business success (Obunike, 2016; Udu, 2015; Onyima, Nzewi & Chiekezie, 2013; Oyewunmi, Oyewunmi & Moses, 2021; Igwe et al, 2018). Onyima, Nzewi & Chiekezie (2013) point to the flourishing Igbo businesses in Taraba and other northern states of Nigeria as evidence of the success of the *Igba Boyi* model. Meagher (2009, p.33) also pointed to the legendary success of Igbo trading and manufacturing networks since the Civil War, which emanated from the cooperative relations across ethnic cleavages rather than ethnic exclusivity. This, however, raises some issues around Igbo Entrepreneurship, and these include the sense of Igbo exclusivity in their business, where, even amongst the Igbo in certain trades, some local communities have a comparative advantage, seeing that line of trade as their exclusive preserve, and working strenuously to keep the secrets of their Trade, even away from other Igbo communities. This study unravelled the trading roots, and trajectory of specific trades amongst Igbo traders.

As penetrating and widespread as apprenticeship had been in Igboland, it is not a juicy endeavour or activity for as Lancy (2012) has so incisively titled his paper, "First You Must Master Pain: The Nature and Purpose of Apprenticeship", it seemed as if he was referring directly to Igbo apprenticeship, for the terrain of *Igba Boyi* is symbolic in many respects. Yes, it goes with tremendous pain and perseverance. It operates without prejudice to the existential danger of bringing someone in the same profession (same trade) who is likely to emerge as a potential competitor. In the *Igba Boyi* model, there seems to be no consideration of self-destruction or elite group interest, but a mixture of charity and utilitarian motives. It also derives momentum from the social exchange, where even the young lad is expected to provide some service in return for the acquisition of relevant knowledge and settlement. Therefore, the *Igba Boyi* apprenticeship resonates well with the Social Exchange Theory

(Nnonyelu, 2009; Eke, 1970; Blau, 1964) where the exchange is not limited to material transactions in the marketplace alone, but involves the exchange of goods, services, and sentiments of various kind. The principle of reciprocity which is at the heart of social exchange is the foundation on which the *Igba boyi* model has stood.

In a sense, there is this umbilical cord that ties the Igbo entrepreneur to his/her home community, or even the extended community of in-laws. This explains the periodic return by successful traders to their home communities to get into their business circuits (networks) new apprentices. This has become a measure of wealth, and a source of fame and popularity. Among *Ụmụ Boyi*, some have relationships (consanguineal or affinal) with the **Oga** and those that are not kin-related. Which one of these is in vogue and why? It needs to be investigated, whether kin- or non-kin-related *Nwa Boyi* has anything to do with the content of knowledge transmitted, duration of the training, certainty of settlement, and the amount (resources) expended in settling the new graduand from the *Igba boyi* school.

Is *Igba Boyi* the exclusive training for young males; as there seems to be a gender bias in the consideration of Igbo apprenticeship? In Igbo society, there has been a genderisation of social relationships where patriarchy is dominant. In Igboland, son preference has been the vogue, as the son is expected to preserve the family lineage, step into the shoes of his father, inherit the family land (if any) and be the custodian of family property. The sons are expected to go into an Apprenticeship (*Igba Boyi*) to make money for the family upkeep. Why is *Igba Boyi* male-dominated, and what are the possible explanations to the gendered demographics in the *Igba Boyi* model? Do we have a changing cohort of female *boyi* or more appropriately, *Igba Geli*? Why is *Igba Geli* a rarity? Girls take the roles of the house helps (housemaids). Housemaids have not transformed into market apprentices, or are they now the new category of sales girls that have become common features in the markets? It is, therefore, necessary to inquire if the sales girls are an emerging replacement of the *Nwa Boyi?* Is it safe to assume that sales girls in the Onitsha markets are likely to become substitutes for *Umu Boyi?* This needs empirical examination, and that forms part of the concern of the current study. There seems to be a growing concern about the declining attraction of *Igba Boyi* among the youth (Oyewunmi et al, 2021). *Igba Boyi* may not be as fashionable as it was in the past. Why? It is therefore the intention of this study to probe deeply into the state of apprenticeship in Igboland, particularly the acclaimed *Igba Boyi* model. Our thesis is that *Igba Boyi*, the significant marker of Igbo entrepreneurial behaviour and launching pad of Igbo ethnic entrepreneurship seems to be fading away, or losing its appeal. There seems to be a precipitous descent, or decline in the *Igba Boyi* apprenticeship model. The *Igba Boyi* Apprenticeship institution seems to be in a state of flux, if not of crisis. This evolving scenario demands serious empirical interrogation, as it is far removed from the dominant, mainstream valorisation and romanticism of *Igba Boyi* as presented by scholars like Adeola (2021), Agu et al (2020), Igwe et al (2018), and Madichie, Nkamnebe & Idemobi (2008).

Is it the changing Social values, or availability and accessibility of education that have combined to turn the youth away from *Igba Boyi*, escalating and swelling the ranks of the unemployed as is reported by the National Bureau of Statistics (NBS, 2020) where 42.5 percent of the Nigerian Youths are unemployed. Those who are supposed to be undergoing apprenticeship, or learning in colleges and universities are no longer there. In the past, social interaction was by and large, based on respect for, and adherence to the values of merit, excellence, objectivity, impartiality, fairness, equity, compassion, humaneness, and reward for productivity and hard work. Today merit and hard work have been unseated, no longer on the throne (Asobie, 2014, p.4)

Arising from these contradictions is the glorification and adoration of money, no matter how ill-gotten, where nondescript persons become role models only on the strength of the amount of money they have. The era of making money through legitimate means and hard work took a back seat as the attention of the youths shifted to other swift money-making ventures like internet/cybercrime (Yahooyahoo) and obtaining by false pretence (a.k.a 419) (Oyewunmi et al, 2021, p.21). This dislocation or disorientation of social values may have been responsible for the "involvement of youths in illegal businesses such as drug trafficking, illegal imports, manufacture, and imports of fake products as well as involvement in money laundering (Igwe et al, 2018, p.44). The general disorientation of values and underlying norms are a critical component of the impairment of cultural influences in the attitudinal dispositions or behavioural tendencies of groups and collectivities, and the dialectics of group transformation. Strong cultural institutions (Igwe & Ochinanwata, 2021) that would serve as a counterpoise to check the effects of these developments with perhaps unpalatable denouement are in themselves almost imperilled. Modernity and the force of globalisation may have challenged the nucleus of the Igbo family, the epicentre of *Igba Boyi*, rendering it incapable of playing its once traditional role(s) in the training of would-be entrepreneurs. Anggadwita, Ramadani & Ratten (2017) reinforced the above assumption when they enthused that socio-cultural systems in transitional societies incentivise latent qualities and features that could impact a person's general wellbeing, industrial potential or passion, perception, and idiosyncrasies. It is, therefore, apposite to investigate, and this study has chosen, the tripartite filial relationship between the Family, *Igba Boyi,* and Igbo entrepreneurship. This triadic linkage suggests that if the family is negated, not playing its usual traditional roles as the bulwark of Igbo enterprise, then its impact on the peoples' behavioural propensity, in this case, appetite or passion for apprenticeship may be affected, or derailed with possible impact on the spirit of enterprise (Agu et al, 2020; Udu, 2015; Kansikas, Laakkonen, Sarpo & Kontinen, 2012).

What is the role of the state in *Igba Boyi*? It seems that the state is absent, minimally involved in the relationship between *Nwa Boyi* and **Ọga**. In some other climes in Africa, and more in the developed societies, the state plays a central role in the apprenticeship scheme. Olulu & Udeorah (2018) report that in South Africa, the state is a party to the apprenticeship contract, playing a central role not only in the certification of qualified apprentices but in the entire apprenticeship scheme. Therefore, it became imperative that the current study extended its binoculars to unravelling the role of the state, or lack of it in the processes of the apprenticeship model.

It is therefore these gaps in the literature that the current study wants to fill by conducting an expansive and elaborate study of traders in Onitsha markets, covering Main Market, Ọchanja, Bridge Head, Building Materials, and Spare Parts markets located in four Local Government Areas of Anambra State. This study is undergirded by the following objectives, research questions, and hypotheses.

1.2 Objectives

1. To identify the socio-cultural characteristics that drive Igbo entrepreneurial success;
2. To examine the influence of participation in apprenticeship scheme on business success of Igbo traders in Onitsha markets;
3. To explore the relationship between the master's trade and the duration of the apprenticeship scheme among Igbo traders in Onitsha markets;
4. To investigate the extent to which level of education influences business success among Igbo traders in Onitsha markets;
5. To determine the likelihood that older apprentices are more involved in a non-kin related apprenticeship than younger ones;
6. To ascertain the level of preference for female apprentices by young *Ndi Ọga* in comparison to older *Ndi Ọga* among Igbo traders in Onitsha markets;
7. To examine the influence of adult education on entrepreneurship and apprenticeship skills development among traders in Onitsha markets;
8. To ascertain the extent to which *Igba Bọyị* influences employment and wealth creation among traders in Onitsha markets;
9. To explore the relationship between acquisition of basic skills and values by *Umu Boyi* and entrepreneurial success in Onitsha markets;
10. To ascertain the extent to which the emergence of sales girls is displacing the *Nwa Boyi* apprenticeship scheme in Onitsha markets;
11. To investigate the relationship between the decline in *Igba Bọyị* and loss of family values among Igbo youths;
12. To examine the level of interference by the Government in the relationship between *Ndị Ọga* and *umu bọyị*.

1.3 Research Questions

1. What are the socio-cultural characteristics that drive Igbo entrepreneurial success among traders in Onitsha markets?
2. To what extent does participation in apprenticeship schemes influence business success among Igbo traders in Onitsha markets?
3. What level of relationship exists between the type of business *Ndị Ọga* deal in and the duration of apprenticeship for *Ụmụ Bọyị in* Onitsha markets?
4. To what extent does the level of education influence the entrepreneurial success of Igbo traders in Onitsha markets?
5. What is the likelihood that older apprentices are more involved in non-kin-related apprenticeships than younger ones among traders in Onitsha markets?
6. What is the preference rate of female apprentices by younger *Ndị Ọga* to older ones among Igbo traders in Onitsha markets?
7. To what level does the adult education program enhance entrepreneurship and apprenticeship skills development among traders in Onitsha markets?
8. To what extent does *Igba Bọyị* influence employment and wealth creation among Igbo traders in Onitsha markets?
9. What is the relationship between the acquisition of basic skills and values by *Ụmụ Bọyị and* entrepreneurial success in Onitsha markets?
10. To what extent does the emergence of sales girls displace the *Nwa Boyi* apprenticeship scheme among *Ndị Igbo* in Onitsha markets?
11. What is the relationship between the decline in *Igba bọyị* and the loss of family values among Igbo youths?
12. To what degree does the government interfere in the relationship between *Ndị Ọga* and *Ụmụ Bọyị?*

1.4 Hypotheses

1. There is a relationship between Igbo socio-cultural characteristics and entrepreneurial success among Igbo traders in Onitsha Markets.
2. *Ndị Ọga* who participated in the *Nwa Bọyị* apprenticeship scheme are more likely to succeed in business than those who did not.
3. There is a relationship between the type of business *Ọga* deals in and the length of stay of *Nwa Boyi* among Igbo Traders in Onitsha Markets.
4. *Ndị Ọga* with a higher level of education are more likely to achieve business success than those with a lower level of education.
5. Older apprentices are more likely to be in a non-kin related apprenticeship than younger apprentices.

6. Younger *Ndi Oga* are more likely to hire female apprentices than older *Ndi Oga.*

7. Availability of adult education enhances entrepreneurship and Apprenticeship skills development among traders in Onitsha markets.

8. There is a relationship between *Igba Boyi*, employment and wealth creation among traders in Onitsha Markets.

9. There is a relationship between the acquisition of basic skills and values by *Umu Boyi* and entrepreneurial success.

10. The emergence of sales girls will likely displace the *Igba Boyi* scheme among *Ndi Igbo* in Onitsha Markets.

11. There is a relationship between the decline in *Igba Boyi* and loss of family values among Igbo youths.

12. Government does not interfere in the relationship between *Ndi Oga* and *Umu Boyi.*

1.5 Description of the Onitsha Markets: History, Population, Location, and Features

1.5.1 Historical Background of Onitsha

Onitsha is a port and market town in Anambra state. The town is located on the eastern bank of the River Niger just south of its confluence with the Anambra River (Tributary of the River Niger). The town was founded by Benin Adventurers in the early 17th century (Encyclopedia Britannica, 1999). It grew to become the political and trading nerve center of the Onitsha Kingdom. Its monarchical system of leadership is very prestigious and rare among other Igbo. It was patterned after the Benin Kingdom. The establishment of a British trading post in Onitsha was negotiated with William Balfour Baikie, a British trader by the then Obi of Onitsha (Amy Mckenna, 2019). Onitsha remains the chief entry port for goods coming upstream from the Niger River Delta and those being transported downstream from towns on the Benue River. Two major roads lead to the Town from Enugu and Owerri respectively. The River Niger Bridge was constructed in 1965 across the River Niger from Onitsha to Asaba. These provide Onitsha with a direct road link to Delta, Edo, Ondo, Ogun, and Lagos states. The length of the Bridge is about 1,404.2 meters (Encyclopedia Britannica, 1998). The most important local exports of Onitsha include yams, cassava, fish, rice, palm produce among others. The popular Roman Catholic cathedral which has been upgraded to a Basilica is located in Onitsha. It was built in 1935. The Anglican All Saints Cathedral built in 1952 is also located in Onitsha. Some of the oldest secondary schools in Anambra state are found in Onitsha Town e.g. Dennis Memorial Grammar School (DMGS) builtin 1925, St. Charles College built in 1928, Christ the King College (CKC) builtin 1933, and others are all located in Onitsha. According to Okechukwu

(2021), the Obi of Onitsha celebrates his *Ọfala* festival annually, where the *Agbalanze* group, *ndị ichie*, *Ọdụ*, other prestigious groups are always integral parts of the ceremony.

1.5.2 Origin and Development of Onitsha Markets

The Onitsha Market is as old as Onitsha town itself. It is said to have started in the 16th Century when the Onitsha indigenes settled at the bank of the River Niger. They settled with their Wooden Gong (a deity) under the Traditional leadership of Ezechima. The deity is known as *Anịọnịcha*. A shrine was built for the deity at *Ose Ọkwọdụ* Market, opposite the present-day Union Bank. According to the report given by (IDI, Male, 78 years), the worshippers usually gather on *Nkwo* days at the shrine or anytime there is a problem in Onitsha to worship the idol and ask for its intercession. Journey to the shrine is between 1 to 2 am. The traditional Onitsha people still worship the deity till today. They normally go through a route near the River Niger to the shrine, and they believe that the deity is responsible for the occasional Fire outbreaks in Onitsha markets whenever the traders commit atrocious acts. No trader is allowed to display his goods around the shrine because Onitsha indigenes have special reverence to the idol. The idol is said to 'give babies' and be very upright and does not condone any form of corrupt practice. In those days, business was by trade by barter, but as time went by, the use of cowry was introduced as a medium of exchange (Ibekwe, 2018).

In the early and mid-eighteenth century, *'ndịọcha Potokị'* (The Portuguese) arrived in Nigeria and navigated inland of the River Niger from the Atlantic Ocean. The first place they encountered human activity was at Onitsha. After the initial hostility by Onitsha indigenes to the foreigners, they were later accepted and both settled down for business. The foreigners brought Christianity, schools, and goods such as clothing, gun, gun powder, hot drinks, cigarettes among others, in exchange for slaves mainly who they exported to their countries to work in their factories and plantations in Europe. They also bought ivory and palm produce among other goods, from Onitsha (Mckenna, 2019).

Towards the end of the eighteenth century, the British came, intending to rule. They sacked the Portuguese and established the Lagos colony, Southern protectorate, and later moved to establish the Northern protectorate all of which they amalgamated in 1914 for easy administration in what we know today as Nigeria. Onitsha River port served the Northern protectorate because bigger vessels could not navigate beyond Onitsha. The British introduced the use of legal tender (money), firstly coins and later notes as a medium of exchange for goods and services (Encyclopedia Britannica, 1999). The Royal Niger Company was brought to Onitsha by the British colonial masters, and this brought modernization to Onitsha Market. Others include John Holt, Kingsway, SCOA,

Supermarkets, among others.

Many people trooped in from southern and northern Nigeria and some West African countries into Onitsha for one commercial activity or another. At this time, the environment became very busy and unconducive for the Obi of Onitsha which led to his relocation to an inland town (Enu-Onitsha) (Encyclopedia Britannica, 1999). Onitsha became very prominent for economic activities, and other countries soon had their interest registered for trade for example; France, Taiwan, Germany, Japan, Korea, Malaysia, and some other Asian tigers. They exported their manufactured goods into Onitsha Market. Initially, most of the non-British products were banned from entering Otu-Onitsha Market because they were seen as inferior goods, this led to the establishment of a new market called the Ochanja Market. Ochanja was a derogatory word for low value (inferior).

Okeke posits (2018) that after Nigeria got her independence in 1960, the premiere of Eastern Nigeria; Dr. M. I. Okpara embarked on the construction of the main market, the biggest market in West Africa; that was among his first post-independence projects. From 1967 to 1970, the period of the Nigerian Civil War, the Main Market was destroyed but the administration of Ukpabi Asika, the then Governor of the East Central State, embarked on its reconstruction in 1973 and was completed in 1975. He ordered the relocation of the timber dealers from the market to the present-day Ọgbọ Osisi market near the River Niger Bridge Head to ease off the congestion at the main market. Ọgbọ Osisi later spread to accommodate dealers on other goods. Today it has turned out to become what we know as Bridge Head Market.

In 1984, tragedy struck again; the Onitsha Main Market was gutted by fire, followed by another fire incident in 1989, and then 1997, respectively, and that was the last fire incident experienced at Onitsha Main Market to date. After the 1984 inferno which also happened at the Ochanja Market, the state government in a bid to relieve the traders at Ọchanja of untold hardship, set up a new area at Iweka Road for them to continue with their business. That new area is what is known today as the Relief Market. The Relief and Head Bridge Markets have expanded tremendously to even compete with the Main Market both in size and volume. The ever-increasing commercial activities in all the Markets have led to the establishment of many new markets and plazas where business is done.

1.5.3 Location and Features of Onitsha Markets

Onitsha is one of the major cities in Eastern Nigeria. It is located precisely in Anambra State which was carved out from the old Anambra State in 1991, (Ibekwe 2019). According to Anazodo (2021), Onitsha houses most of the major and busiest Markets in Nigeria. When we talk of Onitsha Markets, we are talking about all the markets located within and around Onitsha Metropolis in such towns as Obosi, Nkpor, Ogbunike, Ogidi, Nkwelle Ezunaka, and Ogbaru. There are about 63 markets scattered in Anambra State and more than 25 markets of various sizes are spread across Onitsha Metropolis and environs. These markets specialize in different wares. Onitsha Main Market is the mother of all the markets and is divided into three major zones. Each zone specializes in particular goods such as clothing, jewelry, household items, babies' wares, second-hand clothes (*ọkịrịka*). About one pole from the Main Market is the Ose Ọkwọdụ market which specializes in food items. Ọchanja market is located in Onitsha South Local Government Area about half a kilometer from the Main Market. It deals majorly with food items, provisions, and footwear.

Obinze (2021) narrated that the Bridge Head Market as the name implies is situated at the end of the River Niger Bridge in Onitsha. The Market is large geographically and is divided into 5 major zones and other smaller zones. Each zone deals with specific goods and services. For example; Pharmaceuticals (Ọgbọ-ọgwụ), Timber Market (Ọgbọ-Osisi), fairly used items (Akpakala), Tools, Plumbing Materials. The smaller zones include Food Stuff Market (Ọdụ-Igbo), Fabricators, Artisans, Furniture makers, Welder Markets among others. Similarly, the Relief Market is located in Ọgbaru L.G.A and deals mostly in canned foods, spirits, beverages, drinks, and provisions. The Electronic Market is located in Ọgbaru L.G.A. and all types of electronic devices are sold there. The Old Auto Spare Parts Market is located in Ogbaru L.G.A while the New Auto Spare Parts Market is located in Idemili L.G.A. Ọgbọ-Afere Market also located in Ọgbaru LGA deals in all kinds of cooking utensils. The Plastic Market is located very close to Ọgbọ-Afere Market and deals in all kinds of plastic wares. The Tyre Market is located along Enugu-Onitsha express road. According to Anazodo (2021), the Shoe Manufacturing Market is located at Nkwelle Ezunaka Junction. It was launched by the Vice President of Nigeria (Prof. Yemi Osibanjo) in August 2021. The Building Materials Market is located at Idemili LGA and they deal with all kinds of building materials. Onitsha Market is the pride of Old Eastern Nigeria and is the largest market in West Africa.

1.5.4 Population

The population of traders and 'support traders' in Onitsha is well over 1 million and this number places Onitsha as one of the most densely populated cities in Nigeria. In addition, Onitsha Market provides over one million direct and indirect jobs in the areas of haulage, small and medium enterprises (SMEs), artisans, hand/head carriage, wheelbarrow/cart pushers. Loading and off-loading, sales girl/boy, town service, and other transport services (Mycostoma, 2021).

Most of the internally generated revenue of Anambra state comes from trade and commerce and it accounts for over 70% of the state IGR. The traders are mostly importers and exporters.

Arising from the volume of trade and commerce in Onitsha, people from all walks of life - Africa, Europe, America, and other countries have one commercial interest or another in Onitsha. Some of the traders have direct contacts with world-renowned manufacturers in China, Turkey, Indonesia, South Africa, Britain, Singapore, and many others. Many traders from Cameroon, Benin Republic, Ghana, and South Africa feed on Onitsha Markets.

Uniquely, Onitsha Market traders venture into many thriving industries such as shoe manufacturing, textiles, drinks, packaged water, plastics, petrochemicals, polythene, aluminum, cosmetics, food packaging industries. Onitsha Markets receive many customers with over 10 million transactions daily, except Mondays which records over 14 million transactions; thus the traders nick-named Monday transactions Monday Hammer. The annual Volume of trade in Onitsha is about 3.4 Billion Dollars, this has kept the GDP of Anambra State above that of other states in Nigeria (IDI, Male, 78 years).

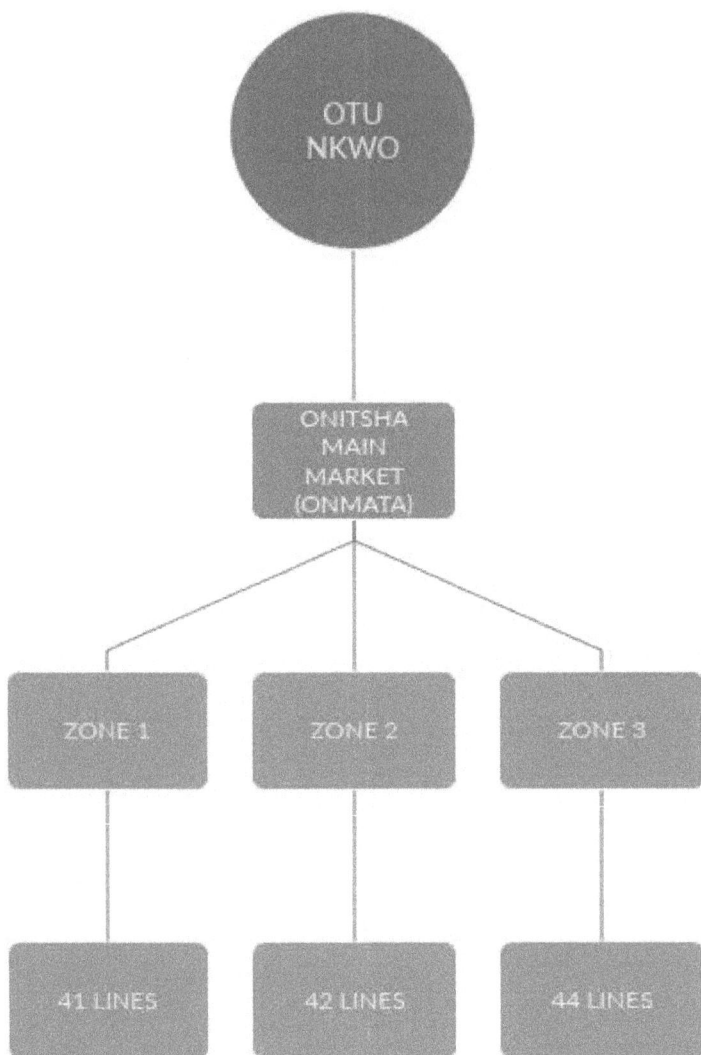

Figure i: Onitsha Main Market

About one pole from the Main Market is the Ose Okwodu market which specializes in food items. Ochanja Market is located in the Onitsha South Local Government Area about half a kilometer from the Main Market. It deals mainly in food items, provisions, and footwear. The population of traders and 'support-traders' in the Ọchanja market that made Ochanja one of the most densely populated markets in Onitsha is above one million. There are jobs provided indirectly by Ọchanja-Market in the areas of small and medium enterprises (SMEs), artisans, and direct manual labour-wheelbarrow/cart, loading, and off-loading among others. This is obtainable in all the markets. Transport businesses and a host of other support businesses are booming.

Undoubtedly, Government internally generated revenue (IGR) is boosted up to 30% by Onitsha Market. Over one million visitors are received in Ọchanja Market with different transactions daily.

Recently, the Ọchanja market was a victim of a fire outbreak in 2019 which destroyed properties of traders worth billions of naira, resulting in painful deaths among victims. A woman, who died with her only child, was consumed by the fire. Their images are constantly circulated on the Nigerian Social Media Space particularly on WhatsApp. Another trader who also died was said to have run into his shop to take his money. "In all, seven persons died (Ojukwu, 2019).Traders in Ọchanja markets have remained apprehensive since that ugly incident. However, with the ever-resilient spirit of *Ndi Igbo* the Ọchanja market traders have bounced back to their characteristic pattern of revival.

1.6 The Triple Helix Model and the Ịgba-Bọyị Apprenticeship Scheme

The triple helix is a model of innovation which refers to a framework that explores the nexus of interactions between academia (science), industry (society), and government (policy) to foster economic and social development. This model was first propounded by Henry Etzowitz and Leydesdorff in the 1990s in their work titled 'The Triple Helix: University-Industry-Government Relations: A Laboratory of Knowledge-Based Economic Development' (Etzkowitz & Leydesdorff, 2000; Leydesdorff & Etzkowitz, 1996). This framework is applied when there is a need for the transformation of each of these sectors and not just that, but also when they are conscientiously integrated. This model stresses the expansion of the traditional research and teaching missions in academia into a new focus on economic and social development (Etzkowitz, 2008). It seeks to bring informality together with formality. This will necessitate informal actors and formal actors or stakeholders coming together towards confronting contemporary complex challenges and by extension holistically drive the socio-economic development of the society. The triple helix model stresses the measures for bringing together science, policy, and societal actors (SPS) towards sustainable development. According to Saviano et al., (2019) strengthening the science-policy-society is the key to progress. This can only be feasible when these SPS stakeholders have imbibed what is known as 'sustainability-thinking. 'Sustainability means meeting our own needs without compromising the ability of future generations to meet their own needs' (Deniz, 2016; Farias et al., 2020). Sustainability thinking implies the attitude, behaviours, values, and mindset expected from an entrepreneur to make ethical decisions and act sustainably. The relevant stakeholders must assess the consequences and impact of their ideas, opportunities, and actions if they must make progress or develop.

Just like in Albert Einstein's words 'the world we have created is the product of our thinking and if we want to change the world, we have to change our thinking.' To achieve sustainable socio-economic development in Igbo land, we must discard all unsustainable thinking and behaviours that prevail in our contemporary Igbo society.

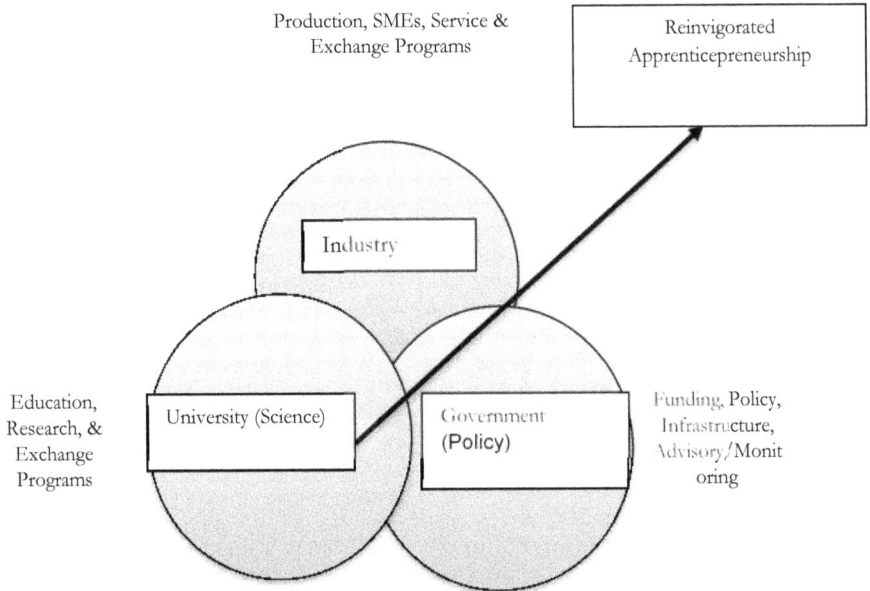

Figure ii: Triple Helix Model

Here, each sector is represented by a circle (helix), with overlapping interactions. The interactions between universities (academia/scientific communities), Industries (societies, Entrepreneurs/SMEs), and Government (policy) give rise to the transformation of the targeted sector(s). In essence, it is expected to give rise to a hybrid as the outcome of these interactions. In relation to this study on 're-invigorating Igbo entrepreneurial behaviour through an enhanced apprenticeship scheme in Onitsha Markets'. Here, the *Igba Boyi* scheme and entrepreneurship space in the selected Onitsha Markets represents the society/industry, the university/academia- represents science/research (like the one currently carried out by this research team), and the government as the third leg of the tripod. Put differently, the universities are supposed to provide the research upon which traders, industries/entrepreneurs will build upon to produce commercial goods/services and, on the reverse side, traders too can tap from the knowledge creation and transfer of the university system in their practice of the trading and apprenticeship system (*Igba bọyị*). This can be feasible through mutual exchange programs between industries and the Universities thereby, enhancing the 'town and gown' interaction. The industries, traders (masters/apprentices), or entrepreneurs engage in producing commercial goods, business/trade skill transfer, and sustenance like in the Igba-bọyị scheme. While the government as the third helix is expected to engage in the provision of adequate infrastructure, regulations of the markets, and also provide relevant funding for the operation of the markets and the apprenticeship scheme. All these are targeted towards socio-economic transformation and development. To achieve this, these actors and stakeholders must adopt some transformative behaviours and actions as well as 'sustainability thinking'. This is proposed in this research as a workable framework for reinvigorating the *Igba Bọyị* apprenticeship scheme and entrepreneurial behaviour in the selected Onitsha Markets. This is feasible because this study has already established that the '*Igba Bọyị*' apprenticeship scheme is a skill-based practice among Ndi Igbo operating on informality, just like the University is a knowledge-based system based on formality. The first helix draws from informality and others are based on formality. Therefore, we propose that there should be an interface between informality and formality to achieve the desired transformation. This can be achieved through a co-transfer and exchange of actors, partners, and stakeholders between the universities and the markets, industries, and entrepreneurs in the selected study area. These transfers can stimulate the integration of the knowledge acquired from academia with the skills from the informal sector- trade and apprenticeship scheme in the various markets. This critical integration and engagement are all bound together in mutual knowledge-skill transfers and exchanges while the government serves as the umpire and regulator. As a regulator, the government is expected to produce goods, roads, and streets to navigate the markets, build market stalls, provide electricity, water, and conveniences like toilets and bathrooms. This nexus would also bridge the gap in the relationship between theory and praxis. This is what this research team proposes to be a scientifically proven strategy for re-invigorating the *Igba-bọyị* apprenticeship scheme in the selected markets studied and by extension in all apprenticeship schemes existing or practiced anywhere.

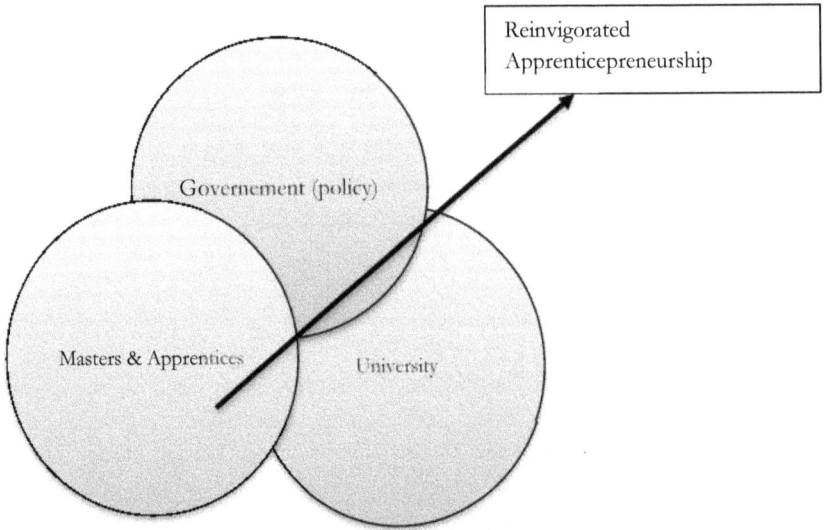

Figure iii: Triple Helix of a Reinvigorated Apprenticespreneurship

Section Two
Review of Related Literature

Section Two
Review of Related Literature

This section examines relevant theoretical and empirical literature on Igbo apprenticeship.

2.1 Conceptual and Theoretical Issues

This subsection explores all relevant conceptual and theoretical issues in the existing literature on apprenticeship.

2.1.1 Igbo Entrepreneurship Behaviour

Entrepreneurship has generally been noted as the bedrock and engine of growth for most developed nations and it has continued to shape developing and emerging economies for many centuries through employment and wealth creation. Entrepreneurship is a process that involves individuals becoming innovative and creative by investing their resources and time in taking various forms of risks; financially, physically, psychologically, and socially to be rewarded with some things that are remarkably different (Hisrich, 2005) in addition to deriving satisfaction. Thus, entrepreneurship is all about creating something new by willingly taking risks and making investments toward creating opportunities within the environment (Akram and Syed, 2017).

Entrepreneurial behavior refers to the discovery and exploitation of a new business opportunity for the purpose of profit and growth: it involves the identification of a new business opportunity, the establishment of a new venture to exploit that opportunity, and the management of the new venture to make it flourish over time (Palma, Cunha, and Lopes, 2009). Entrepreneurs who are curiously ambitious persons willing to take risks in investing their resources with the aim of innovating and creating wealth towards gaining rewards and solving societal problems are behind every entrepreneurial behaviour.

Igbo entrepreneurial behaviour can be related to Bandura's (1977) distinctive social learning process which begins from the family/kindred unit and invests in the entrepreneurial socialization of its members at a very young age (Adebukola, Olabode, and Chinọnye, 2021, p. 15 in Adeola, 2021). Adebukola et al., (2021), insist that Igbo entrepreneurial behaviour encourages traits like effective negotiation, risk-taking, optimism, saving culture, innovativeness, and investment outlook to be learnt in the process (p. 15).

North (1990) had observed that institutions govern individual behaviour and, together with social and cultural elements, determine own behaviour (Anggadwita, Ramadani and Ratten, 2017 in Igwe, Newbery, Amoncar, White, and Madichie, 2018). Studies have also shown that entrepreneurship is inextricably linked to institutions and family (Aldrich and Cliff, 2003; Williams *et al.*, 2013 in Igwe et al, 2018). It was also concluded by Igwe et al. (2018) that Igbo entrepreneurial culture develops from the linked institutions of the extended family and the informal apprenticeship system and institutions. Though the origin of Igbo entrepreneurial behaviour may never be conclusively traced or fully explained, it can be rightly asserted to have been shaped and nurtured by the existing occupational environmental practices over time within existing institutions.

The Igbo of the South-East origin, are characterized as naturally enterprising, ingenious, and industrious (Meagher, 2009); their entrepreneurial orientations steadily distinguished them from other ethnic groups in Nigeria and Africa (Adeola, 2021) and their uncommon entrepreneurial behaviour predates colonialism. Hamza (2013) reported that people of Igbo communities in Nigeria are considered one of the oldest entrepreneurs in history. However, this was brought to the fore and made more manifest by the post-civil war pronouncements by the federal government of Nigeria. Before the outburst of entrepreneurism in Igbo land, they had been predominantly involved in farming, especially in yam cultivation that during the Pre-colonial times, wealthy men in Igbo land were given names like *"Di Ji"*, (king of Yam), based on the number of yam barns they have successfully harvested after each farming season. Therefore, the farming system, in no small measure, also contributed to the nurturing of the Igbo entrepreneurial behaviour. Such a farming system allowed big-time yam farmers to mentor younger ones, mentee as apprentices, who may be their children or relatives, to work with them for many years and thereafter set them free with yam seedlings which enabled them to start their own farming enterprise. This practice has been around before trade and other commercial activities started in Igbo land and predates colonialism. Igbo entrepreneurism is very unique in nature because Igbo are found in every nook and cranny of Nigeria in particular and the African continent and the world, in general. They have been able to turn the most unlikely ventures into viable and flourishing businesses by merely being able to identify the needs of a place or group of people and striving to meet them while making profit in the process (Anyadike et al., 2012).

2.1.2 Apprenticeship Scheme and Igba Boyi in Igbo Land

Historically, apprenticeship, in general, is believed to be the oldest form of training in the world of work and business (Geslaa, 2019). Its emergence predates the medieval era, when guilds, journeymen, and craftsmen flourished, setting the template for the exploitation of productive forces, and the correspo-nding relations of production (Nnonyelu and Onyeizugbe, 2020). This notwithstanding, the age-old practice of apprenticeship did not receive adequate attention until recently. Pre-colonial apprenticeship scheme in Igbo land has been present because people were always seriously engaged in the world of work but it was not as popular as it became in the periods after the Nigeria-Biafran Civil War.

Apprenticeship is a means of training people to learn a trade or craft for their future wellbeing and livelihood and undergoing its training further enables the absorption of extensive skills and erudition in a particular trade or craft under the guidance of an expert (Olulu and Udeorah, 2018, p. 5). This seeks to accelerate the career of an apprentice towards developing into an accomplished tradesperson (Ekesiobi and Dimnwobi, 2020). An apprenticeship is a form of mentorship programme where a younger person, *Nwa Boyi*, goes through the tutelage and intensive training of *Igba Boyi* process expectedly with a high measure of commitment and sacrifice under a Master, the mentor or *Oga*, knowing that one day he will be on his own, managing his own business and possibly, training potential *Ụmụ Bọyị* or Apprentices.

Apprenticeship is an instructional method for teaching an acceptable way of understanding and doing tasks, solving problems, and dealing with problematic situations (Collins, Brown and Newman, 1989 in Ezenwakwelu, Egbosionu and Okwo, 2019). It is a system of training a new generational set of practitioners with a structured competency and expected basic set of skills. It can be likened to a type of vocational but Informal vocational education as well as on-the-job training where the apprentice, *Nwa Boyi*, is expected to graduate at the end of a specified period ready to start his own trade/business with the learnt vocation or skill.

From the definition by the International Labour Organization (ILO, 2012), apprenticeship means

"any system by which an employer undertakes by contract to employ a young person and to train him [or her] or have him [or her] trained systematically for a trade for a period the duration of which has been fixed in advance and in the course of which the apprentice is bound to work in the employer's service" (p. 2). Certain conditions emanate from the definition of apprenticeship by ILO (2012) as follows: it will be based in the workplace supervised by an employer; it will be intended for young people; its fundamental aim is learning a trade/acquiring a skill; the training is 'systematic' ie follows a predefined plan; it will be governed by a contract between apprentice and employer (p. 2). Apprenticeship also means training programmes that combine vocational education with work-based learning for an intermediate occupational skill (i.e., more than routine job training), and that are subject to externally imposed training standards, particularly for their workplace component" (ILO, 2012, p. 3).

In categorizing apprenticeship ILO (2012) maintains that there are informal or formal apprenticeships (ILO, 2012) both still aimed at transmitting the needed skills from an experienced master to the younger learner. Olulu and Udeorah (2018) however, noted that the practice of apprenticeship can be divided into traditional, informal, and modern apprenticeship models. Informal apprenticeship is synonymous with an informal economy and poor societies, where apprentices learn through observation and imitation from experienced masters to acquire the needed skills in particular trade before being inducted into the culture and netwo rks of the business (ILO, 2012). The Informal apprenticeship agreements are mostly oral, yet they are embedded in the society's customs, norms, and traditions (ILO, 2012, p. 4) and this exemplifies the *Igba Bọyi* apprentice scheme in Igbo land. Formal apprenticeship is highly regulated and structured "usually by legislation at the national level, is waged, is based in the workplace, based on a contract which specifies a duration, programme of learning (including transferable skills) assessment and final certification and the entitlement to off-the-job learning" (ILO), 2012; Olulu and Udeorah, 2018).

Igbo apprenticeship scheme of *Igba Bọyi* can be said to have taken its deepest root during the post-war entrepreneurial and commercial activities necessitated by the unwanted treatment meted on Igbo people immediately after the civil war. Therefore, the civil war played an unprecedented role in the furtherance, nurturing, and growth of the Igbo entrepreneurial skills and ventures.

Following the end of the civil war which lasted for three years (1967-1970) where over three million children and women were gruesomely decimated through hunger, not counting those slaughtered cold-bloodedly as the war was starting and the able-bodied men who died as soldiers during the war, there was confusion and utter hopelessness. As if these were not enough, a leveling measure was meted upon the Igbo people when only twenty pounds was given to everyone who had money in the bank irrespective of the amount in the account ab initio. As bad as the twenty pounds was, it ignited the renowned Igbo genetic entrepreneurship skills embedded in their nature as a tribe in Nigeria. The first set that left their homes to nearby cities, Onitsha in particular, came back after a few years to take their kin who were still idle or engaged in peasant farming, fishing, craftsmanship, and even petty trading. Igbo apprenticeship in trade and commerce in the form of *Igba Bọyi*, therefore, was given traction following the immediate post-war events.

With the notable success witnessed from the entrepreneurial and apprenticeship activities, the practice became so famous that parents then had to plead with relatives who were already successful entrepreneurs to take their male children as *Ụmụ Bọyi*. Those successfully trained and settled who could start their enterprises later came back to take others. In this manner, success in trade and commerce became regenerative.

The major advantage of Igbo apprenticeship can be traced to the training of the *Nwa Boyi* in the secrets of a particular trade and commercial venture. Other advantages are embedded in the social, psychological, physical, and spiritual training received by the *Nwa Boyi*, especially if he co-resides with the *Oga*. Successfully trained apprentices also became sources of additional capital before they completely disentangled from their masters arising from the fact that sometimes the masters start a joint business with them as a way of raising funds for their settlement. Freed apprentices who left their masters peacefully and are successful have been known to maintain a very cordial relationship with their masters from which the entire family benefited subsequently.

There are predominantly two patterns of apprentices; kin-related and non-kin-related. While the kin-related were related to the Master (***Oga)***, maternally or paternally, the non-kin-related were not and may not even hail from the same village or town. Moreover, while Kin-related were directly taken as *Umu Boyi* because of the relationship that existed ab initio, the latter are mostly through referrals from friends or at the market.

2.1.3 Socio-Cultural Characteristics of Entrepreneurship

These are characteristics associated with the social system and culture of a people within an environment. They consist of the attitudes, beliefs, thinking patterns, and acceptable behavioural models of the people. Thus, a social-cultural environment, in relation to entrepreneurship, can be seen as consisting of all the elements of the social system and culture of a people which positively or negatively affect and influence entrepreneurial emergence, behaviour, and performance, and entrepreneurship development in general (Akhter and Sumi, 2014). All the elements that influence the values, thinking, and actions of individuals within any environment with regard to entrepreneurship can be seen as comprising the social-cultural environment of entrepreneurship. Both the social and cultural factors are learnt over time as acceptable ways of life and before they manifest in the lifestyle of the people, they have tended to become embedded. Such elements include beliefs, values, attitudes, habits, forms of behaviour, and lifestyles of persons as developed from cultural, religious, educational, and social conditioning (Adeleke, Oyenuga, and Ogundele, 2003 in Akhter and Sumi, 2014).

Therefore, the socio-cultural characteristics of Igbo people, as far as entrepreneurship is concerned, emanate from their belief system that they are entrepreneurial by nature through hard work. The Igbo also believe very strongly in rendering service, not slavery and this singular belief has contributed in no small measure to the success of the Igbo entrepreneurial venture. Some Igbo proverbs that tend to drive home their belief system m are "akpaa na-anwụ, elie na ndo" (no pain, no gain); "Ngana kpuchie ute, agụụ ekpughee ya" (slothfulness and indolence lead to starvation); Ọnye fee eze, eze eluo ya" (he who serves will later be served). All the three point to timely hard work and service.

2.1.4 Genderization/Feminization of Igba Boyi in Igbo Land

The question of why males are predominantly apprentices is traditionally rooted in the notion of patriarchy, where in traditional Igbo society authority and inheritance are traced along male lines. From pre-colonial times, males have always been the breadwinners and heads of families who would usually bring home their venison, harvested crops, or fish to ensure that their families fed well while females were home keepers. The females, as mothers, give birth to children, stay home to care for them, their husbands, and the family as a whole.Therefore, as *Nwa Bọyi* apprentices, the males were trained to prepare them as future fathers and heads of their families.

The females received their own training by staying at homes with their mothers learning the rudiments of housekeeping and going to farms with the whole family, when the need arose. They also received proper and more appropriate training outside the homes in more semi-formal ways as soon as they are married. Recently, however, young females are seen to be serving as *Nwa Bọyi* apprentices in the feminine version known as "*Igba Gelị*" or sales girls and this is a total change in paradigm which has brought in the new perspective "Nwa gelị".

In the households where men are seen as responsible for the financial demands of the family, the global economic downturn has made things tougher for them (Adebisi and Akinsoto, 2016) and this is where women can complement the role of men, especially in the African traditional setting. Females make up 49.4% of Nigeria's population and to ignore their contribution to the economy may not be healthy for holistic Sustainable development. McGowan, Redeker, Cooper, and Greenan, (2011) further emphasize that the motivation, expectations of women to establish entrepreneurial ventures to balance work responsibilities and earning potential with family commitments have not been given much attention. Adebisi and Akinsoto (2016) further enunciated that the necessity to ensure household upkeep has warranted the need for women to seek gainful employment in addition to the ever demanding domestic duties and responsibilities of child bearing, rearing and general welfare of the family (p. 2). Therefore, *Igba Gelị*, as a corresponding requirement for females, is becoming very imperative to enable the almost half of Nigeria's population play the requisite role towards National development.

2.1.5 Entrepreneurship, Apprenticeship, Employment and Wealth Creation

Entrepreneurship which involves the act of starting and managing a business for the purpose of growth and profit (Carland, Hoy, Boulton, & Carland, 1984 in Hisrich, Langan-Fox and Grant, 2007), can be traced back to ancient Greece, where entrepreneurial activity brought independence, economic and social reform (Hisrich et al., 2007). Entrepreneurs through their novel ideas create and innovate ventures that eventually become entrepreneurially successful leading to opportunities that create employment and ultimately manifest in wealth creation. Entrepreneurial activities provide opportunity through their innovative process for employment and wealth creation. Oyo and Oluwatayo (2015) maintain that entrepreneurship can contribute to the reduction of unemployment; reduction in poverty and hunger; reduction in terrorism and criminal activities while Nyeneokpon, (2012) argues that entrpreneurship improves infrastructural development and economic diversification. The aforementioned factors and more can manifest in wealth creation which effect is usually experienced in national growth.

Hisrich et al. (2007), maintain that "entrepreneurship is a major source of employment, economic growth, and innovation, promoting product and service quality, competition, and economic flexibility as well as a mechanism by which many people enter the society's economic and social mainstream, aiding culture formation, population integration, and social mobility" (p. 1). It is a major source of employment, economic growth, and innovation and is an integral part of the economic renewal process (Kuratko, 2003). The impact and contributions made by entrepreneurship to global economies have led to the manifestation of its seeming indispensability.

There is no gainsaying that the *Igba Boyi* apprenticeship scheme has also contributed in no small measures to growth, development and sustenance of entrepreneurship in Igbo land since that is where the incubation and nurturing of successful Igbo entrepreneurship take root. By implication, it has also directly resulted in creating employment and growing wealth in Igbo land, Nigeria and Africa as a whole.

2.1.6 Decline of Apprenticeship Scheme

The Igbo apprenticeship scheme has been proclaimed by many as a sine qua non to the success so far recorded by Igbo entrepreneurship which has produced many wealthy Igbo and contributed immensely to employment and wealth creation. Unfortunately, it is facing many challenges (Nwanoruo, 2004; Fajobi, Olatujoye, Amusa & Adedoyin, 2017 in Ejo-orusa and Destiny, 2019, Nkamnebe and Ezemba, 2021) which may eventually lead to its total collapse. Some of these challenges arise from the non-settlement of apprentices (by the nature of the aggrement which are mostly oral), abuse of apprentices in its various forms (especially through the ill-treatment metted on them by the Ọga's immediate family), child labour abuse, inadequate framework to guide the system, and lack of education during the training period (in Ejo-orusa, and Destiny, 2019, pp. 113-115). Nkamnebe and Ezemba (2021) equally mentioned the issue of weakening *Igba Bọyị* by the actual terms of engagement which are oral and often not rigidly defined making it difficult to be enforced in a court of law (p. 32). However, the society frowns at masters who fail to honour their promises and stigmatises them as dishonest stock (p. 33).

Other issues that have tended to weaken the Igbo apprenticeship scheme arise from norms and ethos. In recent times, the quest for materialism has taken a new dimension and dishonesty and greed have blossomed into the get-rich-quick syndrome which is currently thriving. Lack of patience to learn the necessary skill under the **Ọga** and loss of requisite family values can also result in the decline of the *Igba Bọyị* apprenticeship scheme of the Igbo. In addition are issues like dishonesty, theft, fraud, fear of the future and peer group influence which Nkamnebe and Ezemba (2021), examined as challenges of *Igba Bọyị* (p. 33). The same authors had maintained that the masters and mentors who play crucial roles in sustaining the *Igba-Bọyị* model, can at the same time, become antithetical to its continued existence by weakening the scheme in different ways (p. 32). From the findings of Okeke and Osang (2021), the unwillingness of young men to take up the businesses of their fathers, study courses that will promote their growth and malicious stealing of their masters money by the apprentices are implicated as the key factors that led to the decline of the scheme's potency (p. 129).

2.1.7 The Family, *Igba Bọyị* and the Igbo Entrepreneurship

The family as an institution plays the role of nurturing the children for their future endeavours. The Igbo family lays the foundation for such a future through the values embedded in the Igbo culture which eventually mould the behaviour of the entire members of that institution. Institutions govern individual behaviour (North, 1990) and, together with social and cultural elements, determine their own behaviour (Igwe et. al., 2018; Anggadwita, Ramadani and Ratten, 2017).

Igbo families teach their children the issues of life and living based on the ethos of acceptable and unacceptable behaviour lifestyles. Most families are known to protect their family names by teaching their children *Nsọ Anị* - the abominable things that must be abhorred like stealing, dishonesty, greed, cheating and the likes, as well as the gains of honesty, hard work, contentment among others. It is right to say that one cannot give what one does not have; therefore, only families with credibility were known to give their children credible upbringing. Nkamnebe and Ezemba (2021), maintain that "in the past,

Igbo values govern social relations and conduct and serve as a check against unacceptable behaviour" (p. 33).

2.1.8 Co-Residency of *Oga* and *Nwa Boyi*

Co-residency adult education refers to *Nwa Boyi* sharing same residence with the master. Peil (2012) provided a similar illustration where in Accra, Ghana apprentices live with their masters. *Nwa Boyi* living in the same residence as the *Oga* does not imply equal power relations. It is rather a relationship of two-unequal partners, *Nwa Boyi* being subordinate to the *Oga*. Ndi *Oga* takes *Umu Boyi* for mentoring and would usually prefer to live with them because it affords them the opportunity of deriving more direct benefits from them, at home as well as keeping a close eye on them. *Umu Boyi* who reside with their Masters are expected to grow with the *Oga*'s children and do other chores as may be directed by the Madam who also sees to the training of *Umu Boyi* in the house as her direct responsibility. At the end of the day's trading activities, *Umu Boyi* would come back, sometimes with the *Oga*, at other times, after they had stayed back to lock up the stalls/shops. They usually help out in preparing dinners, washing up cooking utensils, and doing other general cleaning within the house under the direct supervision of the Madam. They are also expected to wake up early in the morning to wash their *Oga*'s cars, assist in preparing Breakfast and sometimes take the children to school, as the case may be. Chrisman (2012) reinforced the above assertion on live-in-apprentices when he argued that craftsmen usually train the young apprentices in the mores and folkways of daily existence.

It is very important that *Umu Boyi* are obedient and maintain a good relationship with the Madam since many benefits are imminent from such, as far as their relationship with the *Oga* is concerned.

Umu Boyi who co-reside with *Ndi Oga* also go early to the markets, open and sweep the shops, arrange the goods and wares in their proper positions for sales for the day. This category of apprentices is also known in the market neighbourhood and lines as working for the particular *Oga*. However, as they obediently but indirectly serve other *Ndi Oga* by running little errands for them, they must be honest and diligent. The co-residence set of *Umu Boyi* are usually different from those that do not. This latter category is those who apply to be taken in as apprentices and are trained for shorter periods of time and this brings to fore the issue of tenureship of apprenticeship which is premised on the pattern. However, Schalk, Wallis, Crowston, Lemercier (2016) opined that living within the master's household is a function of the contractual relationship entered into at the inception of the apprenticeship.

2.1.9 Age and Education of Nwa Bọyị

The ILO has not recommended any age as appropriate since different countries have different reasons and circumstances for the apprenticeship. Among the G20 countries, Austria, France, Germany, Switzerland, and Turkey target apprenticeship age at 25 while Germany's latest recommended age range is 16-24. For the US and Canada, to some extent, apprenticeship is a way of up-skilling adults already at work (ILO, 2012, p. 5). As far as Igbo entrepreneurship is concerned, the age of *Nwa Bọyị* or apprentice starts from 12 years (Igwe, Madichie and Amoncar, 2020; Olulu and Udeọrah, 2018; Nigeria Labour Law, 2004). However, this must be with the approval of the parents or guardian. The Nigeria Labour Law (2004) differentiates between two categories of apprentices, the child apprentices between the ages of 12-16 years and the second category are young persons from 16 years and above.

The critical role of adult education in the development of any society has long been recognized (UNESCO, 2010, p. 12). Since the First International Conference on Adult Education in 1949, UNESCO member states have become committed to ensuring that adults are able to exercise their basic right to formal education.

Even with the afore stated, 10.5 million school age children are out of school (UNICEF, 2017). There are usually no educational qualification requirements for *Ụmụ Bọyị* or apprentices because it is never an issue at the time of engagement. Even some *Ndị Oga* may not have acquired what may be termed requisite education and these make Adult education imperative. Adult education is "the entire body of organized educational processes, whatever the content, level or method, whether formal or otherwise, whether they prolong or replace initial education in schools or colleges and universities as well as in apprenticeship whereby persons regarded as adults by the society to which they belong develop their abilities, enrich their knowledge, improve their technical or professional qualifications or turn them into a new direction and bring about changes in their attitudes or behaviour in two-fold perspective of full personal development and participation in balanced, independent, social, economic and cultural development, implying that adult education is learning that takes place among adults. Adult education, however, must not be considered as an entity in itself, it is a subdivision, and an integral part of, a global scheme for lifelong education and learning." (UNESCO, 1976: 2 in UNESCO, 2010 p. 13). There is also Adult learning which encompasses both formal and continuing education, non-formal learning and the spectrum of informal and incidental learning available in a multicultural learning society, where theory- and practice-based approaches are recognized" (UNESCO, 2010, P. 13).

Non-formal education which is also, by implication, a part of Adult education does not constitute a distinct and separate educational system, parallel to the formal education system (Coombs and Ahmed, 1974 in UNESCO, 2010).

Adult education "is any organized, systematic, educational activity, carried on outside the framework of the formal system, to provide selected types of learning to particular subgroups in the population, adults as well as children"…. and therefore includes, "for example, agricultural extension and farmer training programmes, adult literacy programmes, occupational skill training given outside the formal system, youth clubs with substantial educational purposes, and various community programs of instruction in health, nutrition, family planning, cooperatives, and the like (Coombs and Ahmed, 1974: 8). It would be interesting to explore the existence of Adult learning centres for *Ndị Ọga* in Onitsha.

Adult education can be designed to suit whatever purpose it is intended for and the learning focus is on the individual and its self-development (Coombs and Ahmed, 1974, p. 8). The authors go on to emphasize that each apprentice is expected to assume responsibility about the learning programme which centres on the apprentice's individual needs. Entrepreneurship education seeks to provide students with the knowledge, skills and motivation to encourage entrepreneurial success in a variety of settings (Ozurumba, Echem, Okengwu, Ugwuoke, Umofịa and Ifeanachọ, 2021).

The National Commission for Mass Literacy, Adult and Non-Formal Education (NMEC) provided holistic policy guidelines in 2017 which arose from the National Policy on Education in 2013 for the promotion of mass literacy, adult and non-formal education in Nigeria. Based on that provision, Nigeria, like most countries globally, noted the importance of Adult education and provided adequate strategic objectives to guide its implementation (NMEC, 2017, pp. 5-6).

2.1.10 Formal versus Informal Apprenticeship Agreement

An apprenticeship contract involves the establishment of regulatory provisions that would guide the master (*Ọga*) and the apprentice (Okene 2011 cited in Olulu and Udeorah, 2018). Formal and written agreements are documents that state the facts of an issue between two or more persons to guide the relationship concerning them towards actualizing their goals peacefully. The Nigerian labour Act, (2004) stipulates that apprentices understand the terms of the contract of apprentice; that the apprentice is of the right age and that apprentices are not forced into acceptance of the conditions of apprenticeship. In Igbo land, both in the pre-colonial, colonial, and post-civil war periods, the entrepreneurial relationships between the *Ọga* and *Nwa Bọyị*, were never guided by written Agreements. This can be attributed to the Igbo culture because spoken words used to carry lots of weight and it was generally believed that a man's word was his bond. Moreover, responsible and respected Igbo men would usually stand by words that were never doubted or disputed. This is further given theoretical support by the Social Capital Theory that leverages on trust as glue that ties relationships.

Within the Igbo entrepreneurial arrangements, agreements can be regarded as semi-formal if the *Ọga* arranged for a meeting between the parents of the *Nwa Bọyi* to be, for discussion on the terms and conditions of their relationships. During the discussion, the tenure and settlement, *Idu ụnọ* or "*Ibido Ahịa*", were the two most important issues brought to the table, mostly in the form of oral agreement. The oral discussion also presumes that the *Nwa Bọyi* has become the son of the *Ọga* as he must live with him as a member of the family.

With the informal agreement, no discussions were held as the *Nwa Bọyi* may be sent to the *Ọga* without physically coming to take him. At other times, the parents of the *Nwa Bọyi* to be, may even be the ones to plead for their son to be taken, to serve under a supposed successful Master, or arrangement, may have been made through referrals by a friend who may have been served by the brother of the *Nwa Bọyi* or who is related to the family of the *Nwa Bọyi*.

Therefore, Formal apprenticeship agreements, in the real sense of the word, are alien to the Igbo apprenticeship scheme as what was discussed as "formal agreements" were never written down but usually accepted as "*Ụka Akparakpa, isi ka eji ekwe ya*" (a person's word is his/her bond).

2.1.11 *Rules and Regulations of Apprenticeship*

Different continents and countries have realized the importance of getting involved in the regulation of apprenticeship and entrepreneurial schemes in their domain and are taking necessary steps to address the issue. Cedefop (2018) observes the importance of understanding the relevance and role of apprenticeships in national policies for collective skills formation, as part of human capital development strategies. The European Stakeholders and Member States made efforts to increase the apprenticeship offer and its quality following the launch of the European Alliance for Apprenticeships (EAfA) in 2013 and the focus on the added value of work-based learning, particularly apprenticeships, of the Directors General for VET in the Riga conclusions in 2015 (European Commission et al., 2015 in Cedefop, 2018, p. 4). According to the report, "by the end of 2017, most EU governments submitted concrete commitments on steps to increase the quantity, quality and supply of apprenticeships and by June 2017, 208 pledges for apprenticeships within the EAfA were made by companies and business associations, chambers of commerce, industry and crafts, social partners, regional authorities, education and training providers, youth and non-profit organizations, think tanks and research institutes" (p. 4).

Chankseliani, Keep and Wilde (2017) view the use of Employer bodies as the best form of intermediary bodies in regulating the apprenticeship scheme. The authors describe the German Association of Chambers of Commerce and Industry (DIHK) as having responsibility for the introduction and background; determining the suitability of both companies and trainers; registering training contracts; managing examinations and issuing certificates and mediating in any problems that arise (Chankseliani et al., 2017, p. 66). They further cited Denmark as having a similar level of involvement, while Australia, England and South Africa are to a lesser extent. They argue that "these arrangements, via employer bodies, have evolved organically and therefore are more likely to survive, as well as having gained the trust of all the parties over time" (pp. 6-7).

Rules are written regulations that are provided to guide the actions of groups and organizations. Igbo Apprenticeship scheme is usually guided by Unwritten rules and regulations which are two-sided; on the side of the Master and that of the *Nwa Bọyị*. The major rules on the side of the *Nwa Bọyị* are that he must be honest and obedient to the Master and the Madam of the house, the Master's wife; he will not steal the Master's wares or money and he must be friendly with customers to always win them towards patronizing the Master. These cover the rest like punctuality, running little and major errands at the *Ọga*'s shop and family, being very careful with everybody, being respectful to all elders, etc. The rule on obedience to the Master covers the issues of when the *Nwa Bọyị* will wake up, when he comes home, especially on Sundays that are market-free days. Most rules from the Master or *Ọga* have their advantages since they are meant to guide *Ụmụ Bọyị* toward achieving success in their apprenticeship endeavour.

On the side of the Master, it is expected that he will treat the *Nwa Bọyị* as fairly as his own child, discipline him when the need arises, feed and clothe him adequately and settle him at the end of the agreed time. As simple as these rules may look and sound, abiding by them has proved herculean for some *Ọga* and may likely contribute to the decline of apprenticeship. This agrees with Nkamnebe and Ezemba's view (2021) on the superior position usually assumed by *Ndị Ọga* that may lead to them not keeping their words.

2.1.12 Challenges of Ịgba Bọyị Apprenticeship Model

The major challenge apprentices, *Ụmụ Bọyị*, face is the issue of non-settlement after serving the **Ọga** or Master for many years for which reasons or faults may not always be from the Master. The death of the Master has been known to lead to the problem of non-settlement. It can also result from the harsh economic conditions which may have led to general business failures. Oyewunmi, Oyewunmi and Moses (2021) maintain that the challenges of *Ịgba Bọyị/Ịmụ*

Ahịa within the environment are financial and investment illiteracy, death of mentor or apprentice, institutional disadvantages and policy somersaults, and child labour. Others are decline in apprenticeships, mistreatment, breach of the settlement agreement and, mistrust and insincerity (p. 22). Nkamnebe and Ezemba (2021) also examine the challenges of *Igba Boyi*, the mentees, as dishonesty, theft, fraud, fear of the future, and peer group influence (p. 32).

Ndị Ọga mostly fail in keeping to the agreement which is predominantly oral, mere promises, as a result of the trust arising from the Igbo values that used to work so well in Igbo land. The disadvantaged position of the poor *Nwa Boyi* makes it easier for *Ndị Ọga* to go against their word leaving the mentee *Nwa Boyi* to his "chi" and the ancestors (Nkamnebe and Ezemba, 2021).

2.1.13 Challenges of Igbo Entrepreneurship

The index, furnished by the World Bank, provides at a glance how far any country is faring from the ranking in the ten critical areas of doing business. The rankings, 1-190, of the Ease of Doing Business (EoDB) clearly shows the performance of different economies in specific areas. Applying EoDB therefore reveals that in the year 2020, Nigeria is still far behind in the areas that mostly concern small and medium scale businesses and these are starting a business, getting electricity, registering property and paying taxes (Nnabuife, Okeke and Ndubuisi-Okolo. 2018; Ease of Doing Business, 2020). These and many other challenges still persist as little or no improvement has been noticed over the years. Fong, Jabor, Zulkifli, and Hashim (2019) also raised the problems of adequate capital needed, finding the right business location, dealing with unforeseen business challenges and expenses which involve unexpected lawsuits, inconsistent Government policies, bad debt, unpaid bills, and taxes as daunting problems of new entrepreneurs. Legas (2015) discusses challenges like business regulations, lack of infrastructure and finance, lack of entrepreneurial knowledge, and market size as those delaying entrepreneurial success in Sub-Saharan Africa.

Igbo entrepreneurship generally faces similar and even more seriously environmentally based problems. The harsh global economic realities experienced in many nations, high lending and interest rates, business monetary policies, lack of financial support from the government, general insecurities, irregular power supply, poor infrastructural facilities also replicate itself in Nigeria especially in the South East where the Igbo entrepreneurship is domiciled.

2.1.14 Entrepreneurship and Business Success

Economically, business or entrepreneurial success may be viewed only from profit and its indices within a specified period under consideration. However, it is a complex phenomenon and includes multiple criteria of financial and non-financial character (Gorgievski, Ascalon & Stephan, 2010, Orser & Dyke, 2009, Schenk, 1998, in Wach, 2010). Entrepreneurship success, which is a measure of how successful an entrepreneur fares from all the activities performed over a period of time, may not be measured so easily and therefore offers itself to subjective measurement.

Entrepreneurship or business success can be measured from the innovations arising from noted entrepreneurial activities (Schumpeter, 1993); from market growth and expansion (Littunen, 2000); from economic growth (Carree & Thurik, 2003) from the increase in the Gross Domestic Product (GDP) and from the general welfare and happiness level of the populace all of which depend on the economic approach of evaluating entrepreneurship success. Wach (2010), however, offers a psychological approach which recognizes the importance of entrepreneurs' personal motives, goals and aspirations. These include giving value to personal initiative, autonomy, independence, work-enjoyment, self-directed work and high achievement (McClelland, 1968; Schwartz & Bardi, 1997 in Wach, 2010). Entrepreneurs also strive to maintain positive relationships with their employees and customers, for social recognition and to contribute back to the society or firm continuity (Gorgievski at el., 2010; Kuratko et al., 1997 in Wach, 2010, p. 90).

2.2 Theoretical Reviews

2.2.1 Structural Functionalism theory

Structural Functionalist theory maintains input-output analysis, sees political systems as striving for equilibrium or homeostasis and considers feedback in its analysis" (in Fisher, 2010, p. 74). The theory describes a social institution made up of interdependence and interrelationship of units that exist in the Igbo Entrepreneurial ventures involving the *Oga* and *Nwa Boyi* where functions are based on the roles that must be assumed by the different units to maintain the social system.

The Igbo entrepreneurship is explained by the social systems where the entities depend on each other for sustenance and survival within their environment governed by rules. Easton (1953, 1966) suggests that a political system concerns itself with 'the interactions through which values are authoritatively allocated for a society' (in Fisher 2010. p. 72). The Igbo entrepreneurship has been sustained over the years as the Igbo have been singled out as the most successful entrepreneurs wherever they are found, always maintaining a will of their own and a purpose through the values they have collectively shared.

The inputs and outputs of any social system play major roles in shaping the political system. Easton (1966), insists that "outputs not only help to influence events in the broader society of which the system is a part, but also, in doing so, they help to determine each succeeding round of inputs that finds its way into the political system" (Fisher, 2010, p. 74). Structural functionalism's key elements depend on the social structures and the social functions which must exist within the social systems. The feedback loop, which depends largely on the outputs, helps to explain the processes the social systems can use to cope with the stress and make recommendations that alter the system's future behaviour (Fisher, 2010) and this study also interrogates that too.

Structural Functionalism maintains that each function in a system is important to the survival of the whole system and systems that could not adapt to their function cease to exist. Susser (1992) adopted the analogy of human social life as organic, maintaining that individual elements depend on the whole for their maintenance and functionalists tend to view social and political units in more holistic, organic terms. Most functional approaches share the common element that, an interest in relating one part of a society or social system to another part, or to some aspect of the whole, all work towards enhancing the stability of the social system (Fisher, 2010).

2.2.2 Social Learning Theory

Bandura's Social Learning theory (1977) which maintains that Social behaviour is learnt through observation and imitating the behaviour of others (Nabavi, 2012). The *Igba Boyi* Apprenticeship scheme in the entrepreneurial venture of the Igbo usually involves a period of tutelage under the supervision of the *Oga*, who must have undertaken to train the *Nwa Boyi*, who is either kin-related or non-kin-related. *Nwa Boyi* who has been given over to the *Oga* or Master learns the skills and other rudiments of commercial venture through mostly observation and imitation of what the *Oga* has been doing and teaching. The learning process also involves modelling of the behavioural traits seen in the *Oga* and this aspect can influence the behaviour of the *Nwa Boyi* who prepares himself for the future of his own business venture after he has been freed. The conditions required for the modeling process are attention, retention, reproduction and motivation (Navabi, 2012). Igwe et. al. (2018) also maintain that the Social learning theories explain human behaviour concerning continuous reciprocal interaction between cognitive behavioural and environmental influences. Furthermore, this pertains to the relationship between *Oga* and *Nwa Boyi*.

2.2.3 Social Exchange Theory

Social Exchange theory (SET) is said to be among the most influential conceptual paradigms for understanding workplace behaviour (Cropanzano and

Mitchell, 2005). As explained by Blau (1964), it "… refers to voluntary actions of individuals that are motivated by the returns they are expected to bring and typically do in fact bring from others" p. 91 in Cook, Cheshire, Rice and Nakagawa, 2013, p. 63). Blau also argued that Social Exchange, "involves the principle that one person does another a favour and while there is a general expectation of some future return, its exact nature is definitely not stipulated in advance".

The above explains the exact relationship between the master, *Ọga* and the apprentice, *Nwa Bọyị* who goes into an Informal entrepreneurial relationship under oral agreement with the general expectation of some future return, unspecified and in almost all cases and its exact nature usually not known in advance. The relationship has subsisted for many years contributing to the wellbeing of both the Igbo and Nigeria's economic growth.

2.3 Empirical Studies Reviewed

Ekesiobi and Dimnwobi (2020) carried out a study on economic assessment of the Igbo entrepreneurship model for entrepreneurial development in Nigeria: Evidence from clusters in Anambra State with aim of investigating the entrepreneurship practice of the Igbos of South-Eastern Nigeria in order to deepen entrepreneurial development and employment generation in the country. 1187 respondents were drawn from the Onitsha and Nnewi business clusters in Anambra state and the Propensity Score Matching (PSM) technique was employed. The PSM was employed to perform a counterfactual analysis of the effect of the entrepreneurship model on business outcomes by examining participants and non-participants in the Igbo Entrepreneurship Model (IEM). Their findings reveal that entrepreneurs who participated in the IEM have higher business survival rate, business growth rate and access to trade and informal credit, while those that did not participate have better access to formal credit sources than the IEM graduates.

Onwuegbuzie (2017), conducted a study on learning from the past: entrepreneurship through apprenticeship for more successful outcomes. Qualitative method was applied with three cases involving three successful entrepreneurs of different ages. The first case study was a 70-year-old herbal healer with no formal education and operated in a rural area. The second case was in his forties, highly educated who operated in the agricultural Advances in Economics and Business and grew and supplied tomatoes to buyers in large volumes in a suburban area. The third case study was a wood carver in his fifties, who operated in a rural context and had no formal education, but was rich in indigenous knowledge. Onwuegbuzie (2017, p.283) emphasized that the three entrepreneurs had different educational backgrounds and operated in different contexts which selection was made to illustrate how apprenticeship plays out in different contexts and with people from different industries, backgrounds and age groups. Content analysis was done in three dimensions: from the learning process, from the ability to replicate the learning successfully in a business venture and from the ability to sustain the venture over time (p.283).

The findings revealed that prolonged learning duration through experience has a direct relationship on the chances of a successful entrepreneurial outcome (p. 284). Therefore, this resonates with the duration of apprenticeship of *Nwa Boyi* and the feasibility of business success.

Ezenwakwelu, Egbosionu and Okwo (2019) investigated the effect of apprenticeship training on entrepreneurship development in developing economies: A case study of Nigerian apprenticeship system. The study sought to ascertain how apprentices acquire technical and entrepreneurial skills for self-employment; assess the extent to which apprentices acquire entrepreneurial skills and knowledge for entrepreneurship development, and also identify the challenges encountered by apprentices in the course of skill acquisition. The study adopted the survey design and interview of apprentices in specific locations in Enugu metropolis, Nigeria with a sample size of 64 comprising cabinet makers, carpenters, mechanics and welders. Pearson Chi-Square technique on SPSS (v.20) was used to analyze the collected data. The findings revealed that apprentices acquire technical and entrepreneurial skills for self-employment through formal and Informal apprenticeship training systems. Also, lack of qualified manpower, insufficient training tools, inadequate infrastructure facilities and lack of start-up capital impede the course of skill acquisition and apprentices do ultimately acquire sufficient entrepreneurial skills and knowledge for entrepreneurship development (pp. 17-18). The above study buttresses the need for *Umu Boyi to* acquire relevant skills and Knowledge while being challenged by the scarcity of essential resources.

Onyima, Nzewi and Chiekezie (2017) conducted a study on the effects of apprenticeship and social capital on the new business creation process of Igbo immigrant entrepreneurs in Wukari, Taraba State using 40 businesses from the same location. Questionnaire was used as an instrument for data collection. Percentages and mean scores were used for data analysis. The study revealed that while apprenticeship had significant effects on pre-founding activities-during the business take-off stage, social capital became more important when the business had been established. It was concluded that apprenticeship had significant effects on business idea generation, idea modification, business location and financing while social capital served as a source of insurance services and access to information.

Oregun and Nafiu (2014) in their study, investigated Igbo entrepreneurial activity and business success in Nigeria as the panacea for economic growth and development. The study used personal interviews and questionnaire asinstruments for data collection in Sango-Ota, Ifo, Oshodi and Apapa areas. Descriptive statistics were used for the analysis of data. The study revealed that

Igbo entrepreneurial activities are the panacea for the Nigerian economic growth and development, and that Igbo Trade Apprenticeship Scheme (ITAS) is the business success factor.

Obunike (2016) examined the induction strategy of Igbo entrepreneurs and micro-business success: a study of household equipment line in Main Market, Onitsha, Nigeria covering an assumed population of over five hundred. 300 copies of questionnaire were administered to the Masters/Mistresses and 180 returned but only 107 were valid and used; 73 were invalid. Pearson Product-Moment Correlation analysis, and regression analysis were applied in the analysis of data. The findings reveal a strong positive relationship between induction strategy of Igbo entrepreneurs and micro-business success.

Agu and Nwachukwu (2020), explored the relevance of Igbo Traditional Business School (ITBS) in the development of Entrepreneurial Potential and Intention in Nigeria. The two questions interrogated in the study were, "does the ITBS influence entrepreneurial potential and intention, and does Entrepreneurial potential influence intention?" Data were gathered from a purposive sample of 122 actual micro-entrepreneurs (welders) who passed through the ITBS were analysed with Multiple Regression Analysis (MRA) in SPSS 23.0. The results exposed the fact that the ITBS positively and significantly influences entrepreneurial potential and intention, and that perceived desirability, perceived feasibility and propensity to act are significant predictors of entrepreneurial intention.

Ugboaja, Chinedum, Ejem, Ukpere, and Ọnyemaechi (2013) carried out a study on the role of trade associations on entrepreneurial development in Nigeria's road transport industry with a total of one thousand, three hundred and seventy-seven (1377) copies of questionnaire used for the study. The data collected were measured on a 5-point Likert scale with a hypothesized mean of 3.00. The analysis of data revealed that trade associations practiced pro-competitive and anti-competitive roles with an overall mean score of 1.9516 and 4.0824 respectively. The test of hypothesis using two sample z-tests indicated that the z-calculated value for differences in the two mean scores was 130.6724 with a significance (one-tail) probability of less than 0.0001 which is less than the critical value of 0.05. The study concluded that the extent of practice of anti-competitive roles was significantly higher than the extent of practice of pro-competitive roles by the trade associations in Nigeria's road transport industry. Furthermore, the study found that major roles of trade associations on entrepreneurial development in Nigeria's Road Transport Industry were anti-competitive while pro-competitive roles were considered to be minor roles of the trade associations.

Section Three

Methodology

Section Three
Methodology

This section presents the study design with details on the population sampling, methods of data collection and analysis.

3.1 Study Design

This study employed a concurrent, mixed-method research design which incorporated both quantitative and qualitative approaches of data collection and analysis (Teddlie Charles & Tashakkori Abbas, 2003, 2009). This design demands that both quantitative and qualitative data be collected simultaneously. The data were collected simultaneously but were analyzed separately and then integrated at the stage of interpretation of the findings. Specifically, this implies that the two sets of questionnaire were designed and administered at one end and in-depth interviews (IDI), Key informant interviews (KII) and focus group discussions (FGD) at the other end. Thus, neither the quantitative nor the qualitative approaches informed or influenced each other but rather ran concurrently. This implies that both research approaches have equal weight in terms of importance.

This research examined the state of the Igbo entrepreneurial and apprenticeship scheme to reinvigorate the entrepreneurial behaviour of Igbo people (Ndị Igbo) with a specific focus on Onitsha markets in Anambra State, South-eastern Nigeria. This study was designed in early January, 2020 while fieldwork commenced in late March, 2020 and ended in May, 2021. A two-day training was conducted for 50 (fifty) Research Assistants (RAs) who administered copies of questionnaire, as well as three Supervisors, who were trained by two professional resource persons who exposed the RAs and others to the rudiments of the research. One Principal Investigator (PI) and four Co-Principal Investigators (Co-PIs) were involved during the training. The training focused on the purpose/objectives of the research, exposure to skills on instrument administration and ethical issues during fieldwork data collection, use of Open Data Kit (ODK) for questionnaire administration, and ascertaining Geoinformation System (GIS) coordinates. The study was designed to cover the following Onitsha markets: Main Market, Ọchanja Market, Bridge Head Market, Spare Parts Market Nkpor, Building Materials Markets, Ogidi/Ogbunike; which cut across the following Local Government Areas of Anambra State: Onitsha North, Onitsha South, Idemili North and Oyi.

3.2 Quantitative Methodology

The study adopted a survey research design and judgmental sampling was used to select five (5) markets in the Onitsha metropolis in the order of time of the creation of the markets. The markets selected were:

1. Main Market: .... Onitsha North L.G.A
2. Ọchanja Market: .... Onitsha South L. G. A
3. Bridge Head Market: .... Onitsha South L. G. A
4. Spare Parts Market, Nkpor: .... Idemili North L. G. A
5. Building Materials Markets, Ogidi/Ogbunike... Idemili North/Oyi L. G. A

The markets were visited by the research team comprising of the Principal Investigator (PI) and the Co-Principal Investigators (Co-PIs), research assistants, and interviewers for data collection.

The minimum sample size for a statistically meaningful deduction was determined using the statistical formula of Fisher (1998) for calculating sample size.

$$A = Z^2 \frac{(Pq)}{d^2}$$

Z is normal deviant at the portion of 95/5 confidence level
Deviation – 0.02

P = probability of success
Q = probability of failure
$= \frac{1.96 \ (0.05) \ (0.50)}{(0.02)^2}$
$= \frac{0.9604}{0.0004}$ = $\underline{\underline{2,401}}$

Soft copies of questionnaire were distributed as one of the methods of data collection employed for this study. These questionnaires were hosted using an internet-mediated platform known as Open Data Kit (ODK) - a software for online data collection and management employed to collect the primary data. This meant that we scaled over the challenges of printing thousands of hardcopy questionnaires but were confronted with the need for constant use of the internet to access, administer and transfer the online questionnaire to the ODK managers. Research assistants constantly searched for the GIS coordinates before submitting them online to ascertain the location of data collection. The Research Team and the fifty research assistants were pre-trained on the use of ODK application/software.

Two sets of questionnaire were designed, one for the "*Ndị Oga*" (Masters) and one for the "*Ụmụ Boyi*" (Apprentices). Systematic sampling was used to distribute the copies of questionnaire where the elements of the population (the lines in the markets) were arranged in numerical order and the lines were selected at regular intervals from the list. Cluster sampling (the zoning arrangement) from the administrative wing of the market (ASMATA) was also relied upon by the study. Data was collected at every fourth shop of each line.

3.3 Pre-fieldwork Validity and Reliability Test

A pre-test was conducted at Eke-Awka Market to validate the research instruments before proceeding to Onitsha for the main fieldwork. This revealed the questionnaire items that needed to be expunged or modified.

3.4 Description of the Five (5) Selected Onitsha Markets Compositions

- Main Market comprises Zone I (37 lines), Zone II (39 lines), and Zone III (35 lines) based on the pre-fieldwork interviews that were conducted. The lines in the zones were selected at the interval of three (3). This gave the items in the population equal chances of being selected.
- Bridge Head Market comprises 5 Zones and 27 Unions.
- Building Material Market Zone 2 and 3 Ogidi/Ogbunike comprise fifteen (15) lines and were selected at the interval of three (3).
- Building Materials International, Ogidi comprises ten (10) lines and was also selected at the interval of three (3).

3.5 Sampling Procedure and Sample Size Determination

The sample size was allocated to the markets judgmentally relying on the year the markets were formed and ratios and percentages were employed. The Main Market was the oldest, followed by Ochanja Market, Bridge Head, Spare Parts, and Building Materials Markets.

1. Main Market – 40%
2. Ochanja - 20%
3. Bridge Head – 15%
4. Spare Parts, Nkpor – 15%
5. Building Materials, Ogidi/Ogbunike – 10%

Main Market – $\frac{40}{100}$ x $\frac{2401}{1}$ = 960

Ọchanja – $\frac{20}{100}$ x $\frac{2401}{1}$ = 480

Bridge Head – $\frac{15}{100}$ x $\frac{2401}{1}$ = 360

Spare Parts, Nkpor – $\frac{15}{100}$ x $\frac{2401}{1}$ = 360

Building Materials - $\frac{10}{100}$ x $\frac{2401}{1}$ = 240

Total = 2401

3.6 Assumptions

Assumptions were made due to the difficulty of knowing the exact number of apprentices and masters in the markets. Therefore, the study assumed one apprentice to one master in every shop.

3.7 Analytical Methods for Quantitative Data

Descriptive statistics were adopted to present data and answer research questions using frequency Tables, Pie charts, Bar charts, and line charts. Inferential statistics were employed to test the hypotheses adopting Chi Square, Pearson Product Moment Correlation, and Analysis of Variance (ANOVA).

3.8 Methods for Qualitative Data Collection

The study sites and participants were recruited using purposive sampling and snowball techniques. The following qualitative data collection methods were employed namely: In-depth Interviews (IDI), Key Informant Interviews (KII) and Focus Group Discussions (FGD).

A total of 23 (twenty-three) in-depth interviews were conducted involving 22 males and one female comprising mainly male 'Nḍị Ọga' (masters) and one female 'Ọnye Madam' (madam) aged between 30 and 72 years. At the level of trade masters (Nḍị Ọga), only one female madam was accessible because the business/trading terrain in Onitsha Markets is male-dominated.

For key informants, 18 key informants (KII) were identified through the snowball technique and they include experienced retired traders, owners of industries (both defunct and functional), business owners Nḍị Ọga (masters), and market union leaders. Having obtained oral and written informed consent from each of these key informants where necessary, we conducted interviews with them at their preferred venues. Many preferred that the interviews be conducted in their homes and others preferred their offices or shops. The following list shows a few of these key stakeholders interviews: Chief Sir G. U. Okeke (Ọnwa) of the famous GUO motors was interviewed in his home; former Chairman of Onitsha Market Traders Association (OMATA), Chief Honourable Emeka Asoanya, now current Transition Committee Chairman, Onitsha South LGA; former Chairman, Onitsha Market Amalgamated Traders Association (OMATA) and former Anambra State Market Amalgamated Traders Association (ASMATA); High Chief E. A. Okafor, Chairman/CEO, Awutuolo Group of Companies; Chief Dan Ogbuefi (Ide Agulụ), Chairman/CEO Bekks Biscuits - Bekks Group of Companies; High Chief Frank Obi, CEO Franobi Group of Companies Ltd.; Chief Evaristus Ụba, CEO Polly Foam Nigeria Ltd.; Chief Sam Ihionu, CEO Divine Success Plastics Nig. Ltd.; Chief Jude Nwankwo, Chairman Building Materials International Market, Ogidi; Chief Sunday Obieze, President General, Head Bridge Market, Onitsha; Chief Paulinus Anagboso (Onowu Agulụ), Building Materials Market, Ogidi; Hon. Chief Silas Ejeabocha, Council Member, Anaocha LGA, Building Materials Market, Ogidi, among many others.

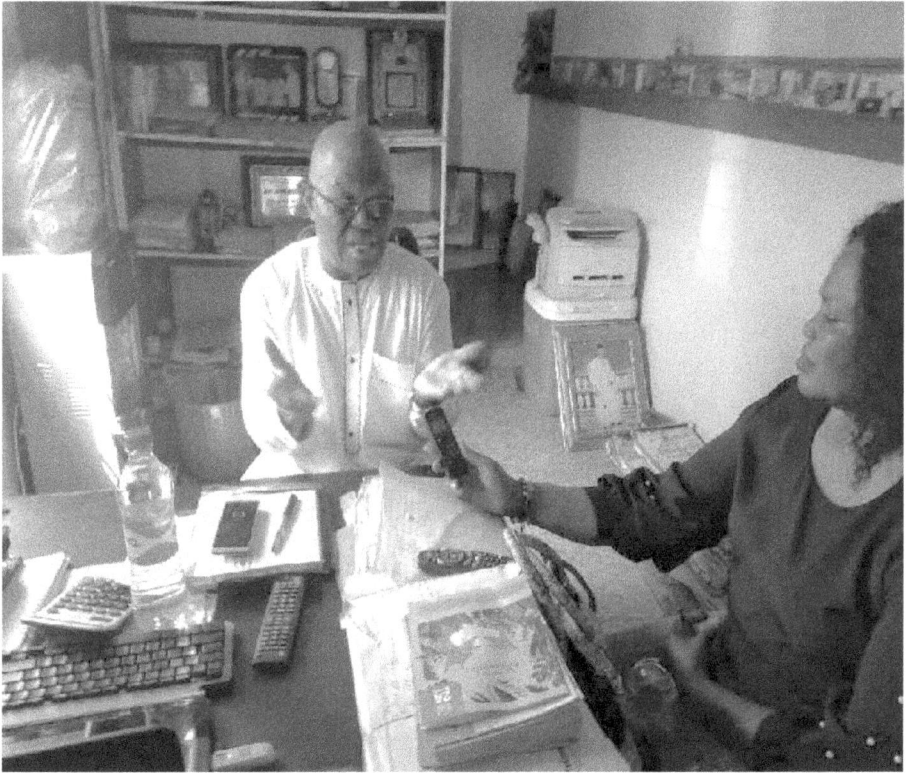

Key Study Stakeholders Interviews

Similarly, for FGD, a total of seven (7) gender-based and mixed sessions of focus group discussions (comprising 6 to 13 participants) were conducted across the various Onitsha markets comprising mainly Market Leaders, masters of trades, apprentices (*Ụmụ Boyi*), sales girls, Learning apprentices (*ndị-na-amụ ahịa*), importers/exporters and leaders of industries within Onitsha, including the Chamber of Commerce. The first FGD took place at the Main Market, Onitsha which involved seven (7) market union leaders who also doubled as *Ndị Oga* (masters/business owners/traders) as study participants with five researchers who served as moderators, time keepers, note-takers, and electronic recorders of all the various FGD sessions. The second FGD also took place at the main market with eight (8) study participants comprising mainly *Ndị Oga* (masters) who were purposively recruited by the Main Market gatekeepers/consultants (insiders) to participate in the study. The third FGD took place at the Bridge Head Market comprising mainly thirteen (13) Market Union leaders cum *Ndị Oga* with five researchers as moderators and one fieldwork research assistant. The fourth FGD comprised mainly of six (6) *Ụmụ Boyi* (servant-apprentices) recruited purposively as study participants with five moderators. At Ọchanja Market, the fifth FGD comprised eight (8) Market Union leaders who also doubled as *Ndị Oga*/shop owners and entrepreneurs with five moderators. At the Building Materials Market, a sixth FGD session was conducted involving 8 study participants mainly *Ndị Oga* and four moderators. Finally, an FGD session was also conducted with eight (8) leaders and members of the Onitsha Chamber of Commerce, Industry, Mines and Agriculture (OCIMMA) with the team of researchers serving as moderators, note-takers, and record keepers.

The research questions for these interviews and discussions centered around the following: history/origin of apprenticeship; structure, practice and management, the influence of relevant institutions like market unions and market governance, families, communities, and chamber of commerce; government influences on the *Igba Boyi* apprenticeship scheme. Others were on the nature of involvement and adaptation to modern online trading/business and transactions. The contributions of *Igba Boyi* to wealth creation, employment creation, and development were explored. We also probed on why *Igba Boyi* and why not *Igba Geli*? This study further explored issues around the challenges of the *Igba Boyi* apprenticeship scheme and the possible solutions and best strategies for the improvement of the scheme to cope with the current realities in the modern world.

To elicit more details about the origin and reasons for apprenticeship among Igbo people in South-eastern Nigeria, the study participants were first asked to narrate what they know or think is the origin and reasons for "*Igba Boyi*" (apprenticeship) in the Igbo society. The study further probed to find out why *Ndị Igbo* place so much value on apprenticeship. Does it have connections to an ancestral linkage, or is it based on the Igbo worldview of "*Onye fe eze, Eze eluo ya*" (when one serves a king, kingship will also get to him)? The study also sought to ascertain if the Igbo apprenticeship culture stems from an act of willingness or compulsion as some may erroneously link the *Igba Boyi* to slavery and servitude. We also tried to find out if it is connected to one's success or failure in business as we found that there are pockets of entrepreneurs who did not undergo apprenticeship or *Igba Boyi* and yet they are in business. Finally, we tried to establish if there is a punishment for not taking an apprentice by a master. All these were explored to get detailed information on the dynamic provenience of the *Igba Boyi* scheme among the Igbo people.

In another vein, attention was also focused on how the *Igba Boyi* scheme is structured and managed in Igbo culture. Are there specific criteria to meet before taking on an apprentice: Terms of Agreement? What happens when the agreement is fulfilled and when it fails? What are the contents of the curriculum? Are there limits to what the apprentice should learn? Is there a structure that stipulates what the apprentice learns at each point? Is the process different when it involves a female?

The study also paid attention to the peculiar nuances (business slangs) applied by apprentices (*Ụmụ Boyi*) and masters (*Ndị Oga*) in their daily business transactions in the selected Onitsha markets. We also tried to understand their business significance and in what instances they are used and ascertained the benefits of the coded language or business slang during trade transactions in the selected Onitsha markets.

In terms of contributions to the development and economy, we explored what lessons the government can take. Are there tribes with a similar system? Will the system be beneficial to Anambra's economy? Will the system be beneficial to the South-east? How can the system be advanced into something national, and what roles can they play?

The influence exerted by institutions in sustaining agreements and the learning process between the apprentice and the boss were investigated such as the influence of family and clan, including spouse and children, the influence of community leadership, influence of the market association and union, influence of ex-apprentices under the same master, influence of religion and spirituality, getting the government to pay part of the settlement fund in settlement of the apprentice, constant reminder of the settlement time of the apprentice by the government.

The traditional significance of the male in the context as against the female, are there verifiable cases of the women getting involved in an apprenticeship?

Are women involved in leadership positions in the markets? Are there plans for the female gender in the *Igba Boyi* scheme?

Issues around adaptation to the use of internet-mediated platforms in the transaction were also explored like; are they involved in drop-shipping (*Igba oso ahia* online), as vendors or owners, which social media outlets do they prefer, and why? Instagram, why? Facebook, why? WhatsApp, why? Twitter, why? YouTube, why? We further explored questions around: acceptance of digital banking, do you accept POS? Do the traders (*Ndi Oga/Umu Boyi*) accept money transfers? If no, why not?

The study also investigated the challenges of the *Igba Boyi* apprenticeship scheme like challenges from the *Nwa Boyi /Oga* (commitment, faithfulness), challenges from family and community institutions, challenges from market institutions, challenges from the government and the wider economy. Are there suggestions to make it better that are to be made more formal if they think it is too informal or otherwise: personal efforts, family efforts, community efforts?

The failures and successes of the discussed institutions were also explored such as the need to enhance the apprenticeship institution; Are there more institutions to carry along? Are present institutions too informal or formal? What are the consequences for formality and informality? The study also tried to ascertain how the apprenticeship scheme contributes to wealth creation and employment generation. Issues around the settlement and the challenges that come with it were interrogated. Finally, the study examined how the apprenticeship (*Igba Boyi*) system can be reinvigorated in Igbo land in terms of funding and its dynamics, payment of stipends/allowances to apprentices if possible, and issues around adult education related to business management.

Table i: Summary of Study Participants in Qualitative Data

Methods of Data Collection	Number of Study Participants	Gender	Age Range	Type of Study Participants	Name of Markets
IDI	23	22 Males, 1 Female	18-72 years	*Ndi Oga, Ndi Madam Umu Boyi*	Main Market, Ochanja Market, Bridge-Head; Spare Parts; Building Materials, Ogidi/Ogbunike
KII	18	All males	50-86 years	Owners of Industries ; Old/Retired Entrepreneurs	All
FGD	7 Sessions (6-13 participants)	68 Males and 12 Females	18 years and above	Market Union Leaders; *Ndi Oga* (masters); *Umu Boyi*	All
Total	121				

3.9 Analytical Procedure for Qualitative Data

Thematic method of analysis was employed to analyze the qualitative data collected for this study. According to Clarke & Braun, (2013); Braun & Clarke (2006), thematic analysis is a qualitative method of data analysis that involves:

> 'Identifying, analyzing, and reporting patterns (themes) within data. It minimally organizes and describes your data set in (thick) detail. However, frequently it goes further than this and interprets various aspects of the research topic' (Braun and Clarke, 2006, p.79).

The intention is to ensure depth and 'thick description' (Geertz, 1973), the relationship between categories of themes, and rigour (Attride-Stirling, 2001; Fereday and Muir-Cochrane, 2006; Vaismoradi et al., 2013). The data collected from the field was translated, transliterated, and transcribed, and stored in electronic gadgets, tape recorders, computers and was also recorded in field notes to ensure no data is lost. This was done first to ensure detailed and accurate emic (insider's) perspectives from the source language (local language/pidgin) which the study participants used during data collection to the target language (English) with aid of a translator or an interpreter. Most of the interviews were conducted in Igbo, Pidgin and English languages. Next, the raw data was imported into the latest version of NVivo (R.1.5) to process the data. Data processing in NVivo involved - cleaning process, editing and analyzing the emerging codes and themes from the reiterative reading of the manuscripts. The study employed the six phases of conducting thematic analysis as prescribed by Braun & Clarke, (2006) namely:

1. Becoming familiar with the data.
2. Generating initial codes.
3. Searching for themes.
4. Reviewing themes.
5. Defining and naming themes.
6. Producing the report

The coding outcomes were later exported into excel/word sheets as 'codebook' to allow for in-depth interpretations, writing up and adequate extrapolations to be made in line with the research objectives. To ensure the reliability and validity of the themes and findings, intra-coder and inter-coder analysis were done. This is where this researcher coded the manuscripts twice within specified time intervals and another coder was allowed to code the same manuscripts to ensure they are arriving at similar themes (Aziato et al., 2014; Cho, 2006; Onwuegbuzie & Leech, 2007). The codes were then categorized into major and minor themes and classifications to enable in-depth extrapolations to be made from the narratives and constructions of the experiences of the traders (*Ndị Ọga* and *Ụmụ Boyi*) in line with the study objectives.

Section Four
Data Presentation and Analysis

Section Four
Data Presentation and Analysis

This section presents both the quantitative and qualitative data of this research concurrently and discursively interprets the data.

4.1 Response Rate

Given the use of an electronic data collection tool – Open Data Kit (ODK), the total number of respondents was 2,401. A total number of 1,201 responses were collected from Ndi Ọga, while 1,200 were collected from Ụmụ Bọyị.

This shows a 100% response rate which was made possible because of the adoption of ODK.

4.2 Socio-demographic Data Presentation of Masters (Ndị Ọga)

This subsection presents the socio-demographic data of the respondents who were administered questionnaires.

Table 1: Local Government Areas (LGAs) covered by the Study

LGAs	Frequency	Percent	Valid Percent	Cumulative Percent
Idemili North	180	15.0	15.0	15.0
Onitsha North	481	40.0	40.0	55.0
Onitsha South	419	34.9	34.9	89.9
Oyi	121	10.1	10.1	100.0
Total	1201	100.0	100.0	

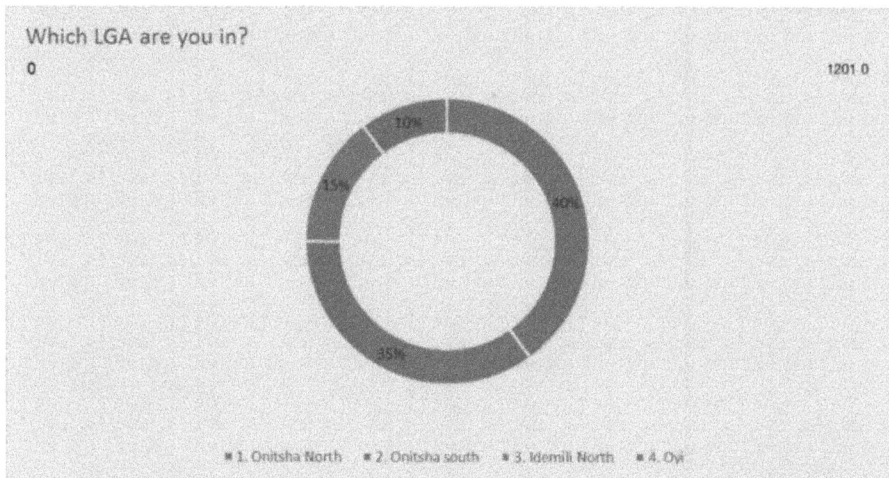

Figure 1: Pie Chart Showing the Number of Local Government Areas (LGAs) covered by the Study.

Table 1 and Figure 1 show that four (4) Local Government Areas were covered in Onitsha Metropolis and the majority of markets studied are situated in Onitsha North Local Government Area representing 40% of the total markets covered. Onitsha South Local Government Area represents 34.9%, Idemili North (15%), Oyi (10.1%).

Table 2: Distribution of *Ndị Ọga* by Age

Age	Frequency	Percent	Valid Percent	Cumulative Percent
20	1	.1	.1	.2
21	3	.2	.2	.4
22	2	.2	.2	.6
23	2	.2	.2	.7
24	6	.5	.5	1.2
25	8	.7	.7	1.9
26	11	.9	.9	2.8
27	10	.8	.8	3.7
28	35	2.9	2.9	6.6
29	31	2.6	2.6	9.2
30	37	3.1	3.1	12.2
31	21	1.7	1.7	14.0
32	29	2.4	2.4	16.4
33	38	3.2	3.2	19.6
34	34	2.8	2.8	22.4
35	79	6.6	6.6	29.0
36	37	3.1	3.1	32.1
37	29	2.4	2.4	34.5
38	40	3.3	3.3	37.8
39	34	2.8	2.8	40.6

40	66	5.5	5.5	46.1
41	30	2.5	2.5	48.6
42	35	2.9	2.9	51.5
43	29	2.4	2.4	54.0
44	24	2.0	2.0	56.0
45	70	5.8	5.8	61.8
46	30	2.5	2.5	64.3
47	30	2.5	2.5	66.8
48	38	3.2	3.2	70.1
49	32	2.7	2.7	72.5
50	49	4.1	4.1	76.6
51	22	1.8	1.8	78.4
52	31	2.6	2.6	81.0
53	25	2.1	2.1	83.1
54	12	1.0	1.0	84.1
55	19	1.6	1.6	85.7
56	24	2.0	2.0	87.7
57	12	1.0	1.0	88.7
58	17	1.4	1.4	90.1
59	16	1.3	1.3	91.4
60	14	1.2	1.2	92.6
61	5	.4	.4	93.0
62	15	1.2	1.2	94.3
63	10	.8	.8	95.1
64	5	.4	.4	95.5
65	9	.7	.7	96.3
66	9	.7	.7	97.0
67	6	.5	.5	97.5
68	9	.7	.7	98.3
69	2	.2	.2	98.4
70	5	.4	.4	98.8
71	3	.2	.2	99.1
72	2	.2	.2	99.3
73	2	.2	.2	99.4
75	2	.2	.2	99.6
76	1	.1	.1	99.7
78	2	.2	.2	99.8
80	1	.1	.1	99.9
81	1	.1	.1	100.0
Total	1201			
		100.0	100.0	

Table 2 and Figure 2 show the age distribution of Ndị Ọga in the five (5)

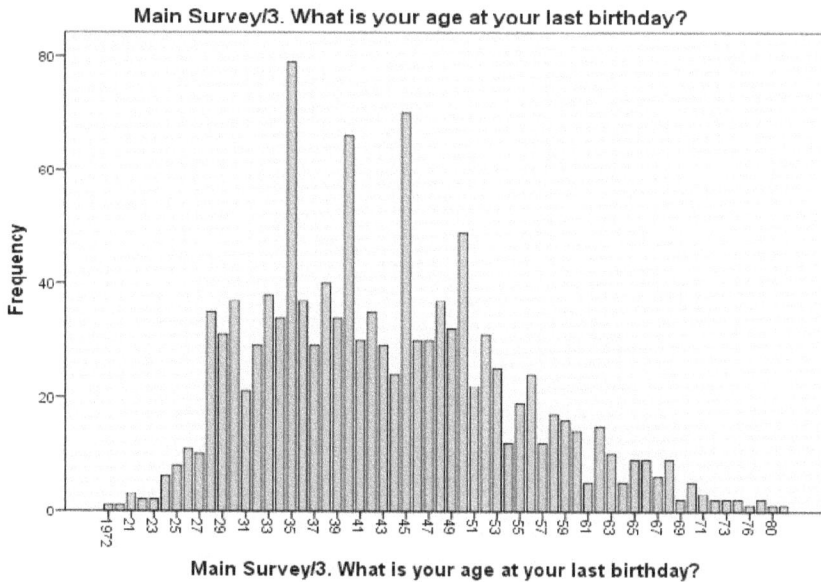

Main Survey/3. What is your age at your last birthday?

Figure 2: Bar Chart Showing the Distribution of Ndị Ọga by Age

markets studied. The frequency table and bar chart depicting that *Ndi Ọga* are in the age bracket of 20 – 81 and the majority are in the age of thirty-five (35) representing 6.67% of the age distribution.

Table 3: Distribution of *Ụmụ Bọyị* by Age

	Frequency	Percent	Valid Percent	Cumulative Percent
14	5	.4	.4	.4
15	14	1.2	1.2	1.6
16	29	2.4	2.4	4.0
17	53	4.4	4.4	8.4
18	72	6.0	6.0	14.4
19	125	10.4	10.4	24.8
20	169	14.1	14.1	38.9
21	150	12.5	12.5	51.4
22	139	11.6	11.6	63.0
23	102	8.5	8.5	71.5
24	87	7.2	7.2	78.8
25	79	6.6	6.6	85.3
26	48	4.0	4.0	89.3
27	30	2.5	2.5	91.8
28	35	2.9	2.9	94.8
29	12	1.0	1.0	95.8
30	20	1.7	1.7	97.4
31	3	.3	.3	97.7
32	2	.2	.2	97.8

33	5	.4	.4	98.3
34	3	.3	.3	98.5
35	8	.7	.7	99.2
36	1	.1	.1	99.3
37	2	.2	.2	99.4
38	2	.2	.2	99.6
39	1	.1	.1	99.7
40	1	.1	.1	99.8
42	1	.1	.1	99.8
45	2	.2	.2	100.0
Total	1200	100.0	100.0	

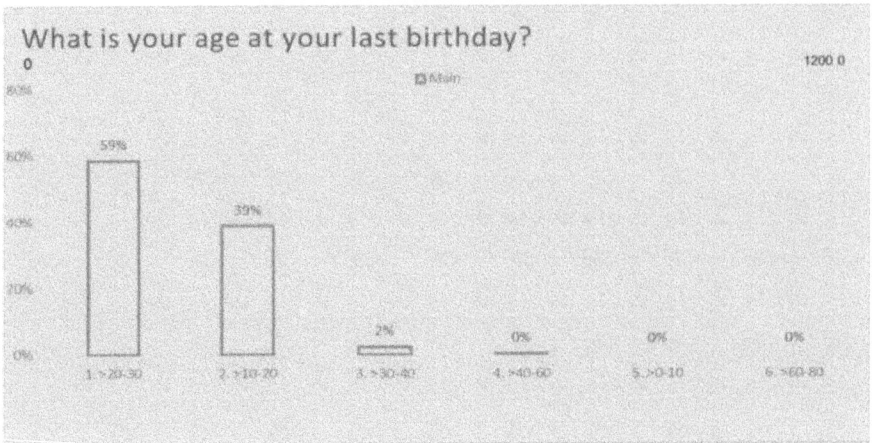

Figure 3: Bar Chart Showing the Distribution of *Ụmụ Boyị* **by** Age

Table 3 (Frequency Table) and Figure 3 (Bar Chart) depict the age distribution of *Ụmụ Boyị* in the markets covered by the study. It reveals that the majority of *Ụmụ Boyị* **are** in the age bracket of 20 – 30 representing 59% of the age distribution.

Table 4: Distribution of *Ndị Ọga* by Age Group

	Frequency	Percent	Valid Percent	Cumulative Percent
20 - 29 years	108	9.0	9.0	9.0
30 - 39 years	381	31.7	31.7	40.7
40 - 49 years	382	31.8	31.8	72.5
50 - 59 years	226	18.8	18.8	91.3
60 - 69 years	83	6.9	6.9	98.3
70 years and above	21	1.7	1.7	100.0
Total	1201	100.0	100.0	

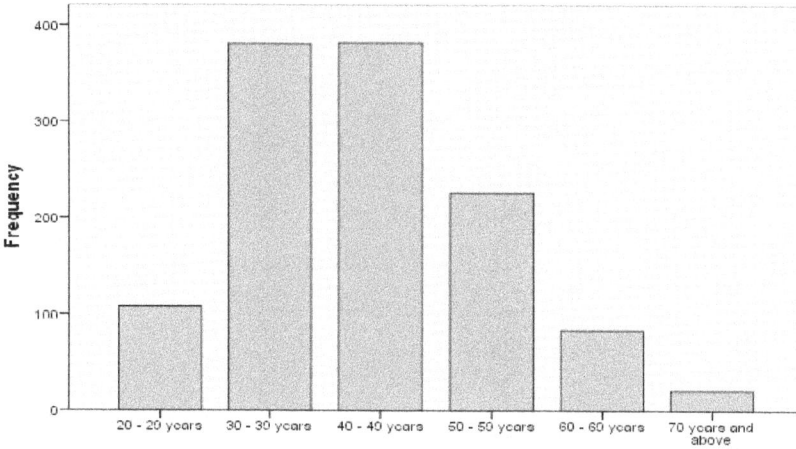

Figure 4: Bar Chart Showing the Distribution of Nḍị Ọga by Age Group

Table 4 (Frequency Table) and Figure 4 (Bar Chart) show the distribution of Nḍị Ọga by age group. The data presentation reveals that the majority are in the age group of 40 – 49 closely followed by those in the age group of 30 – 39. This represents 31.8% and 31.7% of the age group distribution respectively.

Table 5: Distribution of Ụmụ Bọyị by Age Group

	Frequency	Percent	Valid Percent	Cumulative Percent
10 - 19 years	294	24.5	24.5	24.5
20 - 29 years	854	71.2	71.2	95.7
30 - 39 years	48	4.0	4.0	99.7
40 - 49 years	4	.3	.3	100.0
Total	1200	100.0	100.0	

Figure 5: Bar Chart Showing the Distribution of Ụmụ Bọyị by Age Group

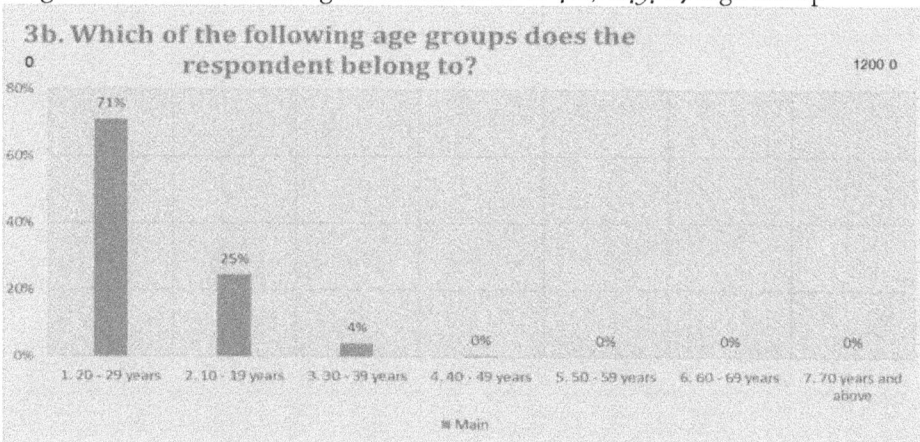

Table 5 (Frequency Table) and Figure 5 (Bar Chart) show the distribution of *Ụmụ Bọyị by* age group. The age group distribution by percentage are 10 – 19 (24.5%), 20 – 29 (71.2%), 30 – 39 (4.0%), 40 – 49 (3.0%). This reveals that the majority of *Umu Boyi* are in the age group of 20 – 29.

Table 6: Distribution of *Ndị Ọga* by Gender

	Frequency	Percent	Valid Percent	Cumulative Percent
Female	97	8.1	8.1	8.1
Male	1104	91.9	91.9	100.0
Total	1201	100.0	100.0	

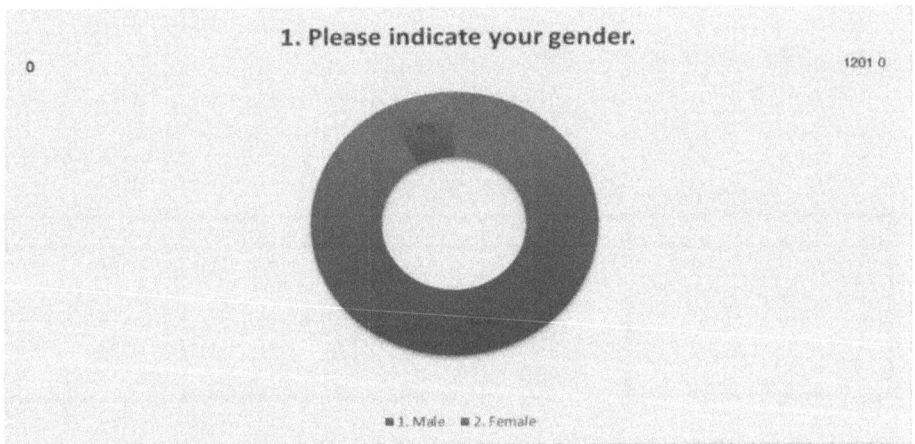

Figure 6: Pie Chart Showing the Distribution of *Ndị Ọga* by Gender

Table 6 (Frequency Table) and Figure 6 (Pie Chart) depict the distribution of *Ndị Ọga* by gender. 8.1% are female and 91.9% are male. This clearly reveals that the majority of *Ndị Ọga* are male.

Table 7: Distribution of *Ụmụ Bọyị* by Gender

	Frequency	Percent	Valid Percent	Cumulative Percent
Female	96	8.0	8.0	8.0
Male	1104	92.0	92.0	100.0
Total	1200	100.0	100.0	

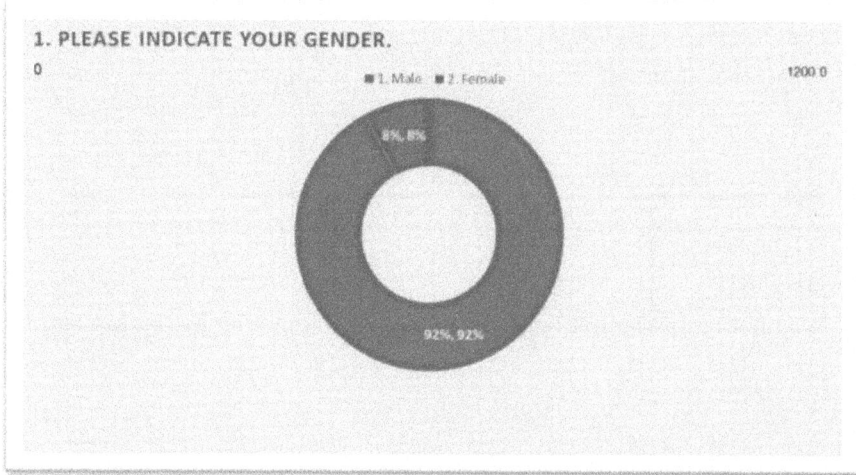

1. PLEASE INDICATE YOUR GENDER.

Figure 7: Pie Chart Showing the Distribution of *Ụmụ Bọyị* by Gender

Table 7 (Frequency Table) and Figure 7 (Pie Chart) show the distribution of *Ụmụ Bọyị* by gender. The females represent 8.0% of the gender distribution while males are 92%. This indicates that males are mostly involved in *Igba Bọyị*.

Table 8: Distribution of *Ndị Ọga* by Marital Status

	Frequency	Percent	Valid Percent	Cumulative Percent
Divorced	2	.2	.2	.2
Married	931	77.5	77.5	77.7
Single	260	21.6	21.6	99.3
Widowed	8	.7	.7	100.0
Total	1201	100.0	100.0	

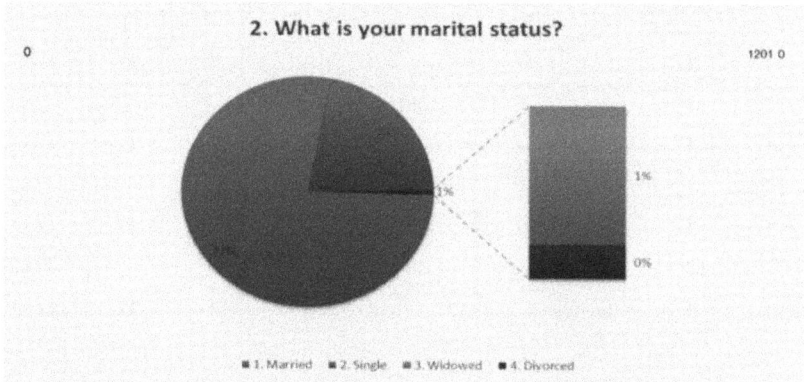

2. What is your marital status?

Figure 8: Pie Chart Showing the Distribution of *Ndị Ọga* by Marital Status

Table 8 (Frequency Table) and Figure 8 (Pie Chart) show the distribution of *Ndị Oga* by marital status. 2.0% are divorced, 77.5% are married, 21.6% are single, 7.0% are widowed. This indicates that the majority of *Ndị Oga* are married.

Table 9: Distribution of *Ụmụ Boyị* by Marital Status

	Frequency	Percent	Valid Percent	Cumulative Percent
Married	20	1.7	1.7	1.7
Single	1180	98.3	98.3	100.0
Total	1200	100.0	100.0	

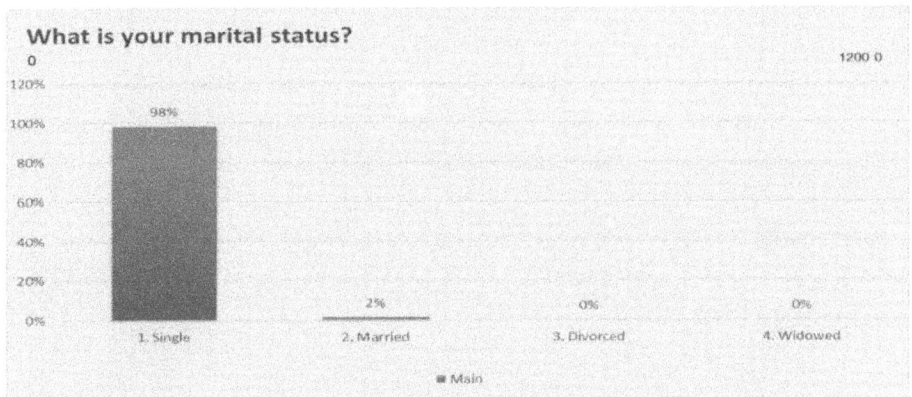

Figure 9: Bar Chart Showing the Distribution of *Ụmụ Boyị* by Marital Status

Table 9 (Frequency Table) and Figure 9 (Bar Chart) depict the distribution of *Ụmụ Boyị* by marital status. From the data presented, married *Ụmụ Boyị* are 1.7% and single *Ụmụ Boyị* are 98.3%. This clearly shows that the majority of *Ụmụ Boyị* are single.

Table 10: Distribution of *Ndị Oga* by Religious Affiliation

	Frequency	Percent	Valid Percent	Cumulative Percent
African traditional religion	27	2.2	2.2	2.2
Christianity	1171	97.5	97.5	99.8
Muslim	1	.1	.1	99.8
Others specify	2	.2	.2	100.0
Total	1201	100.0	100.0	

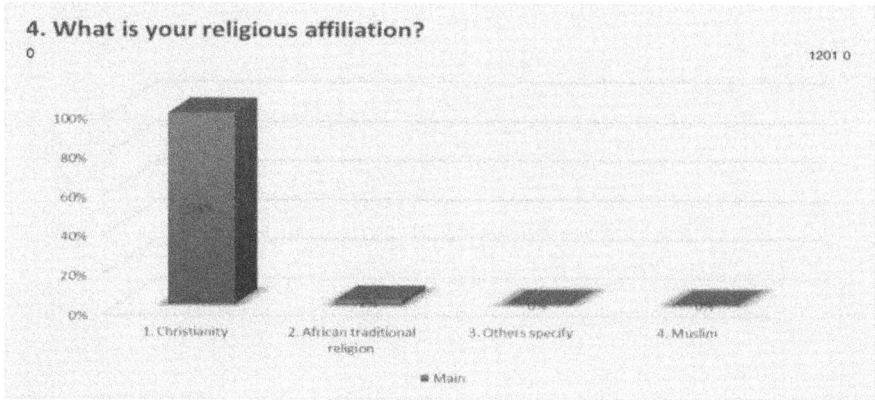

Figure 10: Bar Chart

Indicating the Distribution of *Ndị Ọga* by Religious Affiliation

Table 10 (Frequency Table) and Figure 10 (Bar Chart) show the Distribution of *Ndi Ọga* by religious affiliation. African Traditional Religion represents 2.2%, Christianity (97.5%), Muslim (0.1%), other religions (2.0%). The data distribution indicates that the majority of *Ndị Ọga* that trade in these markets are Christians.

Table 11: Distribution of *Ụmụ Bọyị* by Religious Affiliation

	Frequency	Percent	Valid Percent	Cumulative Percent
African traditional religion	10	.8	.8	.8
Christianity	1189	99.1	99.1	99.9
Muslim	1	.1	.1	100.0
Total	1200	100.0	100.0	

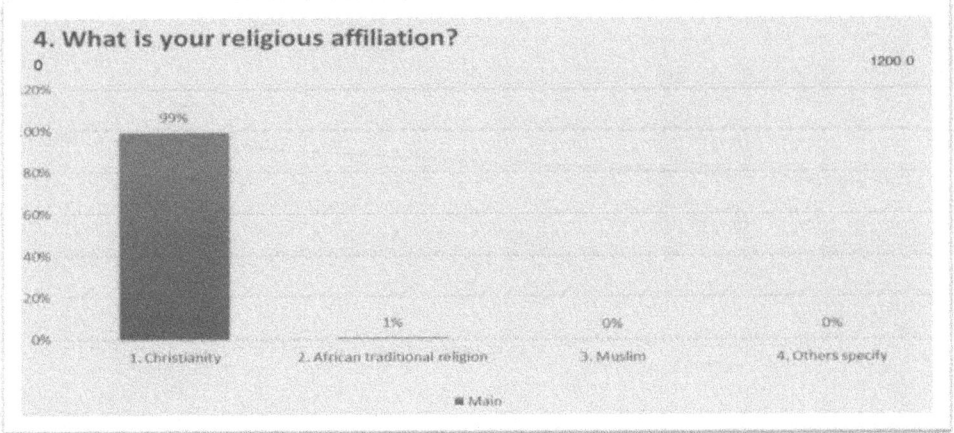

4. What is your religious affiliation?

Figure 11: Bar Chart Showing the Distribution of *Ụmụ Bọyị* by Religious Affiliation

Table 11 (Frequency Table) and Figure 11 (Bar Chart) depict the distribution of *Ụmụ Bọyị* by religious affiliation. African Traditional Religion (0.8%), Christianity (99.1%), Muslim (1.0%). This clearly shows that the majority of *Ụmụ Bọyị are* Christians.

Table 12: Distribution of *Ndị Ọga* by Other Religious Affiliation

	Frequency	Percent	Valid Percent	Cumulative Percent
Other options except (If Others, please specify)	1199	99.8	99.8	99.8
Both a Christian and a traditionalist	1	.1	.1	99.9
Christian and ATR	1	.1	.1	100.0
Total	1201	100.0	100.0	

Table 12 (Frequency Table) shows that those that are both Christian and Traditionalist are 0.1%, Christian and African Traditional Religion (0.1%).

Table 13: Distribution of _Ndị Ọga_ by their Various Trades

	Frequency	Percent	Valid Percent	Cumulative Percent
Automobile Spare Parts	177	14.7	14.7	14.7
Books and Stationeries	22	1.8	1.8	16.6
Building materials/fabrication	151	12.6	12.6	29.1
Carpentry	36	3.0	3.0	32.1
Clothing and textiles	557	46.4	46.4	78.5
Electronics/Electricals	21	1.7	1.7	80.3
Equipment, tools, heavy-duty machinery	33	2.7	2.7	83.0
Foods (provisions)/beverages	19	1.6	1.6	84.6
Forex	5	.4	.4	85.0
General merchandise	64	5.3	5.3	90.3
Home appliances	16	1.3	1.3	91.7
Pharmaceuticals/Cosmetics	100	8.3	8.3	100.0
Total	1201	100.0	100.0	

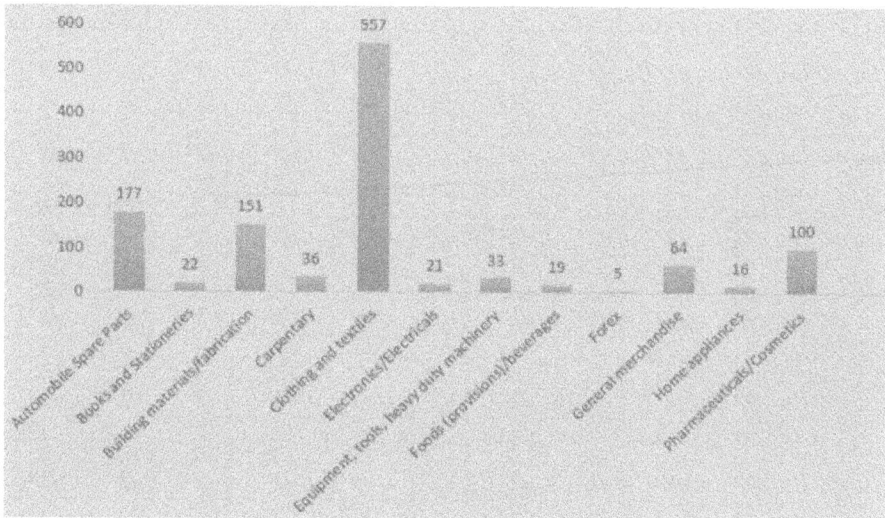

Figure 13: Bar Chart Showing the Distribution of _Ndị Ọga_ by their Various Trades

Table 13 (Frequency Table) and Figure 13 (Bar Chart) indicate the distribution of _Ndị Ọga_ by their various trades. Automobile Spare Parts (14.7%), Books and Stationeries (1.8%), Building Materials/Fabrication (12.6%), Carpentry (3.0%), Clothing and Textiles (46.4%), Electronics/Electricals (1.7%), Equipment, Tools, Heavy Duty Machinery (2.7%), Foods (Provisions)/Beverages (1.6%),

Forex (0.4%), General Merchandise (5.3%), Home Appliances (1.3%), Pharmaceuticals/Cosmetics (8.3%). This data distribution reveals that the majority of N*di Oga* trade in Clothing and Textiles.

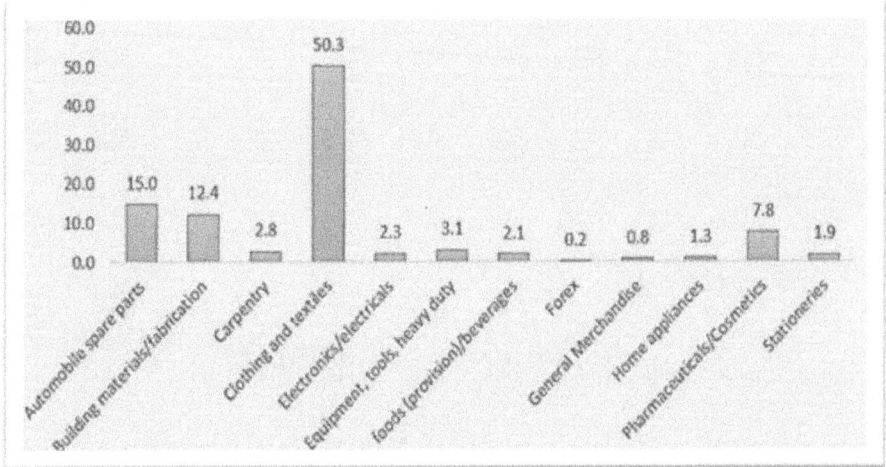

Figure 14: Bar Chart Showing the Distribution of ụmụ bọyị by Trades they are

Table 14: Distribution of Ụmụ Bọyị by Trades they are Learning

	Frequency	Percent	Valid Percent	Cumulative Percent
Automobile spare parts	180	15.0	15.0	15.0
Building materials/fabrication	149	12.4	12.4	27.4
Carpentry	34	2.8	2.8	30.3
Clothing and textiles	604	50.3	50.3	80.6
Electronics/electricals	27	2.3	2.3	82.8
Equipment, tools, heavy duty	37	3.1	3.1	85.9
foods (provision)/beverages	25	2.1	2.1	88.0
Forex	2	.2	.2	88.2
General Merchandise	10	.8	.8	89.0
Home appliances	15	1.3	1.3	90.3
Pharmaceuticals/Cosmetics	94	7.8	7.8	98.1
Stationeries	23	1.9	1.9	100.0
Total	1200	100.0	100.0	

Table 14 (Frequency Table) and Figure 14 (Bar Chart) shows the distribution of *Ụmụ Bọyị* by trades they are learning. Automobile Spare Parts (15.0%), Building Materials/Fabrication (12.4%), Carpentry (2.8%), Clothing and Textiles (50.3%), Electronics/Electricals (2.3%), Equipment, Tools, Heavy Duty Machinery (3.1%), Foods (Provisions)/Beverages (2.1%), Forex (0.2%), General

Merchandise (0.8%), Home Appliances (1.3%), Pharmaceuticals/Cosmetics (7.8%), Stationeries (1.9%). This data distribution reveals that Clothing and Textiles are the trades that *Umu Boyi* majorly learn.

Table 15: Distribution of *Ndi Oga* by Highest Level of Education

	Frequency	Percent	Valid Percent	Cumulative Percent
Bachelors Degree	139	11.6	11.6	11.6
FSLC	218	18.2	18.2	29.7
No formal education	41	3.4	3.4	33.1
OND/HND	86	7.2	7.2	40.3
Postgraduate Degrees	9	.7	.7	41.0
SSCE	708	59.0	59.0	100.0
Total	1201	100.0	100.0	

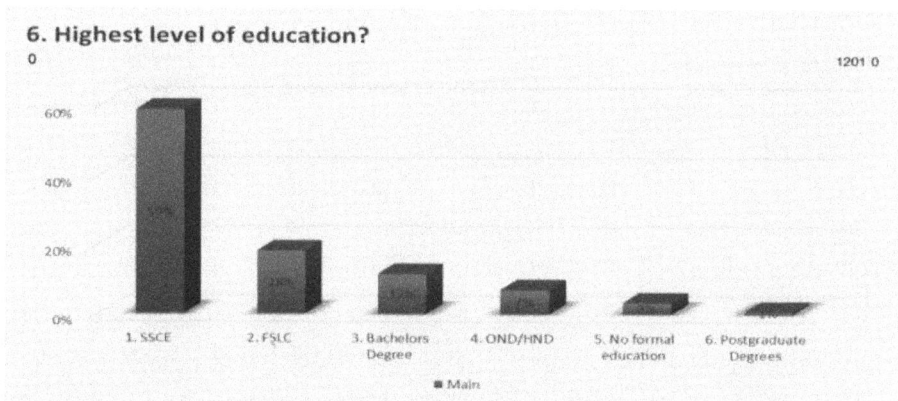

Figure 15: Bar Chart Showing the Distribution of *Ndi Oga* by Highest Level of Education

Table 15 (Frequency Table) and Figure 15 (Bar Chart) show the distribution of *Ndi Oga* by the highest level of education. 11.6% have Bachelor's Degree, 18.2% have First School Leaving Certificate (FSLC), 3.4% have no formal education, 7.2% have Ordinary National Diploma (OND)/Higher National Diploma (HND), 0.7% have Postgraduate Degrees and the majority, which is 59.0% have Secondary School Certificate (SSCE).

Table 16: Distribution of *Ụmụ Bọyị by* Highest Level of Education

	Frequency	Percent	Valid Percent	Cumulative Percent
Bachelor's Degree	26	2.2	2.2	2.2
FSLC	262	21.8	21.8	24.0
No formal education	49	4.1	4.1	28.1
OND/HND	50	4.2	4.2	32.3
Postgraduate Degrees	1	.1	.1	32.3
SSCE	812	67.7	67.7	100.0
Total	1200	100.0	100.0	

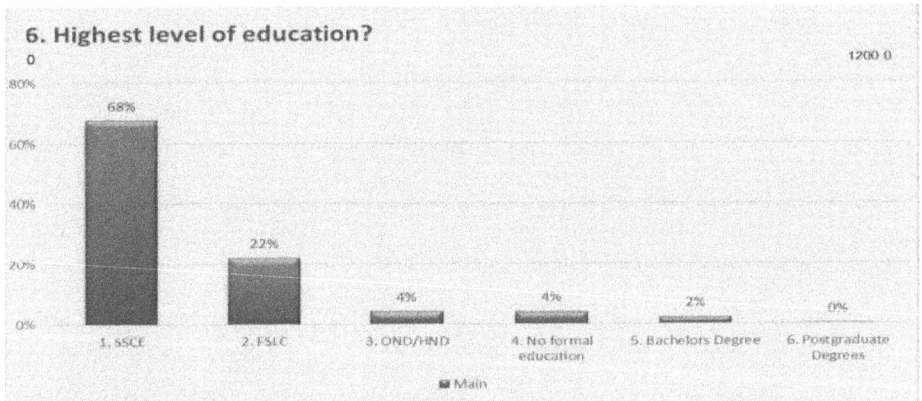

Figure 16: Bar Chart Showing the Distribution of *Ụmụ Bọyị by* Highest Level of Education

Table 16 (Frequency Table) and Figure 16 (Bar Chart) present the distribution of *Ụmụ Bọyị* by highest level of education. Those with Bachelors Degree are 2.2%; 21.8% for First School Leaving Certificate holders; 4.1% have no formal education, 4.2% have OND/HND and 1.7% have Postgraduate Degrees, while majority, which is 67.7%, have Secondary School Certificates.

Table 17: Distribution of *Ndị Oga* by State of Origin

	Frequency	Percent	Valid Percent	Cumulative Percent
Abia State	53	4.4	4.4	4.4
Akwa Ibom State	2	.2	.2	4.6
Anambra State	752	62.6	62.6	67.2
Delta State	4	.3	.3	67.5
Ebonyi State	42	3.5	3.5	71.0
Enugu State	183	15.2	15.2	86.3
Imo State	163	13.6	13.6	99.8
Ondo State	1	.1	.1	99.9
Rivers State	1	.1	.1	100.0
Total	1201	100.0	100.0	

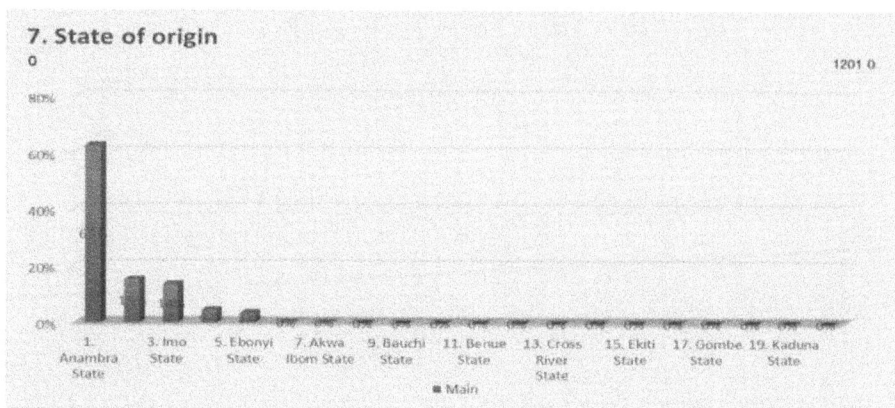

Figure 17: Bar Chart Showing the Distribution of *Ndi Oga* by State of Origin

Table 17 (Frequency Table) and Figure 17 (Bar Chart) indicate the distribution of *Ndi Oga* by State of Origin. Abia State (4.4%), Akwa Ibom State (0.2%), Anambra State (62.6%), Delta State (0.3%), Ebonyi State (3.5%), Enugu State (15.2%), Imo State (13.6%), Ondo State (0.1%), Rivers State (0.1%). This reveals that the majority of *Ndi Oga* come from Anambra State.

Table 18: Distribution of *Ụmụ Bọyị* by State of Origin

	Frequency	Percent	Valid Percent	Cumulative Percent
Abia State	74	6.2	6.2	6.2
Adamawa State	1	.1	.1	6.3
Anambra State	681	56.8	56.8	63.0
Cross River State	2	.2	.2	63.2
Delta State	8	.7	.7	63.8
Ebonyi State	97	8.1	8.1	71.9
Enugu State	241	20.1	20.1	92.0
Imo State	91	7.6	7.6	99.6
Kogi State	1	.1	.1	99.7
Ondo State	2	.2	.2	99.8
Rivers State	1	.1	.1	99.9
Taraba State	1	.1	.1	100.0
Total	1200	100.0	100.0	

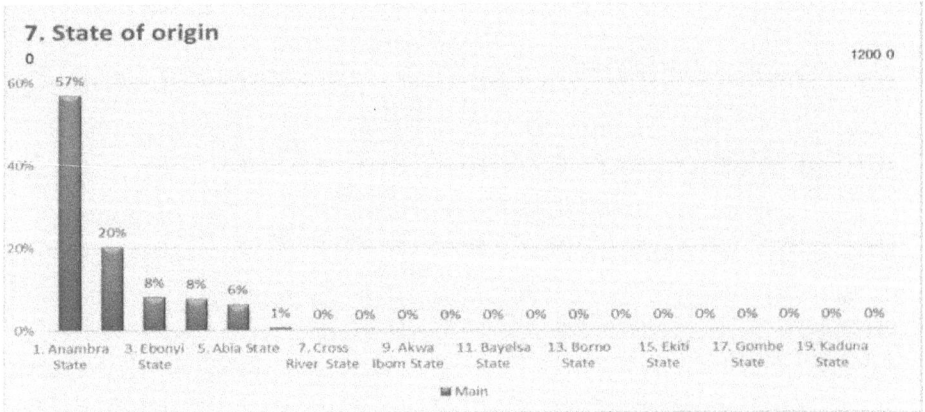

Figure 18: Bar Chart Showing the Distribution of *Ụmụ Bọyị* by State of Origin

Table 18 (Frequency Table) and Figure 18 (Bar Chart) show the distribution of *Ụmụ Bọyị* by State of Origin. 6.2% come from Abia State, 0.1% from Adamawa State, 56.8% from Anambra State, 0.2% from Cross River State, 0.7% from Delta State, 8.1% from Ebonyi State, 20.1% from Enugu State, 7.6% from Imo State, 0.1% from Kogi State, 0.2% from Ondo State, 0.1% from Rivers State and 0.1% from Taraba State. This reveals that the majority of *Ụmụ Bọyị* are from Anambra State.

Table 19: Distribution of *Ndị Ọga* from Anambra State by LGAs

	Frequency	Percent	Valid Percent	Cumulative Percent
Aguata	90	7.5	7.5	44.9
Anambra East	24	2.0	2.0	46.9
Anambra West	27	2.2	2.2	49.1
Anaocha	88	7.3	7.3	56.5
Ayamelum	24	2.0	2.0	58.5
Awka North	32	2.7	2.7	61.1
Awka South	14	1.2	1.2	62.3
Dunukofia	41	3.4	3.4	72.6
Ekwusigo	38	3.2	3.2	75.8
Idemili North	83	6.9	6.9	69.2
Idemili South	35	2.9	2.9	78.7
Ihiala	57	4.7	4.7	83.4
Njikoka	38	3.2	3.2	86.6
Nnewi North	27	2.2	2.2	88.8
Nnewi South	25	2.1	2.1	90.9
Ogbaru	18	1.5	1.5	92.4
Onitsha North	27	2.2	2.2	94.7
Onitsha South	7	.6	.6	95.3
Orumba North	26	2.2	2.2	97.4
Orumba South	14	1.2	1.2	98.6
Oyi	17	1.4	1.4	100.0
Total	1201	100.0	100.0	

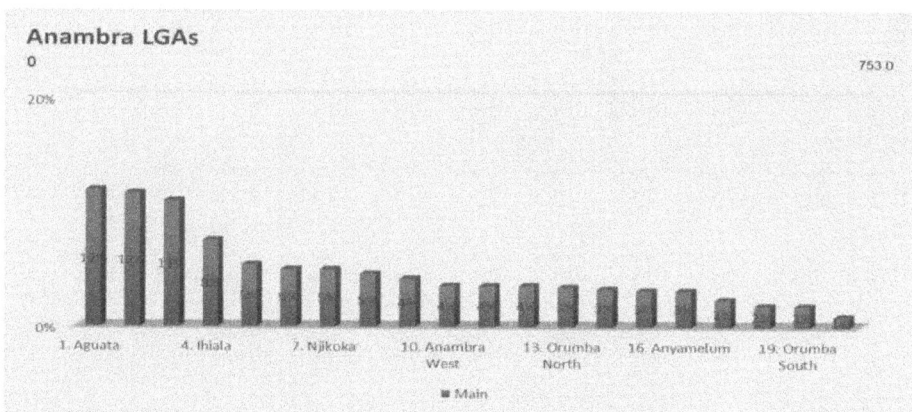

Figure 19: Bar Chart Showing the Distribution of *Ndị Ọga* from Anambra State by their LGAs

Table 19 (Frequency Table) and Figure 19 (Bar Chart) depict the distribution of *Ndị Ọga* from Anambra State by Local Government Areas. This reveals that the majority of *Ndị Ọga* (Masters) in the markets covered come from Aguata which represents 7.5%, followed by Anaocha (7.3%) and then Idemili North (6.9%).

Table 20: Distribution of *Ụmụ Bọyi* from Anambra State by LGAs

	Frequency	Percent	Valid Percent	Cumulative Percent
Aguata	68	5.7	5.7	48.9
Anambra East	24	2.0	2.0	50.9
Anambra West	25	2.1	2.1	53.0
Anaocha	72	6.0	6.0	59.0
Ayamelum	38	3.2	3.2	62.2
Awka North	41	3.4	3.4	65.6
Awka South	28	2.3	2.3	67.9
Dunukofia	46	3.8	3.8	71.8
Ekwusigo	26	2.2	2.2	73.9
Idemili North	71	5.9	5.9	79.8
Idemili South	31	2.6	2.6	82.4
Ihiala	47	3.9	3.9	86.3
Njikoka	32	2.7	2.7	89.0
Nnewi North	14	1.2	1.2	90.2
Nnewi South	13	1.1	1.1	91.3
Ogbaru	16	1.3	1.3	92.6
Onitsha North	23	1.9	1.9	94.5
Onitsha South	10	.8	.8	95.3
Orumba North	20	1.7	1.7	97.0
Orumba South	15	1.3	1.3	98.3
Oyi	21	1.8	1.8	100.0
Total	1200	100.0	100.0	

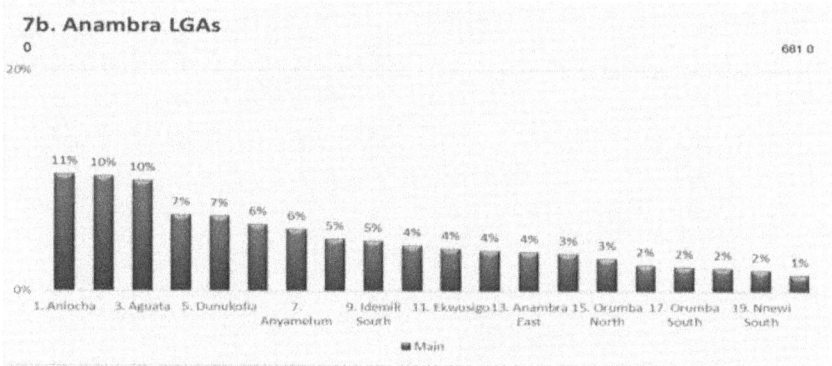

7b. Anambra LGAs

Figure 20: Bar Chart Showing the Distribution of *Ụmụ Bọyị* from Anambra State by LGAs

Table 20 (Frequency Table) and Figure 20 (Bar Chart) show the distribution of *Ụmụ Bọyị* from Anambra State by Local Government Areas. The data presentation reveals that 6.0% of *Ụmụ Bọyị, which* is the majority, come from Onitsha South, followed by Idemili North (5.9%) and then Aguata (5.7%).

Table 21: Distribution of *Ndị Ọga* from Other States

	Frequency	Percent	Valid Percent	Cumulative Percent
Other States	448	100	100	100

Table 22: Distribution of *Ụmụ Bọyị* from Other States

	Frequency	Percent	Valid Percent	Cumulative Percent
Other States	519	100	100	100

Table 23: Distribution of *Ndị Ọga* by Market Location

	Frequency	Percent	Valid Percent	Cumulative Percent
Bridge Head Market	179	14.9	14.9	14.9
Building Materials Market, Ogidi/Ogbunike	117	9.7	9.7	24.6
Main Market	486	40.5	40.5	65.1
Ochanja Market	237	19.7	19.7	84.8
Spare Parts Market, Nkpor	182	15.2	15.2	100.0
Total	1201	100.0	100.0	

10. Market location of your business?

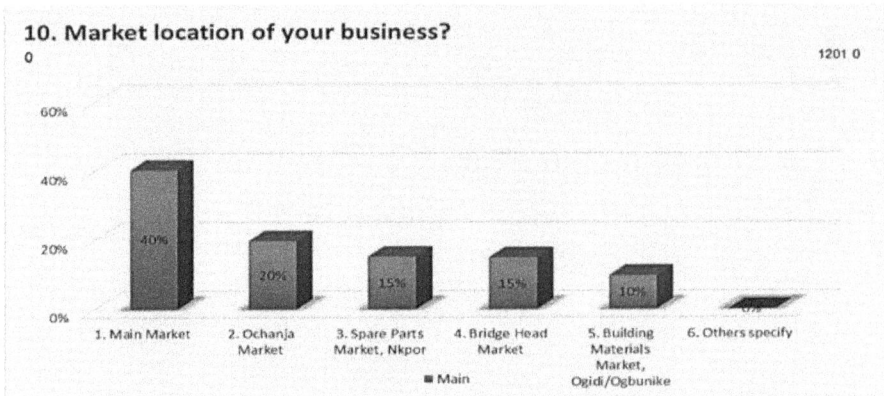

Figure 23: Bar Chart Showing the Distribution of Ndị Ọga by Market Location.

Table 23 (Frequency Table) and Figure 23 (Bar Chart) show the distribution of Ndị Ọga by market location. 14.9% of them are in Bridge Head Market, 9.7% in Building Materials Market, Ogidi/Ogbunike; 40.5% which represents the majority are in Main Market, 19.7% in Ochanja Market and 15.2% in Spare Parts Market, Nkpor.

Table 24: Distribution of Ụmụ Bọyị by Market Location where they are Apprenticing

	Frequency	Percent	Valid Percent	Cumulative Percent
Bridge Head Market	179	14.9	14.9	14.9
Building Materials Market, Ogidi/Ogbunike	118	9.8	9.8	24.8
Main Market	488	40.7	40.7	65.4
Ochanja Market	236	19.7	19.7	85.1
Spare Parts Market, Nkpor	179	14.9	14.9	100.0
Others specify	0	0	0	100.0
Total	1200	100.0	100.0	

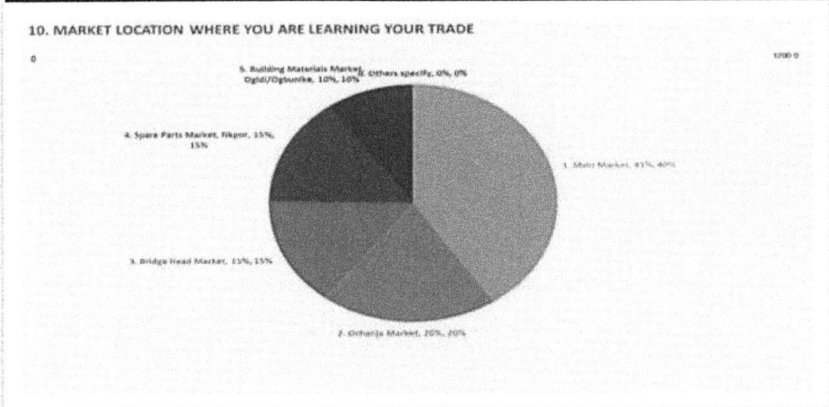

Figure 24: Pie Chart Showing the Distribution of Ụmụ Bọyị by Market Location where they are Apprenticing

111

Table 24 (Frequency Table) and Figure 24 (Pie Chart) show the distribution of *Ụmụ Bọyị* by market location. 14.9% are learning their trade in Bridge Head Market, 9.8% in Building Materials Market, Ogidi/Ogbunike; 40.7% which represents the majority are in Main Market, 19.7% in Ochanja, and 14.9% in Spare Parts Market, Nkpor.

Table 25: Distribution of *Ndị Ọga* by Average Monthly Income

	Frequency	Percent	Valid Percent	Cumulative Percent
10,000.00 - 50,000.00	291	24.2	24.2	54.7
60,000.00 -100,000.00	366	30.5	30.5	30.5
110,000.00 - 150,000.00	205	17.1	17.1	71.8
160,000.00 - 200,000.00	143	11.9	11.9	83.7
210,000 and above	196	16.3	16.3	100.0
Total	1201	100.0	100.0	

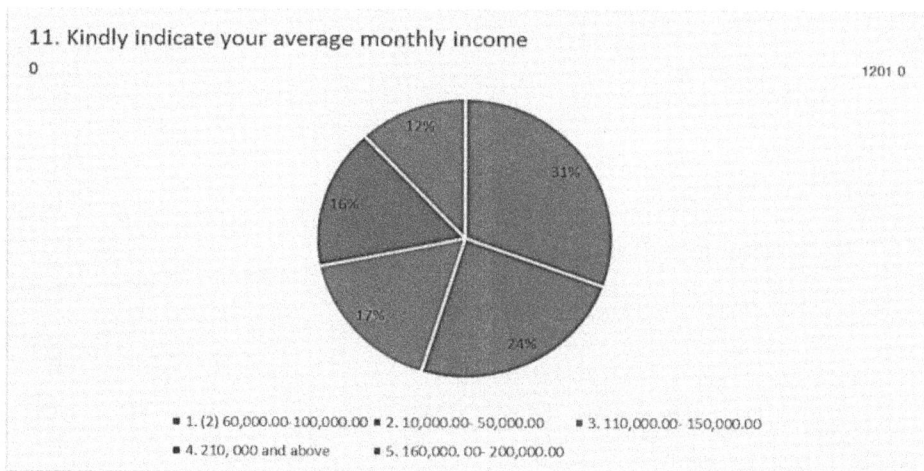

11. Kindly indicate your average monthly income

- 1. (2) 60,000.00-100,000.00 ■ 2. 10,000.00- 50,000.00 ■ 3. 110,000.00- 150,000.00
- 4. 210, 000 and above ■ 5. 160,000. 00- 200,000.00

Figure 25: Pie Chart Showing Distribution of *Ndị Ọga* by Average Monthly Income

Table 25 (Frequency Table) and Figure 25 (Pie Chart) show the distribution of *Ndị Ọga* by average monthly income. 24.2% of *Ndị Ọga* have average income 10,000.00 to 50,000.00, 30.5% have average income of 60,000.00 to 100,000.00, 17.1% have average income of 110,000.00 to 150,000.00, 11.9% have average income of 160,000.00 to 200,000.00 and 16.3% have average income greater than 200,000.00. This reveals that the majority of *Ndị Ọga* has an average income of 60,000.00 to 100,000.00 which represents 30.5%.

Table 26: Distribution of *Ụmụ Bọyị by* Average Monthly Income

	Frequency	Percent	Valid Percent	Cumulative Percent
No income	726	60.5	60.5	60.5
Less than 3,000	189	15.8	15.8	76.3
4,000-6,000	87	7.2	7.2	83.5
7,000 -10,000	49	4.1	4.1	87.6
Above 10,000	149	12.4	12.4	100.0
Total	1200	100.0	100.0	

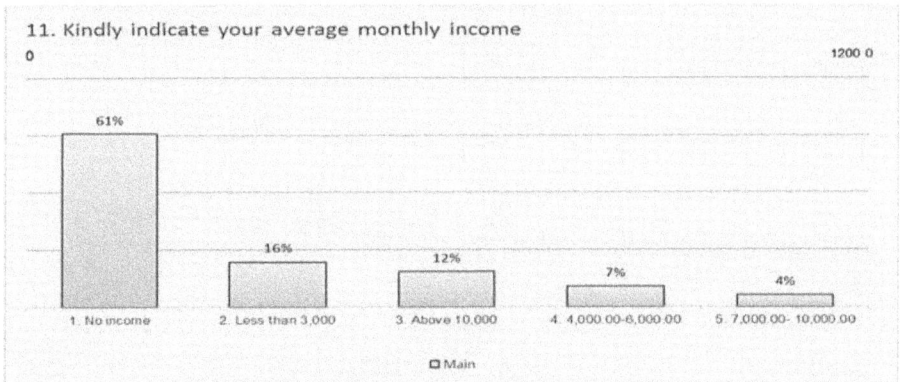

Figure 26: Bar Chart Showing Distribution of *Ụmụ Bọyị by* Average Monthly Income

4.3 Substantive Issues

Table 27: Distribution of *Ndị Ọga* by Number of Apprentices Trained

	Frequency	Percent	Valid Percent	Cumulative Percent
0	302	25.1	25.1	25.1
1	151	12.6	12.6	37.7
10	16	1.3	1.3	39.1
11	7	.6	.6	39.6
12	10	.8	.8	40.5
13	2	.2	.2	40.6
15	11	.9	.9	41.5
16	2	.2	.2	41.7
17	2	.2	.2	41.9
19	2	.2	.2	42.0
2	228	19.0	19.0	61.0
20	4	.3	.3	61.4
23	1	.1	.1	61.4
3	176	14.7	14.7	76.1

30	1	.1	.1	76.2
4	92	7.7	7.7	83.8
40	1	.1	.1	83.9
5	90	7.5	7.5	91.4
50	1	.1	.1	91.5
6	56	4.7	4.7	96.2
7	20	1.7	1.7	97.8
8	19	1.6	1.6	99.4
9	7	.6	.6	100.0
Total	1201	100.0	100.0	

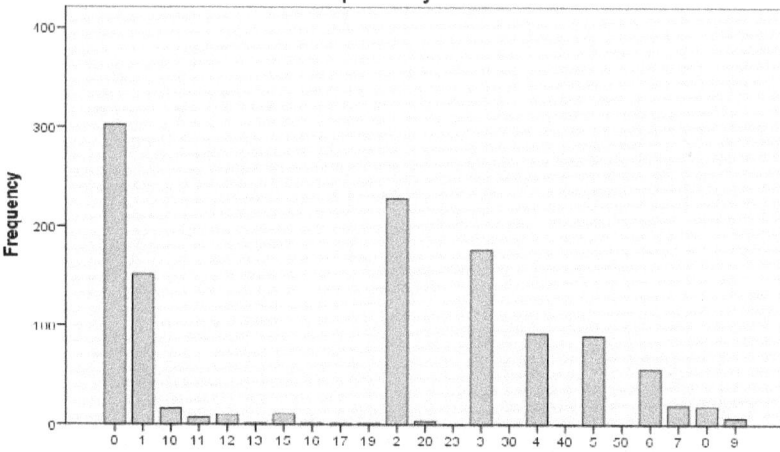

Figure 27: Bar Chart Depicting the Distribution of Ndị Ọga by Number of Apprentices Trained

Table 28: Distribution of *Ndị Ọga* by their Responses on Why They Have Not Trained Any *Nwa Bọyị*

	Frequency	Percent	Valid Percent	Cumulative Percent
Other options except (If none, why?)	899	74.9	74.9	74.9
Beginner	104	8.7	8.7	83.5
Don't have strength for *Umu Boyi* issues	11	.9	.9	84.4
I don't want any apprentice	85	7.1	7.1	91.5
I prefer sales girls	17	1.4	1.4	92.9
No Apprenticeis interested	7	.6	.6	93.5
No money to train anyone	33	2.7	2.7	96.3
Nothing, it's personal	29	2.4	2.4	98.7
Things are difficult	16	1.3	1.3	100.0
Total	1201	100.0	100.0	

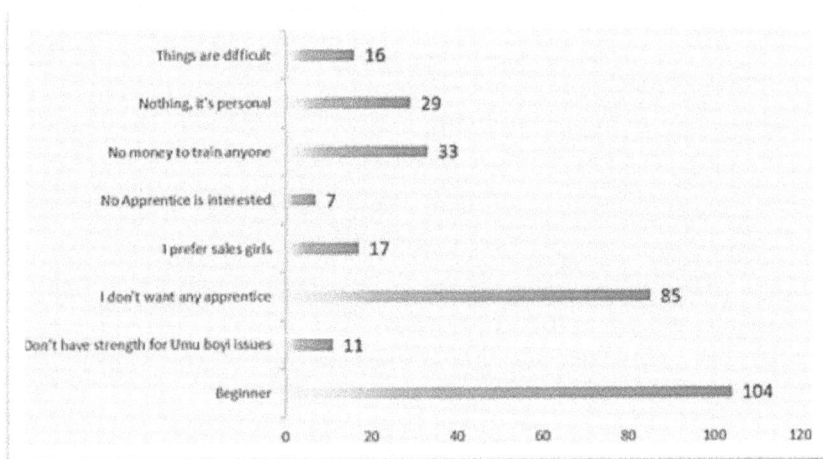

Figure 28: Bar Chart Depicting the Distribution of *Ndị Ọga* by Their Responses on Why They Have Not Trained Any *Nwa Bọyị*

From Table 28 (Frequency Table) and Figure 28 (Bar Chart), data distribution of *Ndị Ọga* by their responses on why they have not trained any *Nwa Bọyị* revealed that being a 'beginner' is the major reason followed by 'not being interested in training *Nwa Bọyị* '.

Table 29: Distribution of Ndị Ọga by their Responses on use of Apprentices that Pay to Learn their Trade (Ịmụ Ahịa)

	Frequency	Percent	Valid Percent	Cumulative Percent
No	997	83.0	83.0	83.0
Yes	204	17.0	17.0	100.0
Total	1201	100.0	100.0	

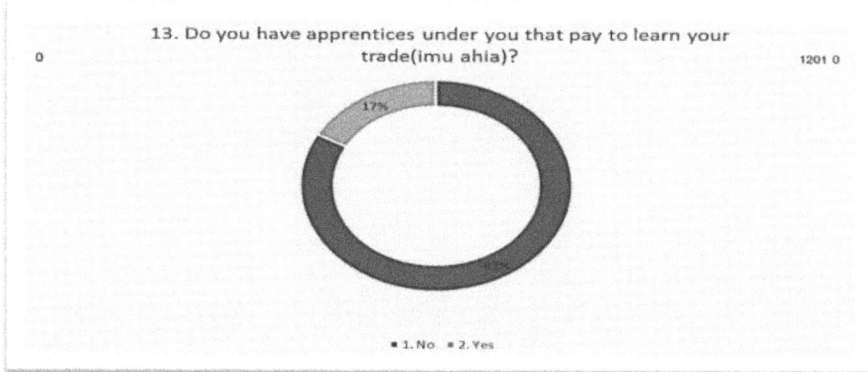

13. Do you have apprentices under you that pay to learn your trade(imu ahia)?

0   1201 0

17%

■ 1. No ■ 2. Yes

Figure 29: Pie Chart Showing the Distribution of Ndị Ọga by their Responses on whether they have Apprentices that Pay to learn their Trade (Ịmụ Ahịa)

Table 29 (Frequency Table) and Figure 29 (Pie Chart) show the distribution of Ndị Ọga by their responses on whether they have apprentices that pay to learn their trade. The majority, which is 83.0%, answered 'No', saying they do not have apprentices that pay to learn their trade, while 17% responded 'Yes.'

Table 30: Distribution of Ndị Ọga by their Responses on Whether the Apprentices that Pay to Learn their Trade (Ịmụ Ahịa) are different from Umu Boyi

	Frequency	Percent	Valid Percent	Cumulative Percent
Other responses except 'Yes' responses to (Do you have apprentices under you that pay to learn your trade?)	997	83.0	83.0	83.0
No	5	.4	.4	83.4
Yes	199	16.6	16.6	100.0
Total	1201	100.0	100.0	

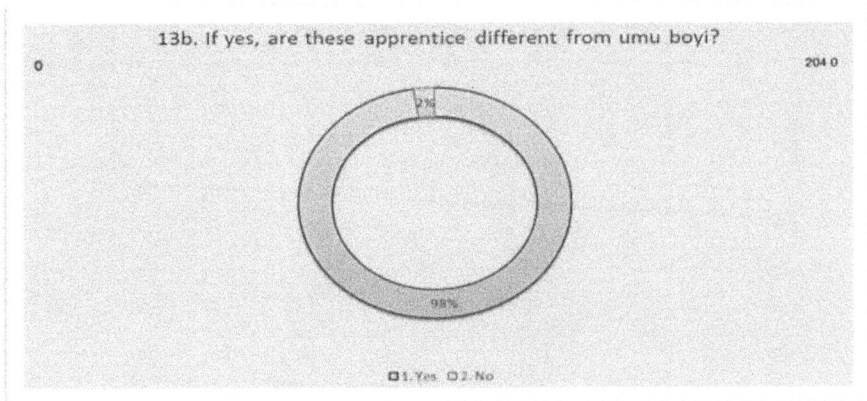

13b. If yes, are these apprentice different from umu boyi?

0   204 0

2%

98%

□1.Yes □2.No

Figure 30: Pie Chart showing Distribution of *Ndị Ọga* by their Responses on Whether the Apprentices that Pay to Learn their Trade (*Imụ Ahịa*) are different from *Ụmụ Bọyi*

Table 30 (Frequency Table) and Figure 30 (Pie Chart) show the distribution of *Ndị Ọga* by their responses on whether the apprentices that pay to learn their trade (*Imụ Ahịa*) are different from *Ụmụ Bọyi* . The majority which is represented by the greater percentage said 'Yes' and also agreed that they have apprentices under them that pay to learn their trade. 5% said 'No'.

Table 31: Distribution of *Ndị Ọga* by their Responses on Reasons Why Apprentices that Pay to Learn their Trade (*Imụ Ahịa*) are different from *Ụmụ Bọyi*

	Frequency	Percent	Valid Percent	Cumulative Percent
Other responses except 'Yes' responses to (Do you have apprentices under you that pay to learn your trade?) and 'No' responses to (If yes, are these apprentices different from *uỤmụ Bọyi* ?)	1002	83.4	83.4	83.4
I make money from those who come to learn	19	1.6	1.6	85.0
None residential except for *Nwa Bọyi*	50	4.2	4.2	89.2
People are no longer interested in bọyi,	4	.3	.3	89.5
settlement, services, duration of years	43	3.6	3.6	93.1
The person paying fends for	25	2.1	2.1	95.2

himself while depends completely on his *Oga*				
Those who pay don't stay for long while N*wa Boyị* does	24	2.0	2.0	97.2
Ụmụ Boyị is hard to get and too expensive	1	.1	.1	97.3
Ụmụ Boyị is more practical than Ụmụahịa	1	.1	.1	97.3
Ụmụ Boyị are not independent while the others are	32	2.7	2.7	100.0
Total	1201	100.0	100.0	

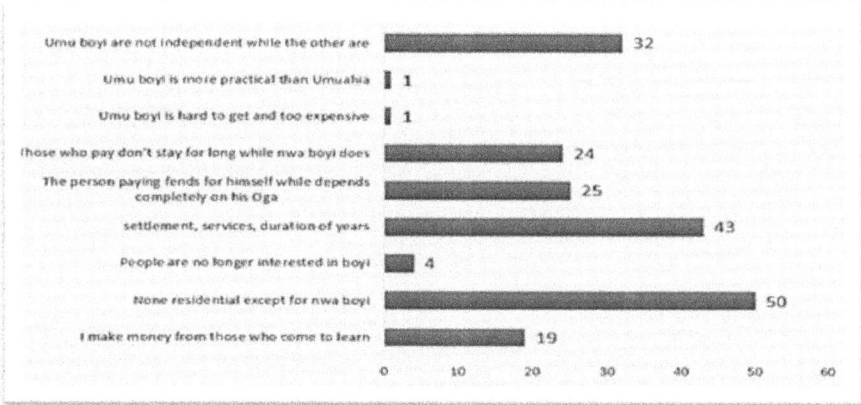

Figure 31: Bar Chart Showing the Distribution of Ndị Oga by their Responses on Reasons Why Apprentices that Pay to Learn their Trade (Ịmụ Ahịa) are different from Ụmụ Boyị

Table 31 (Frequency Table) and Figure 31 (Bar Chart) depict the distribution of *Ndị Oga* by their responses on reasons why apprentices that pay to learn their trade (*Imu Ahia*) are different from *Ụmụ Boyị*. The data distribution shows that *Igba Boyị* is different from *Ịmụ Ahịa*.

Table 32: Distribution of *Ndị Ọga* by their Responses on their Preference for *Nwa Bọyị* to Apprentices who pay to Learn a Trade (*Ịmụ Ahịa*)

	Frequency	Percent	Valid Percent	Cumulative Percent
Other responses except 'Yes' responses to (Do you have apprentices under you that pay to learn your trade?) and 'No' responses to (If yes, are these apprentices different from *Ụmụ Bọyị* ?)	1002	83.4	83.4	83.4
Don't Know	9	.7	.7	84.2
Maybe	15	1.2	1.2	85.4
Not Sure	140	11.7	11.7	97.1
Surely	35	2.9	2.9	100.0
Total	1201	100.0	100.0	

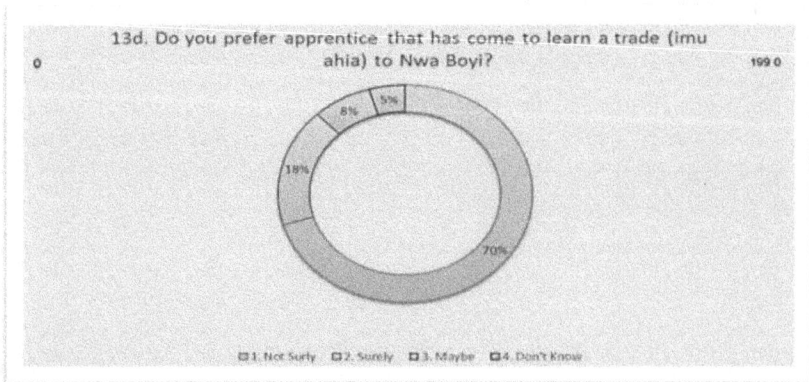

Figure 32: Pie Chart of the Distribution of *Ndị Ọga* by their Responses on their Preference for *Nwa Bọyị* to Apprentices who pay to Learn a Trade (*Ịmụ Ahịa*)

Table 32 (Frequency Table) and Figure 32 (Pie Chart) show the distribution of *Ndị Ọga* by their responses on their preference for *Nwa Bọyị* to apprentices who pay to learn a trade (*Ịmụ Ahịa*). The data distribution depicts that *Ndị Ọga* prefer

Table 33: Distribution of Ụmụ Bọyị by their Responses on Whether they Know Anyone that Currently Pays to Learn a Trade (Ịmụ Ahịa)

	Frequency	Percent	Valid Percent	Cumulative Percent
No	658	54.8	54.8	54.8
Yes	542	45.2	45.2	100.0
Total	1200	100.0	100.0	

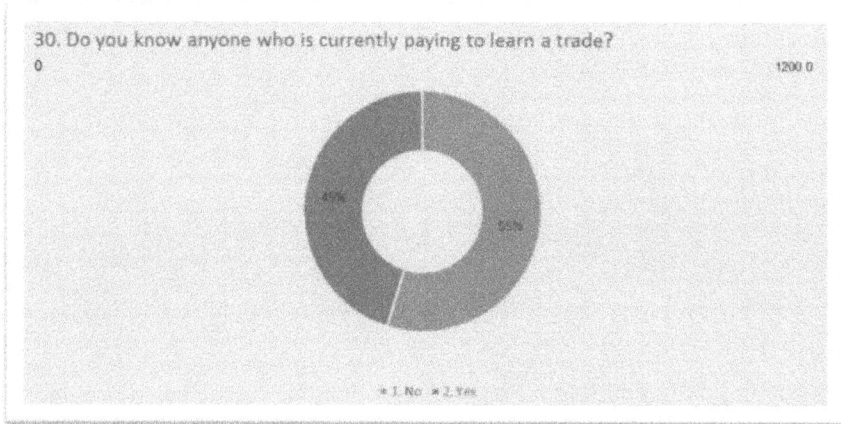

Figure 33: Pie Chart Showing the Distribution of Ụmụ Bọyị by their Responses on whether they know Anyone that Currently Pays to Learn a Trade (Ịmụ Ahịa)

Table 33 (Frequency Table) and Figure 33 (Pie Chart) show the distribution of Ụmụ Bọyị by their responses on whether they know anyone that currently pays to learn a trade. 54.83% of Ụmụ Bọyị answered 'Yes' and 45.2% answered 'No'. Therefore, those that answered 'Yes' are in majority.

Table 34: Distribution of Ụmụ Bọyị by their Responses on Whether the Apprentices that Pay to Learn their Trade (Ịmụ Ahịa) are different from Ụmụ Bọyị

	Frequency	Percent	Valid Percent	Cumulative Percent
No	292	24.3	24.3	24.3
Yes	908	75.7	75.7	100.0
Total	1200	100.0	100.0	

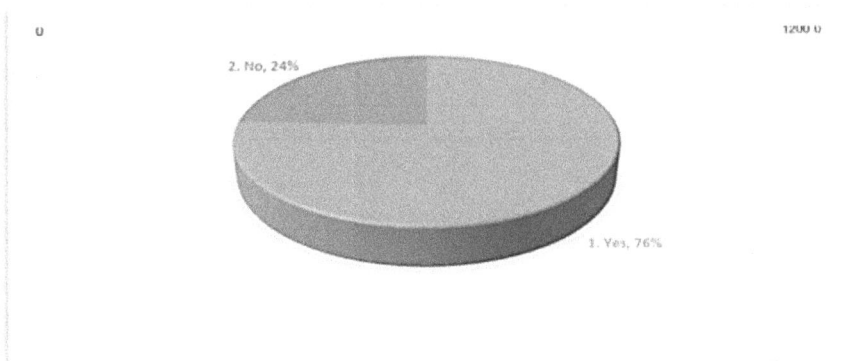

Figure 34: Pie Chart Showing the Distribution of *Ụmụ Bọyị* by their Responses on Whether the Apprentices that Pay to Learn their Trade (*Ịmụ Ahịa*) are different from *Ụmụ Bọyị*.

Table 34 (Frequency Table) and Figure 34 (Pie Chart) show the distribution of *Ụmụ Bọyị* by their responses on whether the apprentices that pay to learn their trade (*Ịmụ Ahịa*) are different from *Ụmụ Bọyị*. 75.7% of *Ụmụ Bọyị* answered 'Yes' which represents the majority, while 24.3% answered 'No'.

Table 35: Distribution of *Ụmụ Bọyị* by their Responses on Reasons Why Apprentices that Pay to Learn their Trade (*Ịmụ Ahịa*) are different from umu bọyị

	Frequency	Percent	Valid Percent	Cumulative Percent	
Other responses except 'Yes' responses to (If yes, are these apprentices different from *Ụmụ Bọyị?*)	292	24.3	24.3	24.3	
Non-residential except for *Nwa Bọyị*	209	17.4	17.4	41.8	
Ọga makes money from it	32	2.7	2.7	44.4	
Settlement, service duration of years	109	9.1	9.1	53.5	
The person paying fends for himself while *Nwa Bọyị* depends completely on *Ọga*	174	14.5	14.5	68.0	
Those who pay don't stay for long while *Nwa Bọyị* does	95	7.9	7.9	75.9	
Ụmụ Bọyị are not independent while others are	231	19.3	19.3	95.2	
Ụmụ Bọyị is hard to get and too expensive	1	.1	.1	95.3	
Ụmụ Bọyị is more practical than *Ịmụ Ahịa*	57	4.8	4.8	100.0	
Total	1200	100.0	100.0		

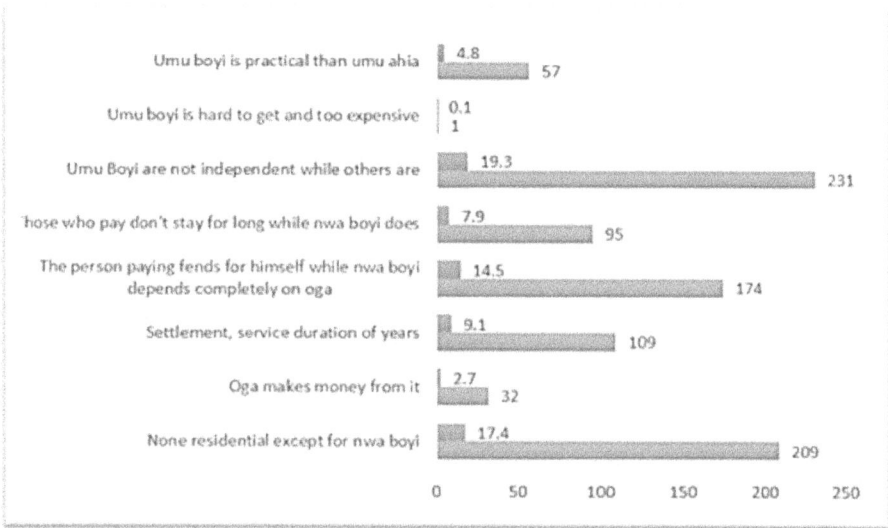

Figure 35: Bar Chart Showing the Distribution of *Ụmụ Bọyị* by their Responses on Reasons Why Apprentices that Pay to Learn their Trade are different from *Ụmụ Bọyị*

Table 35 (Frequency Table) and Figure 35 (Bar Chart) depict the distribution of *Ụmụ Bọyị* by their responses on reasons why apprentices that pay to learn their trade are different from *Ụmụ Bọyị*. 24.3% of *Umu Boyi* answered that they are not different, but 74.7% answered 'Yes' representing the majority. The apprentices gave different reasons for their responses, with the majority saying that *Ụmụ Bọyị* are not independent and they are residential, while those that pay to learn a trade are non-residential.

Table 36: Distribution of *Ndị Ọga* by their Responses on Whether they ever served as *Nwa Bọyị*

	Frequency	Percent	Valid Percent	Cumulative Percent
No	288	24.0	24.0	24.0
Yes	913	76.0	76.0	100.0
Total	1201	100.0	100.0	

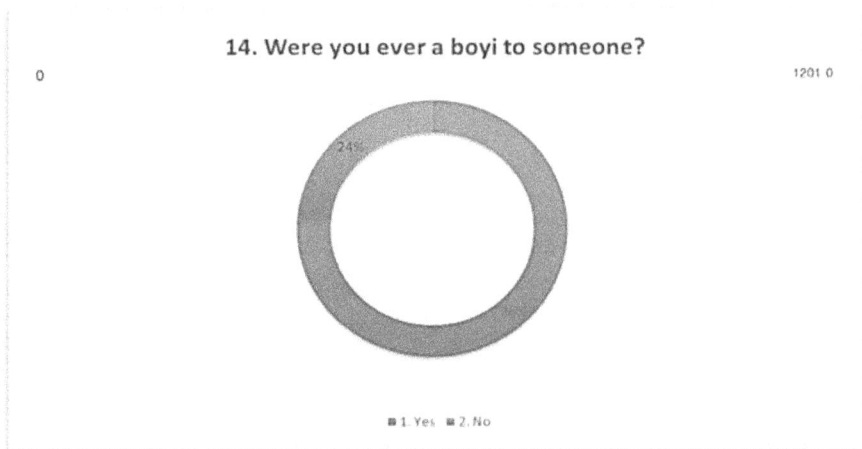

14. Were you ever a boyi to someone?

0   1201 0

■ 1. Yes   ■ 2. No

Figure 36: Pie Chart on the Distribution of *Ndị Ọga* by their Responses on Whether they ever served as *Nwa Bọyị*

Table 36 (Frequency Table) and Figure 36 (Pie Chart) show the distribution of *Ndị Ọga* by their responses on whether they have ever served as *Nwa Bọyị*. 24.0% answered 'No' while 76.0% which represents the majority answered 'Yes'.

Table 37: Distribution of *Ndi Ọga* by their Responses on whether they served as Kin-related *Nwa Bọyị*

	Frequency	Percent	Valid Percent	Cumulative Percent
Other responses except 'Yes' responses to (Were you ever a *boyi* to someone?)	288	24.0	24.0	24.0
No	411	34.2	34.2	58.2
Yes	502	41.8	41.8	100.0
Total	1201	100.0	100.0	

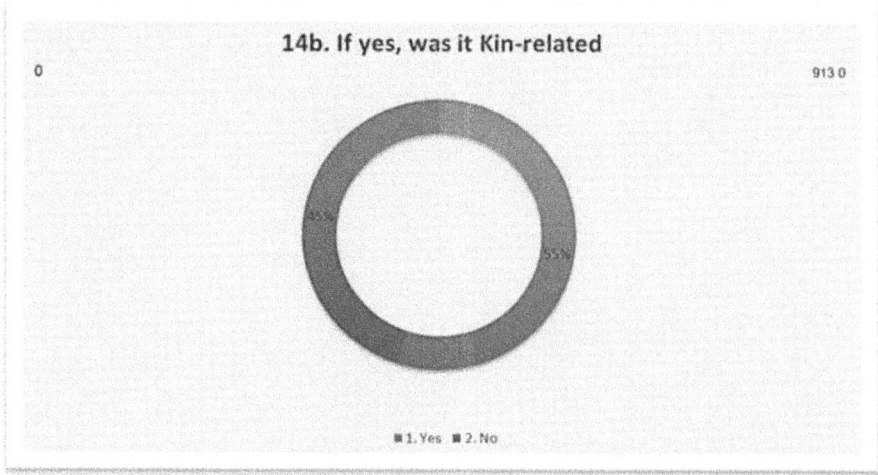

14b. If yes, was it Kin-related

0   913 0

45%

55%

■ 1. Yes   ■ 2. No

Figure 37: Pie Chart Showing the Distribution of *Ndị Ọga* by their Responses on Whether they served as Kin-related *Nwa Bọyị*

Table 37 (Frequency Table) and Figure 37 (Pie Chart) show the distribution of *Ndị Ọga* by their responses on whether they served as kin-related *Nwa Bọyị*. 24.0% never served as *Nwa Bọyị*, 34.2% answered 'No', while 41.8% which represents the majority, responded 'Yes'.

Table 38: Distribution of *Ụmụ Bọyị* by their Responses on Whether they have any Kin relationship to their *Ọga*

	Frequency	Percent	Valid Percent	Cumulative Percent
Yes	462	38.5	38.5	38.5
No	717	59.8	59.8	98.3
Don't know	21	1.8	1.8	100.0
Total	1200	100.0	100.0	

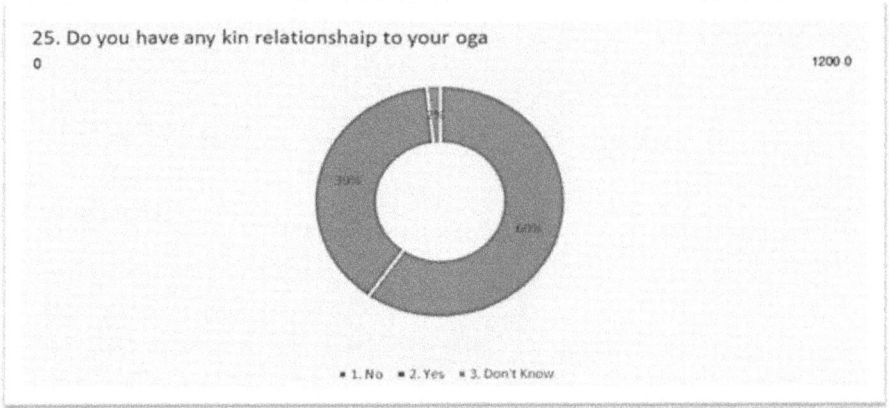

25. Do you have any kin relationshaip to your oga

0   1200 0

■ 1. No ■ 2. Yes ■ 3. Don't Know

Figure 38: Bar Chart showing Distribution of *Ụmụ Bọyị* by their Responses on Whether they have any Kin relationship to their *Ọga*

Table 38 (Frequency Table) and Figure 38 (Pie Chart) depict the distribution of *Ụmụ Bọyị* by their responses on whether they have a kin relationship to their *Ọga*. 38.5% of *bọyị* answered 'Yes', 59.8% answered 'No' representing the majority of responses, 1.8% were indifferent.

Table 39: Distribution of *Ndị Ọga* by their Responses on their Length of Stay as *Nwa Bọyị* before Settlement

	Frequency	Percent	Valid Percent	Cumulative Percent
Other responses except 'Yes' responses to (Were you ever a *boyi* to someone?)	288	24.0	24.0	24.0
1	12	1.0	1.0	25.0
10	57	4.7	4.7	29.7
11	10	.8	.8	30.6
12	9	.7	.7	31.3
13	7	.6	.6	31.9
14	2	.2	.2	32.1
15	2	.2	.2	32.2
16	1	.1	.1	32.3
17	1	.1	.1	32.4
2	13	1.1	1.1	33.5
3	22	1.8	1.8	35.3
4	46	3.8	3.8	39.1
5	118	9.8	9.8	49.0
6	190	15.8	15.8	64.8
7	188	15.7	15.7	80.4
8	149	12.4	12.4	92.8
9	86	7.2	7.2	100.0
Total	1201	100.0	100.0	

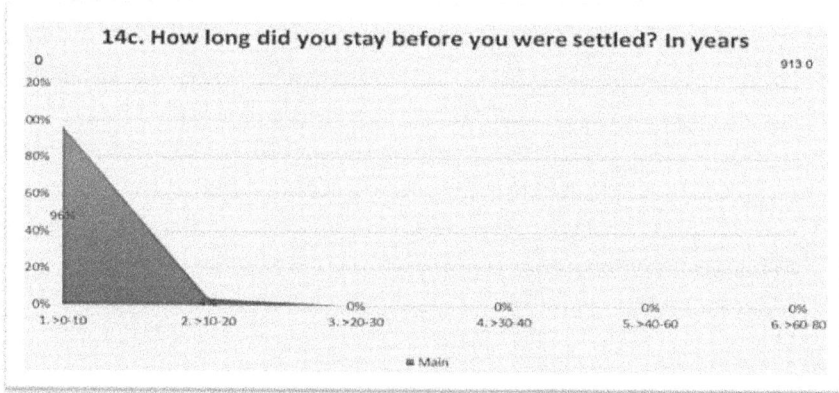

Figure 39: Graph Plot Depicting the Distribution of *Ndị Ọga* by their Responses on their Length of Stay as *Nwa Boyi* before Settlement.

Table 39 (Frequency Table) and Figure 39 (Graph Plot) reveal that the majority (96.50%) of *Ndị Ọga* who had an apprenticeship experience, spent a duration of 1 to 10 years, even though most of them spent 5 to 8 years.

Table 40: Distribution of *Ndị Ọga* by their Responses on Preferred Age for Apprenticeship

	Frequency	Percent	Valid Percent	Cumulative Percent
0	4	.3	.3	.3
1	1	.1	.1	.4
10	4	.3	.3	.7
12	36	3.0	3.0	3.7
13	33	2.7	2.7	6.5
14	53	4.4	4.4	10.9
15	241	20.1	20.1	31.0
16	165	13.7	13.7	44.7
17	164	13.7	13.7	58.4
18	309	25.7	25.7	84.1
19	44	3.7	3.7	87.8
20	114	9.5	9.5	97.3
21	5	.4	.4	97.7
22	5	.4	.4	98.1
23	1	.1	.1	98.2
24	2	.2	.2	98.3
25	1	.1	.1	98.4
35	1	.1	.1	98.5
4	2	.2	.2	98.7
5	2	.2	.2	98.8

	Frequency	Percent	Valid Percent	Cumulative Percent
6	7	.6	.6	99.4
7	2	.2	.2	99.6
8	4	.3	.3	99.9
9	1	.1	.1	100.0
Total	1201	100.0	100.0	

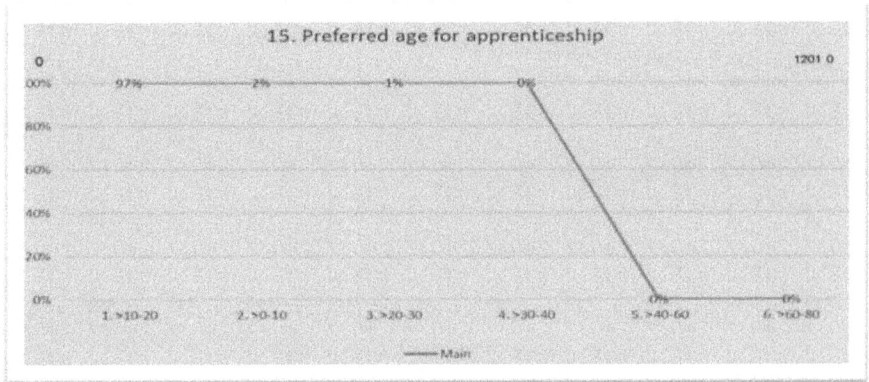

Figure 40: Line Chart Showing the Distribution of Ndị Ọga by their Responses on Preferred Age for Apprenticeship

As shown in Table 40 and Figure 40 with respect to the distribution of Ndị Ọga by their responses on preferred age for an apprenticeship, 97% of the respondents indicated that the preferred age for apprenticeship is 10-20 years while only 3% decided otherwise.

Table 41: Distribution of Ụmụ Bọyị by their Responses on Preferred Age for Apprenticeship

	Frequency	Percent	Valid Percent	Cumulative Percent
0	3	.3	.3	.3
10	8	.7	.7	.9
11	4	.3	.3	1.3
12	24	2.0	2.0	3.3
13	29	2.4	2.4	5.7
14	42	3.5	3.5	9.2
15	209	17.4	17.4	26.6
16	169	14.1	14.1	40.7
17	167	13.9	13.9	54.6
18	383	31.9	31.9	86.5
19	44	3.7	3.7	90.2
20	82	6.8	6.8	97.0
21	7	.6	.6	97.6
22	8	.7	.7	98.3

23	1	.1	.1	98.3
24	3	.3	.3	98.6
25	6	.5	.5	99.1
26	3	.3	.3	99.3
28	2	.2	.2	99.5
35	1	.1	.1	99.6
5	2	.2	.2	99.8
6	3	.3	.3	100.0
Total	1200	100.0	100.0	

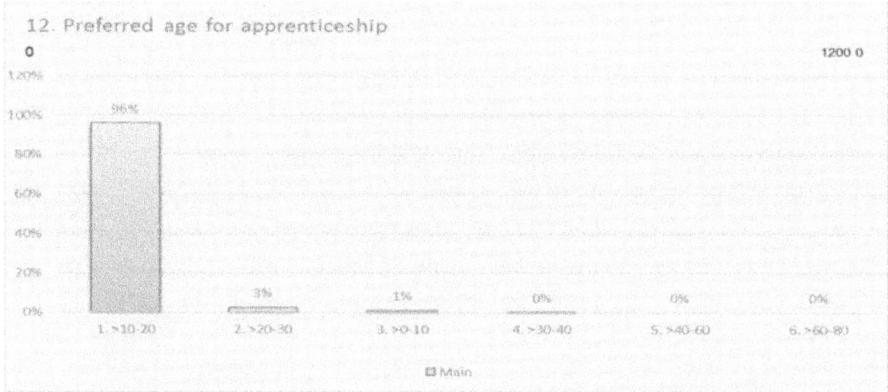

Figure 41: Bar Chart Showing the Distribution of *Ụmụ Bọyị* by their Responses on Preferred Age for Apprenticeship

Table 41 and Figure 41 also showed the distribution of *Ụmụ Bọyị* by their responses on preferred age for the apprenticeship. 96% of the respondents indicated that the preferred age for apprenticeship is 10-20 years while 4% indicated otherwise. The implication here is that both *Ndị Ọga* and *Ụmụ Bọyị* have the same perception of the preferred age for apprenticeship.

Table 42: Distribution of *Ndị Ọga* by their Responses on Preferred Gender for Apprenticeship

	Frequency	Percent	Valid Percent	Cumulative Percent
Female	29	2.4	2.4	2.4
Male	1172	97.6	97.6	100.0
Total	1201	100.0	100.0	

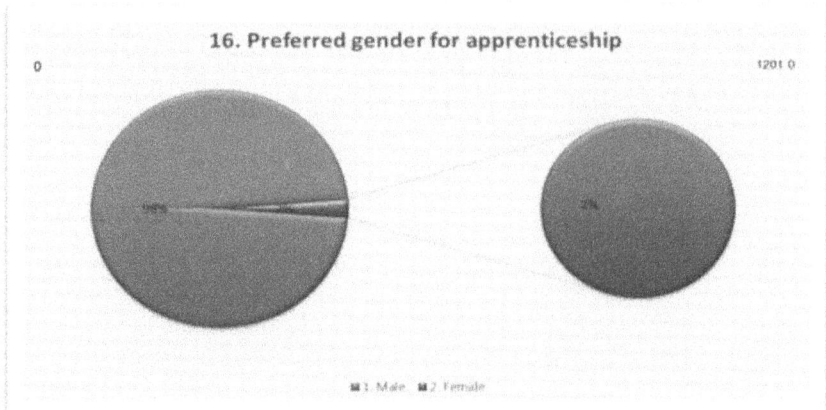

Figure 42: Pie Chart Showing the Distribution of Ndị Ọga by their Responses on Preferred Gender for Apprenticeship

Table 42 and Figure 42 revealed the distribution of *Ndị Ọga* by their responses on preferred gender for the apprenticeship. 96.6% of the respondents indicated that the male gender is preferred for apprenticeships to the female gender. This explains the traditional role of men as head of household in the traditional Igbo society and also the risk of the female gender going to live with the master (which most times are un married for a few years after being settled) for years without being molested sexually.

Table 43: Distribution of *Ndị Ọga* by their Responses on Prevalent Type of Apprenticeship

	Frequency	Percent	Valid Percent	Cumulative Percent
Both	702	58.5	58.5	58.5
kin related	201	16.7	16.7	75.2
Set	298	24.8	24.8	100.0
Total	1201	100.0	100.0	

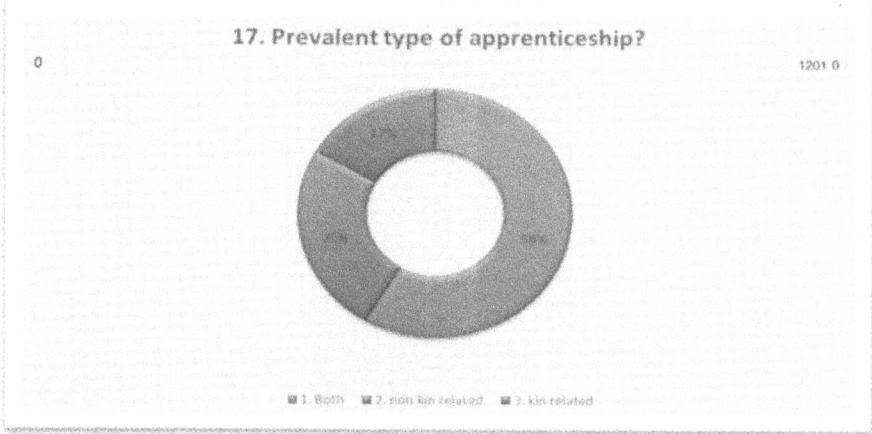

Figure 43: Pie Chart Depicting the Distribution of Ndị Ọga by their Responses on Prevalent Type of Apprenticeship

As shown in Table 43 and Figure 43, with respect to the distribution of Ndị Ọga by their responses on prevalent type of apprenticeship, 58.5% of the respondents indicated that both kin and non-kin are a prevalent type of apprenticeship. 24.8% of the respondents indicated that non kin is the prevalent type of apprenticeship while 16.7% of the respondents indicated that kin is the prevalent type of apprenticeship. The results suggest that both kin and non-kin relationships are prevalent Types of apprenticeship.

Table 44: Distribution of *Umu Boyi* by their Responses on Prevalent Type of Apprenticeship

	Frequency	Percent	Valid Percent	Cumulative Percent
Both	622	51.8	51.8	51.8
kin related	228	19.0	19.0	70.8
Non-kin related	350	29.2	29.2	100.0
Total	1200	100.0	100.0	

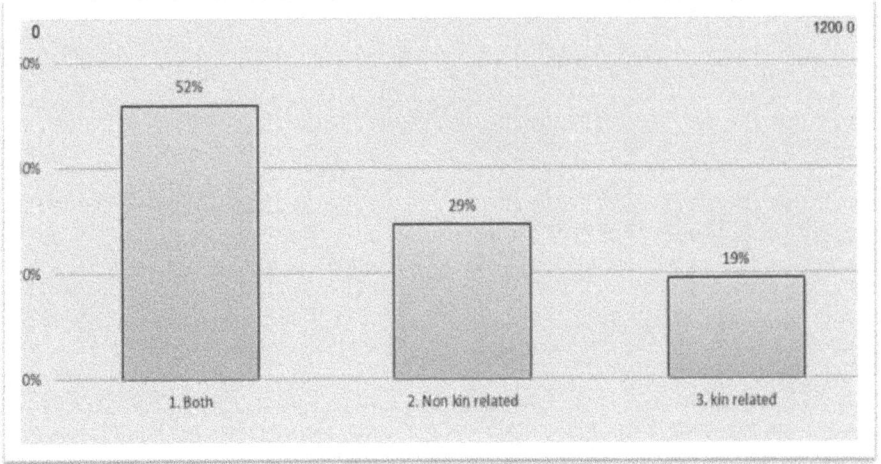

Figure 44: Bar Chart Showing the Distribution of *Ụmụ Bọyị* by their Responses on Prevalent Type of Apprenticeship

As shown in Table 44 and Figure 44, with respect to the distribution of *Ụmụ Bọyị* by their responses on prevalent types of apprenticeship, 51.8% of the respondents indicated that Both kin and non-kin are the prevalent types of apprenticeship. 29.2% of the respondents indicated that non-kin is the prevalent type of apprenticeship while 19.0% of the respondents indicated that kin is the prevalent type of apprenticeship. The results suggest that both kin and non-kin apprenticeships are the prevalent types of apprenticeship. This further revealed that both Ndị Ọga and *Ụmụ Bọyị* have similar perceptions of the prevalent type of apprenticeship.

Table 45: Distribution of *Ndị Ọga* by their Responses on the Type of Apprentices (Kin-related/Non-kin-related) they have

	Frequency	Percent	Valid Percent	Cumulative Percent
Apprentices (*Imu Ahia*)	75	6.2	6.2	6.2
Kin related	221	18.4	18.4	24.6
No boyi for now	460	38.3	38.3	62.9
Non-kin-related	375	31.2	31.2	94.2
Sale girls	70	5.8	5.8	100.0
Total	1201	100.0	100.0	

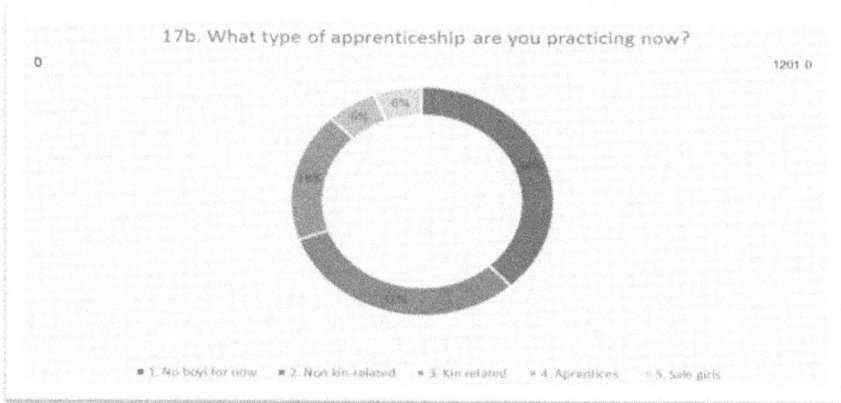

Figure 45: Pie Chart Showing the Distribution of *Ndị Oga* by their Responses on the Type of Apprentices (Kin-related/Non-kin-related) they have

Table 45 and Figure 45 show the distribution of *Ndị Oga* by their responses on the type of apprentices they have. 6.2% of the respondents indicated Apprentices (*Imụ Ahịa*). 18.4% indicated Kin-related apprenticeship. 38.3% indicated 'No *Nwa Boyị* for now'. 31.2% indicated 'Non-kin-related' while 5.8% indicated 'Sale girls'. The implication is that the Igbo apprenticeship system is gradually fizzling out as the majority of *Ndị Oga* no longer have *Nwa Boyị*.

Table 46: Distribution of *Ndị Oga* by their Responses on whether Communities are Identified with Particular Types of Trade

	Frequency	Percent	Valid Percent	Cumulative Percent
No	526	43.8	43.8	43.8
Yes	675	56.2	56.2	100.0
Total	1201	100.0	100.0	

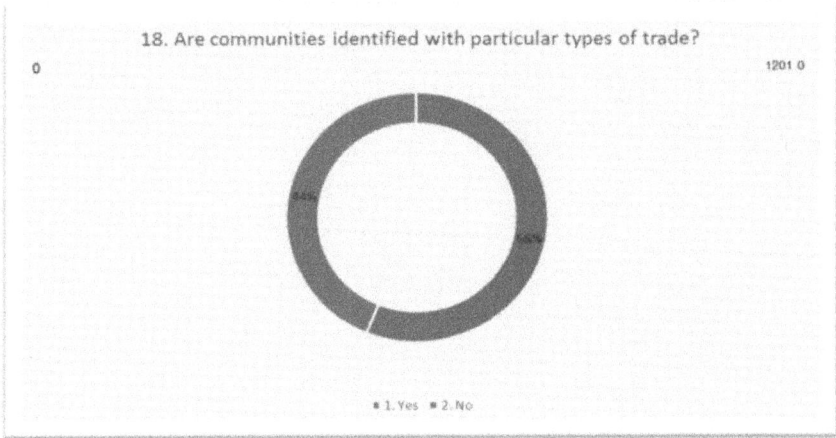

18. Are communities identified with particular types of trade?

0   1201 0

■ 1. Yes ■ 2. No

Figure 46: Ring Chart Showing the Distribution of Ndị Ọga by their Responses on whether Communities are Identified with Particular Types of Trade

Table 46 and Figure 46 reveal the distribution of Ndị Ọga by their responses on whether communities are identified with particular types of trade. Majority representing 56.2% of the respondents indicated that communities are identified with particular types of trade, while 43.8% indicated that communities are not identified with particular types of trade. The results suggest that communitiesare most likely to be identified with particular types of trade as Nnewi is known in most fora as the hub of spare parts. Enugu Agidi is known for timber production among others.

Table 47: Distribution of Ụmụ Bọyị by their Responses on whether Communities are Identified with Particular Types of Trade

	Frequency	Percent	Valid Percent	Cumulative Percent
No	695	57.9	57.9	57.9
Yes	505	42.1	42.1	100.0
Total	1200	100.0	100.0	

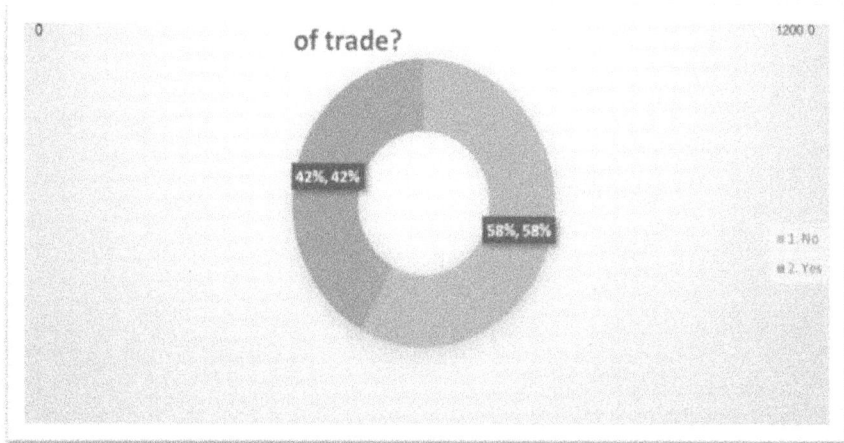

Figure 47: Pie Chart Showing the Distribution of Ụmụ Bọyị by their Responses on whether Communities are Identified with Particular Types of Trade

With respect to the distribution of Ụmụ Bọyị by their responses on whether communities are identified with particular types of trade as shown in Table 47 and Figure 47, 57.9% of the respondents indicated that communities are identified with particular types of trade while 42.1% of the respondents indicated that communities are not identified with particular types of trade. The results are at variance with the perception of Ndị Ọga. The implication is that times are actually changing. What was actually obtainable in the past is no longer fashionable in all cases.

Table 48: Distribution of Ndị Ọga by their Responses on how Ịgba Bọyị Became a Widely Accepted Entrepreneurial Behaviour among Ndị Igbo

	Frequency	Percent	Valid Percent	Cumulative Percent
Advancement in social mobility	53	4.4	4.4	4.4
All of the above	68	5.7	5.7	10.1
Expansion in family business	94	7.8	7.8	17.9
Expansion in trade and industry	273	22.7	22.7	40.6
Increase in wealth for entrepreneurs	462	38.5	38.5	79.1
Modification over time	215	17.9	17.9	97.0
Sustainable social protection system.	36	3.0	3.0	100.0
Total	1201	100.0	100.0	

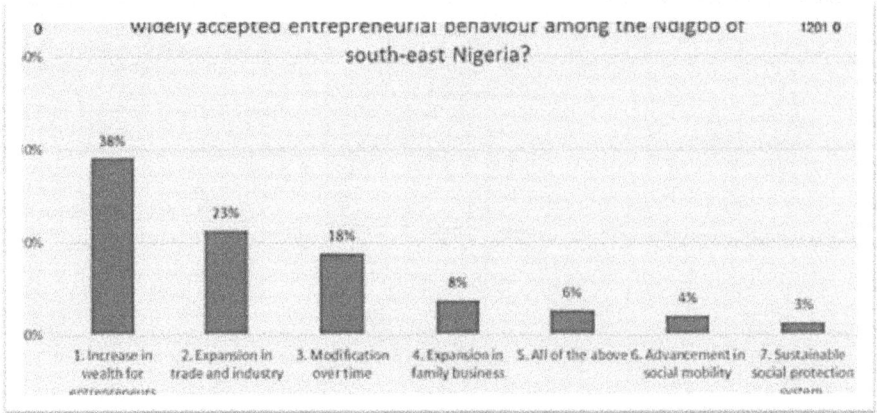

Figure 48: Bar Chart Distribution of *Ndị Ọga* by their Responses on how *Igba Boyi* Became a Widely Accepted Entrepreneurial Behaviour among *Ndị Igbo*

Table 48 and Figure 48 show the distribution of *Ndị Ọga* by their Responses on how *Igba Bọyị* became a widely accepted entrepreneurial behaviour among *Ndị Igbo*. 4.4% indicated that *Igba Bọyị* system became a widely accepted entrepreneurial behaviour among *Ndị Igbo* because of the quest for advancement in social mobility; 7.8% of the respondents indicated that the reason is for expansion in the family business; 22.7% of the respondents indicated that it was due to the quest for expansion in trade and industry; 38.5% of the respondents indicated that it was because of the quest for increase in wealth for entrepreneurs; 17.9% of the respondents identified the reason as modification over time; 3.0% of the respondents stated the reason to be sustainable social protection system while, 5.7% of the respondents chose all the above mentioned reasons. However, increase in wealth for entrepreneurs stands out as the major reason why the *Igba Bọyị* system became a widely accepted entrepreneurial behaviour among *Ndị Igbo*.

Table 49: Distribution of *Ụmụ Bọyị* by their Responses on how *Nwa Boyi* Became a Widely Accepted Entrepreneurial Behaviour among *Ndị Igbo*

	Frequency	Percent	Valid Percent	Cumulative Percent
Advancement in social mobility	50	4.2	4.2	4.2
Expansion in family business	114	9.5	9.5	13.7
Expansion in trade and industry	277	23.1	23.1	36.8
Increase in wealth for entrepreneurs	527	43.9	43.9	80.7

135

Modification over time	177	14.8	14.8	95.4
Others specify	23	1.9	1.9	97.3
Sustainable social protection system.	32	2.7	2.7	100.0
Total	1200	100.0	100.0	

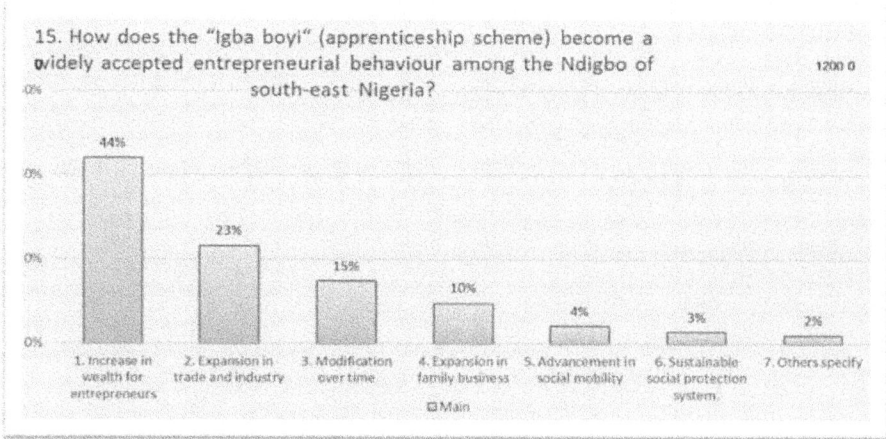

Figure 49: Bar Chart Depicting the Distribution of *Ụmụ Bọyị* by their Responses on how *Nwa Bọyị* Became a Widely Accepted Entrepreneurial Behaviour among *Ndị Igbo*.

As shown in Table 49 and Figure 49 with respect to the distribution of *Ụmụ Bọyị* by their responses on how *Igba Bọyị* became a widely accepted entrepreneurial behaviour among *Ndị Igbo*. 4.2% chose 'the quest for advancement in social mobility'. 9.5% of the respondents selected 'expansion in a family business'. 23.1% indicated 'the quest for expansion in trade and industry'.

43.9% of the respondents indicated 'the quest for increase in wealth for entrepreneurs'. 14.8% of the respondents said 'it resulted from modification over time'.

1.9% insisted that 'it was for sustainable social protection system', while 2.7% of the respondents indicatedall 'the above reasons'. Interestingly, both *Ndị Ọga* and *Ụmụ Bọyị* have the same perception that increase in wealth for entrepreneurs is the major reason why the *Igba Bọyị* system became a widely accepted entrepreneurial behaviour among *Ndị Igbo*.

4.3.1 Igbo Entrepreneurial and Apprenticeship Culture: Origin and Reasons for the Emergence

In a similar vein, the qualitative arm (interviews and discussions) of this research have been able to establish that over many centuries, the *Igba Boyi* (apprenticeship scheme) has become a globally known and widely accepted entrepreneurial behaviour and practice among *Ndi Igbo* of South-eastern Nigeria. From the interviews, the study revealed that historically, the entrepreneurial and apprenticeship culture is mainly associated with the Igbo people of Nigeria and it began in precolonial times before contact with Europeans. The practice had existed long before the birth of most contemporary practitioners in the selected markets studied. It is a trade and skill culture operated by the Igbo people of South-eastern Nigeria and also sparingly observed among other ethnic groups. *Igba Boyi* is a traditional skill-based apprenticeship scheme. It initially began as a skill acquisition enterprise specifically for the transfer, maintenance, and sustenance of inherited skills within notable families known for their expertise in certain crafts. Later there was a shift from not just maintaining the skills within families, but to other families (whose children are willing to learn the craft, trade, or skill) within the extended families, village, and community levels and one of the many reasons is to alleviate the burdens of parents with large family size. These children were sent to learn and acquire some traditional skills in blacksmithing, traditional herbal skills, textile crafts, pottery, oil palm processing, agricultural produce (especially families where you have *Ezeji* - king cultivator of yams and the like), among so many others. The excerpts below give a picture of what the traders think is the origin of *Igba Boyi*:

Igba Boyi started before we were born; we grew to meet the practice. We are not the ones that brought about the practice, it is the practice that the Igbo people use in training themselves and we discovered it is helping us. Even those that went to school are not left out in this practice, but the difference is that theirs (length of apprenticeship) will be shorter than those that didn't go to school. But ours was when we rounded off with secondary or primary school that we went into *Igba Boyi* and afterward, we started ours with what we were settled with. That was when people were submissive. Some apprentices normally serve for four, five, six, or seven years and the practice helped our parents who usually give birth to too many children, not now that people give birth to two or three children and they are ok with them. My dad was a farmer and I did Boyi for 9 years and people that I trained are many as well and we have used this practice to train many young ones but today there is a problem especially in our Anambra (KII with Male, 78 years old Ọga, entrepreneur, and industry owner).

Igba Boyi didn't start today, during the era of my fathers, when a child matures a bit, his people will be looking for a person from the same village that is into business in the town to come and carry their child. So, what am I saying, our forefathers went for *bọyi* and it was that era young ladies that are preparing to marry go for '*ọzụzụ*'- a sort of training in the hands of a mature woman that is living an exemplary life, but I don't know whether such is still in existence? Our forefathers see *Igba Boyi* as someone helping to train their child (ren) to become somebody in life. There is a difference between those that went for *Igba Boyi* and those that remained in the village with their parents and tapping palm wine. So, our people believe that once their child is trained by somebody that is doing well, their child will be like them soonest (Male FGD session at Main Market).

I served as an apprentice. In the olden days, dependent-apprenticeship (*Igba Boyi*) helped the Igbo a lot especially those from very poor families. Like those of us from a poor family, we were handed over to someone and when we were handed over to that person, who may also be poor, that is he may be having a very small business on the table; but some of us helped to grow such a man's business. That time we were trained morally, like now, if your people are not known for stealing, when you come to your master you will not be stealing. So that was what helped in this dependent-apprenticeship; if you can remember in 1982 when the Pope visited Nigeria, he said – that Africa has a lesson they will teach the whole world. He explained it as – in Africa, you can go to a poor man's house and make his son a rich man, but in the other parts of the world it is not like that. He said in their country that if you are a cleaner in a factory, all your children will be factory cleaners and the entire family; but Africa can pick a son of the poor and make him rich. The challenge we had was when I was still active in business, I used to have over 17 to 20 dependent apprentices (KII with a 58 years old Male entrepreneur and industrialist in his factory).

Put differently, *Igba Boyi* is a strategy for *skill and wealth acquisition, transfer and sustenance* within and among various notable Igbo families who were involved in the production of goods and services like blacksmithing artifacts, traditional herbal skills, Textile Crafts, Oil Palm Processing, agricultural produce, among others. It was known as '*Igba-ọdịbọ* (not slavery) or *imu-ahia or imu-ọlu*'. This was the pre-modern way of education in Igbo land and every child was exposed to one skill or the other within families or they were sent to those skills or trade-oriented families to live and learn the intended skill. The *Igba Boyi* system of those days was operated based on the principles of common sense and morality such as *trust, honesty, and humility* as shown in some of these excerpts below:

...those that started a business then, were not all educated; because there is a difference between education and common sense (*passing six abụrọ passing sense*), it is common sense that is the root of business and you cannot have common sense if you don't have a good beginning. A good beginning is that from the onset it is either you are Anglican or Catholic, you must be strong in it and will be serious in the church activities, because that is one of the places you can get a good foundation for you to be a business person. For instance, when we were still in our early childhood, if we swore 'true to God', then be it known that we did not do the crime we are being accused of; but today children are ready to deny even killing a human being that they are guilty of; they will even swear with the road. Such persons, you have seen, lack morals. If such a person is engaged in business, he will embezzle the master's capital. And whoever embezzles someone's capital does not come with clean hands. If you want equity, you must come with clean hands. You must be honest so that you can make your own money. So, those that started this business in the early days, abhor certain things, many of them were not born Christian, and their fathers (parents) were/are always standing on the truth with their/his (*Ofor*) ancestral authority. With this, you will see that he will gradually transfer the *ofor* to his son, by telling him – do this and don't do that (IDI with Male 62 years Old *Ọga*).

4.3.2 Structure, Practice and Management of Igba Boyi Culture among Onitsha Markets Traders in Igboland

In terms of Structure of authority in *Igba Bọyị* (dependent-apprenticeship) scheme, the master (*Ọga*) provides leadership and guidance. For instance, upon the arrival of an intending apprentice to the master's home/house, he takes directives from the master (*Ọga*) and sometimes from the wife of his master (Madam) and the senior '*Nwa Boyi*(s)', relative and children of his master (*Ọga*)

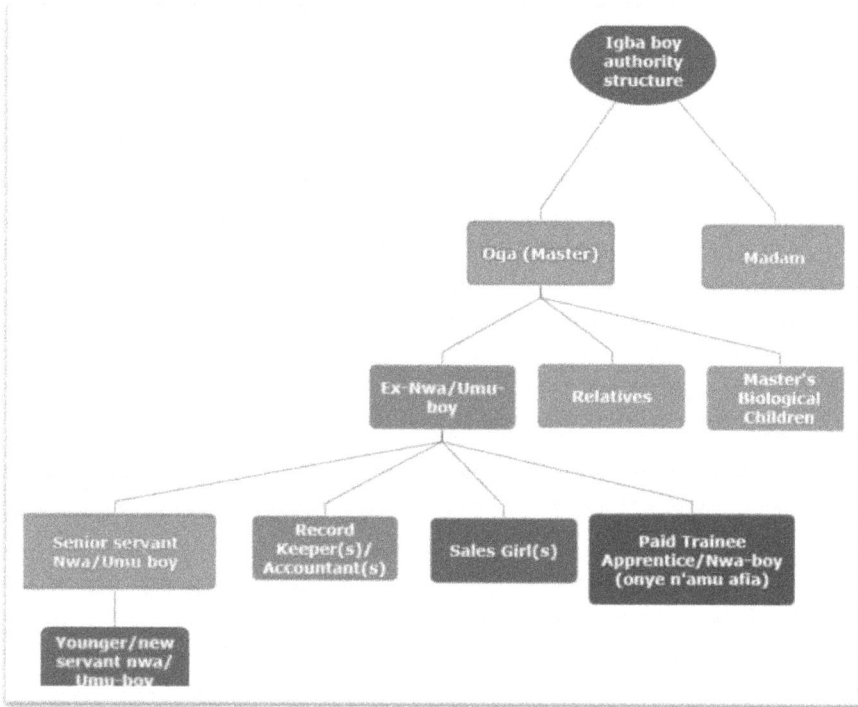

Figure iv: Structure of Authority in the *Igba Boyi* Scheme

The '*Nwa Boyi*' (apprentice) automatically finds himself as a *'live-in'* staff (not a house boy but he is expected to perform similar functions like a *'live-in-maid'* before going to the shop) and behave as a member of his master's household. He takes orders directly from this *Oga* and sometimes from the master's wife especially on domestic chores and related orders like fetching water, washing and cleaning. Apart from the master and wife, the apprentice also takes orders from the master's children especially from those older than him. Similarly, relatives of the master could also give orders which he has to obey and execute.

Away from activities in the master's home, the apprentice must report daily and punctually too to the shop where trading activities occur. These activities range from opening and cleaning the shop, sorting, dusting and arranging goods, hunting for customers (*oso ahja*), loading and off-loading goods, to buying or going home to prepare food (brunch and lunch where/when necessary) among many other expectations. In the process of executing all these responsibilities, he learns the ropes and the nitty-gritty of the trade through observation, imitation and modelling.

4.3.3 Theorization and Conceptualization of 'Ịgba Bọyị'

Ịgba Bọyị as Nkwado Ọgaranya (Apprenticepreneurship): For the purpose of this study, *Ịgba Bọyị is* henceforth described as apprenticepreneurship or *nkwado Ọgaranya* - the sum of the complex exchanges and interactions between an apprentice and an entrepreneur which involve observation and imitation through modelling. This is further conceptualised as the Igbo Entrepreneurial Incubation Scheme (IEIS) that sets the apprentice on a new threshold of gaining the experiential knowledge of a master over a period of time towards sustainable empowerment and sel-factualisation. The foregoing conceptualisation expunges the stigma surrounding apprenticeship that has served to de-incentivise many young persons from getting involved in apprenticeship. This implies that apprenticepreneurship is a mutual relationship that promotes the interests of both the entrepreneur and the apprentice.

With colonialism and the introduction of modern education like primary and secondary schools, technical colleges, and universities, most Igbo children were sent to schools while those whose parents could not afford the cost of western education continued with the existing traditional educational system which is *Igba Bọyị*. This igbo apprenticeship scheme demands patience, and perseverance from the *Nwa Boyi* thereby aligning with the cliche 'no pain, no gain'. This brings to the fore the nexus between hard work and benefits or interface between pain and gain which comes after the long years of training.

Colonialism marked the introduction of foreign languages like English in Igbo land and subsequently an introduction of the concept of 'boy' in the Igbo apprenticeship scheme. This led to the replacement or switch from the usage of the concept of '*Igba ọdịbọ*' to '*Igba Bọyị*'. At this juncture, the attachment of the word '*boy, bọị or boyi*' to '*Igba*' needs a little elaboration. The word 'boy' is an English word, as this seems to portray that '*Igba Boyi*'is a recent practice among the Igbo to a critical mind because English was introduced to Igbo land in colonial times. This is not correct, the concept of the *Igba Bọyị* apprenticeship scheme in Igbo land is best described as a modern way of referring to the pre-colonial *ịmụ-ahịa* (learning a trade), *ịmụ-ọlụ* (learning a handwork/skill).

4.3.4 Types of Igba Bọyị (Apprenticeship)

Kin-related Apprenticeship - Provenance

The interview findings show that the *Igba Bọyị* practice is a *skill incubation* or *skill transfer scheme practiced* among the Igbo people of South-eastern Nigeria for training a new generation of practitioners in a trade or business. Early manifestations of the *Igba Boyi* scheme indicated that many masters of trades and skills brought in their relatives to learn and sustain the trade and skills within families. Thus, this set the stage for the provenience of kin-related apprenticeship practice in Igbo land. Put differently, the Apprenticeship culture (*Igba Boyi*) started with the kin-related among Igbo people. This was subsequently complemented with 'non-kin-related Igba Boyi' but our current findings show that the 'non-kin-related apprenticeship' is on the verge of replacing the 'kin-related apprenticeship'.Currently, this new trend in the *Igba Boyi* apprenticeship scheme is gradually setting the stage for a complete shift of paradigm from kin-related to the prevailing non-kin-related apprenticeship. This gradual change in the practice of *Igba Boyi* is associated with a lot of factors namely: *modern education, the Nigerian-Biafran war, suspicion and lack of trust, accusations and counter-accusations of theft, misappropriation of the master's (Oga's) business capital, and mismanagement, greed and court cases by extended family members who want to take over the business of their brothers/relatives (masters) at their demise thereby leaving the wife and children empty-handed, bickering* and outright conflicts between masters (*Ndi Oga*) and dependent-apprentices (*Umu/ndi*) boyi among many other issues. These identified factors and more, therefore, led to a shift from the familial, consanguineal, affinal, or kin-related dependent apprenticeship to non-kin-related dependent apprenticeship. The length of apprenticeship which is most flexible and not static, the role of *Igba boyi* in alleviating the parental burdens of raising many children in families, the contribution of the *Igba Boyi* scheme in wealth-transfer and upward social stratification of the poor. There is a consensus of opinion among the study participants that *Igba Boyi* scheme in Igbo land has a very long history, almost as old as the Igbo race itself. Like was observed earlier, the Igbo entrepreneurial culture historically began with the 'kin-related *Igba Boyi* practice' otherwise henceforth known in this report as the dependent or live-in (residential) apprenticeship scheme. It is a scheme that thrives on the long standing interaction and exchange of experiential knowledge and skill from masters to apprentices who form a network of his life-long progeny, offspring or descendants. Here, this type of apprentice learns the trade free of charge or may pay to learn depending on the nature of negotiations and agreements during recruitment. The following categorization below is important in this report because this study established diverse forms of apprenticeship discussed and elaborated on later below:

Igba Boyi **(live-in (residential)/Dependent-Apprenticeship):** Here an *Oga* (master) meets with the family of a young boy and says, 'I want to carry this your child to nurture him in business and to make him somebody. In some cases, it could be the parents of the intending apprentice who would approach the master for such negotiations and agreement. In ancient times in Igbo land, there was nothing like written agreement, the only agreement is the spoken words' (Male IDI, Main Market, August 2020). This implies that the agreements were essentially oral. The apprentice goes home with his master/boss, lives in his master's home daily, does home chores like cleaning, washing, and cooking when necessary, and serves his master for many years as often orally agreed. Most times, there is no formal or informal agreement of any sort. *'ekwu-ekwu, aka-aka'* in the words of one apprentice (*Nwa Boyi*) during a Focus Group Discussion (FGD) session with a purposively assembled apprentices at the Bridge Head Market. He was stressing the fact that he was brought from home to serve his *Oga* (master) without any form of agreement on the number of years he would spend. This implies that there could be occasions where agreement (written or oral) is non-existent. Here, even in the contemporary era, it is left at the discretion of the master to decide when to settle the apprentice or not. Many thought that, normally, after 4 years the *Nwa Boyi* will be settled, but sometimes it may not be exactly 4 years some will extend to 5, 6, 7 years, depending on the individual's learning capacity and how fast he is with grasping the skills heis being exposed to. Some masters used to be tricky in such a way that they will overuse the child and sometimes when the time of settlement is near, they will accuse him of one thing or the other and then ask him to go without Settlement.

Apart from the dependent (residential) and independent (non-residential) *Nwa Boyi*, we also have other types of apprentices categorized based on the nature of kinship relations with the masters (*Ndi Oga*) namely: kin-related and non-kin-related dependent-apprentices (*Nwa Boyi*). These are those living within the master's household. They can also be known as dependent apprentices (*Umu Boyi*). Kin-related dependent apprentices are mainly agnates or blood relatives from both the master's father-side and mother-side, Igbo society being a patrilineal society. The non-kin-related dependent apprentices (*Umu Boyi*) are not agnates but may be community members or from other distant towns and states in Nigeria. There are other variants such as the paid and unpaid independent apprentices as discussed below.

Onye na-amu-ahia (Independent apprenticeship): this is a learner or an apprentice but he is of a different type because he is not expected or mandated to live with his *Oga* (master). He comes from home and most times; this type of apprentice is not a child but an already grown-up adult who wants to venture into trading/business. He is independent of his master though under his tutelage. He is not entrusted with finances and capital of the business and he is more or less seen as an outsider in the business unlike the 'dependent apprentice'. This trainee or apprentice is expected to pay for his training under the master (*Oga*). He embarks on this training with a mission to understand the Business skills or trade secrets, nuances, gain knowledge on the basic nitty-gritty of the trade of interest, learn where to source the goods, how to preserve them, and how and when to buy or sell. He is expected to pay a certain amount of fee/money with some items like drinks, kola-nuts, and food where necessary, and sometimes, the skill can be acquired free if the master decides to grant an independent apprentice a waiver. The main difference between this and the former is that this apprentice does not live in his master's home.

Ọsọ-ahịa (Sales/customer-canvaser) or scouting for customers or sales: This occurs when one/trader does not have the capital or even if one has capital but does not have a shop of his own and sometimes one can have a shop. The *ọsọ ahịa* trader tries to identify distributors or big businessmen who brought in some goods that have acquired high patronage or moving sales. This individual goes to him to collect goods for sale. This is dependent on the type of person you are, if you are a friendly fellow, you will definitely have people that will allow you to carry their goods, but if not, people will all run away from giving you such an opportunity. The key factor here is *trust and integrity* to remit what was given to you on trust. This is one way the Igbo entrepreneurship schemes create, distribute and redistribute capital and wealth among Igbo folks, although other ethnic groups are gradually benefiting from this wealth creation process as they are also allowed to venture into *ọsọ ahịa* if they establish a personality of integrity in the mind of other people. All sorts of people get involved in *ọsọ ahịa* namely: ex-*Ụmụ Bọyị* without a shop and/or business capital, current ụmụ-bọyị, and even *Ndi Ọga* just like this master here who was asked if *Ndi Ọga* also participate in *ọsọ ahịa*:

> Yes! You know that some Masters may not have all the goods that the customer requires; like now, I deal in sportswear, there is no way I will have all the goods my customer will need; so, we used to rush out and get it from our neighbors. Similarly, you may have, let's say 500 dozen of a particular product, while the customer requires 800 or 1000 dozens of it – we will then make calls to know the people that have it to make it up. So, by doing this one is chasing for customers or sales (*Igba ọsọ ahịa*) (IDI 45 years Old *Ọga* at Ọchanja Market).

From the findings we established that there are two types of *ọsọ ahịa* namely: direct and indirect *ọsọ ahịa*.

Oche-ọdụ (Journeyman): occurs when the journeyman does not have a shop of his own yet and he stays in any vacant space he sees around, and if the owner of the shop comes, he will pack to another vacant space.

Combined business: this occurs after an apprentice has fully undergone training (graduated) and has been settled by his master. Settlement implies freedom from a master, equipped with goods or capital and shop. He does this for the combined interest of himself and the master. He can decide to go into an arrangement where his capital and that of his master is merged or combined to run a partnership or joint business. This he continues to do until he can fully stand on his own.

Own a Shop: This occurs when an apprentice after 'settlement' or freedom from his master's tutelage is permitted to acquire a shop or own a shop given to him by his *Oga* (master).

Master (*Oga*): This is the skilled trader (expert, trained-trainer, experienced, professional trader) under whose tutelage the apprentice is groomed until he is mature and has acquired relevant trading skills needed in a particular trade. There are about two types of *Oga* namely: the married *Oga* (masters) and the Unmarried/Bachelor *Oga* (master). These two types of masters differ in the type of dynamics that play out in the master's household. The dynamics of interactions that play out in the married master's household are much more complex than that of the master who is a bachelor.

Distributorship: This occurs when a shop owner is fully established and has expanded business linkages, established some form of integrity and trust with a particular company, he can then be invited by the company or request to help distribute the company's goods or products within a particular region or area.

The trajectory of progress from apprenticeship to being a master is dynamic, flexible and the ultimate end is wealth and employment creation.

Table 50: Distribution of *Ndị Ọga* by their Responses on the Most Important Cultural Characteristic that Drives Entrepreneurial Disposition of *Ndị Igbo*

	Frequency	Percent	Valid Percent	Cumulative Percent
Aku luo uno	159	13.2	13.2	13.2
Extended family system	68	5.7	5.7	27.5
*Igwebuike*philosophy	269	22.4	22.4	49.9
Itu mgbele finance support scheme	46	3.8	3.8	53.7
Mgbo olu labour strategy	40	3.3	3.3	57.0

Nwanne di na mba	110	9.2	9.2	66.2
Ogo bu chi onye	56	4.7	4.7	70.9
Onye aghana nwanne ye	329	27.4	27.4	98.3
All of the above	103	8.6	8.6	21.8
Others specify	21	1.7	1.7	100.0
Total	1201	100.0	100.0	

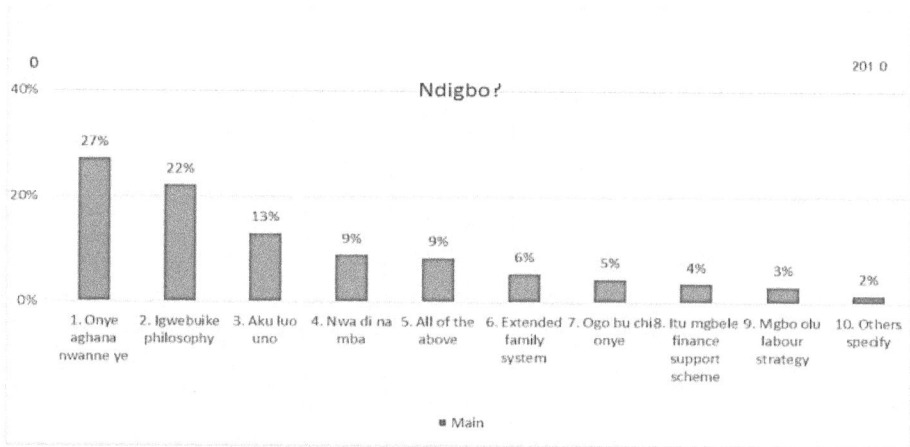

Figure 50: Bar Chart Distribution of Ndị Ọga by their Responses on the Most Important Cultural Characteristic that Drives Entrepreneurial Disposition of Ndị Igbo.

Table 50 and Figure 50 showes the distribution of Ndị Ọga by their responses on the most important cultural characteristic that drives the entrepreneurial disposition of Ndị Igbo. 13.2% of the respondents indicated that 'Aku luo uno' philosophy is the important cultural characteristic that drives the entrepreneurial disposition of Ndị Igbo. 5.7% of the respondents indicated 'extended family system'. 22.4% of the respondents chose 'igwe bụ ike' philosophy. 3.8% of the respondents selected 'itu mgbele finance support scheme'. 3.3% of the respondents indicated that 'mgbọọlụ labour strategy'. 9.2% of the respondents identified 'nwanne dị na mba'. 4.7% of the respondents indicated that 'Ọgo bụ chi ọnye'. 27.4% of the respondents indicated that 'Ọnye aghana nwanne ya' is the important cultural characteristic; 1.7% of the respondents selected 'Ọnye aghana nwanne ya', while 8.6% of the respondents chose all the above responses.

Table 51: Distribution of *Ụmụ Bọyị* by their Responses on the Most Important Cultural Characteristic that Drives Entrepreneurial Disposition of *Ndị Igbo*

	Frequency	Percent	Valid Percent	Cumulative Percent
Aku luo uno	176	14.7	14.7	14.7
Extended family system	73	6.1	6.1	27.7
Igwebuike philosophy	265	22.1	22.1	49.8
Itu mgbele finance support scheme	35	2.9	2.9	52.7
Mgbo olu labour strategy	65	5.4	5.4	58.1
Nwanne di na mba	163	13.6	13.6	71.7
Ogo bu chi onye	56	4.7	4.7	76.3
Onye aghana nwanne ye	284	23.7	23.7	100.0
All of the above	83	6.9	6.9	21.6
Total	1200	100.0	100.0	

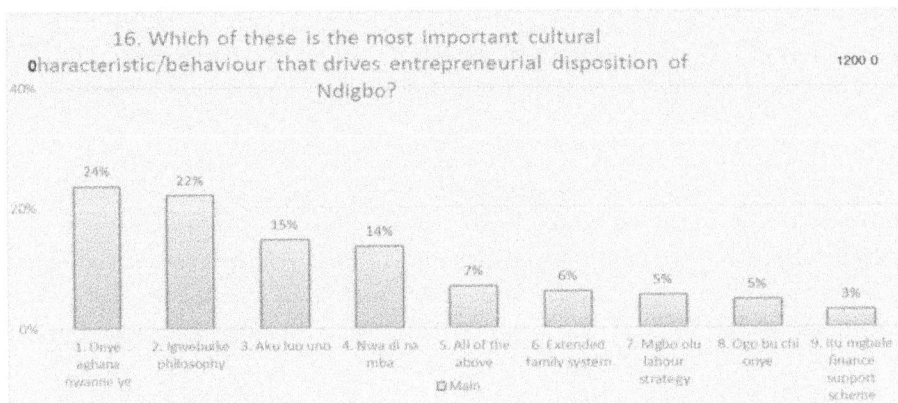

Figure 51: Bar Chart Depicting the Distribution of *Ụmụ Bọyị* by their Responses on the Most Important Cultural Characteristic that Drives Entrepreneurial Disposition of *Ndị Igbo*

As shown in Table 51 and Figure 51 with respect to the distribution of *Ụmụ Bọyị* by their responses on the most important cultural characteristic that drives entrepreneurial disposition of Ndi Igbo. 14.7% of the respondents indicated that '*Akụ luo unọ*'philosophy is the most important cultural characteristic that drives the entrepreneurial disposition of *Ndị Igbo*. 6.1% of the respondents indicated that it is 'the extended family system'. 22.1% of the respondents chose '*igwe bụ ike*' philosophy. 2.9% of the respondents indicated that*itu mgbele* finance support scheme; 5.4% of the respondents identified '*mgbọ ọlụ* labour strategy'. 13.6% of the respondents indicated 'nwanne dị na mba'. 4.7% of the respondents selected '*ọgọ bụ chi ọnye*'. 23.7% of the respondents selected '*Ọnye aghana nwanne ya*', while 6.9% of the respondents chose all the above options. The result suggests that '*Ọnye aghana nwanne ya*' (Be your brother's keeper) is the most important cultural characteristic that drives the entrepreneurial disposition of *Ndị Igbo*.

Table 52: Distribution of *Ndị Ọga* by their Responses on Other Important Cultural Characteristics that Drive Entrepreneurial Disposition of *Ndị Igbo*

	Frequency	Percent	Valid Percent	Cumulative Percent
Other options except (If others, specify)	1180	98.3	98.3	98.3
An average Igboman is arrＯgant and won't want to be belittled. Firstly, it's survival, after the war, they were left without anything and faced business squarely Secondly, it's the normal nature of an Igbo man	1	.1	.1	98.3
Fear of unknown	1	.1	.1	98.4
For cultural perspective of being independent	1	.1	.1	98.5
General poverty elevating scheme	1	.1	.1	98.6
God made it that Igbobe industrious	1	.1	.1	98.7
I don't really know	1	.1	.1	98.8
I dont believe in anyone	1	.1	.1	98.8
I dont know	1	.1	.1	98.9
Igbos are known to have survival instincts	1	.1	.1	99.0
Independence of Igbo	1	.1	.1	99.1
It is a tradition for you to become a student before you become a teacher	1	.1	.1	99.2
Ka enyere ibe ha aka	1	.1	.1	99.3
Ka enyere Mmadu aka	1	.1	.1	99.3

Liberation from government intimidation and shame from the failed war. It will be very hard for an Igboto be president hence we struggle to carve a niche for ourselves, to make sure we are respected amongst men.	1	.1	.1	99.4
Low value of education	1	.1	.1	99.5
Natural for Igboto be independent	1	.1	.1	99.6
No idea	1	.1	.1	99.7
Ọnye fee eze, eze eruo ya	1	.1	.1	99.8
There is no country you will not see an Igboman. With God all things are possible	1	.1	.1	99.8
uba mmadu	1	.1	.1	99.9
Umunna nwezuo aku	1	.1	.1	100.0
Total	1201	100.0	100.0	

4.3.5 Philosophies and the Socio-Cultural Characteristics that Drive Igbo

Entrepreneurial Success

From the interviews and discussions, this study confirmed that the Igbo apprenticeship scheme operates on the following philosophies: the *'Igwe bụ ike'* philosophy, *'Ọnye aghana nwanne ya'* ideology, *'Ọgọ bụ chi ọnye'*, *'Nwanne di na mba'* s*lỌgan*, *'adịghị anọ-ofu ebe ekili mmanwụ'* cliché, among others. Some of these peculiar cultural characteristics have sustained the contemporary vestiges of the original traditional form of *'Igba Bọyị'* practice among *Ndị Igbo*. These characteristics range from its *capacity to adjust to modifications over time, its potentials to increase wealth for Igbo entrepreneurs, ensure expansion in private trade and industry, capacity for sustainable expansion of family business, provide the foundation for advancement in social mobility and ensure sustainable social protection system for Ndị Igbo.* We found that this is anchored on certain philosophies and worldviews upon which *Ndị Igbo* operate.

This study further confirmed that the most important Igbo philosophies and cultural characteristic behaviour that drive the entrepreneurial dispositions of *Ndị Igbo* are: the *'Igwe bụ ike'* philosophy (meaning there is strength in majority/unity); the *'Ọnye aghana nwanne ya'* ideology (be your brother's keeper); the autochthonous social support system of the ever-dynamic extended family system. Further findings reveal that Igbo people uphold the principle that *'Ọgọ bụ chi ọnye'* (your in-law or family relative is your savior/god or helper). This stresses the need to fall back to relatives when business declines or fails. This is one way the Igbo entrepreneurial culture is unique when compared with modern Western-oriented entrepreneurship, and this is because when business capital declines or fails, for instance, the entrepreneur falls back to the banks. This is not so for the Igbo entrepreneur, one can fall back to kin-groups, relatives, and the extended family for social and financial support as they not only give financial support but they can also provide *Nwa Boyi* - (an apprentice) who can learn the trade skill free of charge while providing cheap labour or productivity in furtherance of the master's trade. Also, we found that *Ndị Igbo* upholds the '*Nwanne dị na mba' slOgan which* highlights the already established practice of 'non-kin-related apprenticeship' particularly in city centers when one migrates far away from home. We found that the Igbo man is conscientiously and consciously itinerant and can be found in any part of the world. This itinerant nature of *Ndị Igbo* spells out adaptability, flexibility, and dynamism which were discovered to be key features of any would-be sustainable entrepreneurship, hence the popular maxim '*adighi anọ-ofu ebe ekili mmanwụ*' (meaning that a spectator does not stay at a single location to watch a masquerade). The Igbo itinerant businessman does not fail to tap into the existing 'fictitious kinship relations' in distant lands. Fictitious kinship is an anthropological term referring to the nature of intra/intergroup relations which is often experienced by a migrant in urban/city centers when the migrant is away from home or blood relatives (Leyton, 2018). The other is the Igbo ideology that wealth must get home hence the cliche '*Akụ luo ụnọ*'. This Igbo philosophy contributes a large percentage of the global worldwide remittances from Igbo people back home from abroad (whether from local or international migrants, Legal or Illegal migrants- the idea and motive is always to bring wealth back home). This is the philosophy that drives the annual unique culture 'end-of-the year returns' mostly occurring in December/January. Apart from coming back home for social reintegration, people return home with huge cash for personal and community development projects and businesses of all sorts.

This study also found that the '*Mgbọ ọlụ* labour' strategy among *Ndị Igbo* enables adequate labour distribution among kin groups and also ensures increased productivity. Similarly, the 'Itụ mgbele'- finance support scheme comes across as the bedrock for revitalizing a kin's business capital when bankrupt. All these principles put together remain the superstructure upon which the *Igba Boyi* scheme is operated and sustained.

Table 53: Distribution of *Ndị Ọga* by their Responses on the Main Person during Apprenticeship Negotiation and Placement Process

	Frequency	Percent	Valid Percent	Cumulative Percent
Biological brothers	2	.2	.2	.2
Biological father	1142	95.1	95.1	95.3
Biological mother	24	2.0	2.0	97.3
Biological sisters	2	.2	.2	97.4
Family friends	17	1.4	1.4	98.8
Kinsmen	14	1.2	1.2	100.0
Total	1201	100.0	100.0	

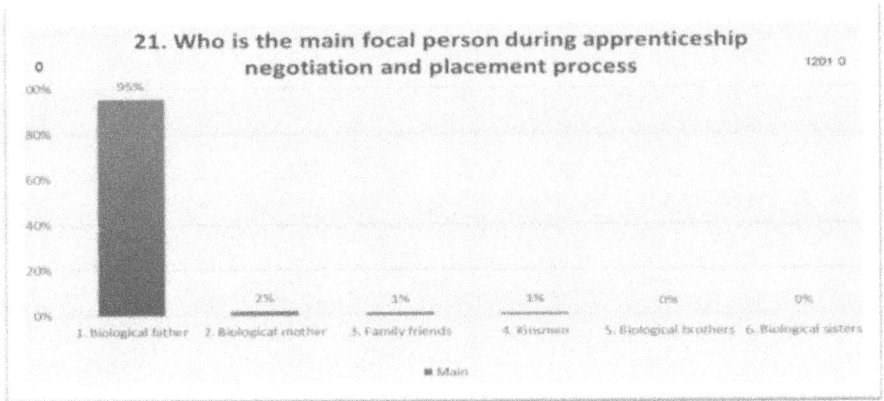

Figure 53: Bar Chart Depicting the Distribution of *Ndị Ọga* by their Responses on the Main Person during Apprenticeship Negotiation and Placement Process.

Table 53 and Figure 53 showed the distribution of *Ndị Ọga* by their responses on the main person during apprenticeship negotiation and placement process. 0.2% indicated 'biological brothers'. 95.1% indicated 'biological father'. 2.0% indicated 'biological mother'. 0.2% indicated 'biological sisters'. 1.4% indicated 'family friends' and 1.2% indicated 'kinsmen'. The results suggestthat the biological father is the main person during apprenticeship negotiation and placement process.

Table 54: Distribution of *Ndị Ọga* by their Responses on the Main Person during Apprenticeship Negotiation and Placement Process if Parents are Dead

	Frequency	Percent	Valid Percent	Cumulative Percent
Biological brothers	458	38.1	38.1	38.2
Biological sisters	8	.7	.7	38.9
Familyfriends	25	2.1	2.1	41.0
Kinsmen	141	11.7	11.7	52.7
Uncle	568	47.3	47.3	99.9
None of the above	1	.1	.1	100.0
Total	1201	100.0	100.0	

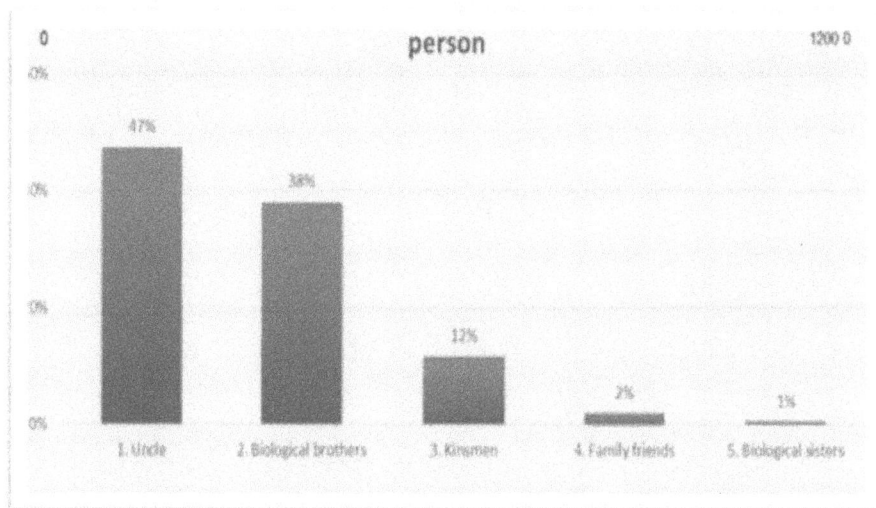

Figure 54: Bar Chart Showing the Distribution of *Ndị Ọga* by their Responses on the Main Person during Apprenticeship Negotiation and Placement Process if Parents are Dead.

Table 54 and Figure 54 reveal the distribution of *Ndị Ọga* by their responses on the main person during apprenticeship negotiation and placement process if parents are dead. 38.1% indicated that 'biological brothers' as the main person during apprenticeship negotiation and placement process if parents are dead. 0.7% chose 'biological sisters'. 2.1% identified 'family friends'. 11.7% selected 'kinsmen'. 47.3% chose 'uncle'. The result revealed that an uncle is the 'main person during apprenticeship negotiation and placement process if parents are dead followed by biological brothers.

Table 55: Distribution of *Ụmụ Boyi* by their Responses on the Main Person during Apprenticeship Negotiation and Placement Process

	Frequency	Percent	Valid Percent	Cumulative Percent
Biological brothers	17	1.4	1.4	1.4
Biological father	1102	91.8	91.8	93.3
Biological mother	35	2.9	2.9	96.2
Biological sisters	6	.5	.5	96.7
Family friends	21	1.8	1.8	98.4
Kinsmen	19	1.6	1.6	100.0
Total	1200	100.0	100.0	

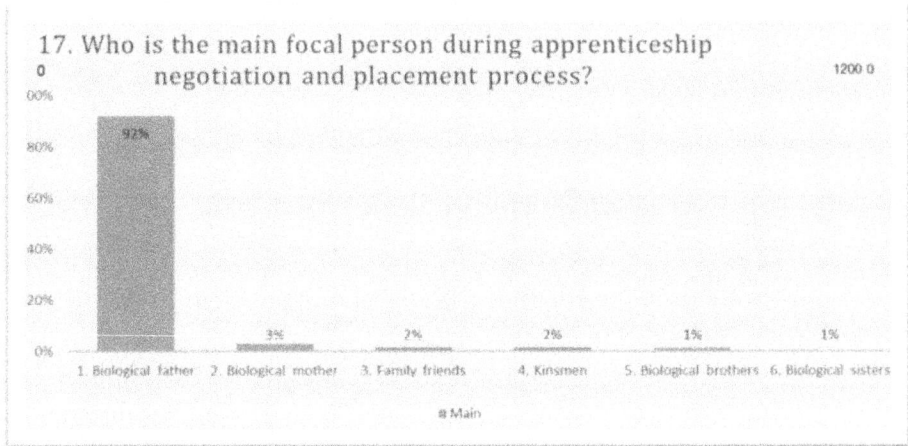

Figure 55: Bar Chart Depicting the Distribution of *Ụmụ Boyi* by their Responses on the Main Person during Apprenticeship Negotiation and Placement Process

Table 55 and Figure 55 showed the distribution of *Ụmụ Boyi* by their Responses on the Main Person during Apprenticeship Negotiation and Placement Process. 1.4% indicated 'biological brothers' as the main person during apprenticeship negotiation and placement process. 91.8% indicated 'biological father'. 2.9% selected 'biological mother'. 0.5% indicated 'biological sisters'. 1.8% chose 'family friends', while 1.6% identified kinsmen. From the perspective of *Ụmụ Boyi*, the result revealed that the biological father is the main person during apprenticeship negotiation and placement process.

Table 56: Distribution of _Ụmụ Bọyị_ by their Responses on the Main Person during Apprenticeship Negotiation and Placement Process if Parents are Dead

	Frequency	Percent	Valid Percent	Cumulative Percent
Biological brothers	745	62.1	62.1	62.1
Biological sisters	17	1.4	1.4	63.5
Familyfriends	50	4.2	4.2	67.7
Kinsmen	364	30.3	30.3	98.0
Uncle	24	2.0	2.0	100.0
Total	1200	100.0	100.0	

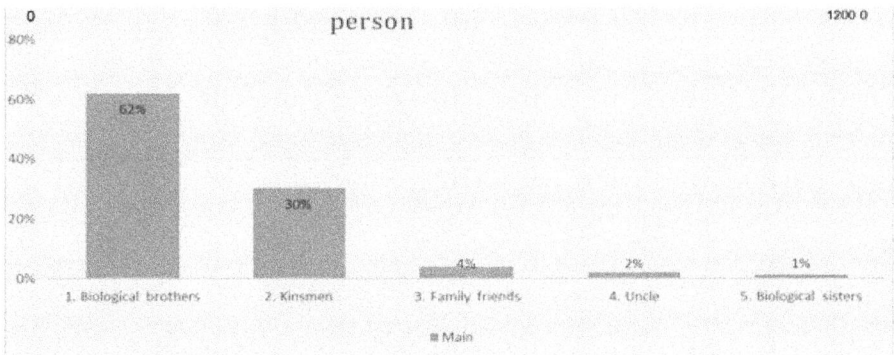

Figure 56: Bar Chart Showing the Distribution of ụmụ bọyị by their Responses on the Main Person during Apprenticeship Negotiation and Placement Process if Parents are Dead.

Table 56 and Figure 56 show the distribution of Ụmụ Bọyị by their Responses on the Main Person during Apprenticeship Negotiation and Placement Process if Parents are Dead. 62.1% indicated 'biological brothers' as the main person during apprenticeship negotiation and placement process. 1.4% indicated 'biological sisters'. 4.2% selected 'family friends'. 30.3% indicated 'kinsmen', while 2.0% identified 'uncle'. From the perspective of Ụmụ Bọyị, the result revealed that the biological brother is the main person during apprenticeship negotiation and placement process if parents are dead.

Table 57: Distribution of Ndị Ọga by their Responses on the Existence of Apprenticeship Agreement between Nwa Bọyị and Ọga

	Frequency	Percent	Valid Percent	Cumulative Percent
No	28	2.3	2.3	2.3
Yes	1173	97.7	97.7	100.0
Total	1201	100.0	100.0	

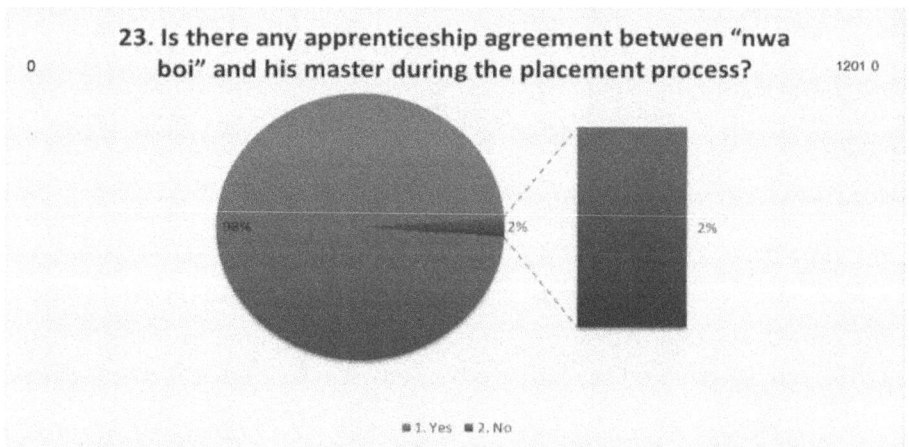

23. Is there any apprenticeship agreement between "nwa boi" and his master during the placement process?

■ 1. Yes ■ 2. No

Figure 57: Pie Chart Showing the Distribution of Ndị Ọga by their Responses on the Existence of Apprenticeship Agreement between Nwa Bọyị and Ọga

As shown in Table 57 and Figure 57 with respect to the distribution of Ndị Ọga by their responses on the existence of apprenticeship agreement between Nwa Bọyi and Ọga. 97.7% of the respondents indicated that 'there is in existence apprenticeship agreement between Nwa Bọyị and Ọga' while 2.3% of the respondents indicated that 'there is no apprenticeship agreement between Nwa Bọyị and Ọga'.

Table 58: Distribution of *Ndị Ọga* by their Responses on the Form of Apprenticeship **Agreement between *Nwa Bọyị* and *Ọga***

	Frequency	Percent	Valid Percent	Cumulative Percent
Other options except for 'Yes' responses to (Is there an apprenticeship agreement between "*Nwa Bọyị*" and his master during the placement process?)	28	2.3	2.3	2.3
All of the above	19	1.6	1.6	3.9
Both written and oral agreement	512	42.6	42.6	46.5
Court/Legal agreement	2	.2	.2	46.7
Oath taking	1	.1	.1	46.8
Oral agreement	403	33.6	33.6	80.3
Others (Please specify)	13	1.1	1.1	81.4
Written agreement	223	18.6	18.6	100.0
Total	1201	100.0	100.0	

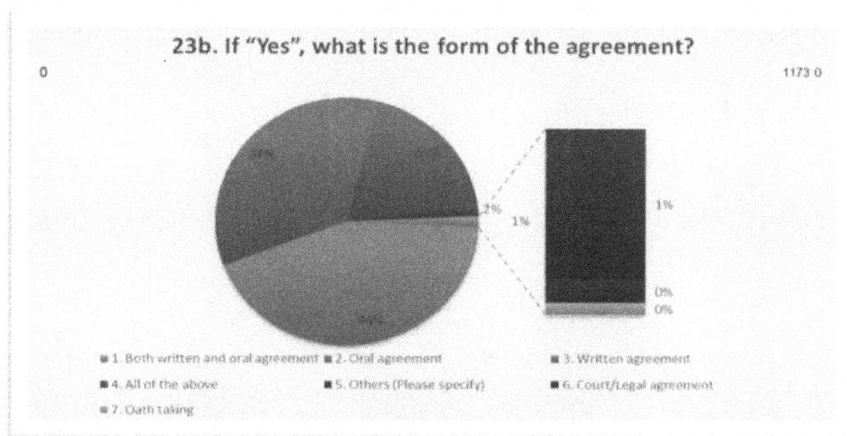

Figure 58: Pie Chart Distribution of *Ndị Ọga* by their Responses on the Form of Apprenticeship Agreement between *Nwa Bọyị* and *Ọga*

Table 58 and Figure 58 show the distribution of *Ndị Ọga* by their responses on the form of apprenticeship agreement between *Nwa Bọyị* and *Ọga*. 42.6% of the respondents indicated that 'there is both written and oral agreement'. 0.2%

indicated that 'Court/Legal agreement exist between *Nwa Bọyị* and *Ọga*'. 0.1% of the respondents indicated that 'oathtaking type of agreement exist between *Nwa Bọyị* and *Ọga*'. 33.6% of the respondents indicated that 'oral agreement exists between *Nwa Bọyị* and *Ọga*'. 18.6% of the respondents indicated that 'written agreement exists between *Nwa Bọyị* and *Ọga*'. 2.3% of the respondents responded to 'other options except 'Yes' responses to whether any form of agreement existbetween *Nwa Bọyị* and *Ọga*'. 1.6% indicated 'all of the above' option while 1.1% specified 'others'. The implication is that the major form of agreement between *Nwa Bọyị* and *Ọga* are both written and followed by just oral agreement between *Nwa Bọyị* and *Ọga*.

Table 59: Distribution of *Ụmụ Bọyị* by their Responses on the Existence of Apprenticeship Agreement between *Nwa Bọyị* and *Ọga*

	Frequency	Percent	Valid Percent	Cumulative Percent
No	58	4.8	4.8	4.8
Yes	1142	95.2	95.2	100.0
Total	1200	100.0	100.0	

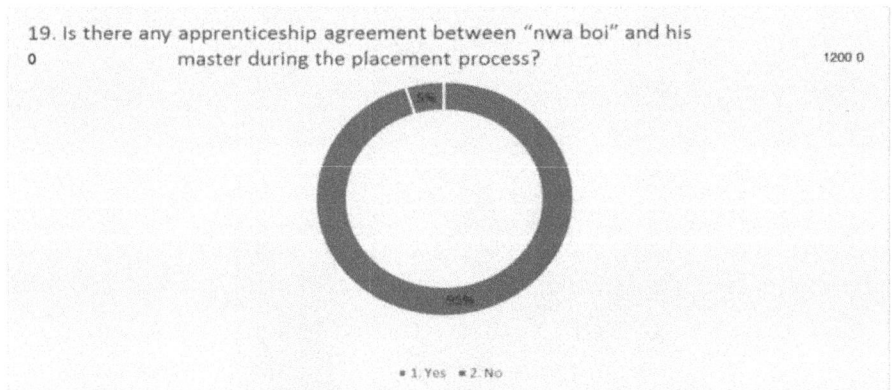

19. Is there any apprenticeship agreement between "nwa boi" and his master during the placement process?

• 1. Yes • 2. No

Figure 59: Pie Chart Depicting the Distribution of *Umu Boyi* by their Responses on the Existence of Apprenticeship Agreement between *Nwa Bọyị* and *Ọga*.

Table 59 and Figure 59 reveal the distribution of *Ụmụ Bọyị* by their responses on the existence of apprenticeship agreement between *Nwa Bọyị* and *Ọga*. 95.2% of the respondents indicated that 'there is in existence apprenticeship agreement between *Nwa Bọyị* and *Ọga*' while 4.8% that 'there is no apprenticeship agreement between *Nwa Bọyị* and *Ọga*'.

Table 60: Distribution of Ụmụ Bọyị by their Responses on the Form of Apprenticeship Agreement between Nwa Bọyị and Ọga

	Frequency	Percent	Valid Percent	Cumulative Percent
Other options except for 'Yes' responses to (Is there an apprenticeship agreement between "nwa boi" and his master during the placement process?)	58	4.8	4.8	4.8
All of the above	18	1.5	1.5	6.3
Both written and oral agreement	427	35.6	35.6	41.9
Oral agreement	462	38.5	38.5	80.4
Others (Please specify)	5	.4	.4	80.8
Written agreement	230	19.2	19.2	100.0
Court/Legal Agreement	0	0	0	100.0
Oath taking	0	0	0	100.0
Total	1200	100.0	100.0	

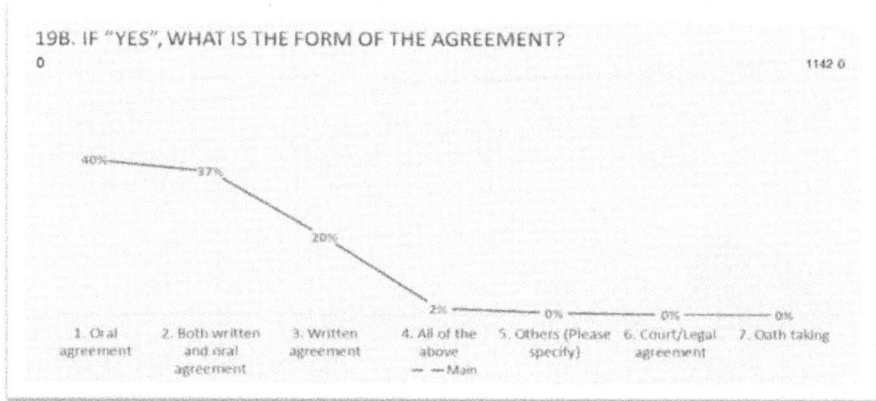

19B. IF "YES", WHAT IS THE FORM OF THE AGREEMENT?

Figure 60: Line Chart representing the Distribution of Ụmụ Bọyị by their Responses on the Form of Apprenticeship Agreement between Nwa Bọyị and Ọga.

Table 60 and Figure 60 show the distribution of Ụmụ Bọyị by their responses on the form of apprenticeship agreement between Nwa Bọyị and Ọga. 35.6% of the respondents indicated 'both written and oral agreement'. 38.5% of the respondents indicated that 'oral agreement exists between Nwa Bọyị and Ọga'.

19.2% of the respondents indicated that 'written agreement exists between *Nwa Boyi* and *Oga*. 4.8% of the respondents responded indicated 'other options except 'Yes' responses to whether any form of agreement exist between *Nwa Boyi* and *Oga*'. 1.5% indicated 'all of the above' options while 0.4% specified 'others'. The implication is that the major form of agreement between *Nwa Boyi* and *Oga* as perceived by *Umu Boyi* are both written and oral agreements followed by just oral agreement.

Table 61: Distribution of *Ndị Oga* by their Responses on the Most Common Provisions in the Agreement between *Oga* and *Nwa Boyi*

	Frequency	Percent	Valid Percent	Cumulative Percent
Apprenticeship code of conduct	56	4.7	4.7	16.6
Duration of the apprenticeship	930	77.4	77.4	94.0
Others (Please specify)	13	1.1	1.1	95.1
Sanctions of erring trainers and trainees	6	.5	.5	95.6
Settlementprocedures	53	4.4	4.4	99.0
All of the above	143	11.9	11.9	100.0
Total	1201	100.0	100.0	

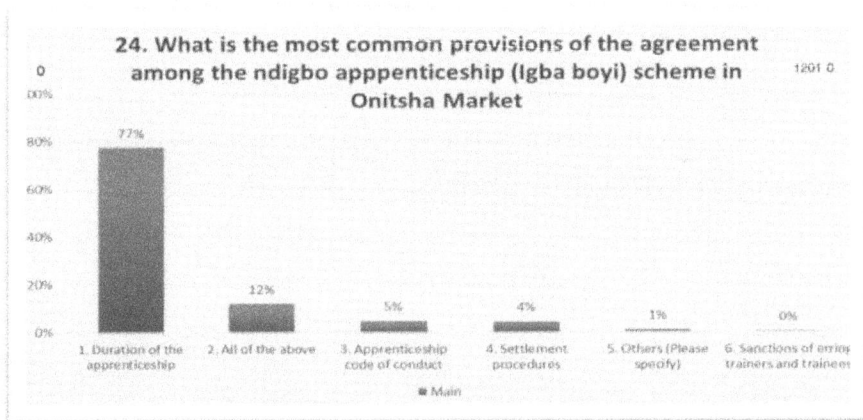

Figure 61: Bar Chart Showing the Distribution of *Ndị Oga* by their Responses on the Most Common Provisions in the Agreement between *Oga* and *Nwa Boyi*

As shown in Table 61 and Figure 61 with respect to the distribution of *Ndị Oga* by their responses on the most common provisions in the agreement between

Ọga and *Nwa Bọyị*, 4.7% indicated 'apprenticeship code of conduct'. 77.4% indicated 'duration of the apprenticeship'. 0.5% of the respondents indicated 'sanctions of erring trainers and trainees'. 4.4% indicated 'settlement procedures'. 1.1% indicated 'Others (Please specify)' while 11.9% indicated 'all of the above'. The results revealed that duration of the apprenticeship is the most common provision in the agreement between *Ọga* and *Nwa Bọyị*.

Table 62: Distribution of *Ụmụ Bọyị* by their Responses on the Most Common Provisions in the Agreement between *Ọga* and *Nwa Bọyị*

	Frequency	Percent	Valid Percent	Cumulative Percent
Apprenticeship code of conduct	72	6.0	6.0	6.0
Duration of the apprenticeship	867	72.3	72.3	78.3
Others (Please specify)	13	1.1	1.1	79.4
Sanctions of erring trainers and trainees	8	.7	.7	80.1
Settlementprocedures	83	6.9	6.9	87.0
All of the above	157	13.1	13.1	100.0
Total	1200	100.0	100.0	

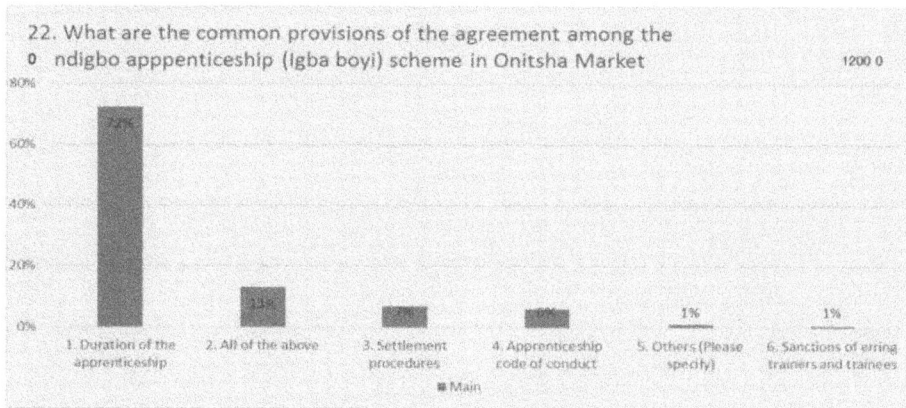

Figure 62: Bar Chart Representing the Distribution of *Ụmụ Bọyị* by their Responses on the Most Common Provisions in the Agreement between *Ọga* and *Nwa Bọyị*.

Table 62 and Figure 62 showed the distribution of *Ụmụ Bọyị* by their responses on the most common provisions in the agreement between *Ọga* and *Nwa Boyi*.

6.0% indicated 'apprenticeship code of conduct'. 72.3% indicated 'duration of the apprenticeship'. 0.7% of the respondents indicated 'sanctions of erring trainers and trainees'. 6.9% indicated 'settlement procedures'. 1.1% indicated 'Others (Please specify)', while 13.1% indicated 'all of the above'. The results revealed that duration of the apprenticeship is the most common provision in the agreement between *Ọga* and *Nwa Bọyị*.

Table 63: Distribution of *Ndi Ọga* by their Responses on Other Provisions in the Agreement between *Ọga* and *Nwa Bọyị*.

	Frequency	Percent	Valid Percent	Cumulative Percent
Other options except (If others, please specify)	1188	98.9	98.9	98.9
All options listed out except settlement procedures	1	.1	.1	99.0
Depends on the type of business	1	.1	.1	99.1
Duration for the boyi and rules to be obeyed by the *Nwa Bọyị* e.g size of hair cut, type of clothes to wear, etc	1	.1	.1	99.2
Duration of time and code of conduct	1	.1	.1	99.3
First, the duration of the apprenticeship, and secondly is the consequences of conduct	1	.1	.1	99.3
I didn't enter into any agreement with my boyi. His mother died and I decided to help him	1	.1	.1	99.4
I don't do such	1	.1	.1	99.5
No agreement made	1	.1	.1	99.6
None	1	.1	.1	99.7
Rulesand regulations also	1	.1	.1	99.8
Some do have agreement while some don't it is not a must	1	.1	.1	99.8
That you will take care of the child without maltreatment and the child also will be obedient	1	.1	.1	99.9
There are no stipulated agreement procedures, it depends on the person and family	1	.1	.1	100.0
Total	1201	100.0	100.0	

Table 63: Distribution of *Ndị Ọga* by their responses on Other Provisions in the Agreement between *Ọga* and *Nwa Bọyị*. Depends on the type of business,

duration for the *boyi* and rules to be obeyed by the *Nwa Boyi* e.g size of haircut, type of clothes to wear, etc; duration of time and code of conduct; First, the duration of the apprenticeship, and secondly is the consequences of conduct; I did not enter into any agreement with my *boyi*. His mother died and I decided to help him; I did not do such; No agreement made; Some do have agreement, while some do not. It is not a must that you will take care of the child without maltreatment and the child also will be obedient; There are no stipulated agreement procedures, it depends on the person and family.

Table 64: Distribution of *Ụmụ Bọyị* by their Responses on Other Provisions in the Agreement between *Ọga* and *Nwa Bọyị*

	Frequency	Percent	Valid Percent	Cumulative Percent
Other options except (If others, please specify)	1187	98.9	98.9	98.9
Duration of time and settlement procedures	1	.1	.1	99.0
Everything is at the will of the *Ọga*	1	.1	.1	99.1
He said no form of agreement	1	.1	.1	99.2
How hardworking or how many sales do you make	1	.1	.1	99.3
I didn't do agreement	1	.1	.1	99.3
I don't know	1	.1	.1	99.4
Mainly option 1 and 2	1	.1	.1	99.5
No agreement of any sort	1	.1	.1	99.6
No agreement, just assurance	1	.1	.1	99.7
None	2	.2	.2	99.8
Options 1 and 3	1	.1	.1	99.9
Said they've not talked on agreement	1	.1	.1	100.0
Total	1200	100.0	100.0	

From Table 64, it could be deduced that a few of those who pointed at other provisions in the agreement identified 'How hardworking or how many sales do you make' and the discretion of the *Ọga* as other provisions of the agreement.

Table 65: Distribution of *Ndị Ọga* by their Responses on the Existence of a Probation Period before Agreement is Signed

	Frequency	Percent	Valid Percent	Cumulative Percent
No	162	13.5	13.5	13.5
Yes	1039	86.5	86.5	100.0
Total	1201	100.0	100.0	

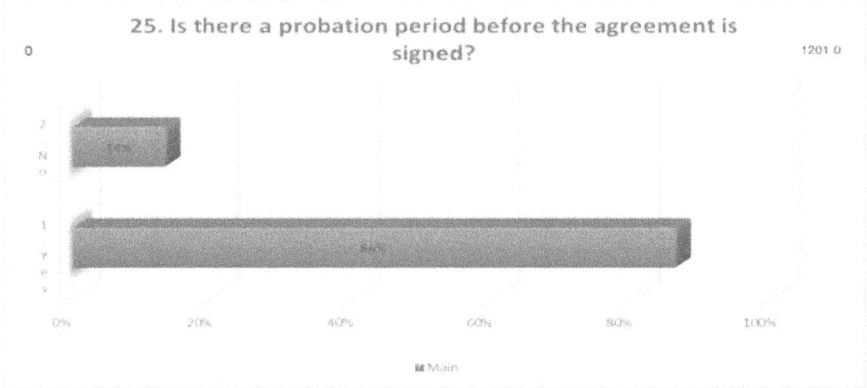

Figure 65: Bar Chart Representing the Distribution of *Ndi Ọga* by their Responses on the Existence of a Probation Period before Agreement is Signed.

Table 65 and Figure 65 show the distribution of *Ndi Ọga* by their responses on the existence of a probation period before agreement is signed. 86.5% of the respondents indicated that there is existence of a probation period before agreement is signed. 13.5% of the respondents indicated that there is no existence of a probation period before agreement is signed. This is clearly evident that agreements are not usually made at the inception of *Igba Boyị* apprenticeship, but there is a waiting period during which the *Nwa Boyị* is observed to see his level of preparedness and interest in the particular trade of the master.

Table 66: Distribution of *Ndị Ọga* by their Responses on the Probationary Period (in Months) before Agreement is Signed

	Frequency	Percent	Valid Percent	Cumulative Percent
Other responses except for 'Yes' responses to (Is there a probation period before the agreement is signed?)	162	13.5	13.5	13.5
1	22	1.8	1.8	15.3
10	2	.2	.2	15.5
12	203	16.9	16.9	32.4
15	1	.1	.1	32.5
18	10	.8	.8	33.3
2	40	3.3	3.3	36.6
24	17	1.4	1.4	38.1
3	213	17.7	17.7	55.8
4	26	2.2	2.2	58.0
5	26	2.2	2.2	60.1
6	456	38.0	38.0	98.1
7	5	.4	.4	98.5
8	12	1.0	1.0	99.5
9	6	.5	.5	100.0
Total	1201	100.0	100.0	

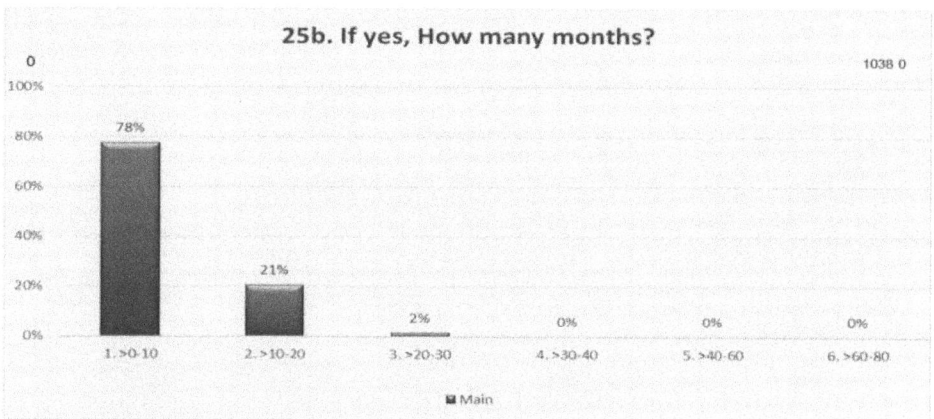

Figure 66: Bar Chart Showing the Distribution of *Ndị Ọga* by their Responses on the Probationary Period (in Months) before Agreement is signed.

The above table reveals that the majority of the respondents identified 3 months, 6 months and 12 months as the preferred probationary period, after which agreement could be signed.

Table 67: Distribution of Ụmụ Bọyị by their Responses on the Existence of a Probation Period before Agreement is Signed

	Frequency	Percent	Valid Percent	Cumulative Percent
No	201	16.8	16.8	16.8
Yes	999	83.3	83.3	100.0
Total	1200	100.0	100.0	

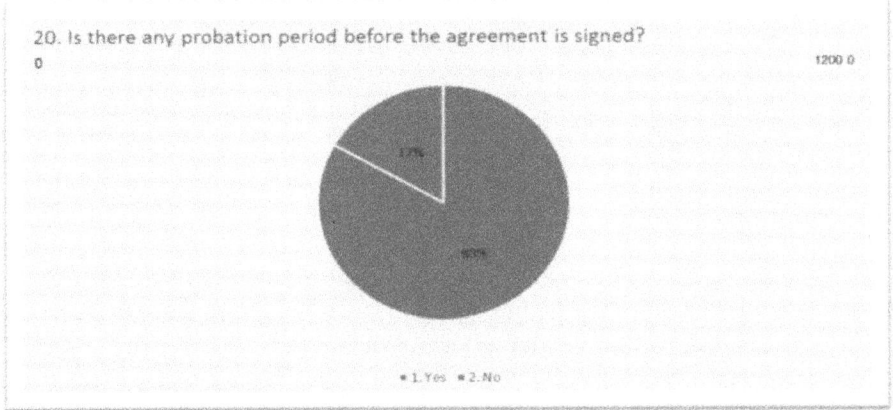

20. Is there any probation period before the agreement is signed?

● 1.Yes ● 2.No

Figure 67: Pie Chart Representing the Distribution of Ụmụ Bọyị by their Responses on the Existence of a Probation Period before Agreement is Signed.

Table 67 and Figure 67 show the distribution of Ụmụ Bọyị by their responses on the existence of a probation period before agreement is signed. 16.8% of the respondents indicated that 'there is no existence of a probation period before agreement is signed', while 83.3% of the respondents indicated that 'there is no existence of a probation period before agreement is signed'. The results show that there is usually a probation period before agreement is signed.

Table 68: Distribution of Ụmụ Bọyị by their Responses on the Probationary Period (in Months) before Agreement is Signed

	Frequency	Percent	Valid Percent	Cumulative Percent
Other responses except for 'Yes' responses to (Is there a probation period before the agreement is signed?)	201	16.8	16.8	16.8
1	25	2.1	2.1	18.8
10	2	.2	.2	19.0
11	1	.1	.1	19.1
12	173	14.4	14.4	33.5

15	1	.1	.1	33.6
18	5	.4	.4	34.0
2	42	3.5	3.5	37.5
24	7	.6	.6	38.1
3	217	18.1	18.1	56.2
4	37	3.1	3.1	59.3
5	41	3.4	3.4	62.7
6	412	34.3	34.3	97.0
7	10	.8	.8	97.8
8	19	1.6	1.6	99.4
9	7	.6	.6	100.0
Total	1200	100.0	100.0	

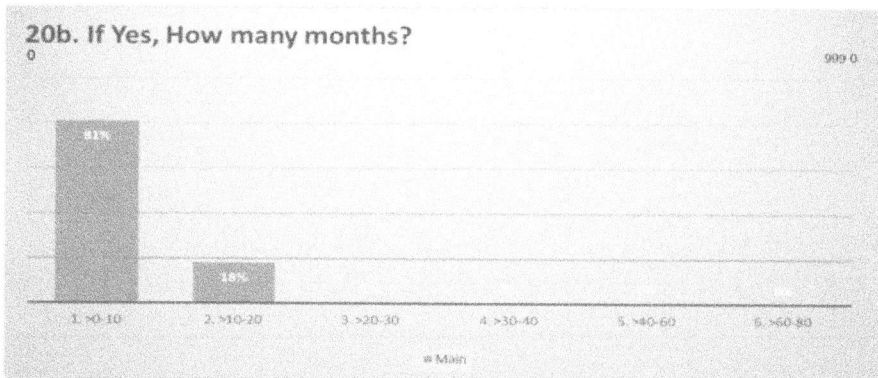

Figure 68: Bar Chart Representing the Distribution of *ụmụ bọyị* by their Responses on the Probationary Period (in Months) before Agreement is Signed

It is evident from Table 68 and Figure 68 above that among *Ụmụ Bọyị* respondents, majority identified 3 months (18.1%), 6 months (34.3%) and 12 months (14.4%) as the preferred months used for probation before agreement is signed.

Table 69: Distribution of *Ndị Ọga* by their Responses on the Class of Igbo People more involved in *Igba Boyi*

	Frequency	Percent	Valid Percent	Cumulative Percent
The wealthy	15	1.2	1.2	1.2
The poor and indigent	742	61.8	61.8	63.0
Both	197	16.4	16.4	79.4
All Igbo indigenous people	247	20.6	20.6	100.0
Total	1201	100.0	100.0	

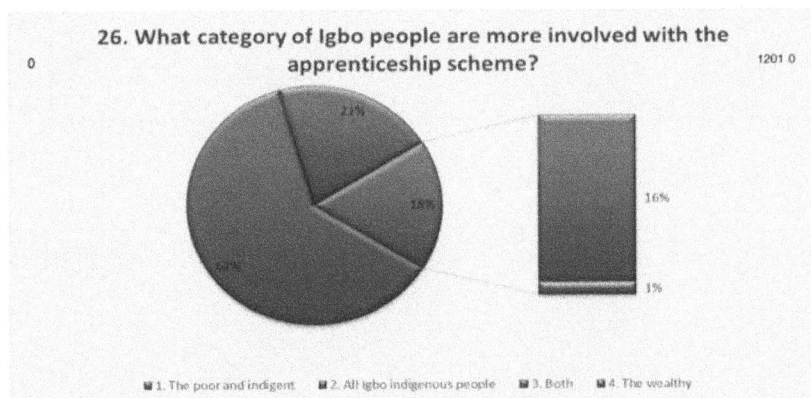

26. What category of Igbo people are more involved with the apprenticeship scheme?

0   1201 0

16%

1%

■ 1. The poor and indigent   ■ 2. All Igbo indigenous people   ■ 3. Both   ■ 4. The wealthy

Figure 69: Pie Chart Showing the Distribution of *Ndị Ọga* by their Responses on the Class of Igbo People more involved in *Igba Boyi*

Table 69 and Figure 69 showed the distribution of *Ndị Ọga* by their responses on the class of Igbo people more involved in *Igba Boyi*. 1.2% of the respondents indicated that 'the wealthy are the class of igbo people more involved in *Igba Boyi*'. 61.8% of the respondents indicated that 'the poor and indigent are the class of Igbo people more involved in *Igba Boyi*'. 16.4% of the respondents indicated that 'both the wealthy and the poor and indigent are the class of Igbo people more involved in *Igba Boyi*. while 20.6% of the respondents indicated that 'all Igbo indigenous people are involved in *Igba Boyi*'. The results revealed that the poor and indigent are mainly the class of Igbo people that are more involved in *Igba Boyi*, followed by all Igbo indigenous people.

Table 70: Distribution of Ụmụ Bọyị by their Responses on the Class of Igbo People more involved in Igba Bọyị

	Frequency	Percent	Valid Percent	Cumulative Percent
The wealthy	7	.6	.6	.6
The poor and indigent	804	67.0	67.0	67.6
Both	167	13.9	13.9	81.5
All Igboindigenous people	222	18.5	18.5	100.0
Total	1200	100.0	100.0	

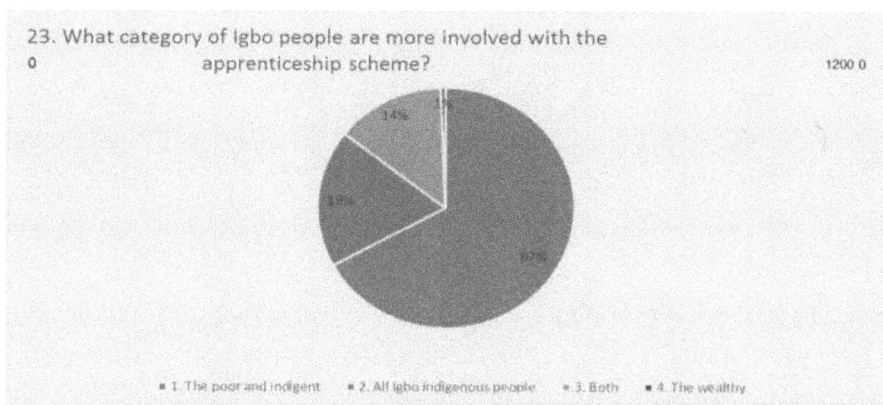

23. What category of Igbo people are more involved with the apprenticeship scheme?

■ 1. The poor and indigent   ■ 2. All Igbo indigenous people   ■ 3. Both   ■ 4. The wealthy

Figure 70: Pie Chart Distribution of Ụmụ Bọyị by their Responses on the Class of Igbo People more involved in Igba Bọyị

Table 70 and Figure 70 showed the distribution of Ụmụ Bọyị by their responses on the class of Igbo people more involved in Igba Bọyị. 0.6% of the respondents Igba Bọyị indicated that 'wealthy are the class of Igbo people more involved in Igba Bọyị'. 67.0% of the respondents indicated that the poor and indigent are the class of Igbo people more involved in Igba Bọyị'. 13.9% of the respondents indicated that 'both the wealthy and the poor and indigent are the class of Igbo people more involved in Igba Bọyị'; while 18.5% of the respondents indicated that 'all Igbo indigenous people are more involved in Igba Bọyị'. The results also revealed that the poor and indigent are mainly the class of Igbo people that are more involved in Igba Bọyị followed by all Igbo indigenous people.

Table 71: Distribution of *Ndị Ọga* by their Responses on Preferred Type of Apprenticeship

	Frequency	Percent	Valid Percent	Cumulative Percent
Both	583	48.5	48.5	48.5
Kin related	237	19.7	19.7	68.3
Non kin related	381	31.7	31.7	100.0
Total	1201	100.0	100.0	

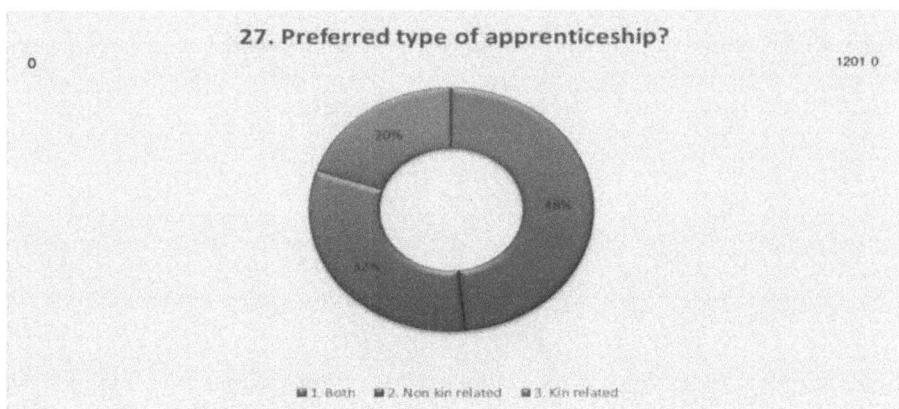

Figure 71: Pie Chart Distribution of *Ndị Ọga* by their Responses on Preferred Type of Apprenticeship

Table 71 and Figure 71 showed the distribution of *Ndị Ọga* by their responses on preferred type of apprenticeship. 19.7% of the respondents indicated that their responses on preferred type of apprenticeship is 'Kin related'. 31.7% of the respondents indicated that their preferred type of apprenticeship is 'non kin related'. 48.5% of the respondents indicated that their preferred type of apprenticeship are 'both Kin related and non kin related'. From the results of the respondents, both Kin related and non kin related types of apprenticeship stand out as the preferred types of apprenticeship.

Table 72: Distribution of Ụmụ Bọyị by their Responses on Preferred Type of Apprenticeship

	Frequency	Percent	Valid Percent	Cumulative Percent
Both	503	41.9	41.9	41.9
Kin related	301	25.1	25.1	67.0
Non kin related	396	33.0	33.0	100.0
Total	1200	100.0	100.0	

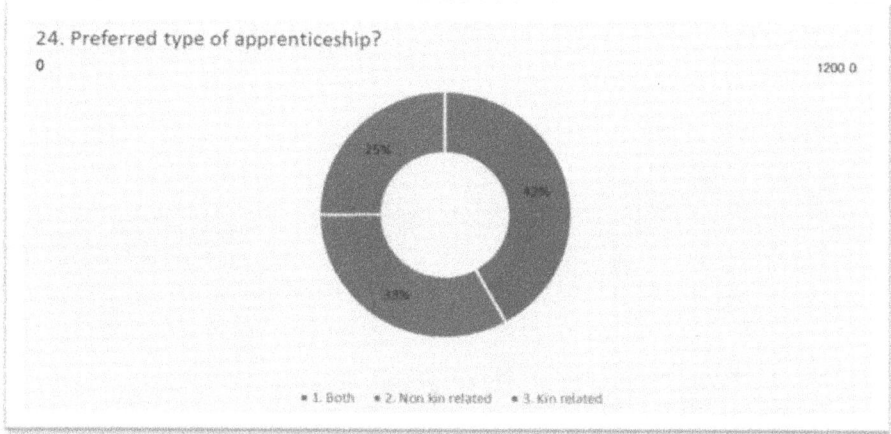

Figure 72: Pie Chart Representing the Distribution of Ụmụ Bọyị by their Responses on Preferred Type of Apprenticeship

Table 72 and Figure 72 showed the distribution of Ụmụ Bọyị by their responses on preferred type of apprenticeship. 25.1% of the respondents indicated that their responses on preferred type of apprenticeship is 'Kin related'. 33.0% of the respondents indicated that their preferred type of apprenticeship is 'non kin related'. 41.9% of the respondents indicated that their preferred type of apprenticeship are 'both Kin related and non kin related'. From the results, Ụmụ Bọyị also confirmed that both Kin related and non kin related types of apprenticeship stand out as the preferred type of apprenticeship. It is interesting to note that amongst Ụmụ Bọyị, a significant proportion identified 'non kin-related' apprenticeship as a preferred type. This shows that non kin-related apprenticeship is becoming a common feature of the Igbo apprenticeship model, unlike what obtained in the past when the kin-related apprenticeship model held sway.

Table 73: Distribution of *Ndị Ọga* by their Responses on Ideal Age Category of *Igba Bọyị*

	Frequency	Percent	Valid Percent	Cumulative Percent
10 – 13 years	46	3.8	3.8	3.8
14 – 17 years	623	51.9	51.9	55.7
18 – 21 years	518	43.1	43.1	98.8
22 – 25 years	13	1.1	1.1	99.9
35 years and above	1	.1	.1	100.0
Total	1201	100.0	100.0	

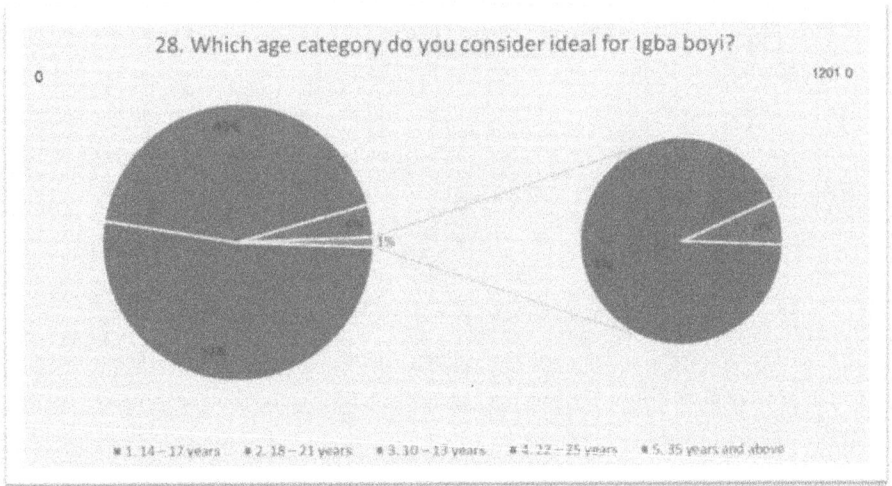

Figure 73: Pie Chart Showing Distribution of *Ndị Ọga* by their Responses on Ideal Age Category of *Igba Bọyị*

Table 73 and Figure 73 show the distribution of *Ndị Ọga* by their responses on the ideal age category of *Igba Bọyị*. 3.8% of the respondents indicated that the ideal age category of *igba boyi* is '10 – 13 years'. 51.9% of the respondents indicated that the ideal age category of *Igba Bọyị* is '14 – 17 years'. 43.1% of the respondents indicated that the ideal age category of igba bọyi is 18 – 21 years'. 1.1% of the respondents indicated that the ideal age category of *Igba Bọyị* is '22 – 25 years', while 0.1% the respondents indicated that the ideal age category of *Igba Bọyị* is '35 years and above'. From the foregoing, *Ndị Ọga* clearly identified the age Categories 14 - 17, 18 - 21 years as the preferred age cohort for *Igba Bọyị*.

Table 74: Distribution of Ụmụ Bọyị by their Responses on Ideal Age Category of Igba Bọyị

	Frequency	Percent	Valid Percent	Cumulative Percent
10 – 13 years	48	4.0	4.0	4.0
14 – 17 years	582	48.5	48.5	52.5
18 – 21 years	543	45.3	45.3	97.8
22 – 25 years	27	2.3	2.3	100.0
Total	1200	100.0	100.0	

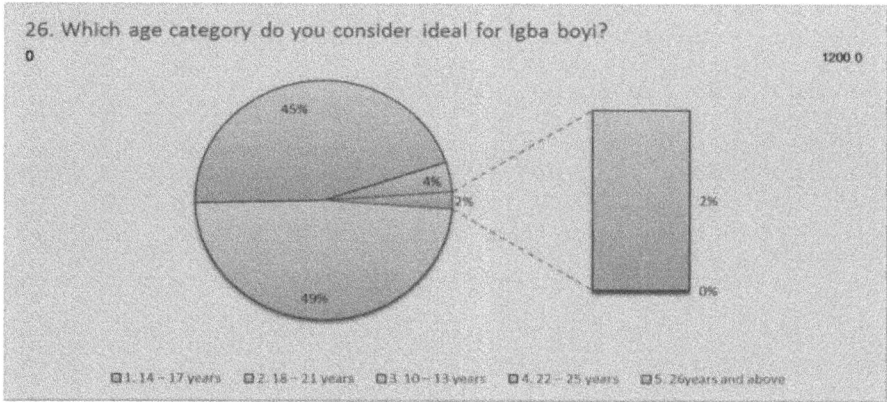

Figure 74: Pie Chart Representing the Distribution of Ụmụ Bọyị by their Responses on Ideal Age Category of Igba Bọyị

Table 74 and Figure 74 show the distribution of Ụmụ Bọyị by their responses on the ideal age category of Igba Bọyị. 4.0% of the respondents indicated that the ideal age category of Igba Bọyị is '10 – 13 years'. 48.5% of the respondents indicated that the ideal age category of Igba Bọyị is '14 – 17 years'. 45.3% of the respondents indicated that the ideal age category of Igba Bọyị is '18 – 21 years', while 2.3% of the respondents indicated that the ideal age category of Igba Bọyị is '22 – 25 years'. From the results of the study both Ndị Ọga and Ụmụ Bọyị indicated that the ideal age category of Igba Bọyị is – 21 years followed by 22 – 25 years. From the responses above, Ụmụ Bọyị reinforced the choice of Ndị Ọga as has earlier been indicated by their clear identification of the age categories 14 - 17, 18 - 21 years as the preferred age cohort for Igba Bọyị.

Table 75: Distribution of _Ndị Ọga_ by their Responses on Adequate Number of Years for Mastering the Trade

	Frequency	Percent	Valid Percent	Cumulative Percent
Less than 2 years	375	31.2	31.2	100.0
2 - 4 years	245	20.4	20.4	20.4
4 - 6 years	385	32.1	32.1	52.5
6 - 8 years	187	15.6	15.6	68.0
8 years and above	9	.7	.7	68.8
Total	1201	100.0	100.0	

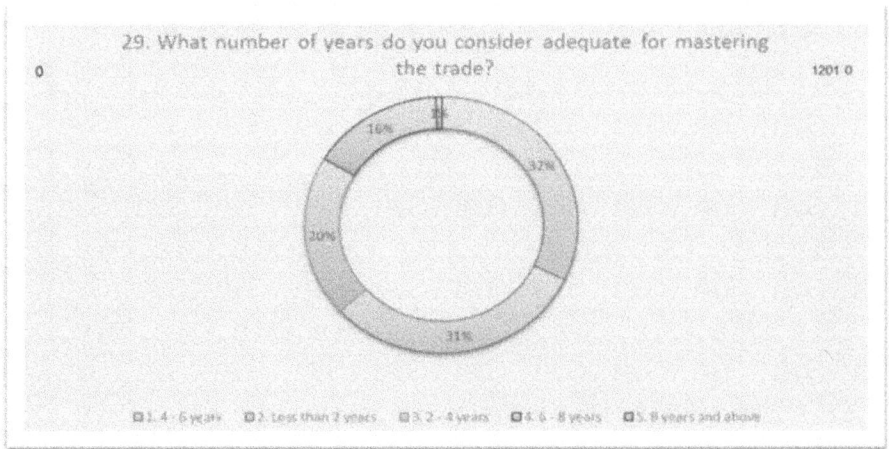

Figure 75: Ring Chart Distribution of _Ndị Ọga_ by their Responses on Adequate Number of Years for Mastering the Trade

Table 75 and Figure 75 show the distribution of _Ndị Ọga_ by their responses on the adequate number of years for mastering the trade. 31.2% of the respondents indicated that 'adequate number of years for mastering the trade is Less than 2 years'. 20.4% of the respondents indicated that 'adequate number of years for mastering the trade is 2 - 4 years'. 32.1% of the respondents indicated that 'adequate number of years for mastering the trade is 4-6 years'. 15.6% of the respondents indicated that adequate number of years for mastering the trade is 6-8years'. 0.7% of the respondents indicated that adequate number of years for mastering the trade is 8 years and above'. From the foregoing, it is evident that the majority of the respondents (817; 68.02%) chose 2 - 8 years as the preferred period for mastery of the trade.

Table 76: Distribution of *Ụmụ Bọyị* by their Responses on Adequate Number of Years for Mastering the Trade

	Frequency	Percent	Valid Percent	Cumulative Percent
2 - 4 years	243	20.3	20.3	20.3
4 - 6 years	370	30.8	30.8	51.1
6 - 8 years	157	13.1	13.1	64.2
8 years and above	12	1.0	1.0	65.2
Less than 2 years	418	34.8	34.8	100.0
Total	1200	100.0	100.0	

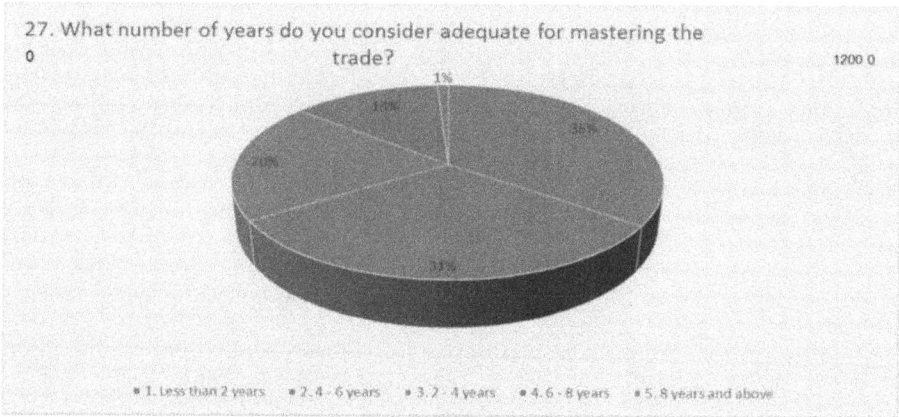

27. What number of years do you consider adequate for mastering the trade?

● 1. Less than 2 years ● 2. 4 - 6 years ● 3. 2 - 4 years ● 4. 6 - 8 years ● 5. 8 years and above

Figure 76: Distribution of *ụmụ bọyị* by their Responses on 'Adequate Number of Years for Mastering the Trade.

Table 76 and Figure 76 showed the distribution of *Ụmụ Bọyị* by their responses on adequate number of years for mastering the trade. 20.3% of the respondents indicated that the adequate number of years for mastering the trade is '2 - 4 years'. 30.8% of the respondents indicated that the adequate number of years for mastering the trade is '4-6 years'. 13.1% of the respondents indicated that the adequate number of years for mastering the trade is '6-8years'. 1.0% of the respondents indicated that the adequate number of years for mastering the trade is '8 years and above'. 34.8% of the respondents indicated that the adequate number of years for mastering the trade is 'less than 2 years'. From the foregoing, amongst the generation of apprentices or *Ụmụ Bọyị* in the different markets, 770 respondents, representing 64.2% chose 2 - 4 years, 4 - 6 year and 6 - 8 years as the best period for *Nwa Bọyị* to gain all the experience needed to master the trade. It is instructive that a significant proportion of *Ụmụ Bọyị* (418; 34.8%) went for the singular category of less than 2 years as the best period during which enough learning would have occurred to master the trade. This may explain that there is a rush to transit to the master stage amongst *Umu Boyi*.

Table 77: Distribution of *Ndị Ọga* by their Responses on Specific Trades that Require Longer Periods of *Igba Bọyị*

	Frequency	Percent	Valid Percent	Cumulative Percent
No	947	78.9	78.9	78.9
Yes	254	21.1	21.1	100.0
Total	1201	100.0	100.0	

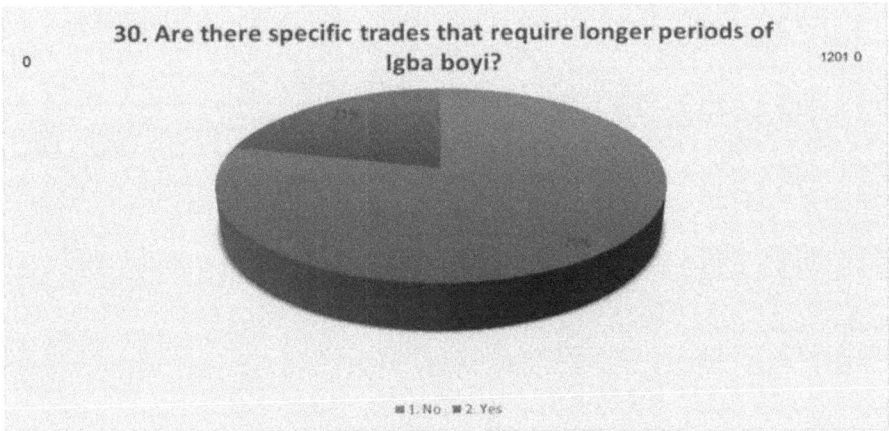

Figure 77: Pie Chart Distribution of *Ndị Ọga* by their Responses on Specific Trades that Require Longer Periods of *Igba Bọyị*

Table 77 and Figure 77 show the distribution of *Ndị Ọga* by their responses on specific trades that require longer periods of *Igba Bọyị*. 78.9% of *Ndị Ọga* indicated that there are no trades that require longer periods of *Igba Bọyị*. 21.1% of *Ndị Ọga* indicated that there are trades that require longer periods of *Igba Bọyị*.

Table 78: Distribution of *Ndị Ọga* by their Responses on Specific Trades that Require Longer Periods of *Igba Bọyị*

	Frequency	Percent	Valid Percent	Cumulative Percent
Other responses except for 'Yes' responses to (Are there specific trades that require longer periods of *Igba Bọyị*?)	947	78.9	78.9	78.9
Automobile spare parts	75	6.2	6.2	85.1
Building materials and fabrication	11	.9	.9	86.0
Carpentry	2	.2	.2	86.2
Clothing and textiles	20	1.7	1.7	87.8
Electronics and Electricals	7	.6	.6	88.4
Equipment, Tools, and Heavy duty	8	.7	.7	89.1
Food and beverages	7	.6	.6	89.7
Forex	8	.7	.7	90.3
General Merchandise	35	2.9	2.9	93.3
Pharmaceuticals and cosmetics	80	6.6	6.6	99.8
Stationeries	2	.2	.2	100.0
Total	1201	100.0	100.0	

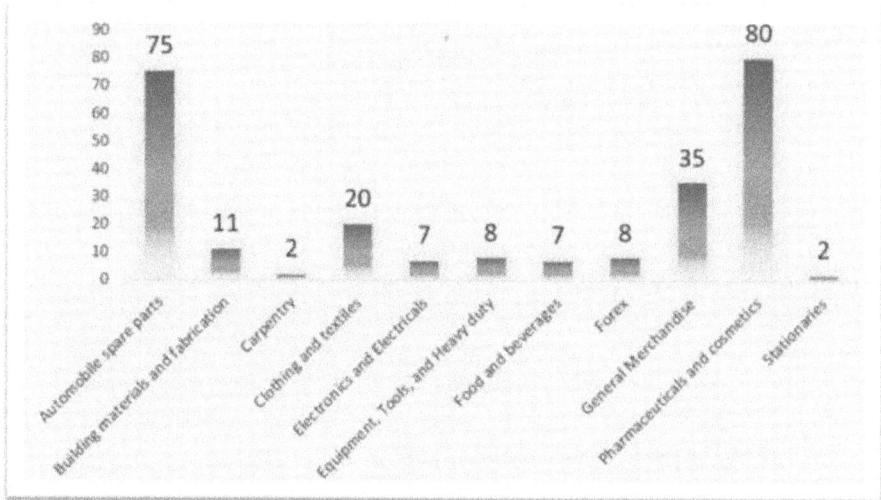

Figure 78: Bar Chart Showing the Distribution of *Ndị Ọga* by their Responses on Specific Trades that Require Longer Periods of *Igba Bọyị*.

Table 78 and Figure 78 showed the distribution of *Ndị Ọga* by their responses on specific trades that require longer periods of *Igba Boyi*. 78.9% of *Ndi Oga* that responded to the questions indicated that there are specific trades that require longer periods of *Igba Boyi*. However, Pharmaceuticals and Cosmetics; and Automobile Spare Parts standout asspecific trades that require longer periods of *Igba Boyi*.

Table 79: Distribution of *Umu Boyi* by their Responses on Specific Trades that Require Longer Periods of *Igba Boyi*

	Frequency	Percent	Valid Percent	Cumulative Percent
No	999	83.3	83.3	83.3
Yes	201	16.8	16.8	100.0
Total	1200	100.0	100.0	

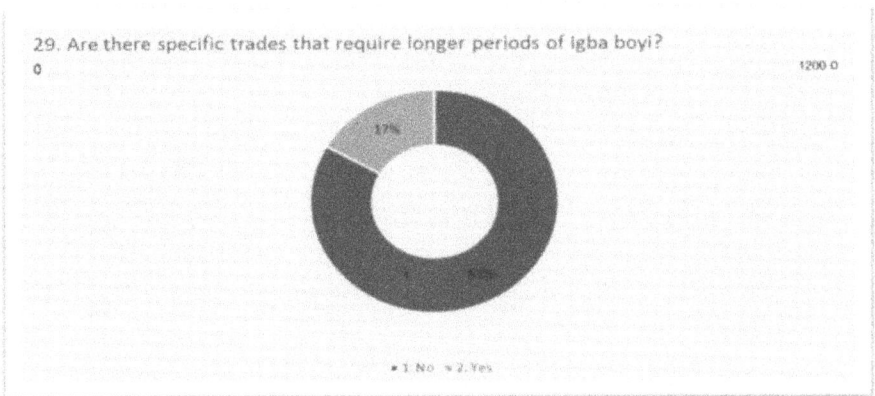

Figure 79: Pie Chart showing the Distribution of *Umu Boyi* by their Responses on Specific Trades that Require Longer Periods of *Igba Boyi*

Table 79 and Figure 79 showed the distribution of *Umu Boyi* by their responses on specific trades that require longer periods of *Igba Boyi*. 83.3% of the respondents indicated that there are no specific trades that require longer periods of *Igba Boyi*. 16.8% of the respondents indicated that there are specific trades that require longer periods of *Igba Boyi*.

Table 80: Distribution of *Ụmụ Bọyị* by their Responses on Specific Trades that Require Longer Periods of *Igba Bọyị*

	Frequency	Percent	Valid Percent	Cumulative Percent
Other responses except for 'Yes' responses to (Are there specific trades that require longer periods of *Igba Boyi?*)	999	83.3	83.3	83.3
Automobile spare parts	63	5.3	5.3	88.5
Building materials/fabrication	5	.4	.4	88.9
Carpentry	3	.3	.3	89.2
Clothing and Textiles	19	1.6	1.6	90.8
Equipment, tools, heavy duty	5	.4	.4	91.2
Electronics/Electricals	9	.8	.8	91.9
Food(Provision)/Beverages	6	.5	.5	92.4
Forex	6	.5	.5	92.9
General Merchandise	41	3.4	3.4	96.3
Home Appliances	1	.1	.1	96.4
Pharmaceuticals/Cosmetics	43	3.6	3.6	100.0
Total	1200	100.0	100.0	

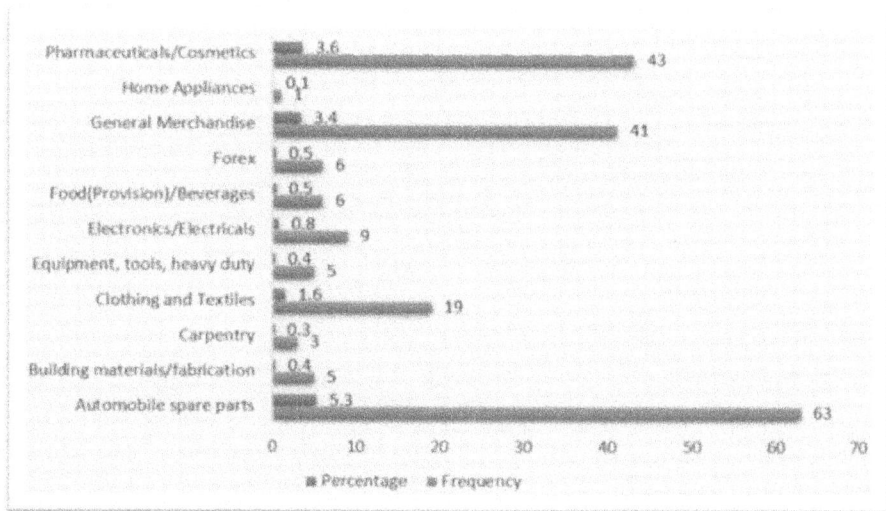

Figure 80: Bar Chart Depicting the Distribution of *Ụmụ Bọyị* by their Responses on Identified Specific Trades that Require Longer Periods of *Igba Bọyị*

Table 80 and Figure 80 show the distribution of *Ụmụ Bọyị* by their responses on specific trades that require longer periods of *Igba Bọyị*. From the perspectives of

Ụmụ Bọyị, 83.3% of *Ụmụ Bọyị* that responded to the questions indicated that there are no specific trades that require longer periods of *Igba Bọyị*. However, Automobile Spare Parts, General Merchandise and Pharmaceuticals/Cosmetics standout as specific trades that require longer periods of *Igba Bọyị* from the limited number of *Ụmụ Bọyị* that maintained that there are specific trades that require longer periods of *Igba Bọyị*.

Table 81: Distribution of *Ndị Ọga* by their Responses on Preferred Gender for Apprenticeship

	Frequency	Percent	Valid Percent	Cumulative Percent
Female	40	3.3	3.3	3.3
Male	1161	96.7	96.7	100.0
Total	1201	100.0	100.0	

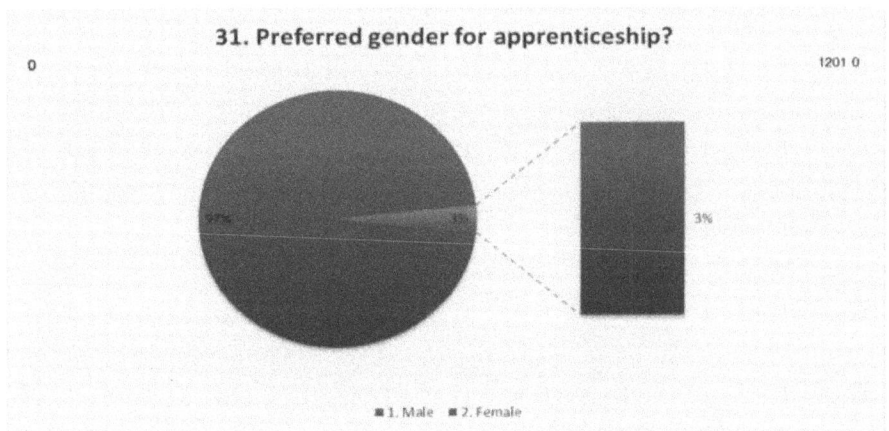

Figure 81: Pie Chart Representing the Distribution of *Ndị Ọga* by their Responses on Preferred Gender for Apprenticeship

Table 81 and Figure 81 showed the distribution of *Ndị Ọga* by their responses on preferred gender for apprenticeship. 96.7% of the respondents indicated that 'the male gender is the preferred gender for apprenticeship'. 3.3% of the respondents indicated that 'the female gender is the preferred gender for apprenticeship'.

Table 82: Distribution of *Ndị Ọga* by their Responses on Reasons for Preferred Gender for Apprenticeship

	Frequency	Percent	Valid Percent	Cumulative Percent
Agility and strength of *Nwa Boyi*	563	46.9	46.9	46.9
Females attract more customers	4	.3	.3	47.2
Girls are good for sales girl	100	8.3	8.3	55.5
It's traditional for males to be *Nwa Boyi*	239	19.9	19.9	75.4
Nature of business	111	9.2	9.2	84.7
To avoid sexual harassment	73	6.1	6.1	90.8
We don't take girls as boyi	111	9.2	9.2	100.0
Total	1201	100.0	100.0	

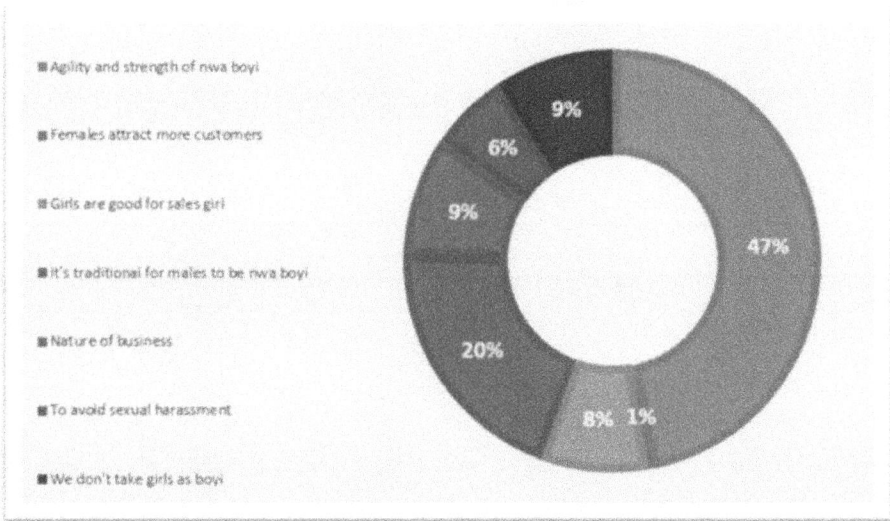

Figure 82: Pie Chart Showing the Distribution of *Ndị Ọga* by their Responses on Reasons for Preferred Gender for Apprenticeship

Table 82 and Figure 82 show the distribution of *Ndị Ọga* by their responses on reasons for preferred gender for apprenticeship. 46.9% indicated that the agility and strength of *Nwa Boyi* is the reason for preferred gender for apprenticeship.0.3% of the respondents said that females attract more customers. 8.3% of the respondents indicated that girls are good for sales girls. 19.9% of the respondents said that it is traditional for males to be *Nwa Boyi*. 9.2% of the respondents indicated that it is the nature of business. 6.1% of the respondents indicated that it is to avoid sexual harassment and 9.2% indicated that they do not take girls as boyi. Results revealed that the agility and strength of *Nwa Boyi* is the reason for preferred gender for apprenticeship and that it is traditional for males to be *Nwa Boyi*.

Table 83: Distribution of *Ndị Ọga* by their Responses on Trade Specificity of *Igba Geli*

	Frequency	Percent	Valid Percent	Cumulative Percent
No	1053	87.7	87.7	87.7
Yes	148	12.3	12.3	100.0
Total	1201	100.0	100.0	

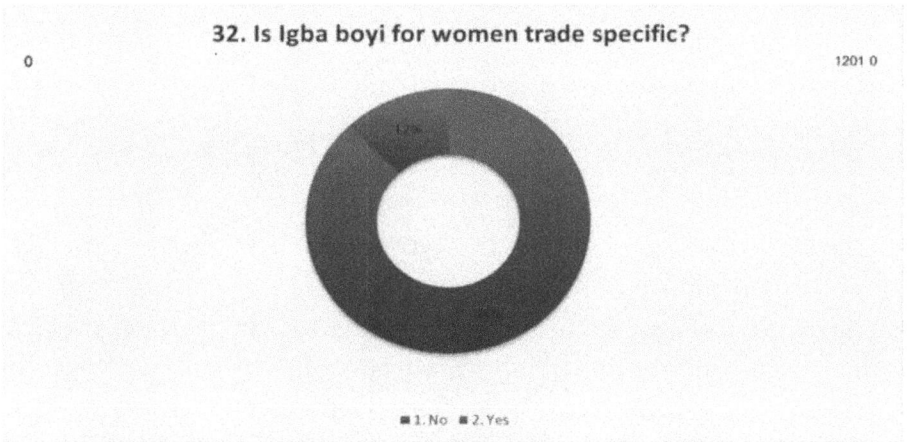

Figure 83: Pie Chart Showing the Distribution of *Ndị Ọga* by their Responses on Trade Specificity of *Igba Geli*

Table 83 and Figure 83 showed the distribution of *Ndị Ọga* by their responses on trade specificity of *Igba Geli*. 87% of the respondent indicated No to the trade specificity of *Igba Geli* while 12.3% of the respondents indicated Yesto the trade specificity of *Igba Geli*.

Table 84: Distribution of *Ndị Ọga* by their Responses on Specific Trades for *Ịgba Gelị* (Female Apprentice)

	Frequency	Percent	Valid Percent	Cumulative Percent
Other responses except 'Yes' responses to (Is *Ịgba Boyi* for women trade specific?)	1053	87.7	87.7	87.7
Cosmetics	18	1.5	1.5	89.4
Fashion and designing	54	4.5	4.5	93.7
Food and Beverages	20	1.7	1.7	95.3
Haircare and Saloon	40	3.3	3.3	98.7
Phones/Electrical/Electronics	3	.2	.2	98.9
Sales girl	13	1.1	1.1	100.0
Total	1201	100.0	100.0	

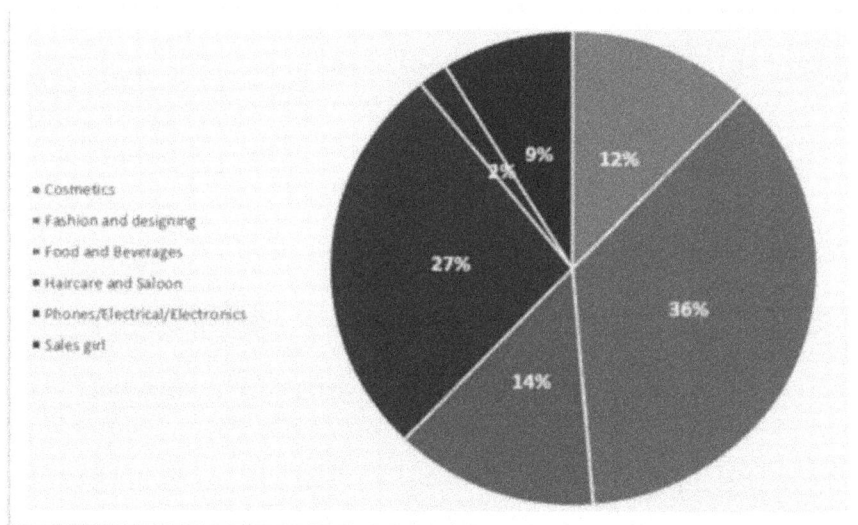

Figure 84: Pie Chart Showing the Distribution of *Ndị Ọga* by their Responses on Specific Trades of *Ịgba Gelị* (Female Apprentice)

Table 84 and Figure 84 showed the distribution of *Ndị Ọga* by their responses on specific trades of *Ịgba Gelị* (Female Apprentice).From the perspectives of *Ndị Ọga*, 87.7% of *Ndị Ọga* that responded to the question did not welcome the idea of *Ịgba Gelị* (Female Apprentice). However, 12.3% of the available respondents indicated that cosmetics and fashion and designing are specific trades of *Ịgba Gelị* (Female Apprentice).

Table 85: Distribution of *Ndị Ọga* by their Responses on Preference for *nwa gelị* to *Nwa Bọyị* as Apprentice

No	976	81.3	81.3	88.9
Yes	133	11.1	11.1	100.0
Both	92	7.7	7.7	7.7
Total	1201	100.0	100.0	

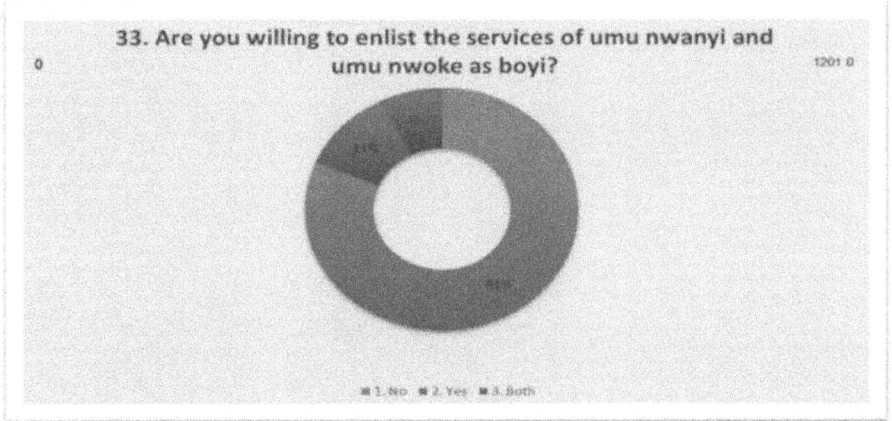

Figure 85: Pie Chart Showing the Distribution of *Ndị Ọga* by their Responses on Preference for *Nwa gelị* to *Nwa Bọyị* as Apprentice

Table 85 and Figure 85 showed the distribution of *Ndị Ọga* by their responses on preference for *nwa gelị* to *Nwa Boyi* as Apprentice. 81.3% of the respondents indicated 'No' to on preference for *nwa gelị* to *Nwa Boyi* as Apprentice. 11.1% of the respondents indicated 'Yes' to on preference for *nwa gelị* to *Nwa Bọyị* as Apprentice while 7.7% of the respondents indicated both *nwa gelị* and *Nwa Boyi* as their preference for Apprentice.

Table 86: Distribution of *Ndị Ọga* by their Responses on Reasons for their Preference

	Frequency	Percent	Valid Percent	Cumulative Percent
Boys are more hardworking and capable	119	9.9	9.9	9.9
Domestic and takes care of the shop	215	17.9	17.9	27.8
I can have both	116	9.7	9.7	37.5
I cannot live with a woman	23	1.9	1.9	39.4
Nature of the business	50	4.2	4.2	43.5
No reason	121	10.1	10.1	53.6
Security (stealing)	21	1.7	1.7	55.4
Sexual issues/gender issues	323	26.9	26.9	82.3
Women are weaker vessels	20	1.7	1.7	83.9
Women don't do *Nwa Boyi*	193	16.1	16.1	100.0
Total	1201	100.0	100.0	

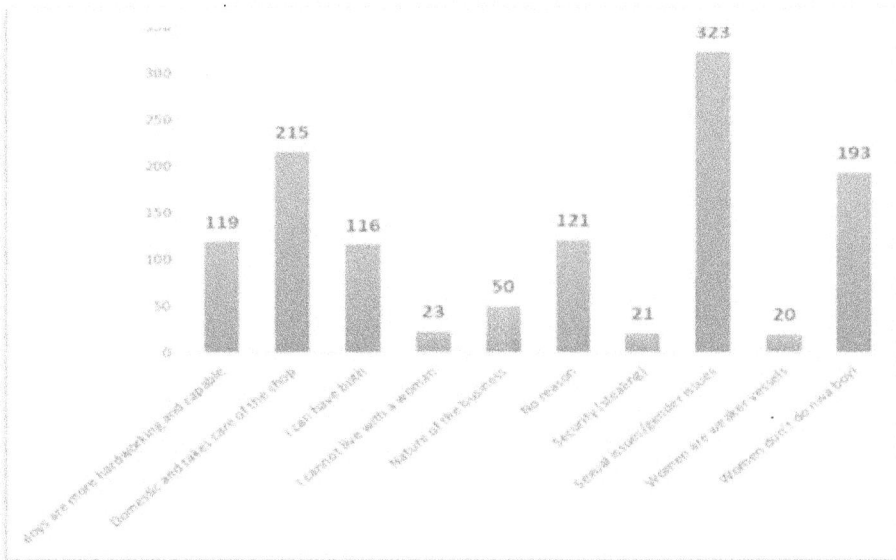

Figure 86: Bar Chart Showing the Distribution of Ndị Ọga by their Responses on Reasons for their Preference

Table 86 and Figure 86 showed the distribution of Ndị Ọga by their responses on reasons for their preference for Nwa Bọyi to Nwa gelị as Apprentice. 9.9% of the respondents indicated that boys are more hardworking and capable as their reason why they prefer Nwa Bọyi to Nwa gelị as Apprentice. 17.9% of the respondents indicated that boys are more hardworking and capable as their reason why they prefer Nwa Bọyi to Nwa gelị as Apprentice. 9.7% of the respondents said "I can have both". 1.9% of the respondents selected that they cannot live with a woman as their reason why they prefer Nwa Bọyi as Apprentice. 4.2% of the respondents chose nature of the business as their reason why they prefer Nwa Bọyi. 10.1% of the respondents chose no reason. 1.7% of the respondents mentioned security (stealing) as their reason. 26.9% of the respondents identified sexual issues/gender issues as their reason why they prefer Nwa Bọyi to Nwa gelị. 1.7% of the respondents said that women are weaker vessels, while 16.1% of the respondents indicated that Women do not do Nwa Bọyi as their reason. The results revealed that sexual issues/gender issues, domestic duties/taking care of the shop as their reasons for preferring Nwa Boyi to Nwa gelị as Apprentices.

4.3.6 Why "Ịgba Bọyị" and not "Ịgba Gelị"?: Gender Dimensions and Discourses on Feminization in the Ịgba-Bọyị Scheme

From the interviews, themes such as *'energy-demanding nature of ịgba-boyị, females being excluded automatically by nature, and the need for the maintenance of division of labour or gender-based division of labour and strict gender roles as structured by the Igbo society'* were the primary reasons for the male-centeredness of *Igba Bọyị scheme* in Igbo land. These findings reflect that the *Igba Bọyị* scheme remains a male-dominated apprenticeship scheme even in the 21st century (specifically 2021) and this is informed by the fact that the Igbo society is a patrilineal society. In ancient Igbo society, women only go through the traditional training known as *'Ọzụzụ'* where they are exposed to the rudiments of domestic chores, caring for babies and husbands, while the responsibility of 'winning bread' rests on the male. In response to this, many of the traders stressed that the Igbo society and families operate on the philosophy that women are traditionally *'ori-akụ'* (wealth consumers) not *'ọkpata-akụ'* (wealth creator/producer) which is the traditional role of Igbo men as shown in some of these interview responses below: "*Igba Bọyị* is used for males who went for apprenticeship under somebody, while that of female training is called training (*ọzụzụ*) (In-depth Interview with 56 years old *Ọga* at Building Materials Market). Another study participant noted that:

> it is not possible to take a girl as (*nwa gelị/Ịgba Gelị*) dependent-apprentice. Women are meant not to suffer, instead, they are called "*ori akụ*"- wealth eater/consumer. In Igbo land, it is difficult for girls to be engaged in dependent-apprenticeship, instead, they will be asked to go and nurse children of another family (housemaid). So that is what I thought is the reason why they are not engaged. In Igbo settings, women are supposed to be in the house, while males hustle for what the family will eat; not because things have changed now, a man will take his bag off for business and the wife will also move for a business too. Owing to the hardship we are facing in the country; women have joined in the pursuit of money to enable the family to make ends meet (In-depth Interview 49 years Old *Ọga*, (Building Material Market, 2020).

Why the name *Igba Bọyị* is because it is only boys that can go on such trades. But women who go on similar missions are said to have gone for "*Ọzụzụ*" family training. A boy, after *Igba Bọyị*, will be settled to start up his own life and live on his own and carter for himself; but a woman that is sent on "*Ọzụzụ*" cannot be allowed to stay alone unless she is a married woman (FGD Comment from Respondent 2 at Building Material Market, 2020).

For so many of the traders, the exclusion of girls in the Igbo apprenticeship scheme is driven by forces of gender role and division of labour and the conception that women are 'weaker vessels' and as such should not be conceived as discrimination against women as most radical feminists would like to presume as shown below in the interview responses below:

> We know that there is some work a woman ca not work, some tedious jobs that can be done only by men. *Igba Boyi* is not just for the *Nwa Boyi* to be going to shop, like in our market here that some people are into tiles, you can not ask women to go and be carrying tiles, like at home where the master is leaving in a five-story building and water is not running in the building, you won't expect a lady to be fetching water from downstairs and be bringing it upstairs, so if I'm to say it is not an easy task (58 years old *Oga* at Building Materials Market, Onitsha, 2020).

One of the respondents stressed that 'men are known to be the owners of the house/home- the pillar of the house. The family responsibility lies on the head of men.' When further probed if there are women in the Market Union executive, he opined that 'yes there are women in our executive. Since, girls do not participate in the apprenticeship scheme, they are engaged as sales girls. They are well paid and we also lecture them against molestation that may arise from (*Ndi Oga*) Masters.'

Another respondent observed that this practice of leaving women behind at home is changing as women are also participating in Wealth hunting but not as apprentices as shown here "it's well known in Igbo culture that females do not go for "*boyi*". It is mostly males that go for *boyi* that is why it is called *boyi*. But the economic situation of things now has discouraged women from staying idle and you see women hustling like men now".

Beyond all these, *Igba Boyi* is too demanding mentally and energy-wise and many women/girls may not cope with these demands and that is why they are naturally excluded in the *Igba Boyi* apprenticeship scheme in Igboland. The interview excerpt below captures this vividly:

> forget that saying that says "what a man can do, a woman can also do" some will even do better. It is not everything a woman can do. What *Igba Boyi* entails is much, as a *boyi* you will go to the warehouse to bring goods, assist in off-loading goods from the truck, go to Lagos to buy goods. Therefore, it is not everything that women can do; they can only

act as sales girls" (FGD Respondent 4 with Market Union Executives at Ochanja Market, 2020).

Table 87: Distribution of *Ndị Ọga* by their Responses on whether they Prefer Sales Girls to *Nwa Bọyi*

	Frequency	Percent	Valid Percent	Cumulative Percent
Yes	157	13.1	13.1	100.0
No	966	80.4	80.4	86.9
Don't Know	78	6.5	6.5	6.5
Total	1201	100.0	100.0	

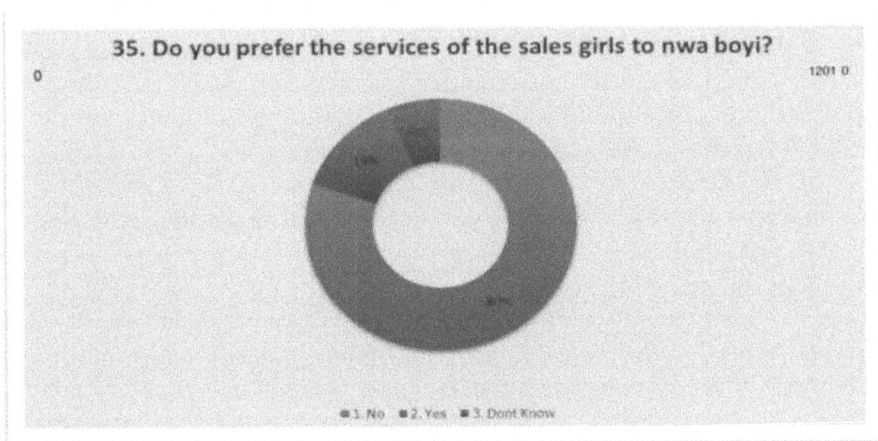

Figure 87: Pie Chart Indicating the Distribution of *Ndị Ọga* by their Responses on whether they prefer Sales Girls to *Nwa Bọyi*

The majority of *Ndị Ọga* (966; 80.4%) are opposed to taking Sale Girls as *nwa boyi* indicating that their roles are not the same, but complementary, while 157 (13.1%) expressed their preference for Sales Girls.

Table 88: Distribution of *Ndị Ọga* by their Responses on Reasons for their Preference for Sales Girls to *Nwa Bọyi*

	Frequency	Percent	Valid Percent	Cumulative Percent
Other options except (If "Yes", state your reasons for your answer)	969	80.7	80.7	80.7
A salesgirl doesn't need to live with me. She comes and goes	9	.7	.7	81.4
Can be sacked at anytime	7	.6	.6	82.0
I don't need *Nwa Boyi*	14	1.2	1.2	83.2
It makes stock	17	1.4	1.4	84.6

taking/management easy			
Nature of business	107	8.9	8.9	93.5
No settlement for sales girls	19	1.6	1.6	95.1
Nobody wants to be boy these days	6	.5	.5	95.6
Stealingand sexually harassment of *Oga*'s family members	32	2.7	2.7	98.3
They incure less expenditure	8	.7	.7	98.9
To attract more customers	13	1.1	1.1	100.0
Total	1201	100.0	100.0	

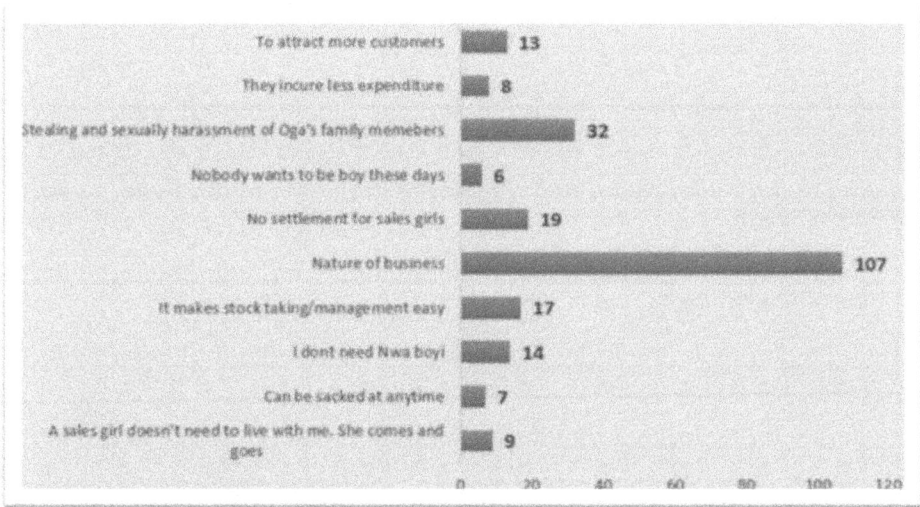

Figure 88: Bar Chart Depicting the Distribution of *Ndị Ọga* by their Responses on the Reasons for their Preference for Sales Girls to *Nwa Bọyi*

Table 88 and Figure 88 show the distribution of *Ndị Ọga* by their responses on the reasons for their preference for sales girls to *Nwa Bọyi*. 80.7% of *Ndị Ọga* that responded to the questions indicated that there are other reasons for their preference for sales girls to *Nwa Bọyi*. However, the few that responded to the options given indicated that the nature of their business is the main reason for their preference for sales girls to *Nwa Bọyi*.

Table 89: Distribution of *Ndị Ọga* by their Responses on the Basic Skills and Knowledge Needed by *Ụmụ Boyi*

		Frequency	Percent	Valid Percent	Cumulative Percent
Honesty	No	173	14.4	14.4	14.4
	Yes	1028	85.6	85.6	100.0
	Total	1201	100.0	100.0	
Good Customer Relationship	No	512	42.6	42.6	42.6
	Yes	689	57.4	57.4	100.0
	Total	1201	100.0	100.0	
Literacy	No	796	66.3	66.3	66.3
	Yes	405	33.7	33.7	100.0
	Total	1201	100.0	100.0	
Knowledge of ICT	No	1140	94.9	94.9	94.9
	Yes	61	5.1	5.1	100.0
	Total	1201	100.0	100.0	
Good Negotiation Skills	No	656	54.6	54.6	54.6
	Yes	545	45.4	45.4	100.0
	Total	1201	100.0	100.0	
Accounting Skills	No	729	60.7	60.7	60.7
	Yes	472	39.3	39.3	100.0
	Total	1201	100.0	100.0	
Self Control/Resilience	No	686	57.1	57.1	57.1
	Yes	515	42.9	42.9	100.0
	Total	1201	100.0	100.0	
Others (Please Specify)	No	946	78.8	78.8	78.8
	Yes	255	21.2	21.2	100.0
	Total	1201	100.0	100.0	
	N Total	3970			

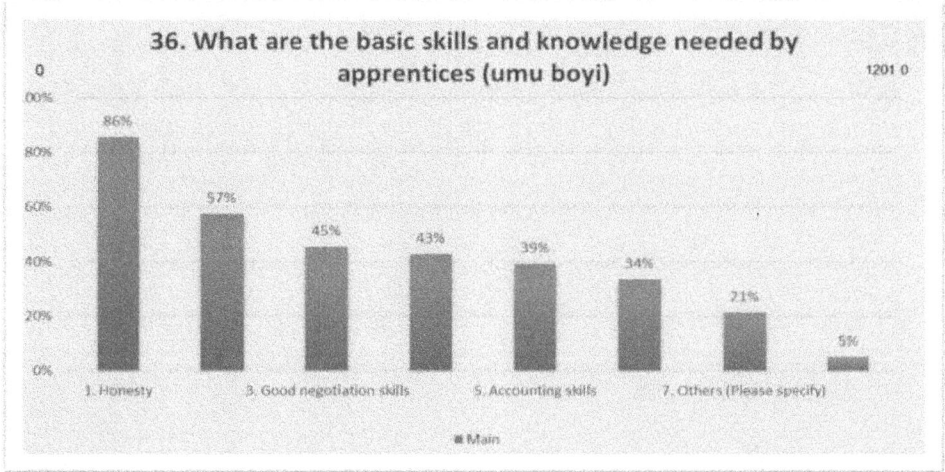

36. What are the basic skills and knowledge needed by apprentices (umu boyi)

Figure 89: Bar Chart Indicating *Ndị Ọga*s' Responses on the Basic Skills and Knowledge Needed by *Ụmụ Bọyị*

Table 89 and Figure 89 showed the distribution of *Ndị Ọga* by their responses on the basic skills and knowledge needed by *Ụmụ Bọyị*. The basic skills that were outlined for respondents to respond to include honesty, Good Customer Relationship, Literacy, Knowledge of ICT, Good Negotiation Skills, Accounting Skills, Self Control/Resilience and Others. From the analysis on the table and the bar chart, honesty (85.6%) and good customer relationship(57.4%) stand out to be the basic skills and knowledge needed by *Ụmụ Bọyị* as perceived by *Ndị Ọga*.

Table 90: Distribution of *Ụmụ Bọyị* by their Responses on the Basic Skills and Knowledge Needed by *Ụmụ Bọyị*

		Frequency	Percent	Valid Percent	Cumulative Percent
Honesty	No	172	14.3	14.3	14.3
	Yes	1028	85.7	85.7	100.0
	Total	1200	100.0	100.0	
Good Customer Relationship	No	475	40.6	40.6	40.6
	Yes	725	60.4	60.4	100.0
	Total	1200	100.0	100.0	
Literacy	No	859	71.6	71.6	71.6
	Yes	341	28.4	28.4	100.0
	Total	1200	100.0	100.0	
Knowledge of ICT	No	1143	95.2	95.2	95.2
	Yes	57	4.8	4.8	100.0

	Total	1200	100.0	100.0	
Good Negotiation Skills	No	686	57.2	57.2	57.2
	Yes	514	42.8	42.8	100.0
	Total	1200	100.0	100.0	
Accounting Skills	No	723	60.2	60.2	60.2
	Yes	477	39.8	39.8	100.0
	Total	1200	100.0	100.0	
Self Control/Resilience	No	691	57.6	57.6	57.6
	Yes	509	42.4	42.4	100.0
	Total	1200	100.0	100.0	
Others (Please Specify)	No	998	83.2	83.2	83.2
	Yes	202	16.8	21.2	100.0
	Total	1200	100.0	100.0	
	N Total	3853			

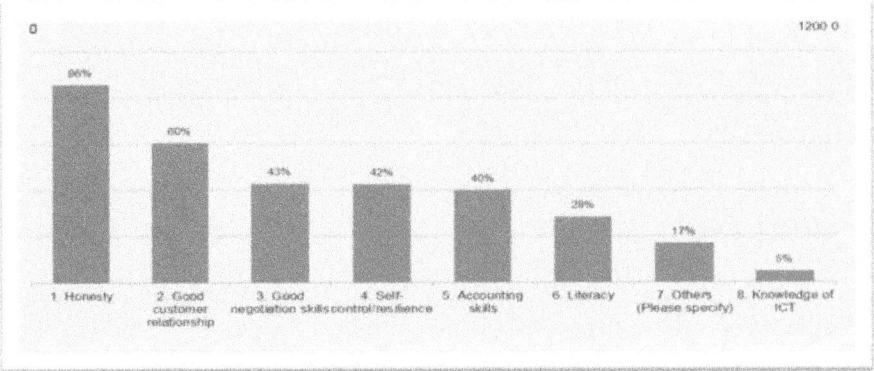

Figure 90: Bar Chart Showing the Distribution of *I̩Imu̩ Bo̩yi̩* by their Responses on the Basic Skills and Knowledge Needed by *I̩Imu̩ Bo̩yi̩*

Table 90 and Figure 90 show the distribution of *U̩mu̩ Bo̩yi̩* by their responses on the basic skills and knowledge needed by *U̩mu̩ Bo̩yi̩*. The basic skills that were outlined for respondents to respond to include honesty, Good Customer Relationship, Literacy, Knowledge of ICT, Good Negotiation Skills, Accounting Skills, Self Control/Resilience and Others. From the analysis on the table and the bar chart, honesty (85.6%) and good customer relationship (57.4%) stand out among the basic skills and knowledge needed by *U̩mu̩ Bo̩yi̩* as perceived by *U̩mu̩ Bo̩yi̩*. The results aligned with the perception of *Ndi̩ O̩ga*.

The excerpts from the In-depth Interviews support the above claim as shown below: "for a business to thrive and this dependent-apprenticeship (*Igba Bo̩yi̩*) to continue, there will be a need to have honest *U̩mu̩ Bo̩yi̩*, there must be humility, there must be endurance – these three cardinal things are very important" (Key Stakeholder, 68 years old in his office, 2020).

4.3.7 The Challenges and Dynamics of Online Businesses

From the interviews, many of the study participants did not fail to highlight the challenges associated with the use of internet-mediated platforms such as the challenge of 'waiting for bank alerts as customers often get debited first whereas the traders wait for minutes, hours, and even days before they get alerts, confirmation of payment by placing a call to the trader's bank account officers which they say cost money and time, the difficulty of older entrepreneurs and traders to operate the new Internet-mediated platforms and as such are still stuck with the use of cheques and constant visits to the banks for 'face-to-face' transactions in the banks.

There is also the challenge of being asked by *robbers to supply account codes and ATM PINs* and this could lead to huge capital losses if not the loss of lives, others feel that the use of internet-mediated platforms for transactions does not feel real as they want to see and count their money physically (some form of self-actualization and satisfaction is derived from touching and counting cash). This spells out the role of satisfying this emotional need of feeling and touching cash in making traders remain stuck with older ways of transactions, cash handling, and management. The interviews also established this was common among traders or shop owners with a small business base. Most big entrepreneurs such as importers, exporters, manufacturers, and industry owners prefer the transfer of cash directly to their bank accounts as none of them want to take the risks of carrying huge cash which can expose them to attacks by robbers and hoodlums. During an FGD session, some discussants were asked: 'Has there been any misfortune arising from using these internet-mediated platforms particularly the social media to transact?' Discussant 2 during an FGD session said: 'To me, I have never experienced any. The only risk in it is that someone can be defrauded through this medium. But we are always careful when dealing with online customers.' While Discussant 6 observed that:

> Another risk that is there is that sometimes you will order for a particular quality of goods, but they will go and manufacture sub-standard or lesser quality to you, this is commonly experienced especially by those that import goods.' Furthermore, they were probed to talk further about the use and acceptance of mobile and internet transfers- 'do you accept it in the market?' Some of the study participants noted that 'Traders have improved, we are now comparable to the civil servants. We make use of all electronic mediums in transacting business, ranging from mobile transfers, internet banking, POS services among others (FGD Participant 5 at Bridge Head Market). Another FGD discussant opined that: 'another risk is that, if armed robbers get you, they will ask you to give them your pin and they

will collect your phone from you, by this, they have access to your bank account' (FGD Participant 3 at Bridge Head Market).

A lot of dynamics play out in the adoption of internet-mediated platforms for transactions among these traders as many still do not accept online banking or internet banking, some do not use the point-of-sale machines (POS), nor do they want to use anything that has to do with social media and the issues of mistrust of the quality of security in the Nigerian banking system as many of the banks are constantly plagued by the activities of hackers. This is driven by lots of factual and non-factual tales about the activities of fraudsters on social media and other platforms. These negative standpoints are peculiar to older persons but the younger businessmen and traders (*Ndị Ọga*) have swiftly adapted to the new modes of internet transactions. Be that as it may, the rate of positive response in the use of internet-mediated platforms for transactions among the traders in the Onitsha Markets is high although their usage still requires carefulness, security consciousness, and tact.

Table 91: Distribution of *Ndị Ọga*s' Responses on Other Basic Skills and Knowledge Needed by *Ụmụ Bọyi*

	Frequency	Percent	Valid Percent	Cumulative Percent
Other options except (If Others, please specify)	945	78.7	78.7	78.7
Agility	74	6.2	6.2	84.8
Dedication	28	2.3	2.3	87.2
Intelligence	19	1.6	1.6	88.8
Loyalty	74	6.2	6.2	94.9
Obedience	61	5.1	5.1	100.0
Total	1201	100.0	100.0	

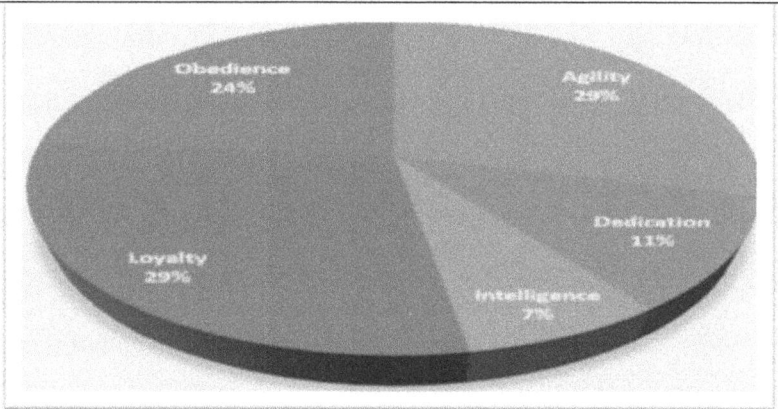

Figure 91: Pie Chart Depicting the Distribution of *Ndị Ọga*s' Responses on Other Basic Skills and Knowledge Needed by *Ụmụ Bọyi*

Table 91 and Figure 91 showed the distribution of *Ndị Ọga*s' responses on other basic skills and knowledge needed by *Ụmụ Bọyi* .78.7% of *Ndị Ọga* that responded to the question indicated that there are other basic skills and knowledge needed by *Ụmụ Bọyi*.

However, the few that responded to the options given indicated that agility, loyalty and obedience are other basic skills and knowledge needed by *Ụmụ Bọyi*.

**Table 92: Distribution of *Ụmụ Bọyị by* their Responses on Other Basic Skills and Knowledge Needed by *Ụmụ Bọyị:*

	Frequency	Percent	Valid Percent	Cumulative Percent
Other options except (If Others, please specify)	998	83.2	83.2	83.2
A boy should be focused on learning the trade and trying to please the *Ọga* so that he can be settled well at the end of the day.	1	.1	.1	83.3
A good attitude to work, be trustworthy	1	.1	.1	83.3
Active and Hustling spirit	1	.1	.1	83.4
Age, hustling spirit, knowledge of business	1	.1	.1	83.5
Agile, humble	1	.1	.1	83.6
Agile, obedience, not being playful	1	.1	.1	83.7
Avoidance of bad company	1	.1	.1	83.8
Be agile, hardworking	1	.1	.1	83.8
Be tolerant, patient, being polite	1	.1	.1	83.9
Being agile, be active	1	.1	.1	84.0
Being respectful	1	.1	.1	84.1
Being smart	1	.1	.1	84.2
Being social, humble	1	.1	.1	84.3
Boldness, respect, and contentment	1	.1	.1	84.3
Character	4	.3	.3	84.7
Character, hard work, smart	1	.1	.1	84.8
Dedication to work	1	.1	.1	84.8
Determination hardworking endurance	1	.1	.1	84.9
Diligent and quick learner	1	.1	.1	85.0
Don't steal	1	.1	.1	85.1
Endurance, humble, patience	1	.1	.1	85.2
Endurance, humility and truthful	1	.1	.1	85.3
Familybackground	2	.2	.2	85.4
Familybackground and Character	1	.1	.1	85.5
Familybackground, hardworking	1	.1	.1	85.6
Fast	1	.1	.1	85.7

Fear of God	1	.1	.1	85.8
Financial management skills	1	.1	.1	85.8
Focus, determination, and endurance.	1	.1	.1	85.9
Follow all instructions	1	.1	.1	86.0
Forget about your people in the meantime, be focused, be wise, respect your madam	1	.1	.1	86.1
Frugal with money	1	.1	.1	86.2
Godliness	1	.1	.1	86.3
Good behavior and disciplined	1	.1	.1	86.3
Good character,	1	.1	.1	86.4
Good character, God Fearing, hardworking	1	.1	.1	86.5
Good habit, obedient	1	.1	.1	86.6
Good relationship with the master	1	.1	.1	86.7
Hard work, smart, character	1	.1	.1	86.8
Hard working	1	.1	.1	86.8
Hard-working	3	.3	.3	87.1
Hard-working and humble	1	.1	.1	87.2
Hard-working and smart	1	.1	.1	87.3
Hard-working and zealous	1	.1	.1	87.3
Hard-working, law-abiding and Obedient...	1	.1	.1	87.4
Hardworking	8	.7	.7	88.1
Hardworking and faithful.	1	.1	.1	88.2
Hardworking and Humble	1	.1	.1	88.3
Hardworking and obedient.	1	.1	.1	88.3
Hardworking, focused	1	.1	.1	88.4
Hardworking, obedient	1	.1	.1	88.5
He has to have patience.	1	.1	.1	88.6
He must be respectful and obedient.	1	.1	.1	88.7
He should have basic education. And must be very honest and obedient and humble	1	.1	.1	88.8
How fit the person is and his background	1	.1	.1	88.8
Humble	7	.6	.6	89.4
Humble and agile	1	.1	.1	89.5
Humble and hard-working	1	.1	.1	89.6
Humble and respectful	2	.2	.2	89.8
Humble and smart	1	.1	.1	89.8

Humble, agile, loyal, truthful	1	.1	.1	89.9
Humble, obedience	1	.1	.1	90.0
Humble, obedient, focused	1	.1	.1	90.1
Humble, social, good to people,	1	.1	.1	90.2
Humble, trustworthy	1	.1	.1	90.3
Humility	3	.3	.3	90.5
Humility and obedience	1	.1	.1	90.6
Humility and smartness	1	.1	.1	90.7
Humility, hardworking, hustling	1	.1	.1	90.8
Humility, he should be smart and should be sharp in learning.	1	.1	.1	90.8
Humility, obedience, agility	1	.1	.1	90.9
Humility.	1	.1	.1	91.0
Hustling	1	.1	.1	91.1
Hustling spirit	2	.2	.2	91.3
Intelligent, perseverance, humble	1	.1	.1	91.3
Loyal, hard-working, profitable, and Obedient...	1	.1	.1	91.4
Loyal, hardworking, obedience, trustworthy	1	.1	.1	91.5
Loyalty	1	.1	.1	91.6
Loyalty and humility	1	.1	.1	91.7
Management of funds	1	.1	.1	91.8
Must be intelligent	1	.1	.1	91.8
Neatness, Hard Work	1	.1	.1	91.9
No particular skills, you have to teach the person that skill	1	.1	.1	92.0
Non. He will be trained when he comes to his *Oga*'s house	1	.1	.1	92.1
Not stealing, fast learner	1	.1	.1	92.2
Obedience	4	.3	.3	92.5
Obedience and humility	1	.1	.1	92.6
Obedience and patience	1	.1	.1	92.7
Obedience and willingness to serve	1	.1	.1	92.8
Obedience Respect Humble Hardworking	1	.1	.1	92.8
Obedience, agile, truthful	1	.1	.1	92.9
Obedience, avoid bad friends	1	.1	.1	93.0

Obedience, endurance and patience	1	.1	.1	93.1
Obedience, humble, truthful	1	.1	.1	93.2
Obedience, humility, agile	1	.1	.1	93.3
Obedience, not steal, respect *Ọga* and madam	1	.1	.1	93.3
Obedience, patience	3	.3	.3	93.6
Obedience, patience,	1	.1	.1	93.7
Obedience, patience, good behavior	1	.1	.1	93.8
Obedience, respectfulness, humility	1	.1	.1	93.8
Obedience, stop stealing, no follow woman	1	.1	.1	93.9
Obedience, truthfulness	1	.1	.1	94.0
Obedience,respect	1	.1	.1	94.1
Obedient	6	.5	.5	94.6
Obedient and hardworking	1	.1	.1	94.7
Obedient to your master	1	.1	.1	94.8
Obedient, no stealing, no bad friends, down to earth, not be distracted, patience, being God-fearing	1	.1	.1	94.8
Once the Person decides	1	.1	.1	94.9
Patience	3	.3	.3	95.2
Patience and endurance, humble	1	.1	.1	95.3
Patience, obedience, respect, humility	1	.1	.1	95.3
Principled and morals	1	.1	.1	95.4
Reduce the number of friends, avoid loitering and focus on what he came to learn. He should also be humble	1	.1	.1	95.5
Respect your master and neighbours in the shop lines and *Ọga*'s wife. Also avoid bad friends, women, and thievery.	1	.1	.1	95.6
Respect, obedience, be trustworthy	1	.1	.1	95.7
Respect, self contentment, humility ,	1	.1	.1	95.8
Respect, truthfulness, patience, endurance	1	.1	.1	95.8
Self dedication	1	.1	.1	95.9

Self discipline	1	.1	.1	96.0
Seriously minded in business	1	.1	.1	96.1
Sharp and smart	1	.1	.1	96.2
Sharp, trustworthy, avoid bad friends, mindful of his environment, agile, not stealing	1	.1	.1	96.3
Should be focused and prioritized, should also be good with time management	1	.1	.1	96.3
Should be humble and respectful	1	.1	.1	96.4
Should be obedient	1	.1	.1	96.5
Should be painstaking	1	.1	.1	96.6
Should be very hardworking	1	.1	.1	96.7
Sincerity, trustworthy	1	.1	.1	96.8
Smart and hard-working	3	.3	.3	97.0
Smart and very fast, agile in working, and to be very calculative.	1	.1	.1	97.1
Smart, endurance	1	.1	.1	97.2
Smart, humble, respectful	1	.1	.1	97.3
Smart, humble, sincere	1	.1	.1	97.3
Smart, respectful and agile	1	.1	.1	97.4
Smartness, ability to observe customers,	1	.1	.1	97.5
Someone who's not living an illegal life, obedience	1	.1	.1	97.6
Someone your spirit accepts	1	.1	.1	97.7
Steady and been serious	1	.1	.1	97.8
Strong and respectful	1	.1	.1	97.8
Submissive	1	.1	.1	97.9
The most important skill is that the person must be very hardworking	1	.1	.1	98.0
The most important thing is that he knows how to hustle.	1	.1	.1	98.1
The most important thing is that the person is hardworking	1	.1	.1	98.2
The most important thing is to get a boy that has a good character. It covers all other qualities.	1	.1	.1	98.3
The person must have patience and must be sharp so as not to be deceived by	1	.1	.1	98.3

other boys				
They set trap for you to huddle over	1	.1	.1	98.4
To be smart	1	.1	.1	98.5
To be smart and always willing to work and learn.	1	.1	.1	98.6
To ensure he avoids bad friends because they cause a lot of problems if you're not careful.	1	.1	.1	98.7
To understand the person his working with and to also avoid been influenced by the other boy's	1	.1	.1	98.8
Transparent, Hardworking	1	.1	.1	98.8
Trustworthy	1	.1	.1	98.9
Trustworthy, hardworking, truthfulness	1	.1	.1	99.0
Trustworthy, obedience	1	.1	.1	99.1
Truthful	1	.1	.1	99.2
Truthfulness, hustling, respectful, wisdom	1	.1	.1	99.3
Very hard-working	1	.1	.1	99.3
Very smart	1	.1	.1	99.4
Vibrant and sharp, being able to interpret customers movements..hustling for customer	1	.1	.1	99.5
Well mannered, social, and hardworking	1	.1	.1	99.6
Wisdom and knowledge	1	.1	.1	99.7
Wisdom, patience, respectful	1	.1	.1	99.8
You can train him to learn any other skill. The most important is literacy.	1	.1	.1	99.8
Zeal for the trade	1	.1	.1	99.9
Zealous, hardworking	1	.1	.1	100.0
Total	1200	100.0	100.0	

Table 93: Distribution of *Ndi Ọga* by their Responses on Benefits of the Apprenticeship Scheme to *Nwa Bọyi*

		Frequency	Percent	Valid Percent	Cumulative Percent
Learning of Skills and/or Trade	No	383	31.9	31.9	31.9
	Yes	818	68.1	68.1	100.0
	Total	1201	100.0	100.0	
Raising Capital	No	495	41.2	41.2	41.2
	Yes	706	58.8	58.8	100.0
	Total	1201	100.0	100.0	
Building Business Contacts	No	749	62.4	62.4	62.4
	Yes	452	37.6	37.6	100.0
	Total	1201	100.0	100.0	
All of the Above	No	898	74.8	74.8	74.8
	Yes	303	25.2	25.2	100.0
	Total	1201	100.0	100.0	
No Benefits	No	1198	99.8	99.8	99.8
	Yes	3	.2	.2	100.0
	Total	1201	100.0	100.0	
Others (Please Specify)	No	1075	89.5	89.5	89.5
	Yes	126	10.5	10.5	100.0
	Total	1201	100.0	100.0	
	N Total	2408			

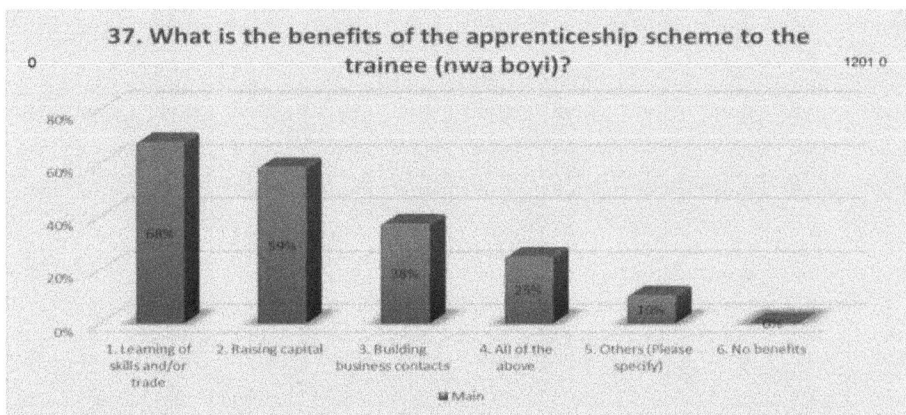

Figure 93: Bar Chart Indicating the Distribution of *Ndi Ọga*s' Responses on Benefits of the Apprenticeship Scheme to *Nwa Bọyi*.

Table 93 and Figure 93 show the distribution of *Ndi Ọga* by their responses on the benefits of the apprenticeship scheme to *Nwa Bọyi*. From Table 93 and Figure 93, learning of skills and/or trade (68.1%) and raising capital (58.8%) stand out to be the main benefits of the apprenticeship scheme to *Nwa Bọyi*.

Table 94: Distribution of Ụmụ Bọyị by their Responses on Benefits of the Apprenticeship Scheme to Nwa Bọyị

		Frequency	Percent	Valid Percent	Cumulative Percent
Learning of Skills and/or Trade	No	381	31.7	31.7	31.7
	Yes	819	68.3	68.3	100.0
	Total	1200	100.0	100.0	
Raising Capital	No	509	42.4	42.4	42.4
	Yes	691	57.6	57.6	100.0
	Total	1200	100.0	100.0	
Building Business Contacts	No	728	60.7	60.7	60.7
	Yes	472	39.3	39.3	100.0
	Total	1200	100.0	100.0	
All of the Above	No	927	77.2	77.2	77.2
	Yes	273	22.8	22.8	100.0
	Total	1200	100.0	100.0	
No Benefits	No	1199	99.9	99.9	99.9
	Yes	1	0.1	0.1	100.0
	Total	1200	100.0	100.0	
Others (Please Specify)	No	1112	92.7	92.7	92.7
	Yes	88	7.3	7.3	100.0
	Total	1200	100.0	100.0	
	N Total	2344			

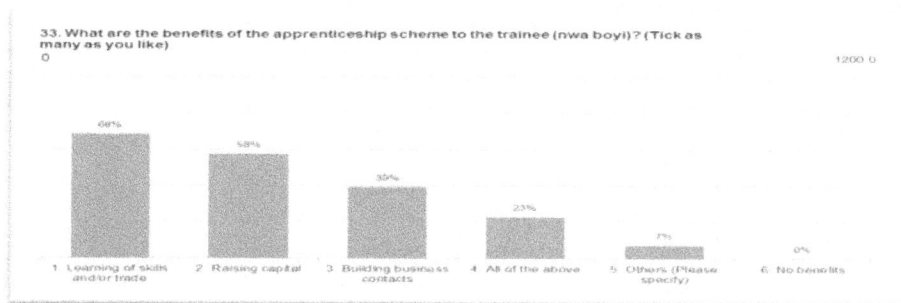

Figure 94: Bar Chart Showing the Distribution of Ụmụ Bọyị by their Responses on Benefits of the Apprenticeship Scheme to Nwa Bọyị

Table 94 and Figure 94 show the distribution of Ụmụ Bọyị by their responses on the benefits of the apprenticeship scheme to Nwa Bọyị. From the analysis on the table and the bar chart, learning of skills and/or trade (68.3%) and raising capital (57.6%) stand out to be the main benefits of the apprenticeship scheme to Nwa Bọyị. The results corroborate that of Ndị Ọga on the benefits of the apprenticeship scheme to Nwa Bọyị.

Table 95: Distribution of *Ndị Ọga* by their Responses on Other Benefits of the Apprenticeship Scheme to *Nwa Bọyị*

	Frequency	Percent	Valid Percent	Cumulative Percent
Other options except (If Others, please specify)	1075	89.5	89.5	89.5
Agility	8	.7	.7	90.2
Connections	7	.6	.6	90.7
Exposure	33	2.8	2.8	93.4
Learn the secrets of the business	34	2.8	2.8	96.4
Management skills	34	2.9	2.9	99.5
To be taken care of by *Ọga*'s	10	.8	.8	100.0
Total	1201	100.0	100.0	

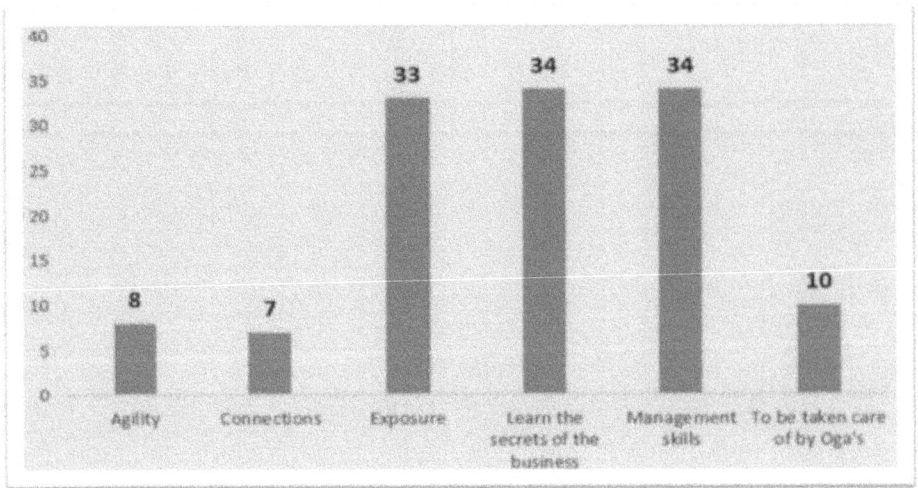

Figure 95: Bar Chart Showing the Distribution of *Ndị Ọga* by their Responses on Other Benefits of the Apprenticeship Scheme to *Nwa Bọyị*

Among those who chose others outside those already indicated, Exposure (33), Learn the Secrets of the Master (34), Management Skills (34) are the other major benefits of the apprenticeship scheme to *Nwa Bọyị*.

4.3.8 Business Secrets: Peculiar Trading Nuances and Business Slangs Utilized and Applied by Apprentices (Ụmụ/Nwa Bọyị) and Master(s) (Ọga/Ndị Ọga)

From the interviews, the following Business slangs and trade tricks were identified as currently used in trade transactions in the studied Onitsha Markets namely: *'ọ mere isi eze nwekwe'* (Is he a stubborn customer); *'is Esau around?';* *'ọ kwa aka ịtọ';* *akwa ezuro ezu';* *were iruro jide akwa ahụ; ogbu laka; tinyere ya C kwọlity/quality;, igotekwe ị kwụọụgwọ; bie ya ebie ma ọ bụ sụa ya asụa; iwerezia afọ nkịta ị wụnye n'afọ ewu';* among so many others. Each of these identified trade slangs has been interpreted below.

These trade slangs used by the traders (*Ndị Ọga* and *Ụmụ Bọyị*) can be categorized into sub-themes such as 'Cheating/Fraud-Oriented Slangs and Profit Maximization Slangs: The excerpts below capture these peculiar trade nuances and business slangs in the studied Onitsha Markets as shown in some of the in-depth interview excerpts below:

Do you know, one day I went to Iweka to buy something and they didn't know I was from the market. The owner of the shop left his shop for the market runner/mobile marketer/drop shipper (*ọnye ọsọ ahịa*). Though, currently drop shipping is prevalent in most social media where people display Pictures of their wares and goods on their Facebook and Instagram pages and when a customer demands it, they go to different physical shops scouting for that particular good in terms of texture and quality and then waybills it to the customer after payment has been made. Many of the Onitsha Market Traders are yet to venture into online *Ọsọ-afịa*, though they have been involved in face-to-face or physical dropshipping (*Ọsọ-ahịa*). The market runner came and positioned himself as the owner of the shop. So, he asked *(ọ mere isi eze nwekwe)* meaning if I am a stubborn customer. I ordered what I wanted to buy i.e., Television and it was brought to me, then immediately another person entered; immediately he entered, he praised the television and began to ask, if I want to give it out as a gift or do I want to make use of it in my house. I then told him I want to make use of it in the house. He maliciously advised that I should not use it instead I should buy another one he pointed. That the one I chose will not last. If you are not careful, they will deceive you by giving you a fake in the name of the original. But if you understand their tricks and insist on the one you have chosen, they sometimes will tell you that they will bring the one in the parking store for you, and when they go there, they will swap the original with the fake and seal it in the carton of original (IDI with a 46 years old *Oga* at Building Materials Market).

Sometimes these market runners/drop-shippers (ndị ọso-afịa) will take you to the owner of the business, and you will hear him say 'Is **Esau around?'** The owner of the business will not say anything and **what that means is that the owner of the business should add his own.** If the price of the good is supposed to be 100 but because he said 'Is Esau around?' the pricing will then be 200 from where you can bargain it to say 150 after he will come back and collect his 50.

This thing is rampant in Emeka **Ọfọr**, where they sell phones. Like on Monday when it was raining, around 10 am I was with my task force and we were hunting for them, and anyone that is caught we hand them over to security (IDI with 41 years old male at Main Market, August 2020).

There are slangs in the market like when a customer comes the master can tell his houseboy (**ọkwa aka ịtọ**), meaning that the price is three thousand naira. Or he can say (**Akwa ezuro ezu**) – that the price the customer is pricing is remaining small to complete, which will help the boy to decide on the price to sell the goods. You can tell him (*were iruro jide akwa ahu*), meaning you should be tactful in measuring the clothes. On the other hand, he can say (**Mere ya aka ịtọ, mere ya aka ịnọ, ma ọbụ mere ya aka ịnọ naọ kara**) – meaning, you should sell to the customer at say – three thousand, four thousand or four thousand five hundred naira, as the case may be. So, these were what we will be discussing without our customers knowing what we are saying. There is one they use when they want to cheat, they call it (ogbu laka), meaning that the customer is a novice, therefore he should add something for him that brought the customer. Or they will say (**Tinyere ya C kwọlity/quality**) – meaning you should add money for him on the amount the customer will buy the goods. But if the customer asked, you will tell him that you want him to give him quality ones; then the customer will feel at home (IDI with a 34 years old *Oga* at Building Materials Market).

Some of these slangs are used by the traders (*Ndị Oga* and *Ụmụ Boyi*) to ascertain the level of the ignorance of the potential customer in order to ascertain if he or she can be cheated or defrauded with recklessness as described by this Key Informant, entrepreneur, and politician whom we interviewed:

…the market that normally has these slangs are markets where there are swindlers; in all the markets where dishonest deals are allowed. Like there was someone I went to the market with. In fact, as the…

somebody from the environment, there was a chemical that they want to mix that will be used to fumigate against rodents. So I went with him to the market where they sell chemicals, and he said "*Ọga I were afọ ewu I wụnye n'afọ nkịta- Ọga put goat intestine into dog intestine*, which one is this..*I werezja afọ nkịta I wụnye n'afọ ewu*" then put the dog intestine into the goat intestine. He then said bring this chemical. We entered the shop and sat down, and he said – that DD force, *Ọga "I were afọ ewu I wịi n'afọ nkịja, I were afọ nkịta ị wịi n'afọ ewu"*. Bring that DD force let me see; he does not know that I am a street man; that the person who came to the market is more experienced than him. He does not know that we are area boys. He does not know that I know what he is doing even more than him. I laughed and called the man and said "*I nwaa anwaa were afọ nkịta wụnye n'afọ ewu, ewu ahụ ya anwụ kwa ebea oo*" if you try it here the goat will die here. The owner of the shop shouted – is this the person you want to cheat? He has passed the message that the owner of the shop should bring out his own cut. The meaning of what he told him to do is this – if a particular product is sold for 1500 and another on for 500, then he is telling him to sell the one of 500 for like 1700 and confuse you that the inferior one is better because they have hiked the price. Then he will say the one of 1500 he should bring 5 cartons and the one of 1700 he should sell 1500. You know that the actual price for the one of 1700 was 500, so if it is sold to us at 1500 too, so he has made 1000 on each of the cartons. That he should look for the one he will put something for him. And the person I came with after this, became frustrated. The slang is used when they want to swindle someone. When they want to dupe, they will start to use slang, and once it is used, they have cheated whom they want to cheat. Do you get me? (In-depth Interview with Key Study Stakeholder, Male, 52 years old in his office)

This key stakeholder further went ahead to disclose another trade slang:

Like when you go to the electronics market, he will say – bring that fan, is it England that was made in China? Do you understand the meaning? I have dealt with you. I can say to him, is it England made in China or is it Indonesia made in China or is it Malaysia that was made in China. And he will say, nooo! He will say this is original China? What this means is that he should give you the inferior ones in the name of the quality ones that you do not know. He has given him the sign language to call me an amateur. He has told him that you don't know anything in the market, that you are a novice. By –is it Malaysia made in China? He has said you look like an experienced person but you don't know anything. That anyone they agree on, you will pay. At this point, they have sold you. Then they will go and get you cold drinks and meat pie to appease your attention. So, this is only done in a market where the dubious character is allowed (In-depth Interview with Key Study Stakeholder, Male, 52 years old in his office).

These dubious trade slangs are prevalent and rampant in the studied Onitsha markets, although most of the traders kept accusing and counter accusing each of the neighbouring markets as guilty, the findings show that there are none of the studied markets that was not accused of perpetrating such vices as stated by this interviewee 'These slangs are not in the Main Market but in Upper-Iweka (*opiweka*) where they sell electronics, the aim of the slangs is to cheat people (IDI with a 56 years old *Oga* in the Main Market). During an FGD session with Ndị *Oga* at the 'Building Materials Market,' a discussant opined 'we don't have that (trade slangs/tricks) in building material section, where you will find such are those that are into electronics'. He further argued that 'there is nothing like ọsọ ohịa here (ọsọ ahọa was not practiced in Building Materials Markets but on the contrary, we observed many people were even inviting the research team to come and buy), but there are people that wanted to start doing it but our President wrote against it.' When further probed with this: 'what if you don't have what a customer is looking for and you go to your neighbour's shop to get the product and add money to the original price, is that not ọsọ ahịa?' The study participants noted that: you can call it 'ọsọ ahịa', but you know somebody that has an address doesn't run after customers/people, your colleague may inform you that he has a particular product in case someone needs it, fortunate to you somebody that needs the product came around and you went to get the goods and topped little money on it, that is not ọsọ afịa' per-say. Otherwise, in a case where you just alighted from a vehicle and somebody just meets you and start asking you what you want and once you tell him, he takes you to the shop of his colleague that will cheat you, that is ọsọ ahịa' and we don't tolerate that in the building materials section, once we catch anyone doing that the person will be handed over to the police.

Another study participant in the Main Market also stressed: 'as far as the main market is concerned; we don't have business slang.' Some other study participants at (Ọgbọ-Abada) Textile Market shifted the blame on the use of dubious trade slangs to swindle customers as exclusively practiced by those he branded as 'Ndị-ọsọ-ahịa' (shopless customer-hunters) as shown here: 'in the line, we have (ndị ọsọ-ahịa), they are people that don't have a shop in the market, but they look out for customers, negotiate the price with them and then go to get the product from the shop of somebody that has the product.' But when probed further to ascertain if *Ndị Ọga* engages in *ọsọ-ahịa*, he entangled himself as practicing what he called indirect *ọso-ahịa* (customers/sales hunting) in the excerpt below:

> yes, they do, the difference is that they stay in their shops. As for me, I'm into sport wears and a customer may need 150 dozens of particular wear and what I have maybe 100 dozen, I may make a call to find out who has that product, that is *ọsọ ahịa* indirectly (46 years old *Ọnye Ọga* at Abada line).

These dubious trade slangs do not reflect the feature of a scheme that is aimed at survival (sustainability thinking is absent) as it is operated on the principle of cheating and fraud and this could be a factor in low patronage thereby contributing to the decline observed. Here, the customer unknowingly is subjected to double jeopardy of buy 'inferior goods and defrauded with hiked prices for inferior substances. This is why lots of people prefer to buy things in closed formal supermarket settings than in the open market such as these Onitsha markets.

Table ii: Summary of Trade Slangs and their Meanings

SN	Slang	Meaning
1	**'is Esau around?'**	**the owner of the business should add his own.**
2	*ọ mere isi eze nwekwe*	Is s/he a stubborn customer.
3	*ọ kwa aka ịtọ*	the price is a thousand naira
4	*akwa ezuro ezu* (the cloth is not complete)	The price is not complete yet (that will help the boy to decide on the price to sell the goods).
5	*were iruro jide akwa ahụ*	you should be tactful in measuring the clothes.
6	*ogbu laka*	the customer is a novice; therefore he should add something for the person that brought the customer (Oso-afia gangster/hunter)
7	*tinyere ya C kwọlity/quality ogbolaka or C quality*	you should add money for him on the amount the customer will buy the goods. But if the customer asked, you will tell him that you want him to give him quality ones; then the customer will feel at home. means the person selling should top extra money on the goods.

8	*eye wey see* (commission)	"Eye wey see" is used to convey information to the owner of the business that you brought the customer and you will come and collect cut from the sales. it means that the person that brought the customer has his own share in the business.
9	Bie ya ebie ma ọ bụ sụa ya asụa	give him the lower quality of higher quality as the case may be.
10	*Ị gotekwe Ị kwụọụgwọ*	
11	*Ị werezịa afọ nkịta ị wụnye n'afọ ewu*	telling him to sell the one of 500 for like 1700 and confuse you that the inferior one is better because they have hiked the price.
12	when you go to the electronics market, he will say – bring that fan, is it England that was made in China? I can say to him, is it England made in China or is it Indonesia made in china or is it Malaysia that was made in China. And he will say, nooo! He will say this is the original china?	The customer should be deceived into receiving a lower quality for a higher one s/he requested and payed for.
13	were ililo jide akwa	which means- measuring the cloth with wisdom.

4.3.9 Contexts for the Usage of Trade/Business Slangs

In the era immediately after independence, many *Ndị Ọga* (masters) noted that the use of trade slangs and tricks was not prevalent as it is today in these Onitsha
Markets and this was attributed to the level of moral decadence in the contemporary world as shown by this retired *Ọga* and elder Statesman cum entrepreneur when he was asked: 'When you people were in active trade, was there any slang you people used that customer don't understand, was it in existence then?

> ...no, the kind of lies and tricks in business now weren't in existence then, and one will tell his *Ụmụ Bọyị* then that their customers have trust in them that is while the business is moving. Let me give you an example, there was one time they gave Udeọjị award around 1975/1976. The army was everywhere. Even if it's teacup you bought from the army and you bring it to the market, you will sell it thrice the price you bought it. There were no articles for sale but there was enough money, then when I was in Lagos. I will just be way-billing/sending stuff down the east. My *Ụmụ Bọyị* have prices they sell but because of the rush, they will top money to the initial price I asked

them to sell. If I come back my customers will come to show me the invoice indicating the price. They sold the goods for them. I will tell my *Ụmụ Bọyị* that the prices were much/high and they will tell me that I shouldn't border myself that they have sold higher for some people than those that came complaining, I will tell them they shouldn't worry. Then money had value, I can refund 1000 naira back to them just to maintain their patronage. So you see once they have trust in you, your business will be moving (78 years Male Key Study Stakeholder, in his home).

These Trade nuances could be classified as **sales slangs,** Dubious/trick trade slangs**, Profit-maximizing slangs, shop/line slangs,** Trade/sales signs' among many others. According to some study participants, it is not everyone that gets involved but many traders use them during transactions with potential customers either *to convince a customer to buy a fake product in exchange for an original or to convince customers to buy more than necessary* based on a false promised value as shown in the contribution below:

to tell you the truth, such exist but it's not everybody that is into it. There are some market lines that have their slangs once a customer comes, they will be relating with such slangs so that the customer won't understand what they are saying. When customers come, both when they want to cheat the customer and when they want to sell well for the customer. These slang users make up to 90% of profit (IDI, 46 years old Male *Ọga*, at Ọchanja Market).

Table 96: Distribution of *Ụmụ Bọyị* by their Responses on Other Benefits of the Apprenticeship Scheme to *Nwa Bọyị*

	Frequency	Percent	Valid Percent	Cumulative Percent
Those who already identified stated options outside 'Others'	1112	92.7	92.7	92.7
And know business secrets	1	.1	.1	92.8
Be useful, how to manage funds	1	.1	.1	92.8
Blessing, learn to be God Fearing	1	.1	.1	92.9
Common sense	1	.1	.1	93.0
Common sense, home training	1	.1	.1	93.1

Common sense, training	1	.1	.1	93.2
Creating relationship	1	.1	.1	93.3
The creation of jobs can turn you into a breadwinner	1	.1	.1	93.3
Daily allowance	1	.1	.1	93.4
Experience	2	.2	.2	93.6
Experience in business and business tricks	1	.1	.1	93.7
Experience... practicals.	1	.1	.1	93.8
Exposure	2	.2	.2	93.9
Exposure to business life	1	.1	.1	94.0
Exposure and experience, an advantage over people that pay to learn,	1	.1	.1	94.1
Exposure to business tricks	1	.1	.1	94.2
Exposure to township	1	.1	.1	94.3
Finance control learns the tricks and secrets of the business, learn that aku by ntutu,	1	.1	.1	94.3
For future purposes	1	.1	.1	94.4
For one's own good and guide your own money	1	.1	.1	94.5
Get perfect experience	1	.1	.1	94.6
Godfatherism	1	.1	.1	94.7
He will be economically	1	.1	.1	94.8
He will be very exposed and learn how to close sales easily	1	.1	.1	94.8
He will make friends with his master's customers. He will know where his master gets his goods from.	1	.1	.1	94.9
Help you to save and start your own business	1	.1	.1	95.0
Helps to learn management skills, Self Control, It help to control anger issues, It helps you not to spend much while running your own business	1	.1	.1	95.1
Helps you to know all bout the business both the tricks	1	.1	.1	95.2
His *Ọga* will also pray for him	1	.1	.1	95.3
Home training	2	.2	.2	95.4
Home training, experience, secrets of trade	1	.1	.1	95.5

Home training, the way of the lord (*Oga* is a pastor), committed...I moderate my eating now, management, I have to come home on time	1	.1	.1	95.6
Home training....have sense	1	.1	.1	95.7
How best to make use of money	1	.1	.1	95.8
How to manage funds	1	.1	.1	95.8
How to spend, get your shop, experience	1	.1	.1	95.9
I do him wayo	1	.1	.1	96.0
I want to be like my master	1	.1	.1	96.1
I will learn how to serve	1	.1	.1	96.2
I will value money, once I start the business I will take it serious	1	.1	.1	96.3
It helps the apprentice to be very successful	1	.1	.1	96.3
It is a learning process and the Boyi learns a lot while living with his *Oga*	1	.1	.1	96.4
It teaches character and also business acumen and secrets and tricks	1	.1	.1	96.5
It's a big school of life, teaches you to be patient, calm, how to spend judiciously	1	.1	.1	96.6
Its a university of business that teaches all about business and also life, they learn how to manage, how to train money	1	.1	.1	96.7
Know places especially where to get goods from	1	.1	.1	96.8
Knowledge	1	.1	.1	96.8
Knowledgeand experience	1	.1	.1	96.9
Knowledgeof Business secrets, how to manage money	1	.1	.1	97.0
Knows how to control money	1	.1	.1	97.1
Learn how to economize	1	.1	.1	97.2
Learning of different strategies in business	1	.1	.1	97.3
Learning the secrets of the trade,	1	.1	.1	97.3

Learning the secrets shows me where to buy goods from at a cheaper rate	1	.1	.1	97.4
Learning to put up with njo ahia	1	.1	.1	97.5
Learns it more than an apprentice...home training, hard work, serving both *Ọga* and madam	1	.1	.1	97.6
Make you become social	1	.1	.1	97.7
Morals in life	1	.1	.1	97.8
No jobs	1	.1	.1	97.8
Nwa Boyi will learn the business and also raise capital to start his own some *Ọga* will even pay shop and house rent for 1 year for the newsboy when he is settled.	1	.1	.1	97.9
One is to know the secret of the business, know customers, etc	1	.1	.1	98.0
Patience and money management	1	.1	.1	98.1
Prepares them for the future,	1	.1	.1	98.2
Rentage of Shop	1	.1	.1	98.3
Secrets, control of funds, spending	1	.1	.1	98.3
Security,clothing ,shelter, advice, home training	1	.1	.1	98.4
Settlement	1	.1	.1	98.5
The benefits are many	1	.1	.1	98.6
The difference is clear...the relationship exists over time, the secrets of the business	1	.1	.1	98.7
The family expense of the boy is reduced from his family's hands.	1	.1	.1	98.8
They become experts in the business	1	.1	.1	98.8
They learn how to manage and control money, you will be more experienced and knowledgeable than your age mates, they learn business tricks	1	.1	.1	98.9
They will know the secrets of the business	1	.1	.1	99.0

Those suggested listed above is for the lazy person, every well-trained *Ụmụ Bọyị* will survive after settlement		1	.1	.1	99.1
To be a better person		1	.1	.1	99.2
To become somebody in future		1	.1	.1	99.3
To become someone in future		1	.1	.1	99.3
To get Wisdom and business contact		1	.1	.1	99.4
Truth in the business, customer relationship		1	.1	.1	99.5
Will be able to take care of my family		1	.1	.1	99.6
You can get shop, training		1	.1	.1	99.7
You get experience about the trade		1	.1	.1	99.8
You learn how to manage money when you start your own		1	.1	.1	99.8
You will learn how to drive a car, You will learn how to manage		1	.1	.1	99.9
You will learn wisdom and management skills		1	.1	.1	100.0
Total		1200	100.0	100.0	

Table 96 showed the distribution of *Ụmụ Bọyị* by their responses on other benefits of the apprenticeship scheme to *Nwa Bọyị*. 92.7% of *Ụmụ Bọyị* had already indicated benefits of the apprenticeship scheme to *Nwa Bọyị*. The other 7.3% chose a potpourri of benefits.

Table 97: Distribution of *Ndị Ọga* by their Responses on Benefits of the Apprenticeship Scheme to *Ndị Ọga*

		Frequency	Percent	Valid Percent	Cumulative Percent
It Renders Help	No	191	15.9	15.9	15.9
	Yes	1010	84.1	84.1	100.0
	Total	1201	100.0	100.0	
Ensures Continuity of the Enterprise/Growth of the Business	No	381	31.7	31.7	31.7
	Yes	820	68.3	68.3	100.0
	Total	1201	100.0	100.0	
Giving Back to the Community	No	1040	86.6	86.6	86.6
	Yes	161	13.4	13.4	100.0

		Total	1201	100.0	100.0	
Satisfaction from Helping a Relation	No		1009	84.0	84.0	84.0
	Yes		192	16.0	16.0	100.0
	Total		1201	100.0	100.0	
No Benefits	No		1193	99.3	99.3	99.3
	Yes		8	.7	.7	100.0
	Total		1201	100.0	100.0	
Others (Please Specify)	No		1116	92.9	92.9	92.9
	Yes		85	7.1	7.1	100.0
	Total		1201	100.0	100.0	
	N Total		2276			

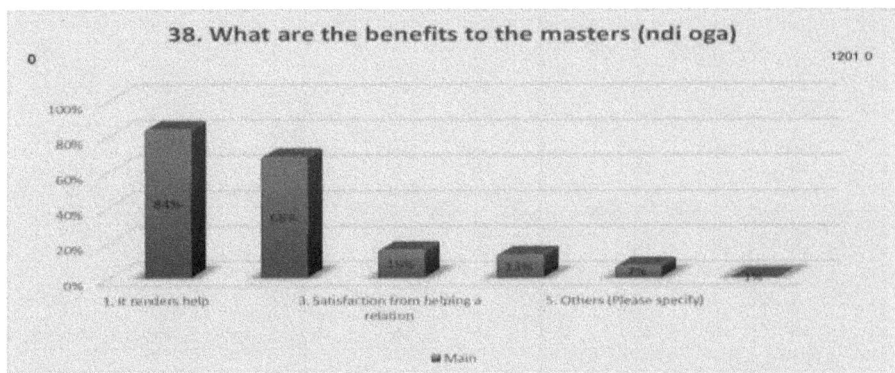

Figure 97: Bar Chart Showing the Distribution of *Ndị Ọga* by their Responses on Benefits of the Apprenticeship Scheme to *Ndị Ọga*

Table 97 and Figure 97 show the distribution of *Ndị Ọga* by their responses on the benefits of the apprenticeship scheme to *Ndị Ọga*. The following benefits were outlined as benefits of the apprenticeship scheme to *Ndi Ọga*. It renders help, ensures continuity of the enterprise/growth of the business, giving back to the community, satisfaction from helping a relation, no benefits, and others. From the analysis on the table and the bar chart, it renders help (84.1%) and ensures continuity of the enterprise/growth of the business (68.3%) stand out to be the main benefits of the apprenticeship scheme to *Ndị Ọga*.

Table 98: Distribution of *Ụmụ Bọyị* by their Responses on Benefits of the Apprenticeship Scheme to *Ndị Ọga*

		Frequency	Percent	Valid Percent	Cumulative Percent
It Renders Help	No	241	20.1	20.1	20.1
	Yes	959	79.9	79.9	100.0
	Total	1200	100.0	100.0	

Ensures Continuity of the Enterprise/Growth of the Business	No	435	36.3	36.3	36.3
	Yes	765	63.7	63.7	100.0
	Total	1200	100.0	100.0	
Giving Back to the Community	No	1084	90.3	90.3	90.3
	Yes	116	9.7	9.7	100.0
	Total	1200	100.0	100.0	
Satisfaction from Helping a Relation	No	1073	89.4	89.4	89.4
	Yes	127	10.6	10.6	100.0
	Total	1200	100.0	100.0	
No Benefits	No	1194	99.5	99.5	99.5
	Yes	6	0.5	0.5	100.0
	Total	1200	100.0	100.0	
Others (Please Specify)	No	1139	94.9	94.9	94.9
	Yes	61	5.1	5.1	100.0
	Total	1200	100.0	100.0	
All of the above	No	1096	91.3	91.3	91.3
	Yes	104	8.7	8.7	100.0
	Total	1200	100.0	100.0	
	N Total	2138			

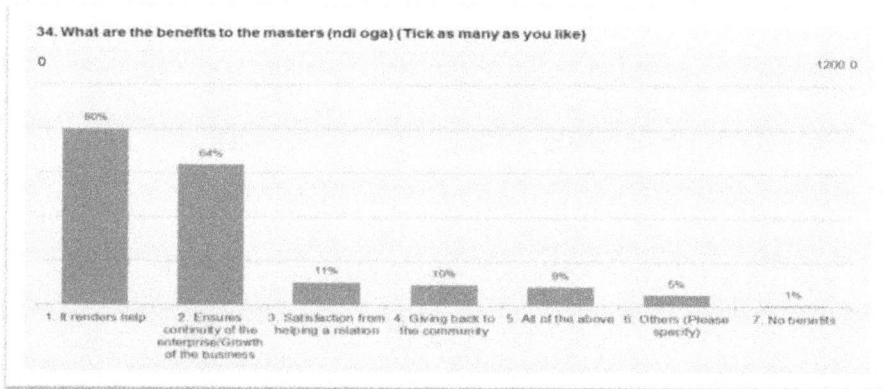

Figure 98: Bar Chart Showing the Distribution of *Ụmụ Bọyị* by their Responses on Benefits of the Apprenticeship Scheme to *Ndị Ọga*

Table 98 and Figure 98 showed the distribution of *Ụmụ Bọyị* by their responses on the benefits of the apprenticeship scheme to *Ndị Ọga*. The following benefits were outlined as benefits of the apprenticeship scheme to *Ndị Ọga*. It renders help, ensures continuity of the enterprise/growth of the business, giving back to the community, satisfaction from helping a relation, no benefits, others, and all of the above. From the analysis on the table and the bar chart, it renders help

(79.9%) and ensures continuity of the enterprise/growth of the business (63.7%) stand out to be the main benefits of the apprenticeship scheme to *Ndị Ọga* from the perspective of *Ụmụ Bọyị*.

Table 99: Distribution of *Ndị Ọga's* Responses on Other Benefits of the Apprenticeship Scheme to *Ndị Ọga*:

	Frequency	Percent	Valid Percent	Cumulative Percent
Those who already chose options apart from 'Others'	1115	92.8	92.8	92.8
Business Growth	26	2.2	2.2	95.0
Get help/assistance from already settled *Umu Boyi*	7	.6	.6	95.6
Helping in domestic chores	33	2.7	2.7	98.3
Personal satisfaction	6	.5	.5	98.8
Societal recognitions, community titles	6	.5	.5	99.3
Stress reduction	8	.7	.7	100.0
Total	1201	100.0	100.0	

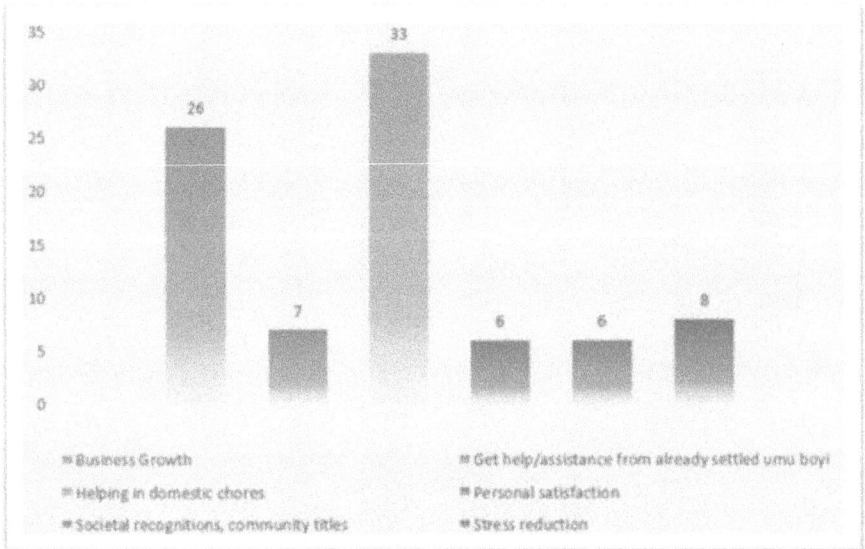

Figure 99: Bar Chart Indicating the Distribution of *Ndị Ọga's* Responses on Other Benefits of the Apprenticeship Scheme to *Ndị Ọga*

Table 99 and Figure 99 show the distribution of *Ndị Ọga's* responses on other benefits of the apprenticeship scheme to *Ndị Ọga*. 92.8% of the respondents already indicated responsesfrom the ones listed earlier. 86 other respondents who chose 'Others' identified 'Business Growth', 'Get help/assistance from already settled *Umu Boyi*', 'Helping in domestic chores', 'Personal satisfaction', 'Societal recognition/community titles' and 'Stress reduction' as other benefits of *Igba Boyi* scheme to *Ndi Oga*.

Table 100: Distribution of *Umu Boyi's* Responses on Other Benefits of the Apprenticeship Scheme to *Ndi Oga*

	Frequency	Percent	Valid Percent	Cumulative Percent
Those who already chose options apart from 'Others'	1139	94.9	94.9	94.9
Able to engage in other business	1	.1	.1	95.0
Affords him time to travel and buy goods	1	.1	.1	95.1
Also acts as sales boy	1	.1	.1	95.2
And look after the shop when *Oga* is not around	1	.1	.1	95.3
Assists both at home and in the market	1	.1	.1	95.3
Attending to a customer, wash the cars, do waybill, stay in the shop in the absence of *Oga*, bathe the children	1	.1	.1	95.4
Been proud that he has trained someone successfully	1	.1	.1	95.5
Being happy to have trained someone successfully	1	.1	.1	95.6
Blessings	1	.1	.1	95.7
Carry of heavy market goods	1	.1	.1	95.8
Carrying heavy cartons, going to the warehouse, looking for customers	1	.1	.1	95.8
Chores,and servitude	1	.1	.1	95.9
Cooking for *Oga*, washing plates and cars and clothes	1	.1	.1	96.0
Domestic chores included	1	.1	.1	96.1
Domestic works	1	.1	.1	96.2
Early-bird, very hardworking, to help her business	1	.1	.1	96.3
Future allies and business associates. Also, the boyi turned *Oga* can also be a helper at some other point in the future	1	.1	.1	96.3

Gives him the chance to travel and do other outside businesses	1	.1	.1	96.4
Gives him time to take care of other businesses	1	.1	.1	96.5
He also acts as sales boy to *Oga*	1	.1	.1	96.6
He can easily expand his business through the help of *Umu Boyi*	1	.1	.1	96.7
He can now go on a vacation freely	1	.1	.1	96.8
He can't be everywhere at the same time. Generally, *Nwa Boyi* renders a lot of help domestically and at the shop	1	.1	.1	96.8
He eases the burden of the business and no matter where the *Oga* is, his business continues	1	.1	.1	96.9
He gets customer from my hand	1	.1	.1	97.0
He has a extra hand	1	.1	.1	97.1
He is his *Oga*'s leg	1	.1	.1	97.2
Help control other businesses	1	.1	.1	97.3
Helps at home	1	.1	.1	97.3
Helps him achieve more gain than he ordinarily wouldn't if he were alone	1	.1	.1	97.4
Home training....	1	.1	.1	97.5
Honour and future allies	1	.1	.1	97.6
I stay in the shop when he travels, make money for him	1	.1	.1	97.7
I wash his car	1	.1	.1	97.8
I wash motor for my *Oga*, do house chores and help this business. I dey learn too	1	.1	.1	97.8
I will raise business contact and more money for him	1	.1	.1	97.9
If things turn around for *Oga*, boys that he settled can rally around and help him up again	1	.1	.1	98.0
It gives pride to the master after settling the apprentices	1	.1	.1	98.1
It reduces the amount of	1	.1	.1	98.2

stress the Oga undergoes			
Looking for customers	1	.1	.1	98.3
Looks after the business when you travelled	1	.1	.1	98.3
Might loan the Oga money when he is settled	1	.1	.1	98.4
More people to attend to customers	1	.1	.1	98.5
Oga also gets the time to travel outside for business and do other things while the boy takes care of the shop.	1	.1	.1	98.6
Other house services	1	.1	.1	98.7
Prestige/ fame	1	.1	.1	98.8
Reduces stress for the Oga	1	.1	.1	98.8
Respect within the boyis community	1	.1	.1	98.9
Running errands	1	.1	.1	99.0
Saves them time and energy	1	.1	.1	99.1
Serve as a sales boy too	1	.1	.1	99.2
Taking care of the children because my Oga is dead	1	.1	.1	99.3
The boyi is the business controller when the Oga isn't around	1	.1	.1	99.3
The master can get help from the boyi that he settles when he needs help	1	.1	.1	99.4
The Oga will always benefit from the Nwa Boyi at anytime	1	.1	.1	99.5
The reward of a good man is in heaven	1	.1	.1	99.6
Traveling	1	.1	.1	99.7
Washing cars	1	.1	.1	99.8
Washing clothes and doing house chores and coming to the shop	1	.1	.1	99.8
When Oga is not around Nwa Boyi control the shop	1	.1	.1	99.9
You can have the time to pursue other things without having to lock your shop	1	.1	.1	100.0
Total	1200	100.0	100.0	

Table 100 shows the distribution of *Ụmụ Bọyị's* responses on other benefits of the apprenticeship scheme to *Ndị Ọga*. 94.9% of the respondents had already indicated benefits other than these ones identified above.

4.3.10 Contributions of Ịgba Bọyị to Society

The interviews revealed that the *Igba Bọyị* scheme has 'lifted people out of poverty, contributed to capacity building, wealth creation, ensuring wealth succession, and sustainability, producing informal professors in trade and business:

i. Lift people out of poverty: Findings under this theme show upward social mobility (*Nkwado Ọgaranya* or apprenticepreneurship) from one social class to another, culminating in a different social status. The *Igba Bọyị* scheme in selected markets, therefore, contributes to lifting people out of poverty as shown in some of these excerpts below: 'my plan is to start up my own business after my apprenticeship and if I raise money, I will train others to help them come out of poverty. People are really passing through difficulties' (23 years old Discussant 4 during the FGD session for *Ụmụ Bọyị* at Bridge Head Market).

ii. Capacity building: the findings also revealed that the *Igba Bọyị* scheme or Igbo Entrepreneurial Incubation Scheme (IEIS) builds people's capacity in trading and business and this is why some young men are still in the scheme even in contemporary times. This scheme creates a 'sense of future hope and anticipated future achiever'. It is this desired future that draws out the mindset of patience, endurance, and hope in a typical Igbo apprentice in these selected Onitsha Markets as shown below: "I think anyone that wants to serve as an apprentice is here to build himself. So, when he is settled, he would not want all his effort to be futile. It is just for us to start building ourselves and plan on how to have our own family and business" (20 years old Discussant 3 during the FGD for *Ụmụ Bọyị* at Bridge Head Market).

Nwa Bọyị will be trained in every aspect of the business. The thing is that when a master recruits a boyi, he and the parents of the boy will agree on the number of years the boy will stay with him. Some parents will pay some amount of money for their child to learn the business for two years and they will be the ones to set up something for their child. Like me, I spent 9 years with my master and I spent 3years in school and served as a *boyi* for 6 years. There are some that spend 7 years or 5 years serving, and it depends on the capacity of the family (58 years old *Ọga*, Ọchanja Market during an IDI, in 2020).

iii. Wealth Creation: one of the major contributions of the *Igba Boyi* scheme is wealth creation as it spreads, distributes, and redistributes wealth from masters to their progeny and apprentices directly and indirectly. One of the key study stakeholders stated: 'I have trained over a million people; yearly I settle 3 to 5 persons.' Another said 'around twelve or thirteen and the people that I trained are over 20 people and all of them are not our people'.

Yes! I said in 1982 that the Pope said that there are things that Africa will teach the western world. That at their place, if your parent is a cleaner all his lineage will all be cleaners, that it is not like that here in Africa, where a rich man will pick a child of the poor and make him rich. I then remembered myself from a very poor background but was picked and made rich. When I came my master was not too rich but I stayed and we worked together and before I left him, he had become an importer.

That is the problem, when you engage a child today that thinks only on what he will gain or eat, there will not be growth in that business (68 years old Manufacturer during a KII in 2020).

iv. Employment Creation: *Igba Boyi* helps in engaging youths who are not in schools and prevents them from loitering and engaging in crimes. Given the fact that an idle mind is the devil's workshop, apprenticeship removes the youth from drudgery, indolence and idleness. Apprenticeship affords *Ụmụ Boyi* the opportunity to become wealth creators.

It also creates jobs for educated people too as shown in some of the comments below:

Like in the 70s and 80s Alor people and Ọraukwu people are known with Hollandaise (*abada*), but now, there is no particular community that is known with a particular trade. Presently, Abakaliki and Enugu people are now dominating the market, because they are the people that are coming now to become dependent-apprentice (*Igba Boyi*). They have dominated every market, many of our children are feeling I am too big for this and that, so, the humble people are now taking over the market. But today, due to the low rate of employment in the country, those that have graduated from the university are now coming back to join the business. In the 80s, when the economy of the country was booming, at that time no one was interested in business. I remember when I traveled abroad for the first time, $1 was equal to 43 kobo, then if you change N10,000 it will give you about $43,000. So, it is only if we can go back and educate our children of the importance of this, that will make it possible (87 years old retired trader during an In-depth Interview in his home in 2020).

The government should create jobs and build industries so that our people can be gainfully employed. There are many traders and entrepreneurs today that employ and are paying up to a thousand people like Dozzy Oil and others. Many people are working for them. So, we want the government to create this job opportunity in Nigeria (IDI with a 58 year old Master in his office).

v. Wealth Succession and Sustainability: *Igba Boyi* is considered as one of the succession plans a trader or entrepreneur can engage in for the sustenance of his wealth as he can fall back to his apprentices who are doing well to help him start-up or build up his capital again if his business fails or collapses. *Igba Boyi* sometimes replaces the roles of amaster's biological children as a social and financial support system and even masters who have no biological children have nothing to fear if they produce high profile apprentices with whom they maintain amicable relationships for years after their settlement or freedom from training. However, many of the Igbo traders harbour a lot of fears for the future as their children are unwilling to ply their trade as shown in the excerpt below:

...So you cannot combine business with leisure, you must separate all of them; so that if you want to go for leisure it will be once in a blue moon. Let your business be your priority, like now when I was building my factory I left Onitsha by 5:00 am before it was 6:00 am. I am already in the factory. I am always number one, I was able to monitor my workers, and I will make sure I am healthy because no successful businessman will survive under ill-health – make sure you take your water, fruits and always exercise your body. Have equipment to check your blood pressure and all that. That is what makes a good businessman. But in our society today at the age of 60, children will be praying for the man to die, and if he dies, what will they do? They don't have that spirit; what I am looking for now is that if I can see a foreigner that can buy me up and give me some percentage, so that if I am no more, the factory can still function, but 95% of Igbo businessmen, once the man is dead the business is gone. This is because there are nosuccession plans, our children have no plan. Look at all the big guys in Anambra state that set up big factories and what have you. They set up all these out of hardship and their children will come up and sell all of them. ...And on the side of the master, he must encourage his *Umu Boyi* to be of good behavior. It is not when your *Nwa Boyi* does something you will start harassing him, you will have to endure some things. Bring him up with the fear of God that he may be richer than you (Key Stakeholder, 68 years old in his office, 2020).

vi. Informal professors in business and trade: the *Igba Boyi* apprenticeship scheme produces informal professors in business and trade. This draws from long years of experiential knowledge and skills in trading impacted into the apprentices by the trade master or trade gurus in the Onitsha Markets as shown in this statement by this entrepreneur cum master:

The master will train the dependent-apprentice in trading that when he must have mastered the trade, he becomes a 'professor' in his business line! So, parents may sometimes have not done what is expected of them, the children will be lacking good morals and when they are engaged in an apprenticeship, if they have good morals but are not educated, they will still help in making the master rich (68 years old male factory owner during an in-depth interview in 2020).

Table 101: Distribution of Responses by *Ndị Ọga* on the Most Common Challenges Encountered by *Ụmụ Bọyị*

	Frequency	Percent	Valid Percent	Cumulative Percent
Accusing *Umu Boyi* falsely and unjustly	55	4.6	4.6	4.6
Breach of apprenticeship agreement	159	13.2	13.2	17.8
Maltreatment by *Ndị Ọga*, nwunye *Ọga*, ụmụ*Ọga*, ụmụnne *Ọga* or older bọyị, others	328	27.3	27.3	45.1
Non-settlement of *Nwa Bọyị* after the agreed years	212	17.7	17.7	62.8
Quest for materialism (Igbu ozu/Ibute ike/Ibute nku)	305	25.4	25.4	88.2
Weakening of traditional kinship ties/belief system	7	.6	.6	88.8
Others (Please specify)	135	11.2	11.2	100.0
Total	1201	100.0	100.0	

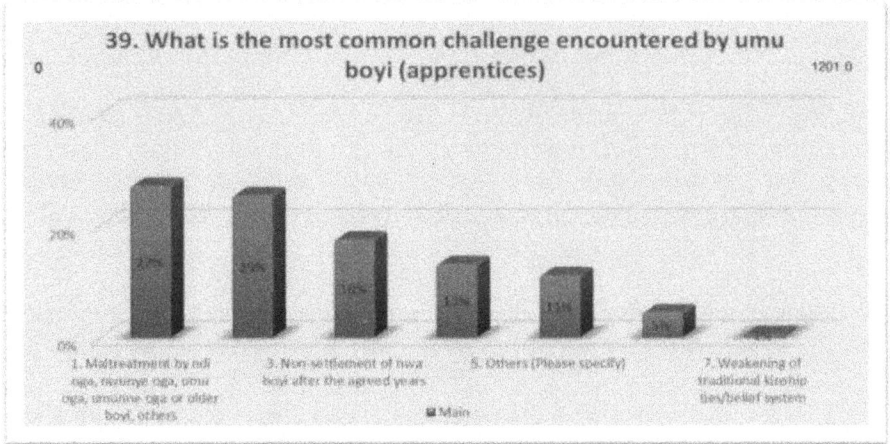

Figure 101: Bar Chart Indicating the Distribution of Responses by *Ndị Ọga* on the Most Common Challenges Encountered by *Ụmụ Bọyị*

Table 101 and Figure 101 showed the distribution of responses by *Ndị Ọga* on the most common challenges encountered by *Ụmụ Bọyị* .4.6% of the respondents indicated 'accusing *Ụmụ Bọyị* falsely and unjustly'. 13.2% of the respondents indicated 'breach of apprenticeship agreement'. 27.3% of the respondents indicated 'maltreatment by *Ndi Ọga*, *nwunye Ọga*, *umụ Ọga*, *umunne Ọga* or older *bọyị*, others'. 17.7% of the respondents 'non-settlement of *Nwa Bọyị* after the agreed years'. 11.2% of the respondents indicated 'other's. 25.4% of the respondents indicated that the 'quest for materialism (*Igbu ozụ/Ibute ike/Ibute nku*)' and 0.6% of the respondents indicated 'weakening of traditional kinship ties/belief system'. The results reveal maltreatment by *Ndị Ọga*, *nwunye Ọga*, *umụ Ọga*, *umụnne Ọga* or older *bọyị*, others and quest for materialism (*Igbu ozụ/Ibute ike/Ibute nku*) as the most common challenges encountered by *umụ bọyị*.

Table 102: Distribution of Responses by *Ụmụ Bọyị* on the Most Common Challenges Encountered by *Ụmụ Bọyị*

	Frequency	Percent	Cumulative Percent
Breach of apprenticeship agreement	265	22.1	22.1
Maltreatment by *Ndi Ọga*, *nwunye Ọga*, *umu Ọga*, *umunne Ọga* or older *boyi*	500	41.7	63.7
Non-settlementof *Nwa Boyi* after the agreed years	177	14.8	78.5
Accusing *Umu Boyi* falsely and unjustly	97	8.1	86.6
Quest for materialism (*Igbu ozu/Ibute ike/Ibute nku*)	61	5.1	91.7
Weakening of traditional kinship ties/belief system	5	.4	92.1
All of the above	52	4.3	96.4
Others (Please specify)	43	3.6	100.0
Total	1200	100.0	

225

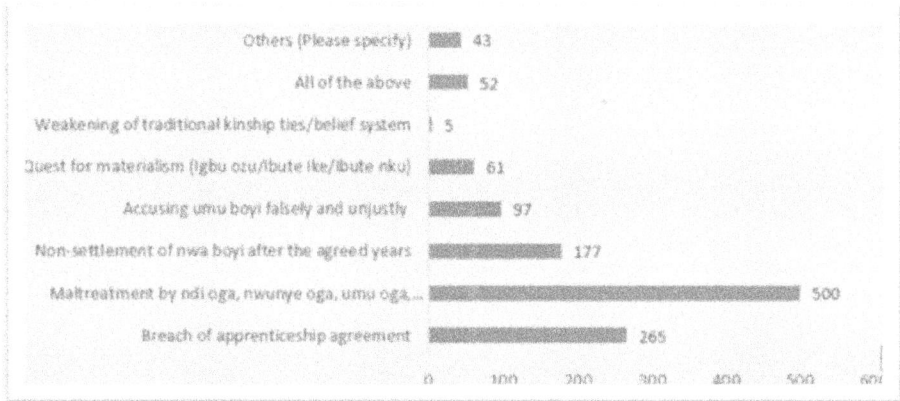

Figure 102: Bar Chart Showing the Distribution of Responses by *Ụmụ Bọyị* on the Most Common Challenges Encountered by *Ụmụ Bọyị*

Table 102 and Figure 102 show the distribution of responses by *Ụmụ Bọyị* on the most common challenges encountered by *Ụmụ Bọyị*. 22.1% of the respondents indicated 'breach of apprenticeship agreement'. 41.7% of the respondents indicated 'maltreatment by *Ndị Ọga, nwunye Ọga, ụmụ Ọga, ụmụnne Ọga* or older *boyi*'. 14.8% of the respondents indicated 'non-settlement of *Nwa Bọyị* after the agreed years'. 8.1% of the respondents indicated 'accusing *Ụmụ Bọyị* falsely and unjustly'. 5.1% of the respondents indicated 'quest for materialism (*Igbu ozu/Ibute ike/Ibute nku*)'. 0.4% of the respondents indicated weakening of traditional 'kinship ties/belief systems'. 4.3% of the respondents indicated 'all of the above' and 3.6% indicated 'others' as the most common challenges encountered by *Ụmụ Bọyị*.

Table 103: Distribution of Responses by *Ndị Ọga* on Other Common Challenges Encountered by *Ụmụ Bọyị*

	Frequency	Percent	Valid Percent	Cumulative Percent
Those who already chose options apart from 'Others'	1065	88.7	88.7	88.7
Adaptation due to change in environment	11	.9	.9	89.6
Alcoholism	2	.2	.2	89.8
Character of *Nwa Boyi*	30	2.5	2.5	92.3
Not well Cater for by *Ọga*	7	.6	.6	92.8
Peer influence	33	2.7	2.7	95.6
Restriction of freedom	8	.7	.7	96.3
Seduction/Sexual harassment by *Ọga*'s wife	17	1.4	1.4	97.7
Stealing	28	2.3	2.3	100.0
Total	1201	100.0	100.0	

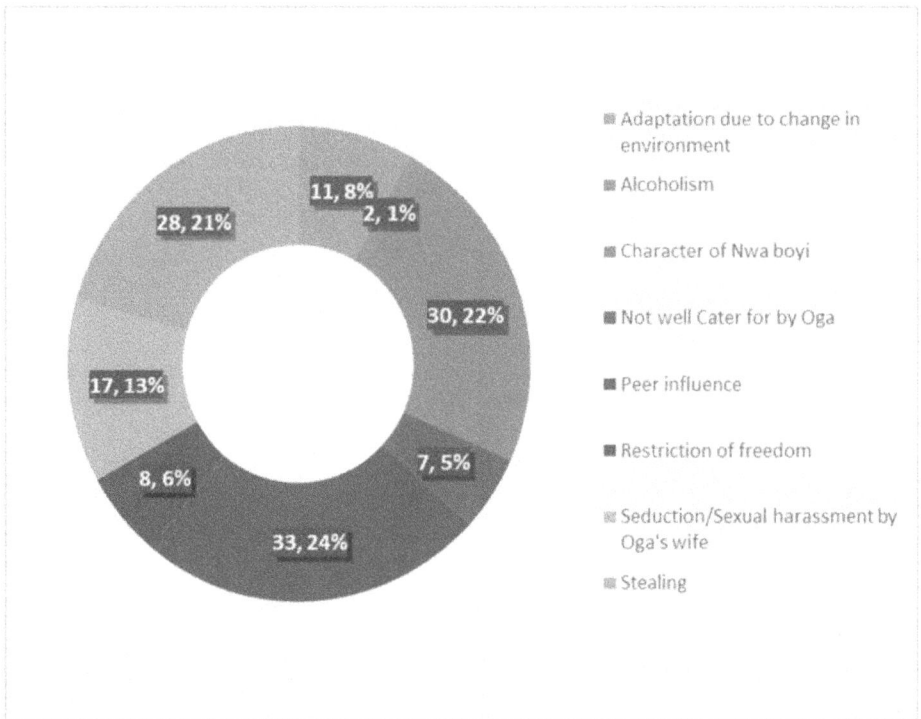

Figure 103: Pie Chart Showing the Distribution of Responses by Ndị Ọga on Other Common Challenges Encountered by Ụmụ Bọyị

Table 103 and Figure 103 show the distribution of responses by Ndị Ọga on other common challenges encountered by Ụmụ Bọyị .88.7% of the respondents indicated other options other than the ones listed on Table 103 and Figure 103 as other common challenges encountered by Ụmụ Bọyị, while 11.3% chose other common challenges as indicated in the table.

Table 104: Distribution of Responses by Ụmụ Bọyị on Other Common Challenges Encountered by Ụmụ Bọyị

	Frequency	Percent	Valid Percent	Cumulative Percent
Those who already chose options apart from 'Others'	1115	92.9	92.9	92.9
Lack of Freedom	1	.1	.1	93.0

After the whole stress in the shop, one has to go home and continue with Domestic works	1	.1	.1	93.1
Alcohol and women	1	.1	.1	93.2
Always pray to good to avoid temptations	1	.1	.1	93.3
Always shouting, always interested in what I do	1	.1	.1	93.3
Any shortage in the business, you will pay it yourself	1	.1	.1	93.4
Bad and terrible treatment from the family	1	.1	.1	93.5
Bad friends	5	.4	.4	93.9
Bad friends,	1	.1	.1	94.0
Bad friends, women, clubbing	1	.1	.1	94.1
Being greedy, stealing	1	.1	.1	94.2
Breach of contract (Patience and malicious acts)	1	.1	.1	94.3
Challengesare based on the personality of *Oga* and capacity of *Oga*	1	.1	.1	94.3
Challengesare much but it takes endurance	1	.1	.1	94.4
Chasing girls, stubbornness	1	.1	.1	94.5
Deprivation of certain rights	1	.1	.1	94.6
Disobedience	1	.1	.1	94.7
Disobedience of the *Nwa Boyi*, Misunderstanding	1	.1	.1	94.8
Doing all sorts of things...	1	.1	.1	94.8
Flexing	1	.1	.1	94.9
Following women, spending on drinks	1	.1	.1	95.0
Freedom	1	.1	.1	95.1
Friends	1	.1	.1	95.2
Generally, it's fear of the unknown	1	.1	.1	95.3
Harassment	1	.1	.1	95.3
High demands	1	.1	.1	95.4
Humiliation	1	.1	.1	95.5
I don't think there's any challenge, they will treat you the way you behave	1	.1	.1	95.6
I'm still new, i don't know	1	.1	.1	95.7

If you try to avoid problems *Oga*'s wife ....they will be no challenges	1	.1	.1	95.8
Insultive, you must obey them whether right or wrong, no freedom, no food when you do wrong	1	.1	.1	95.8
Lack of capital to start	1	.1	.1	95.9
Lack of freedom	2	.2	.2	96.1
Lack of freedom and insults	1	.1	.1	96.2
Lack of freedom and self will	1	.1	.1	96.3
Lack of freedom to date,have phone, come late	1	.1	.1	96.3
Lack of freedom, u can end up in jail	1	.1	.1	96.4
Lack of owners capital in terms of the business	1	.1	.1	96.5
Lack of patience	1	.1	.1	96.6
Limited freedom	1	.1	.1	96.7
Low self-esteem due to lack of Educationcompared to *Oga*'s children	1	.1	.1	96.8
Malnutrition	1	.1	.1	96.8
Misunderstanding	1	.1	.1	96.9
Moneyissues	1	.1	.1	97.0
most of the challenges are from *Umu Boyi*	1	.1	.1	97.1
Naughtiness	1	.1	.1	97.2
No care, spirit of oneness, and others	1	.1	.1	97.3
No challenges	1	.1	.1	97.3
No freedom	2	.2	.2	97.5
No freedom and can't have a personal life	1	.1	.1	97.6
No freedom of life	1	.1	.1	97.7
None as every wrong doing against you will pass away	1	.1	.1	97.8
Not around to mingle with our customers, not allowed to make use of phone	1	.1	.1	97.8
Not praising you when you did the right thing, maltreatment from madam, not making use of phone	1	.1	.1	97.9
Oga's daughter, and theft	1	.1	.1	98.0
One can never please an	1	.1	.1	98.1

Ọga

Our people want to make quick money. Nobody wants to work hard anymore	1	.1	.1	98.2
Over expectation	1	.1	.1	98.3
Over expectation in sales and always demanding	1	.1	.1	98.3
Peer pressure	1	.1	.1	98.4
Promiscuous	1	.1	.1	98.5
Sleeping with madam	1	.1	.1	98.6
Some *Ọga* is harsh, very strict	1	.1	.1	98.7
Some *Ọga* use their *Umu Boyi* for money rituals	1	.1	.1	98.8
Sometimes excessive restrictions by the *Ọga*. No freedom	1	.1	.1	98.8
Sometimes...the fault normally come from *Ụmụ Bọyị*	1	.1	.1	98.9
Stealingfrom *Ọga*	1	.1	.1	99.0
Stealingfrom *Ọga*, suffering	1	.1	.1	99.1
Stealing,	1	.1	.1	99.2
Stealing, charms	1	.1	.1	99.3
That some masters don't like writing agreement	1	.1	.1	99.3
The work is too hard and strenuous	1	.1	.1	99.4
U might die in the process	1	.1	.1	99.5
We don't make use of phone	1	.1	.1	99.6
When *Ọga* doesnt trust the boy that's when challenges come in and vice versa	1	.1	.1	99.7
Women	2	.2	.2	99.8
Women and phone	1	.1	.1	99.9
Women, or parents pressure	1	.1	.1	100.0
Total	1200	100.0	100.0	

Table 104 shows the distribution of responses by *Ụmụ Bọyị* on other common challenges encountered by *Ụmụ Bọyị*. 7.1% chose a potpourri of options as Table 104 shows.

4.3.11 Challenges of the Igbo Apprenticeship Culture

Emerging themes from the interview data collected revolve around the *decline and contemporary challenges of the Igba Boyi apprenticeship scheme* in studied Onitsha Markets and they include: Many believe that the *Igba Boyi* scheme is its current status because 'early Igbo entrepreneurs were not educated and as such do not possess the required prerequisites to cope with the challenges of trading in the contemporary world. Others are the desire to steal, meet up, and loot among apprentices (*Umu Boyi*). There are also a whole lot of settlement issues, distractions from modern gadgets and social media, divulging trade secrets due to the failure to use Igbo by some apprentices and masters including their wives and children, failure by parents to identify ward's areas of strengths early while they are growing up so as to ascertain if they are better fit for *Igba Boyi* or schooling, preference to serve the rich and not the poor *Oga* by apprentices, Unwilling and un-submissive apprentices, the introduction of formality to a trading culture run via shift to sales girls, informality, Little or no orientation for youths in the market, sale of inferior and expired goods, tricycle role in the decline, poor moral upbringing by parents, perception as suffering and descension to a lower level after education, people gaining formal educational & knowledge, the role of *Oso ahia* and fraudulent folks, bad and wicked masters among many others.

4.3.12 Specific Issues with the Current Way/Pattern the "Igba Boyi" (Apprenticeship) System is Structured

The emergent themes from the study on contemporary factors influencing the *Igba Boyi* scheme are but are not limited to: the shift from the engagement of non-Anambrarians to other Igbo people even non-Igbo people are currently being engaged in the scheme and many are of the opinion that this is the key issue resulting to the decline as the younger Anambrarians no longer want to be associated with *Igba Boyi*. Since they consider it as demeaning and descending to a lower level. Other factors are the advent of sales girls which comes with a lot of hazards on the masters as they run down the business when they loot money and send to their boyfriends and family members, some seduce or are seduced by *Ndi Oga* and they get pregnant and are forced to marry the *Oga*, unplanned polygamy and final collapse of the business or trade.

It will be very difficult to bring back the *Igba Boyi* scheme to its original status, even the Abakiliki people have started misbehaving and people started going for sales girls and those sales girls started stealing their master's money and are giving it to their boy friends in the market, there was a case of a young lady that was caught stealing and when she was taken to the police and she received serious torture she now mentioned the boy she was giving the money and that the boy promised to marry her, so the problem is everywhere both with boys and girls, and many a times it is the masters people will starting pointing accusing fingers on (IDI with a male 46 years old *Oga* at Main Market).

> … a serious-minded sales girl will always further her education while she is with the master. She may be impregnated in the process of serving as an apprentice. Sometimes when we see a girl that we like, we may be tempted to marry a second wife. But if you are a man that was trained as an apprentice, you will be told not to be involved in such immorality that it will not help you. You will be told not to engage in marrying two wives, for this will ruin you. But the children of this generation will be carried away with greed, and flashy things of the world. A lot of them that tried to marry two, have failed in this business (IDI with male 67 years old *Oga* at building Materials Market).

Other factors responsible for the observed decline in interest for apprenticeship are: formal education, corrupt family influence on *Nwa Boyi*, unfaithful *Nwa Boyi*, poor moral upbringing by parents, uncommitted *Nwa Boyi*, market union influence, troublesome community influence on *Nwa Boyi*, government and wider economic influences.

4.3.13 Changes and Transformations in the Igba Boyi System

A lot of changes have been observed both in the structure, practice and management of the *Igba Boyi* system. One is prompted to probe the nature of these changes and issues in the practice of apprenticeship in Igboland particularly in the selected Onitsha Markets studied. Some of the prevailing noticeable changes in the practice of the *Igba Boyi* scheme are the unrelenting increasing switch from the engagement of relatives to *non-relatives as apprentices, the advent of sales girls, recruitment of paid staff instead of engaging apprentices, skyrocketing levels of dishonest and greedy apprentices with 'get-rich syndrome', use or employment of the master's wives as staff instead of Nwa Boyi. Others are court cases and counter court cases with kin-related apprentices who want to take over the Oga's (master's) business especially at his demise thereby leaving the widow and children (heirs) empty without inheritance from their father's business; advent of corrupt sales girls, store-keepers, record-keepers and accounting staff mutilate and doctor* figures *to cover their misappropriations and thefts, among many others. Again, a remarkable change is that many apprentices (boyi) do not understand that Igba*

*Boyi is like a **relay race and progenetics** as shown in this excerpt from study participant 8 during a focus group discussion (FGD):*

> what changed is that people do not understand that this is like relay-race – handing over relay stick to the next person. Why we engage these children is for them to take care of us at old-age or in a time we have a slow down in business. It is the children you trained that will come to your aid in these instances.

The magnitude of intractable problems associated with recruiting one's relatives as apprentices are sometimes cantankerous ranging from broken family relations, rancor, bickering, confrontations, infractions of agreements, accusations and counter accusations, court cases and counter cases, acid attacks, exchange of diabolic effects on each other which may result to protracted illnesses; assassinations, to outright fights and murder between family members. The major issue driving these changes is dishonesty, theft, misappropriation of funds which often lead to the collapse of the business if the master is not careful and tactful as shown in the interview excerpts below:

> What the children of this generation want is to be a master without serving. They want it sharp-sharp. That is what has changed. None of them is ready to serve; instead, they want to be the master and that has caused a lot of damage. There is an Igbo adage that says – (Onye fee eze, eze *eruo ya*)- when you serve, you will be served. But this generation does not want it. The level of moral degradation has made it that if you engage a dependent-apprentice today, when he sees the way the master is living, the type of food he eats; he will be thinking that his master started eating that type of food from the on-set. Then they start living like their master, which will affect the capital negatively. When he is accosted, he will say I don't know what has happened; but the type of food he eats everyday – say 2 times every day at N500.00 in a day it is N1000.00 added to your transport and other expenses, at the end of the month will amount to a huge sum, but he will be claiming there has never been a time he misused his master's money. Some will even deep hands into the money bag. I have met many of them inside the public transport where they will be spending so much money, eating laps of chicken, yoghurt, and all sorts of things in the bus, but he ate morning and afternoon food (Male, 55 years, In-depth Interview Participant in 2020).

...not because things have changed now, a man will take his bag off for business and the wife will also move for a business too. Owing to the hardship we are facing in the country; women have joined in the pursuit of money to enable the family to make ends meet (Male, 47 years old, IDI Study Participant in 2020). To me the issue is **the quest to be a master (*Ọga*)** without deep or complete training that is what the children of this generation desire. The children of today do not want to have the patience to serve.

That has been a problem with the continuity of the '*Igba Boyi*' scheme. Because they want to get rich overnight, they tend to be tampering with their masters' business funds, and that has made so many masters not to believe in engaging *Umu Boyi* any longer. Secondly, this time around, because of what is happening between *Ndi Ọga* and *Umu Boyi*, so many Anambra boys dislike taking up *Igba Bọyi*, instead, Enugu and Ebonyi people are gradually taking over the *Igba Bọyi*. Before now, if you engage an Enugu boy, he will serve you very well, but now they are tilting towards Anambra style. When they start mingling with bad friends, they will start looting their master's funds, squandering it with their friends; sometimes some of them do have love affairs with their master's wife. So, this has made so many masters lose interest in engaging *Nwa Bọyi*, like me I have not engaged any for the past 8 years. If I engage *Nwa Bọyi*, I always open a separate shop to be able to know what he will make within the next 4 years. It is from what he made that will be used to settle the *boyi*. He will prefer not to be coming closer to the master for you not to know what he is doing. So, such *Nwa Bọyi* will not like to continue because if the shop is going down, he knows that his settlement will not be sure, because he may have messed up the funds that would be used to start business for him (Male key informant during an in-depth interview in 2020).

You know things have changed to the extent that children who could b serving as apprentices now are on the street doing nothing. You will also find out that the internet has made it possible for them to know all forms of criminal acts and how to carry them out. So to engage this *Nwa Bọyi* now is becoming difficult on a daily basis. The only thing that will be needed to do, is to continue to encourage these children to be disciplined. If they are wise enough, they will see that their master served someone and his master's master served someone also, which means, that one day you will also be master to someone. But this is difficult for them, rather they will prefer to be master without serving. Children nowadays should be made to develop enduring spirit, no matter the number of years they have to serve, the can still become masters if they become patient enough (KII with a 52 years old master, in 2020).

The advent of Plazas and Street market: Several factors including impatience and dishonesty among apprentices led to the advent of Street market particularly in the Main Market as captured by this key informant:

> ...People having shops in the streets. There are a lot of factors that led to that. Selling in front of the shops on the road, there factors that led to that: One of the factors is that the main market was becoming too congested. All the parks in the main market were filled up with shops, and no more ventilation people started moving out. Secondly, there were bad eggs amongst Ụmụ Bọyị. Greed came in; Nwa Bọyị now,

> instead of humbling himself to complete his training, he will now look for an avenue to be richer than his master overnight. We used to engage our relations for *Igba Bọyị* and in – laws too. It was very easy for us, but later, these relations are no longer controllable because of over familiarity, we now changed to neighboring states. They came and formed an association of non-indigenes. Then the *Nwa Boyi* that is now coming from Abakaliki or Enugu sees it as if he is traveling overseas. So he is just coming to reap from you. He would like to make it overnight! So, he will be looking for a way to take away your money (In-depth Interview with Key Stakeholder, Male, 58 years old at Ọchanja Market).

***Igba Bọyị* as pro-genetics or a process of replicating the master:** Inability to understand apprenticeship as pro-genetics or an effort in producing your kind as a master in trade by the apprentices (*Ụmụ Bọyị*). As pro-genetics- it is where the apprentices after undergoing some rigorous years of training are produced by the masters as offspring. This was captured by excerpts below from this key study stakeholder:

> The concept of dependent/residential apprentice (*Igba Bọyị*) is what is called in **Biology as 'pro-genetics' that is to produce your kind.** So you train him to be like you, you tell him every secret in the business, you give him your key to your warehouse. He will be selling and going to the bank. Even when you are not in town no matter how much sales he makes, he is the one that will go to the bank and pay in. That was how stealing started. Assuming he sold goods worth 40 million. He will pay into the master's account 20 million naira into his master's account and pay the other 20 million into his own. The funny part is that you will still be seeing him with his normal shirts and trousers without knowing he has up to 50 million in his account. You know he is not

from here, so he believes – if he stole your money he will go back to his village. So this corruption came in as we started bringing *Umu Boyi* from other areas. Initially, where you will get good *Umu Boyi* were communities like Anam, Qmambala, Otuọcha, Agụleri, Ụmụleri, Qmọ,

Igbaakwu, Qmasị, Innọma and Nzam. When they come, their interest will be to see food and eat, they are very honest. The best *Umu Boyi* that served my father were Chuma and Joseph from Anam. That is where we normally get good *Umu Boyi*, until at a point we stopped getting. We now started engaging from Ebonyi, Nsụkka, Nkanụ and that was the end of discussion (Interview with Key Stakeholder, Male, 49 years, Main Market).

Absence of respect in the Onitsha Markets: Many of the study participants who are *Ndị Qga*, stressed the loss of values and morals by *umu boyi* as a trend which heightened in recent years as shown in the comment below: "what has changed is that, the children of this generation want to make it by all means and when it is made dishonestly, it will disappear because he they will not manage it well. They don't understand the fundamentals and at the end there will not be respect in the market". This, according to him, is caused by insatiable pursuit for money as shown here:

What has caused this is as a result of too much pursuit for money, greed and disrespect. We that were the older generation will not be tactful on who to engage or may recruit people that you will be paying salary monthly because of the fear of the changes that are taking place in *Igba Boyi*." (Male 56 during an In-depth Interview in 2020). Another key informant observed that "Children in this dispensation don't want to serve anybody, those that agree to serve will involve themselves in pilfering and stealing their *Qga*'s money (Male, 68 years, Key Study Stakeholder in factory during an in-depth interview, 2020).

One other respondent observed:

...then it was like our culture because we are known to be respectful and you will hardly see a child that will disrespect his or her parents. It was known then that if one stays with his parents, he may not be able to learn what he is supposed to learn. But as time goes on things begin to change and other things followed suit. What encourages *Igba Boyi* then was that "he that serves others will be served". Most of the people that are doing well now served under somebody, they didn't wake up one morning and became rich. Like me I served somebody and there are people that are serving under me now (In-depth Interview with an *Ọga*, 45 years in 2020).

Advent of evil masters and the distrust between Masters and Apprentices:
Many masters fail to settle their apprentices who have graduated and leave them without capital as Journeymen as described in detail by this key study participant below:

...Look at the problem, it is simple – immorality in our society is so much! When you take someone as *Nwa Boyi*; when he comes in, he will be stealing your money and handing it over to his family and some will give to their girlfriends to keep for them, while some give to their friends and once the master discovers, the *Igba Bọyi* will end. Because they were not honest to their master. Some of them will even carry your money and run to South Africa and with such money the person cannot prosper.

So, that is the reason why there is no trust between the master and his *Nwa Bọyi*. So, that is the problem we have now – dishonesty. *Ụmụ Bọyi* that are expected to be honest are not, then the master, as well, will not give them a second chance to manage them further. He may decide to change them. So, they don't have a second chance to steal again. *Umu Boyi* must endeavor to be honest, they should not steal their master's money. Some parents used to put pressure on them, to steal money from their masters, and eventually 90% of them will be discovered and it becomes a problem. For instance, you can now see some masters operating warehouses, they don't let the servant have the key to the warehouse; because if yhey give the key to the warehouse to them, imagine what will happen to the goods in the warehouses. There was one that happened in my village last month, over 10 million naira. The *Nwa Bọyi* bought a tipper. He gave one lady money, and this 10 million naira, at the end of the day it was difficult to recover up to 1 million. And this is peculiar to *Ụmụ Bọyi* from Anambra state because they are mixing up with people that are above their levels. *Ụmụ Bọyi* do not go clubbing because if their masters discover that they are gone. There was one that happened – *Nwa Boyi* that had 10 girls' phone numbers in his phone. I now asked him how he intended to survive by having 10 different girls' phone numbers. I pleaded with the master and he took him back after he was sent away. It was later discovered that he raped the daughter of their landlord. I still pleaded with the master to settle him. The father sold his land and gave him ₦300,000 to start a business.

One day the guy came back and I noticed that he was smoking what they call grass. I called him and asked him why he sold his father's other land. Three days ago he sold that land for ₦7 million and after selling the land they took him to Benin. What I am telling you is what happened the day before yesterday. He now smokes cocaine, that is the one they call grass. You know when someone is smoking, he will not be in his right mind and he will not have a secret again. So, that is the reason why *Nwa Boyi* should not be engaged in clubbing until he graduates or his master settles him. He can now stand on his feet. If he sees someone to marry or a girlfriend, he should not allow her to disturb him in business. Some of these guys that are doing well can even abandon their girlfriends in a hotel and go for their business.

Table 105: Distribution of Responses by *Ndị Oga* on whether Workshops/Seminars are Organized for *Umu Boyi* by Government Agencies

	Frequency	Percent	Valid Percent	Cumulative Percent
Always	2	.2	.2	.2
Don't know	141	11.7	11.7	11.9
Never	897	74.7	74.7	86.6
Rarely	71	5.9	5.9	92.5
Sometimes	90	7.5	7.5	100.0
Total	1201	100.0	100.0	

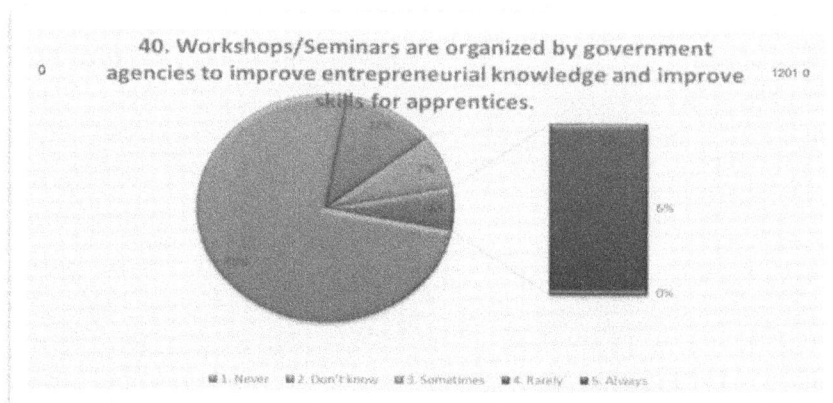

Figure 105: Pie Chart Depicting the Distribution of Responses by *Ndị Oga* on whether Workshops/Seminars are Organized for *Nwa Boyi* by Government Agencies

Table 105 and Figure 105 showed the distribution of responses by *Ndị Ọga* on whether workshops/seminars are organized for *Ụmụ Bọyị* by government agencies. 0.2% of the respondents indicated that 'workshops/seminars are organized for *Ụmụ Bọyị* by government agencies'. 11.7% of the respondents indicated that they 'Do not know whether workshops/seminars are organized for *Ụmụ Bọyị* by government agencies'. 74.7% of the respondents indicated that workshops/seminars are 'Never organized for *Ụmụ Bọyị* by government agencies'. 5.9% of the respondents indicated that workshops/seminars are Rarely organized for *Ụmụ Bọyị* by government agencies'. 7.5% of the respondents indicated that workshops/seminars are 'Sometimes organized for *Ụmụ Bọyị* by government agencies'.

Table 106: Distribution of Responses by *Ụmụ Bọyị* on whether Workshops/Seminars are Organized for *Ụmụ Bọyị* by Government Agencies

	Frequency	Percent	Valid Percent	Cumulative Percent
Always	15	1.3	1.3	1.3
Don't know	243	20.3	20.3	21.5
Never	800	66.7	66.7	88.2
Rarely	61	5.1	5.1	93.3
Sometimes	81	6.8	6.8	100.0
Total	1200	100.0	100.0	

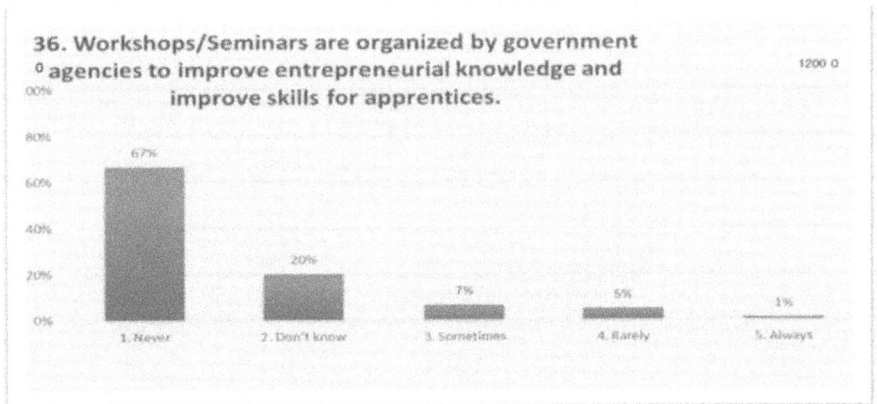

Figure 106: Bar Chart showing the Distribution of Responses by *Ụmụ Bọyị* on whether Workshops/Seminars are Organized for *Ụmụ Bọyị* by Government Agencies.

Table 106 and Figure 106 showed the distribution of responses by *Ụmụ Bọyị* on whether workshops/seminars are organized for *Ụmụ Bọyị* by government agencies. 1.3% of the respondents indicated that workshops/seminars are organized for *Ụmụ Bọyị* by government agencies. 20.3% of the respondents indicated they don't know whether workshops/seminars are organized for *Ụmụ Bọyị* by government agencies. 66.7% of the respondents indicated workshops/seminars are never organized for *Ụmụ Bọyị* by government agencies. 5.1% of the respondents indicated workshops/seminars are rarely organized for *Ụmụ Bọyị* by government agencies. 6.8% of the respondents indicated workshops/seminars are Sometimes organized for *Ụmụ Bọyị* by government agencies.

Table 107: Distribution of Responses by *Ndị Ọga* on Institutional Strategies that can best enhance Entrepreneurship and Apprenticeship among Igbo Traders

	Frequency	Percent	Valid Percent	Cumulative Percent
Adult education strategy	208	17.3	17.3	17.3
Formation of *Isusu* and cooperatives	258	21.5	21.5	38.8
Others (Please specify	145	12.1	12.1	50.9
Seminarsand workshops	235	19.6	19.6	70.4
Tax waivers	355	29.6	29.6	100.0
Total	1201	100.0	100.0	

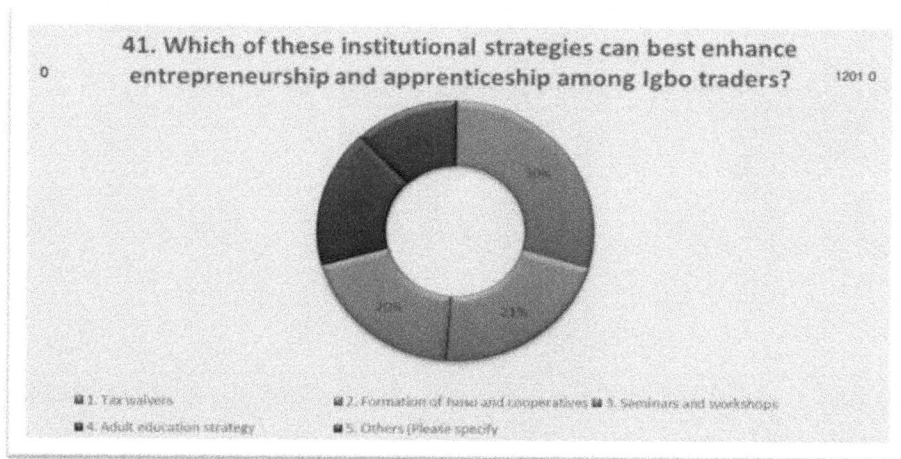

41. Which of these institutional strategies can best enhance entrepreneurship and apprenticeship among Igbo traders?

- 1. Tax waivers
- 2. Formation of Isusu and cooperatives
- 3. Seminars and workshops
- 4. Adult education strategy
- 5. Others (Please specify

Figure 107: Pie Chart Showing the Distribution of Responses by *Ndị Ọga* on

Institutional Strategies that can best enhance Entrepreneurship and Apprenticeship among Igbo Traders.

Table 107 and Figure 107 showed the distribution of responses by *Ndị Ọga* on institutional strategies that can best enhance entrepreneurship and apprenticeship among Igbo traders. 17.3% indicated that 'adult education strategy is an institutional strategy that can best enhance entrepreneurship and apprenticeship among Igbo traders'. 21.5% indicated 'formation of *isusu* and cooperatives'; 12.1% selected 'Others'. 19.6% chose seminars and workshops, while 29.6% indicated that 'tax waiver' is the best institutional strategy that can best enhance entrepreneurship and apprenticeship among Igbo traders. It is evident that *Ndị Ọga* are looking up to the government to create the enabling business landscape like a favourable environment to help in growing their businesses.

Table 108: Distribution of Responses by *Ụmụ Bọyị* on Institutional Strategies that can best enhance Entrepreneurship and Apprenticeship among Igbo Traders

	Frequency	Percent	Valid Percent	Cumulative Percent
Adult education strategy	258	21.5	21.5	21.5
Formation of Isusu and cooperatives	315	26.3	26.3	47.8
Others (Please specify)	95	7.9	7.9	55.7
Seminarsand workshops	263	21.9	21.9	77.6
Tax waivers	269	22.4	22.4	100.0
Total	1200	100.0	100.0	

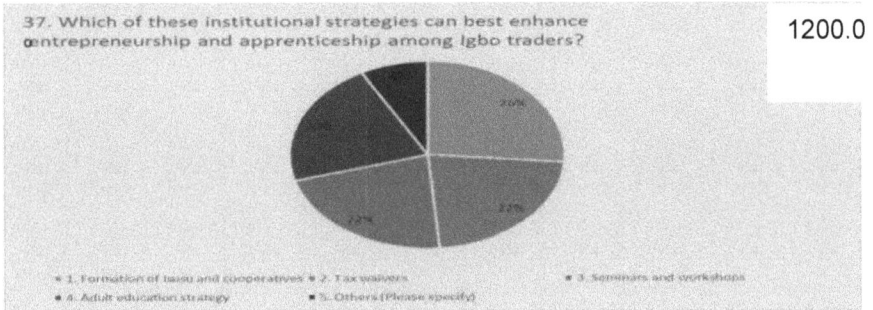

Figure 108: Distribution of Responses by *Ụmụ Bọyị* on Institutional Strategies that can best enhance Entrepreneurship and Apprenticeship among Igbo Traders.

Table 108 and Figure 108 show the distribution of responses by *Ụmụ Boyi* on institutional strategies that can best enhance entrepreneurship and apprenticeship among Igbo traders. 21.5% indicated that 'adult education strategy' is the institutional strategy that can best enhance entrepreneurship and apprenticeship among Igbo traders; 26.3% selected 'formation of *isusu* and cooperatives'. 21.9% identified 'seminars and workshops'. 22.4% chose 'tax waivers' as the institutional strategy that can best enhance entrepreneurship and apprenticeship among Igbo traders, while 7.9% chose 'Others' outside the listed options aforestated.

Table 109: Distribution of Responses by *Ndị Ọga* on Other Institutional Strategies that can best enhance Entrepreneurship and Apprenticeship among Igbo Traders

	Frequency	Percent	Valid Percent	Cumulative Percent
Other options except (If Others, please specify)	1056	87.9	87.9	87.9
Free trade zone	34	2.8	2.8	90.8
Infrastructures (good roads, electricity, seaport, airport)	63	5.2	5.2	96.0
Interest free loan	38	3.2	3.2	99.2
Stable exchange rate and economy	10	.8	.8	100.0
Total	1201	100.0	100.0	

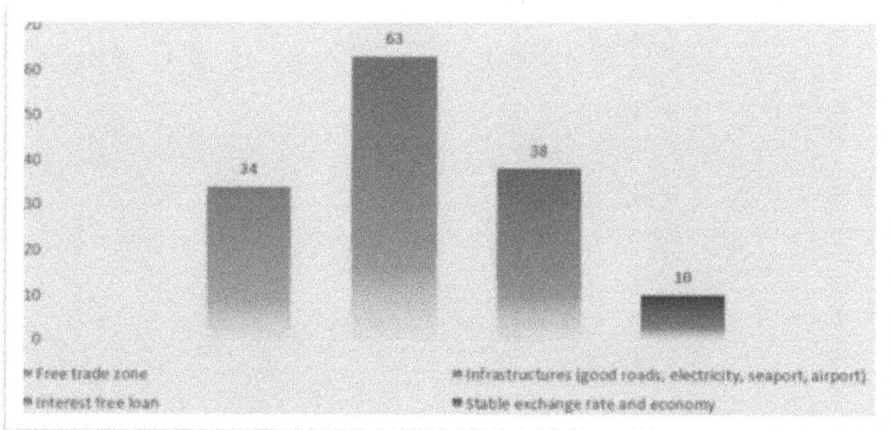

Figure 109: Bar Chart Showing the Distribution of Responses by *Ndị Ọga* on Other Institutional Strategies that can best enhance Entrepreneurship and Apprenticeship among Igbo Traders.

Table 109 and Figure 109 show the distribution of responses by *Ndị Ọga* on other institutional strategies that can best enhance entrepreneurship and apprenticeship among Igbo traders. 87.9% of the respondents indicated 'other options apart from the ones listed on Table'. 109. 2.8% of the respondents indicated 'free trade zone' as the institutional strategy that can best enhance entrepreneurship and apprenticeship among Igbo traders. 5.2% of the respondents indicated 'infrastructure (good roads, electricity, seaport, airport)'. 3.2% of the respondents selected 'interest free loan', while 0.8% of the respondents indicated 'stable exchange rate and economy'.

Table 110: Distribution of Responses by *Ụmụ Bọyị* on Other Institutional Strategies that can best enhance Entrepreneurship and Apprenticeship among Igbo Traders

	Frequency	Percent	Valid Percent	Cumulative Percent
Other options except (If Others, please specify)	1105	92.1	92.1	92.1
Free trade zone	39	3.3	3.3	95.3
Infrastructure (good roads, electricity, seaport, airport)	19	1.6	1.6	96.9
Interest free loan	28	2.3	2.3	99.3
Stable exchange rate and economy	9	.8	.8	100.0
Total	1200	100.0	100.0	

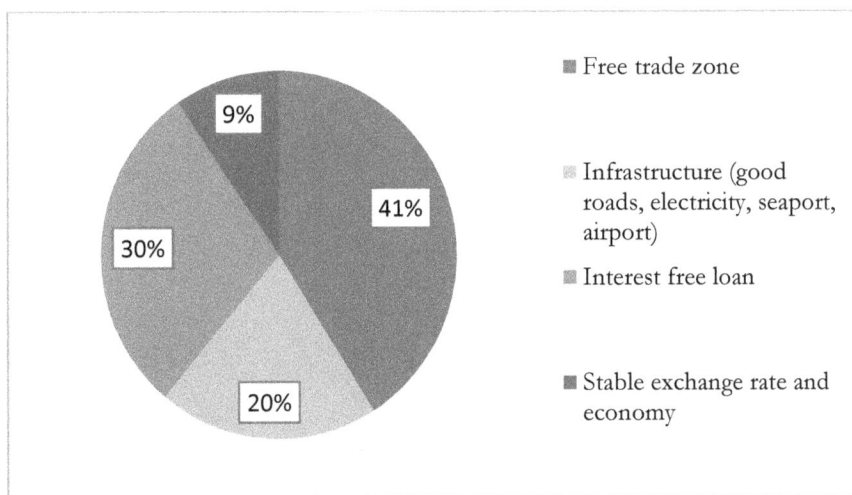

Figure 110: Pie Chart Showing Distribution of Responses by *Ụmụ Bọyị* on Other Institutional Strategies that can best enhance Entrepreneurship and Apprenticeship among Igbo Traders.

Table 110 and Figure 110 show the distribution of responses by *Ụmụ Boyị* on other institutional strategies that can best enhance entrepreneurship and apprenticeship among Igbo traders. 92.1% of the respondents indicated 'other options not listed on Table'. 110. 3.3% of the respondents indicated 'free trade zone' as an institutional strategy that can best enhance entrepreneurship and apprenticeship among Igbo traders. 1.6% of the respondents selected 'infrastructure (good roads, electricity, seaport, airport)'. 2.3% of the respondents chose 'interest free loans', while 0.8% of the respondents selected 'stable exchange rate and economy'.

Table 111: Distribution of *Ndị Ọga* by their Views on Specific Regulations provided by Local and State Governments to guide the Relationship between *Ọga* and *Nwa Bọyị*

	Frequency	Percent	Valid Percent	Cumulative Percent
I don't know	145	12.1	12.1	12.1
Largely true	6	.5	.5	12.6
Maybe	52	4.3	4.3	16.9
Not true at all	941	78.4	78.4	95.3
True	57	4.7	4.7	100.0
Total	1201	100.0	100.0	

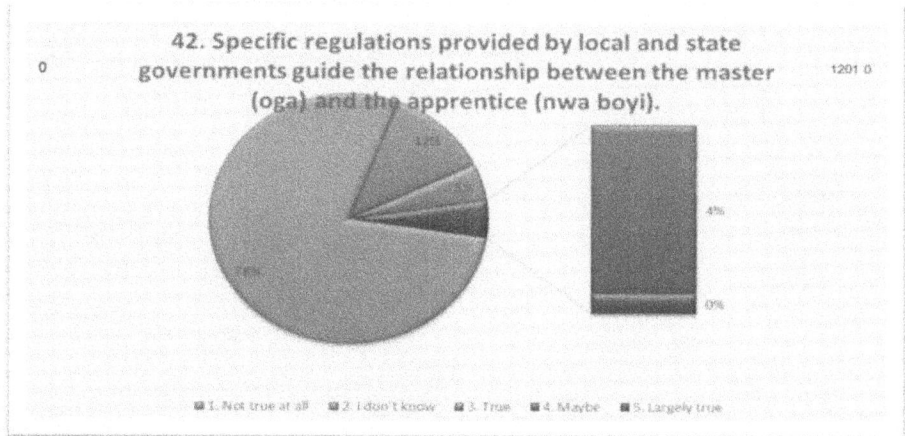

Figure 111: Pie Chart Showing the Distribution of *Ndị Ọga* by their Views on Specific Regulations Provided by Local and State Governments to guide the Relationship between *Ọga* and *Nwa Bọyị*

Table 111 and Figure 111 show the distribution of *Ndị Ọga* by their views on specific regulations provided by Local and State Governments to guide the relationship between *Ọga* and *Nwa Bọyị*. 12.1% indicated 'I don't know'. 0.5% indicated 'Largely true'. 4.3% indicated Maybe. 78.4% indicated 'Not true at all' while 4.7% indicated 'True'.

Table 112: Distribution of *Ụmụ Bọyị* by their Views on Specific Regulations provided by Local and State Governments to guide the Relationship between *Ọga* and *Nwa Bọyị*

	Frequency	Percent	Valid Percent	Cumulative Percent
I don't know	270	22.5	22.5	22.5
Largely true	11	.9	.9	23.4
Maybe	57	4.8	4.8	28.2
Not true at all	803	66.9	66.9	95.1
True	59	4.9	4.9	100.0
Total	1200	100.0	100.0	

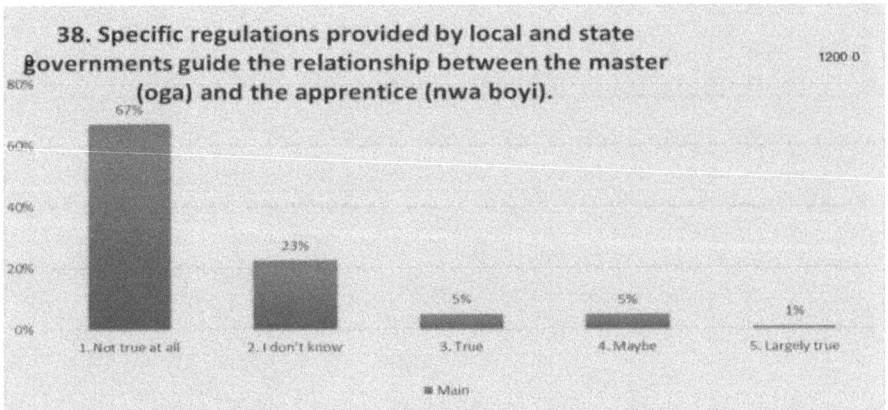

Figure 112: Bar Chart showing the Distribution of *Ụmụ Bọyị* by their Views on Specific Regulations provided by Local and State Governments to guide the Relationship between *Ọga* and *Nwa Bọyị*

Table 112 and Figure 112 showed the distribution of *Ụmụ Bọyị* by their views on specific regulations provided by Local and State Governments to guide the relationship between *Ọga* and *Nwa Bọyị*. 22.5% indicated 'I don't know'. 0.9% indicated 'Largely true'. 4.8% indicated 'May be'. 66.9% indicated 'Not true at all' while 4.9% indicated 'True'.

Table 113: Distribution of *Ndị Ọga* by their Views on the absence of Government monitoring in the Relationship between *Ọga* and *Nwa Bọyị*

	Frequency	Percent	Valid Percent	Cumulative Percent
I don't know	113	9.4	9.4	9.4
Largely true	326	27.1	27.1	36.6
Maybe	24	2.0	2.0	38.6
Not true at all	400	33.3	33.3	71.9
True	338	28.1	28.1	100.0
Total	1201	100.0	100.0	

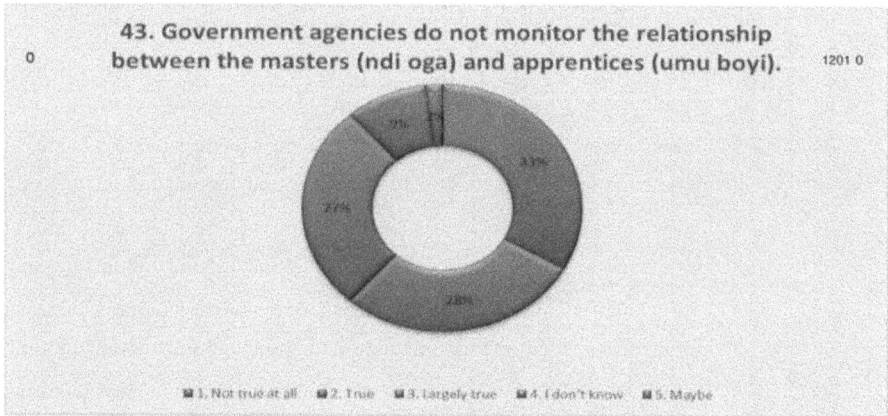

Figure 113: Pie Chart Depicting the Distribution of *Ndị Ọga* by their Views on the absence of Government monitoring in the Relationship between Master (*Ọga*) and *Nwa Bọyị*.

Table 113 and Figure 113 showed the distribution of *Ndị Ọga* by their Views on the absence of Government monitoring in the Relationship between Master (*Ọga*) and *Nwa Bọyị*. 9.4% indicated 'I don't know'. 27.1% indicated 'Largely true'. 2.0% indicated Maybe. 33.3% indicated 'Not true at all' while 28.1% indicated 'True'.

Table 114: Distribution of *Ụmụ Bọyị* by their Views on the absence of Government monitoring in the Relationship between *Ọga* and *Nwa Bọyị*

::	Frequency	Percent	Valid Percent	Cumulative Percent
I don't know	229	19.1	19.1	19.1
Largely true	269	22.4	22.4	41.5
Maybe	34	2.8	2.8	44.3
Not true at all	366	30.5	30.5	74.8
True	302	25.2	25.2	100.0
Total	1200	100.0	100.0	

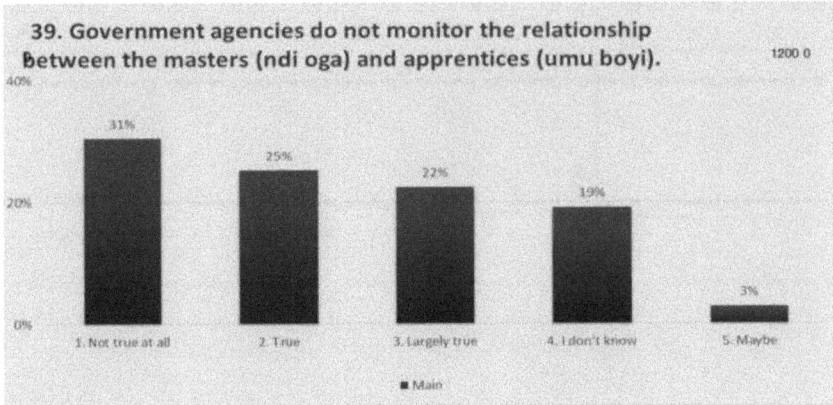

39. Government agencies do not monitor the relationship between the masters (ndi oga) and apprentices (umu boyi).

Figure 114: Bar Chart Showing the Distribution of *Ụmụ Bọyị* by their Views on the absence of Government monitoring in the Relationship between *Ọga* and *Nwa Bọyị*

Table 114 and Figure 114 show the distribution of *Ụmụ Bọyị* by their views on the absence of Government monitoring in the Relationship between Master (*Ọga*) and *Nwa Bọyị*. 19.1% indicated 'I don't know'. 22.4% indicated 'Largely true'. 2.8% indicated 'May be'. 30.5% indicated 'Not true at all' while 25.2% indicated 'True'.

Table 115: Distribution of *Ndị Ọga* by their Views on the extent to which Market Associations intervene in the Relationship between *Ọga* and *Nwa Bọyị*

	Frequency	Percent	Valid Percent	Cumulative Percent
Don't know	82	6.8	6.8	6.8
Great extent	91	7.6	7.6	14.4
Large extent	336	28.0	28.0	42.4
Not at all	242	20.1	20.1	62.5
Rarely	450	37.5	37.5	100.0
Total	1201	100.0	100.0	

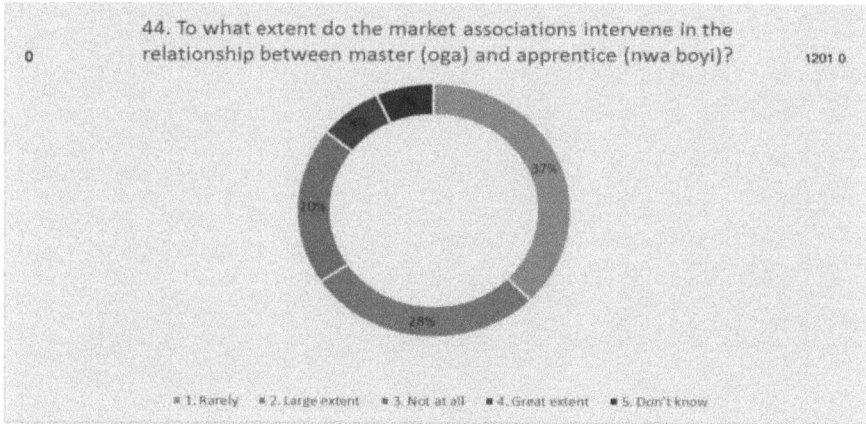

Figure 115: Pie Chart Indicating the Distribution of *Ndị Ọga* by their Views on the extent to which Market Associations intervene in the Relationship between Master (*Ọga*) and *Nwa Bọyị*.

Table 115 and Figure 115 show the distribution of *Ndị Ọga* by their views on the extent to which market associations intervene in the relationship between Master (*Ọga*) and *Nwa Bọyị*. 6.8% indicated 'I don't know'. 7.6% indicated 'Great extent'. 28.0% indicated a 'Large extent'. 20.1% indicated 'Not at all' while 37.5% indicated 'Rarely'.

Table 116: Distribution of *Ụmụ Bọyị* by their Views on the extent to which Market Associations intervene in the Relationship between *Ọga* and *Nwa Bọyị*

:::	Frequency	Percent	Valid Percent	Cumulative Percent
Don't know	191	15.9	15.9	15.9
Great extent	64	5.3	5.3	21.3
Large extent	249	20.8	20.8	42.0
Not at all	286	23.8	23.8	65.8
Rarely	410	34.2	34.2	100.0
Total	1200	100.0	100.0	

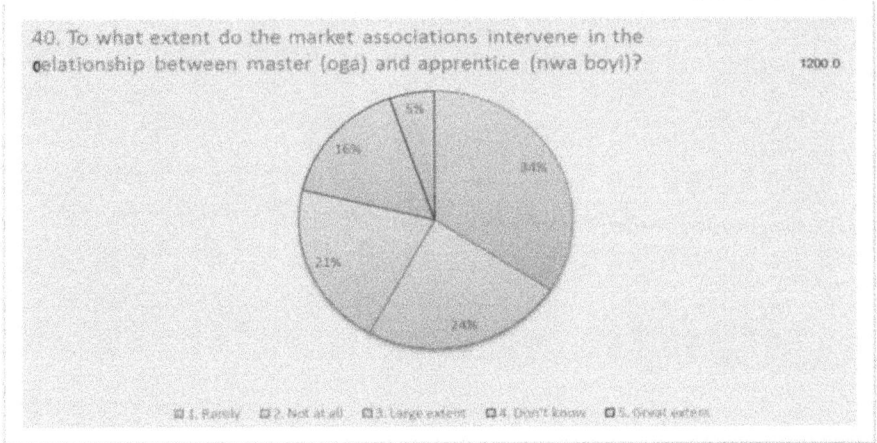

Figure 116: Pie Chart showing the Distribution of *Umu Boyi* by their Views on the extent to which Market Associationsintervene in the Relationship between *Oga* and *Nwa Boyi*

Table 116 and Figure 116 show the distribution of *Ndi Oga* by their Views on the extent to which market associations intervene in the relationship between Master (*Oga*) and *Nwa Boyi*. 15.9% indicated 'I don't know'. 5.3% indicated great extent. 20.8% indicated a 'Large extent'. 23.8% indicated 'Not at all' while 34.2% indicated 'Rarely'.

Table 117: Distribution of *Ndi Oga* by their Views on whether Adult Education Programmes are organized by the State Government for Masters (*Ndi Oga*) and Apprentices (*Umu Boyi*)

	Frequency	Percent	Valid Percent	Cumulative Percent
Don't know	216	18.0	18.0	18.0
Largely true	16	1.3	1.3	19.3
Never	668	55.6	55.6	74.9
Rarely	176	14.7	14.7	89.6
True	125	10.4	10.4	100.0
Total	1201	100.0	100.0	

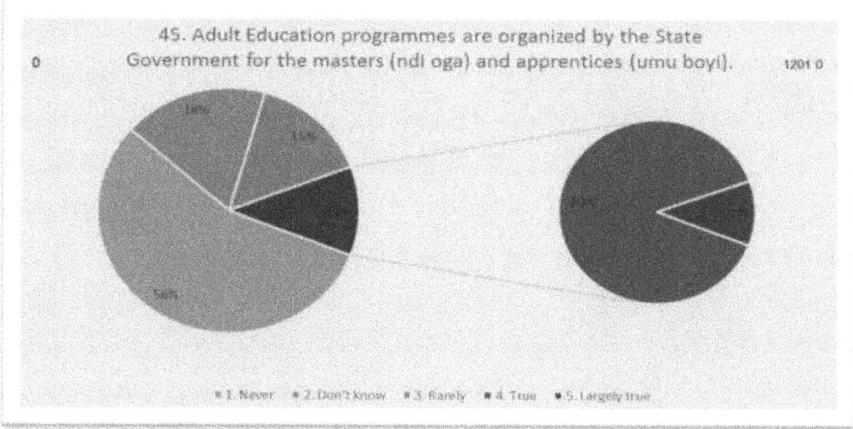

Figure 117: Pie Chart Showing the Distribution of Ndị Ọga by their Views on whether Adult Education Programmes are organized by the State Government for Masters (Ndị Ọga) and Apprentices (Ụmụ Bọyị).

Table 117 and Figure 117 shows the distribution of Ndị Ọga by their views on whether adult education programmes are organized by the State government for masters (Ndị Ọga) and apprentices (Ụmụ Bọyị). 18.0% indicated 'I don't know'. 1.3% indicated 'largely true'. 55.6% indicated 'Maybe'. 14.7% indicated 'Not true at all', while 10.4% indicated 'true'.

Table 118: Distribution of Ụmụ Bọyị by their Views on whether Adult Education Programmes are Organized by the State Government for Ndị Ọga and Ụmụ Bọyị

	Frequency	Percent	Valid Percent	Cumulative Percent
Don't know	391	32.6	32.6	32.6
Largely true	15	1.3	1.3	33.8
Never	590	49.2	49.2	83.0
Rarely	110	9.2	9.2	92.2
True	94	7.8	7.8	100.0
Total	1200	100.0	100.0	

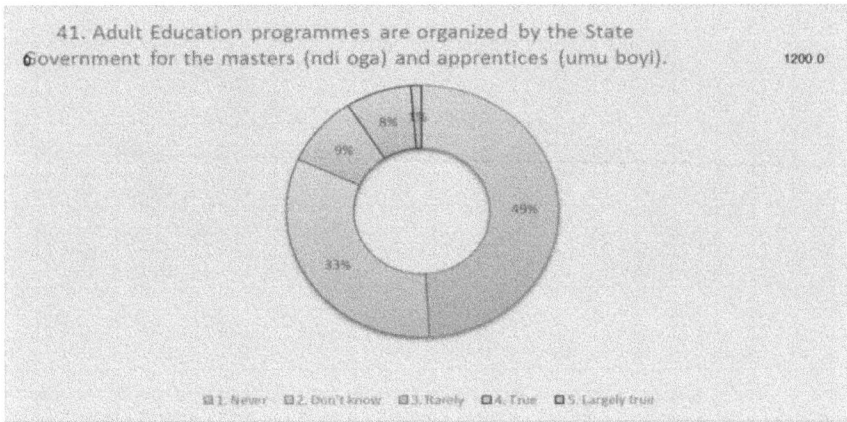

Figure 118: Pie Chart showing the Distribution of *Ụmụ Bọyị* by their Views on whether Adult Education Programmes are organized by the State Government for *Ndị Ọga* and *Ụmụ Bọyị* .

Table 118 and Figure 118 show the distribution of *Ụmụ Bọyị* by their views on whether adult education programmes are organized by the State government for masters (*Ndị Ọga*) and apprentices (*Ụmụ Bọyị*). 32.6% indicated 'I don't know'. 1.3% indicated 'largely true'. 49.2% indicated 'Maybe'. 9.2% indicated 'Not true at all' while 7.8% indicated 'true'.

Table 119: Distribution of *Ndi Ọga* by their Views on how often *Ndị Ọga* and *Ụmụ Bọyị* make use of Adult Education facilities

	Frequency	Percent	Valid Percent	Cumulative Percent
Never	440	36.6	36.6	36.6
Rarely	293	24.4	24.4	61.0
I don't know	251	20.9	20.9	81.9
Often	193	16.1	16.1	98.0
Very often	24	2.0	2.0	100.0
Total	1201	100.0	100.0	

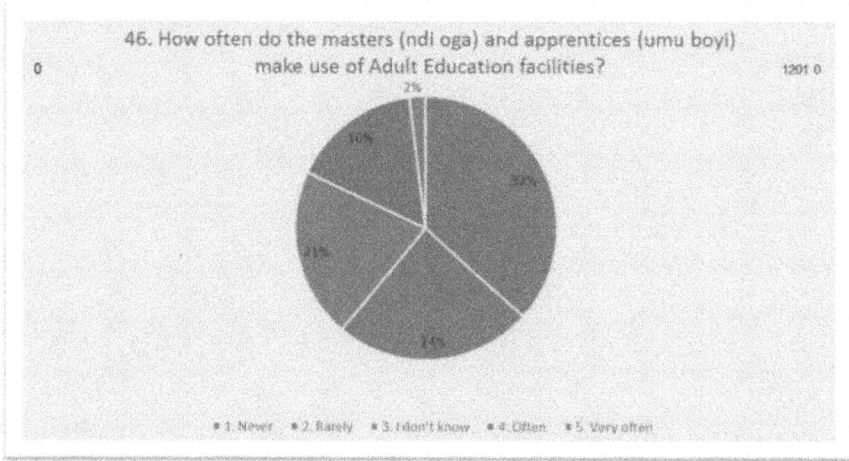

Figure 119: Pie Chart Showing the Distribution of *ndị Ọga* by their Views on how often *Ndị Ọga* and *Ụmụ Bọyị make* use of Adult Education facilities

Table 119 and Figure 119 show the distribution of *Ndị Ọga* by their views on how often *Ndị Ọga* and *Ụmụ Bọyị* make use of adult education facilities. 36.6% of the respondents indicated 'never'. 24.4% of the respondents indicated 'rarely'. 20.9% of the respondents indicated 'I don't know'. 16.1% of the respondents indicated 'often', while 2.0% of the respondents indicated 'very often'.

Table 120: Distribution of *Ụmụ Bọyị* by their Views on how often *Ndị Ọga* and *Ụmụ bọyị* make use of Adult Education facilities

	Frequency	Percent	Valid Percent	Cumulative Percent
I don't know	394	32.8	32.8	32.8
Never	430	35.8	35.8	68.7
Often	136	11.3	11.3	80.0
Rarely	224	18.7	18.7	98.7
Very often	16	1.3	1.3	100.0
Total	1200	100.0	100.0	

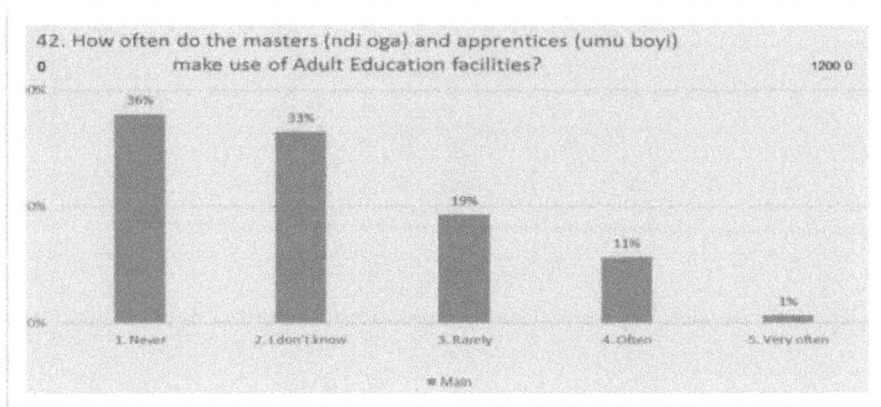

Figure 120: Bar Chart showing the Distribution of *Ụmụ Bọyị* by their Views on how often *Ndị Ọga* and *Umu Boyi* make use of Adult Education facilities.

Table 120 and Figure 120 show the distribution of *Ụmụ Bọyị* by their Views on how often *Ndị Ọga* and *Ụmụ Bọyị* make use of Adult Education facilities. 32.8% of the respondents indicated 'I don't know'. 35.8% of the respondents indicated 'never'. 11.3% of the respondents indicated 'often'. 18.7% of the respondents indicated 'rarely', while 1.3% of the respondents indicated 'very often'.

Table 121: Distribution of *Ndị Ọga* by their Responses on whether further education is necessary in their daily Business Transactions

	Frequency	Percent	Valid Percent	Cumulative Percent
Not needed	243	20.2	20.2	20.2
Maybe	108	9.0	9.0	29.2
I don't know	41	3.4	3.4	32.6
Necessary	530	44.1	44.1	76.7
Very necessary	279	23.2	23.2	100.0
Total	1201	100.0	100.0	

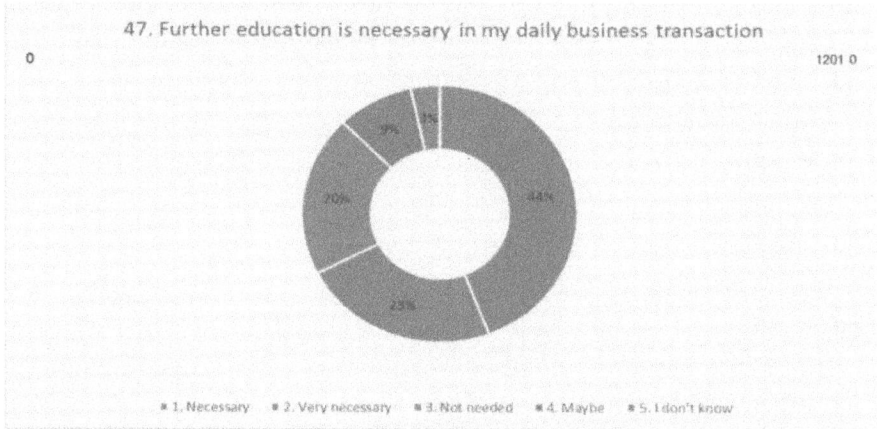

47. Further education is necessary in my daily business transaction

■ 1. Necessary ■ 2. Very necessary ■ 3. Not needed ■ 4. Maybe ■ 5. I don't know

Figure 121: Pie Chart Showing the Distribution of Ndị Ọga by their Responses on whether further education is necessary in their daily Business Transactions.

Table 121 and Figure 121 show the distribution of Ndi Ọga by their responses on whether further education is necessary in their daily business transactions. 20.2% of the respondents indicated not needed. 9.0% of the respondents indicated 'may be'. 3.4% of the respondents indicated 'I don't know'. 44.1% of the respondents indicated necessary while 23.2% of the respondents indicated very necessary. This further highlights the necessity for further education as a way of enhancing the apprenticeship scheme.

Table 122: Distribution of Ụmụ Bọyị by their Responses on whether further education is necessary in their daily Business Transactions

	Frequency	Percent	Valid Percent	Cumulative Percent
I don't know	74	6.2	6.2	6.2
Maybe	123	10.3	10.3	16.4
Necessary	564	47.0	47.0	63.4
Not needed	186	15.5	15.5	78.9
Very necessary	253	21.1	21.1	100.0
Total	1200	100.0	100.0	

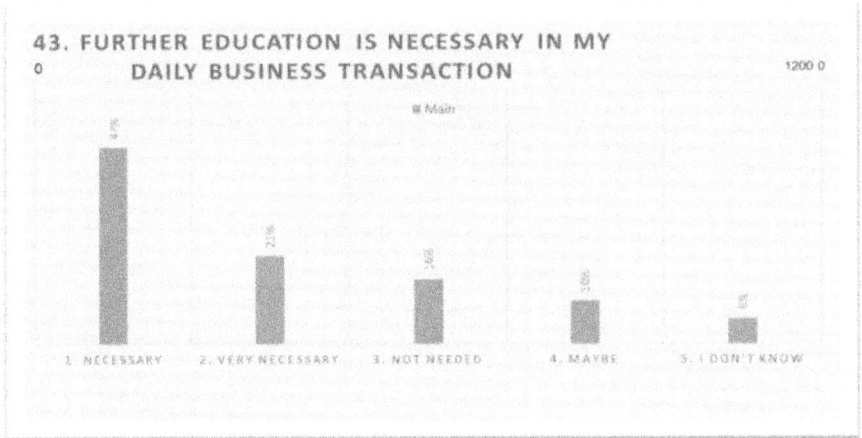

43. FURTHER EDUCATION IS NECESSARY IN MY DAILY BUSINESS TRANSACTION

Figure 122: Bar Chart showing the Distribution of *Ụmụ Bọyị* by their Responses on whether further education is necessary in their daily Business Transactions.

Table 122 and Figure 122 shows the distribution of *Ụmụ Bọyị* by their Responses on whether further education is necessary in their daily Business Transactions. 6.2% of the respondents indicated 'I don't know'. 10.3% of the respondents indicated 'may be'. 47.0% of the respondents indicated 'necessary'. 15.5% of the respondents indicated 'not needed', while 21.1% of the respondents indicated 'very necessary'. The position of *Ụmụ Bọyị buttresses* the views of *Ndị Ọga* when they affirmed the necessity for further education in the Institution of apprenticeship.

Table 123: Distribution of *Ndị Ọga* by their Responses on whether Apprenticeship as a Strategy of Entrepreneurship is on the decline

	Frequency	Percent	Valid Percent	Cumulative Percent
False	229	19.1	19.1	19.1
Don't know	47	3.9	3.9	23.0
True	925	77.0	77.0	100.0
Total	1201	100.0	100.0	

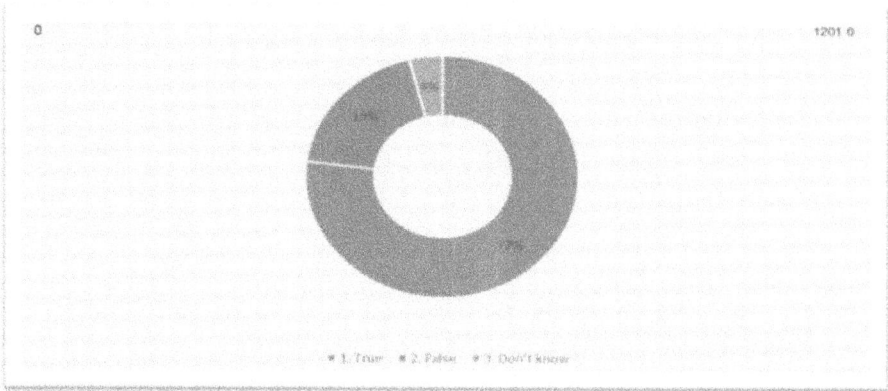

Figure 123: Pie Chart Indicating the Distribution of *Ndị Ọga* by their Responses on whether Apprenticeship as a Strategy of Entrepreneurship is on the decline.

Table 123 and Figure 123 show the distribution of *Ndị Ọga* by their responses on whether apprenticeship as a strategy of entrepreneurship is on the decline. 19.1% indicated 'false'. 3.9% indicated 'I don't know' while 77.0% of the respondents indicated 'it is on the decline'. The implication here is that the apprenticeship as a strategy of entrepreneurship is on the decline.

Table 124: Distribution of *Ụmụ Bọyị* by their Responses on whether Apprenticeship as a strategy of Entrepreneurship is on the decline

	Frequency	Percent	Valid Percent	Cumulative Percent
Don't know	87	7.2	7.2	7.2
False	289	24.1	24.1	31.3
True	824	68.7	68.7	100.0
Total	1200	100.0	100.0	

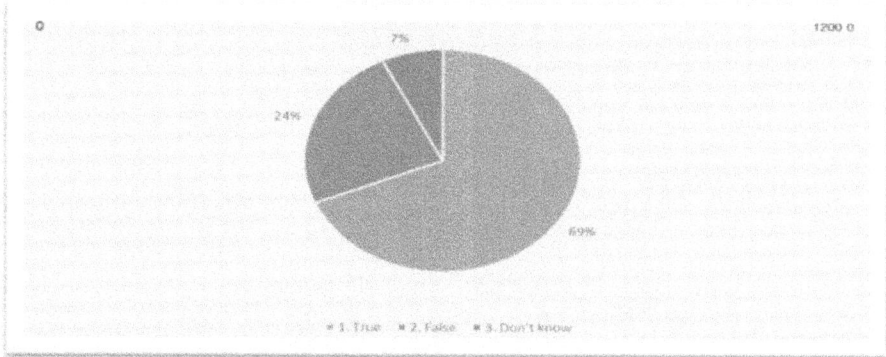

Figure 124: Pie Chart Indicating the Distribution of *Ụmụ Bọyị* by their Responses on whether Apprenticeship as a strategy of Entrepreneurship is on the decline.

Table 124 and Figure 124 show the distribution of *Ụmụ Bọyị* by their Responses on whether Apprenticeship as a strategy of Entrepreneurship is on the decline. 7.2% indicated 'I don't know'. 24.1% indicated 'false' while 68.7% of the respondents indicated that 'it is on the decline'. Results revealed that apprenticeship as a strategy for entrepreneurship is on the decline as also perceived by *Umu Boyi*.

4.3.14 Perspectives on the Decline in Ịgba Bọyị Apprenticeship Scheme in the Selected Onitsha Markets

The *Ịgba boyi* practice has continued over centuries though not in its autochthonous form because of its flexible nature to adapt to the ever erratic systemic and structural changes and demands of the modern business world. However, the perceived or supposed decline in the *Ịgba bọyị* scheme in the studied Onitsha Markets is the fulcrum upon which this study is anchored in order to ascertain why the decline and how it can be reinvigorated. The choice of Onitsha markets is based on the fact that this location in South-eastern Nigeria plays host to a lot of commodities, skill, and service-oriented markets with far-reaching global influence in the world of entrepreneurship. For instance, most importers and exporters of goods to and from China and other business-oriented and productivity-driven economies/countries emanate from Onitsha and contribute a large percentage of Nigeria's foreign exchange transactions. One common opinion among the traders (*Ndị Ọga* and *Ụmụ Bọyị*) is that the practice of *Ịgba Bọyị* in the selected Onitsha markets studied is on the decline, although some of the study participants are of the opinion that it is not totally dead but it is no longer what it used to be. Emergent themes reflecting this observed downward trend was associated with diverse factors namely: *'desire to steal, meet up, and loot' among contemporary apprentices, and many think 'poor moral upbringing by parents, peer pressure and the advent of social media expose young people to ostentatious living; bad and wicked masters were accused by many of the Ụmụ Bọyị (apprentices) as responsible for the prevailing decline;* others were of the opinion that the prevalence of 'fraudulent folks' especially those who defraud customers in the guise of *ọsọ-ahịa* (hunting for customers) and many of them *'sell inferior and expired goods'* to intending customers, hence portraying the traders in these markets in a bad light. In the traders' opinion, this trend among young Igbo people is exacerbated by 'little or no orientation for youths in the markets' organized by relevant institutions like families, communities, market unions, and the chamber of commerce.

The *advent of formal education* which pulled a majority of the prospective or potential '*Ụmụ Bọyị*' (apprentices) into schools led to less patronage of the apprenticeship scheme in the studied Onitsha markets, hence the decline. The excerpt below captures the above-discussed factors responsible for the decline:

> That informal structure of apprenticeship actually has been the area that had striven and gotten to this level of awareness globally about the Igbo people. But when you veer off that particular informal structure looking at a well-organized business in the *Igba Boyi* system, you will be experiencing a decline. We are observing the decline in the *Igba Bọyị* system and it has to do with the trend of people gaining educational knowledge because you cannot come in a structure or in a system where somebody passes through some level of academics like after secondary education, or the tertiary level you now expect the person to descend to such level of apprenticeship? It will not really work in this particular structure that is the reason for the decline (IDI, Male *Ọga* 56 years, Main Market, September 2020).

From another perspective, many traders were of the opinion that most 'early Igbo masters of trade (*Ndị Ọga*) and entrepreneurs' *were not educated and the rate of illiteracy* seems to be a contributing factor to the perceived decline in the Igbo apprenticeship scheme. Another perspective of the study participants is that many people hold, believe, and perceive *Igba Bọyị* as '*suffering and descending to a lower level after formal education*'. Hence, *Igba Bọyị* is *now less appealing to the younger educated Igbo population* and their parents and as such, no one is ready to send his or her wards to *Igba Bọyị*, including most of the contemporary *Ndị Ọga* (masters). This has led to the 'shift to sales girls' and other paid staff as 'trade assistants'. Again, the advent of 'tricycles (*Keke*) and motorcycles (*Ọkada*)' has played a role in the decline of *Igba Bọyị* as many young boys would rather venture into these than go for *Igba Bọyị*. The reasons are because Keke and *Ọkada* expose many young boys to 'quick cash' and they would not spend the number of years demanded in (*Igba Bọyị*) apprenticeship. The few young people who end up as *Nwa Bọyị* (apprentices} prefer to serve the rich masters and not the poor masters (*Ọga*). Many elderly masters (*Ndị Ọga*) also hold the opinion that 'distractions from the use of modern gadgets and social media' prevent apprentices from gaining adequate knowledge of the trade which they have come to learn. In another vein, some very critical traders, are of the opinion that the 'introduction of formality to a trading-culture traditionally run via informality' as a factor for the decline of *Igba Bọyị*. One prevalent issue mentioned by most *Ndị Ọga* is the 'unwilling and un-submissive apprentices' to bend and learn under the tutelage and guidance of masters (*Ndị Ọga*), many masters find these expressions of disrespect agonizing.

Many traders who participated in these interviews stressed the *'failure by parents to identify ward's areas of strengths'* before sending them to either schools or apprenticeship but parents would rather send their wards to schools by default not minding if the child has got the capacity or not. In this case, many ill-advised wards come into apprenticeship unmotivated thereby contributing to the gradual decline of *Igba Boyi*. Hence, unmotivated apprentices contribute to the decline especially those who are cajoled or forced into Igba Boyi. Another factor highlighted in the decline of *'Igba Boyi'* is the *'failure to use Igbo language'* in trading thereby divulging business secrets and this was attributed to the failure of families in teaching their children the Igbo language right from a tender age. This reflects that 'business or trade secrets' occupy a central place in the operation and processes of apprenticeship and entrepreneurship in the studied Onitsha Markets, known as *'Apprenticepreneurship'* as this study has earlier indicated. In the world of apprenticeship among the Igbo, there are complex exchanges that are seen in the challenges, misunderstanding, confrontations, and extreme outright conflicts. There is also an avalanche or humongous array of issues around *'Settlement of apprentices'* after or upon completion of apprenticeship (*Igba Boyi*) like 'accusations and counter-accusations on stealing money and goods from the master's warehouses, looting, court cases, breach of agreements by masters (*Ndị Oga*), market union and police interventions, among many other issues. Some excerpts from the interviews and discussions highlight some of these settlement issues:

> the thing is that in a situation say – as I am here now, maybe discussing with my neighbour, and he will tell me that one of his dependent apprentices is due for settlement and that he is in need of another *Nwa Boyi* to replace the one that will be settled, and asked if I have or I know someone who is trustworthy that I can bring for him. Being that we have been together, I know how he treats his apprentices, I will then refer him to any *Nwa Boyi* that I can attest to his behaviour. But in a situation where it has been known to me that he will not treat the *boyi* very well, I will tell him that I don't have. But if he is a good man, I can tell him that one of my sister's sons or aunties' sons just finished school and he is idle. So, I will make him take my relative's son as his dependent-apprentice. This is because just as the *Nwa Boyi* (dependent-apprentice) do misuse or disobey their master, so we have some masters who do treat their dependent-apprentices badly. Everyone knows how he behaves. Some of the wicked masters, after they have served for years when your settlement time is near, will level all sorts of allegations

against the dependent-apprentice in order not to settle him. All the sufferings of the *Nwa Boyi* will be in vain (IDI with a 67 years-old Male ex-Market Union Leader at Main Market).

...Any *Nwa Boyi* who stole his master's money will be shown the way out. Like a case we are handling now, *Nwa Boyi* bought a phone worth 180 thousand naira. When he was caught, ... he used to keep the phone in the shop when he closed, because he is the person manning the shop, his master is in a different shop. When they were asked, he said it was another dependent-apprentice that owns the phone. Not until the master of the one he claims that bought the phone came and asked him if he is the one that bought the phone, and reminded him that his settlement is near; that was when he confirmed it was the other Nwa Boyi that owns the phone. Can you see? (IDI with a 52 years old key study stakeholder in the Main Market).

...for you to be settled you will have to do some domestic work if I want, - like washing my car and clothes. All of these will amount to what will be considered while settling the *Nwa Boyi*. But anyone that comes for the non-residential apprentice (*Onye n'amu ahia*), the master does not give anything to him but his family will. Such does not require settlement but residential apprentices (*Nwa Boyi*) will be settled (IDI with a 62 years old key study stakeholder in the Main Market).

Like if you have an agreement to serve for 7 years, and on that 7th year the master will approach the *Nwa Boyi* and dialogue with him to stay till another year. Some *Umu Boyi* do consider the extension while some do not. Some wicked masters (*Oga*) within this extension alleged that the servant had committed one thing or the other and threw him out without settlement. This was what my junior brother suffered. After my brother had served for the agreed 7 years, they pleaded for an extension by one year after which they pleaded for another one year, which made 9 years. The news we heard later was that my brother is now in Zone 9, Umuahia, and the funny part of it was that the person that did this to him was our brother who claimed to be a born-again. They said I should not come to Umuahia. If I come, they will arrest me also. It got to a point that we sold our land to rescue our brother. I was in our house when my brother came back with a wrapper and shorts, immediately hot water was provided to disinfect him and his clothing. This to tell what happen in some cases. (In-depth Interview with *Oga*, Male, 41 years at Building Materials).

Table 125: Distribution of *Ndị Ọga*'s Responses on the State of Apprenticeship among Igbo Entrepreneurs

	Frequency	Percent	Valid Percent	Cumulative Percent
Declining very fast and will soon be completely supplanted	266	22.1	22.1	22.1
It is becoming weak but cannot ever die completely	644	53.6	53.6	75.7
Don't know	28	2.3	2.3	78.0
Still strong and ever-expanding	263	21.9	21.9	100.0
Total	1201	100.0	100.0	

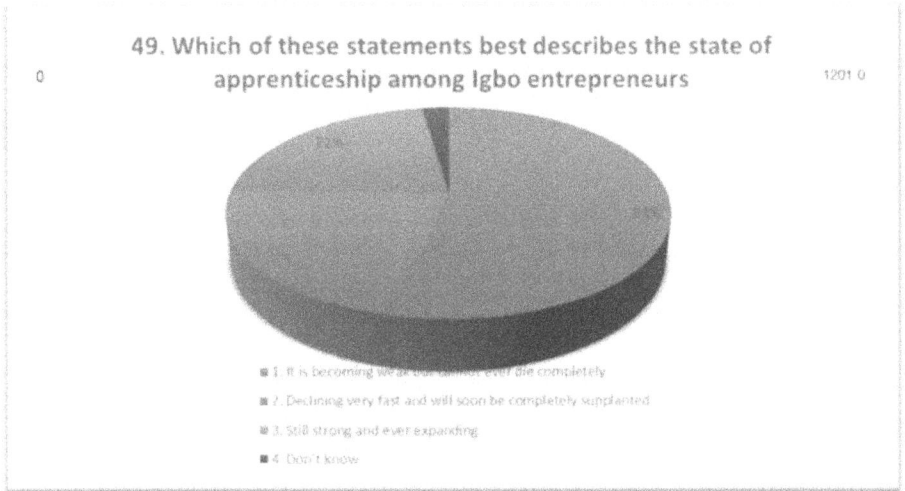

49. Which of these statements best describes the state of apprenticeship among Igbo entrepreneurs

- 1. It is becoming weak but cannot ever die completely
- 2. Declining very fast and will soon be completely supplanted
- 3. Still strong and ever expanding
- 4. Don't know

Figure 125: Pie Chart Showing the Distribution of *Ndị Ọga*'s Responses on the State of Apprenticeship among Igbo Entrepreneurs

Table 125 and Figure 125 show the distribution of *Ndị Ọga*'s responses on the state of apprenticeship among Igbo entrepreneurs. 22.1% of the respondents indicated that the state of apprenticeship among Igbo entrepreneurs is declining very fast and will soon be completely supplanted. 53.6% of the respondents indicated that the state of apprenticeship among Igbo entrepreneurs is becoming weak but cannot ever die completely. 2.3% of the respondents indicated that they do not know the state of apprenticeship among Igbo entrepreneurs. 21.9% of the respondents indicated that the state of apprenticeship among Igbo entrepreneurs is still strong and ever expanding.

Table 126: Distribution of Ụmụ Bọyị's Responses on the State of Apprenticeship among Igbo Entrepreneurs

	Frequency	Percent	Valid Percent	Cumulative Percent
Declining very fast and will soon be completely supplanted	218	18.2	18.2	18.2
Don't know	71	5.9	5.9	24.1
It is becoming weak but cannot ever die completely	577	48.1	48.1	72.2
Still strong and ever expanding	334	27.8	27.8	100.0
Total	1200	100.0	100.0	

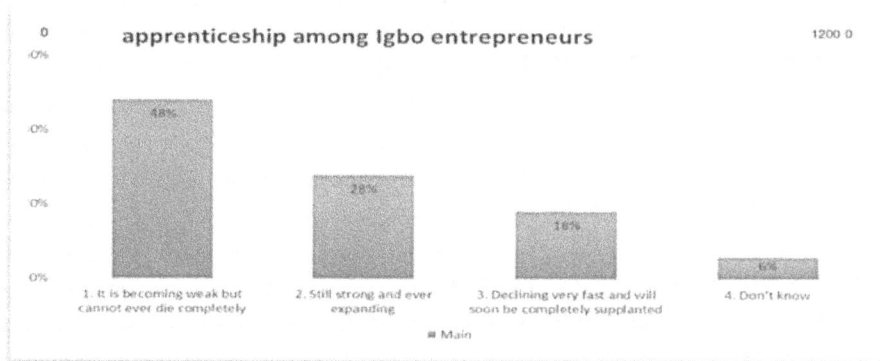

Figure 126: Bar Chart Showing the Distribution of *ụmụ bọyị*'s Responses on the State of Apprenticeship among Igbo Entrepreneurs.

Table 126 and Figure 126 show the distribution of Ụmụ Bọyị's responses on the state of apprenticeship among Igbo entrepreneurs. 18.2% of the respondents indicated that the state of apprenticeship among Igbo entrepreneurs is declining very fast and will soon be completely supplanted. 5.9% of the respondents indicated that they don't know the state of apprenticeship among Igbo entrepreneurs. 48.1% of the respondents indicated that the state of apprenticeship among Igbo entrepreneurs is becoming weak but cannot ever die completely. 27.8% of the respondents indicated that the state of apprenticeship among Igbo entrepreneurs is still strong and ever-expanding.

4.3.15 Measures Currently Employed in Improving and Proposed Strategies to Reinvigorating the Ịgba Bọyị Scheme

Many of the study participants are of the opinion that the solution to the decline should begin with all relevant stakeholders having some form of responsibility in the *Igba Boyi* scheme in the selected Onitsha Markets, beginning from the level of the individual before proceeding to the family level, Market Union, community, Chamber of Commerce, Mines, Industry and Agriculture and finally to the wider role of the Government's trade policies which are sometimes unfavourable to the Igbo entrepreneurial and apprenticeship scheme. The excerpts below show the suggestions by some of the traders:

The role of parents:

> ...the only way I think families can contribute to what is happening in *Igba Boyi* is when they do not give their children proper training. There is no parent that will support his child to be stealing and a child that has a proper upbringing will not misbehave. So, proper training is good (IDI, 66 years old *Oga*, Building Materials Market).

Gender dimension to the decline and solutions:

the way they can help is to scold their children when they err because most at times mothers do not accept that their children are wrong but if it is a man, he will not condole any act of misconduct from his child because he knows that if the child becomes responsible tomorrow, it will be of benefit to everyone (IDI, 66 years old **Oga**, Building Materials Market).

The role of language and individual efforts in reviving the *Igba Boyi* scheme:

Another problem is speaking our language – Igbo. You people will help in making sure that Igbo language is being spoken everywhere at every point in time. This language helped us a lot, when me and my wife travelled for business, we would be discussing in our mother tongue and the white man would not hear us. Even when they ask, we would tell them a different thing. It is disheartening that some of the children born and brought up in Onitsha here do not know how to speak Igbo. There is one of my cousins that I brought down here to attend a seminary school. In their exam, he had English 100, mathematics 100, and one other course 100, but Igbo he scored 0; because he does not know Igbo before now. Even with that three that he passed, he was admitted and because of that I made it compulsory that he will learn Igbo. Do you know, within one year he perfected in Igbo, to tell you that some parents are just punishing their children for nothing. Parents do not know the importance of this language. They do not know that they can use it to discuss with their children in front of their teacher, assuming they are living in other parts of the country, and the teacher will not know what they are discussing. I have told people how I was helped in the embassy by a frontline officer because I shouted in Igbo that I do not have cash with me. He called me and spoke Igbo with me and I did as he told me and I succeeded. But the funny part of it is that some of them that grew in the Yoruba or Hausa part will not even learn the language also – Igbo you don't know, Hausa you don't know, Yoruba you don't know, it is a very big problem. So those of you in our institutions of learning should be encouraging our children to learn how to speak Igbo language. Tell them that they will not pay to learn Igbo, just to speak it at all times, it will master you. There is one Indian citizen that works for me, he did not go to school but it was their native tongue that he used in learning the job that is feeding him today. But our people have gone to school, but nothing to show. So you people should help in breaking this barrier. Do you know that when the boy went back to Lagos he forced the mother to teach them Igbo. The woman called me that I have implicated her, that her children now force her to teach them Igbo. I told her that it is good for her. Do you know my strategy; the strategy I used was that no one will come and ask me anything in English language, that everything must be said in Igbo. Even when it was difficult for some of them to speak what they wanted to tell me in Igbo, I still insisted that it must be said in Igbo – that was how I managed to help them to learn Igbo. Now many of them can now speak Igbo fluently (KII with a retired 78 years old entrepreneur and *Ọga* in his house).

The role of masters and the market unions and mediatory roles:

'If as a master your *Nwa Boyi* commits an offence, you have to report him to the market union first for them to handle. But if it is beyond their power, then the police will be involved (IDI with a 46 years old Master at Ọchanja Market).

The role of Government in the markets:

If the government can organize special lectures for the youth and invite those that did well in *Igba Boyi* to come and speak with them it will go a long way, the challenge is that most of these substances that these young people smoke won't allow them to concentrate, some will prefer going to ride Okada and keke to serving someone not knowing that they can't achieve more with such lifestyle (IDI, 44 years *Ọga*, Bridge Head Market).

Currently used strategies for checkmating the decline in *Igba Boyi* scheme:

Some other solutions are best categorized into sub-themes such as: currently used and proposed strategies suggested by the traders in revitalizing the *Igba Boyi* scheme in the studied Onitsha Markets are: Recruiting sales girls, Parents should identify areas of strengths, Orientation of traders on current realities, Funding the system, Formalizing informality, Adult education, Educational restructuring, Public sensitization by Chamber of Commerce, Encouraging graduates to join entrepreneurship, Monitoring apprentices, Speak Igbo language by the traders, Conduct research and involve stakeholders, Documentation, Orientation of traders on current realities, Train *Oga*'s kids in the trade for succession, Building capital through combined business between *Oga* and *Nwa Boyi*, Early and proper settlement of *Nwa Boyi*, Interventions by Chamber of Commerce, Public Private Partnership among others.

Many of the traders believe that the introduction of formal education dealt a blow on the *Igba Boyi* scheme and has led to the decline of the number of *Umu Boyi willing* to go through the rigors of *Igba boyi*. Many suggested formalizing the *Igba Boyi* scheme since it operates on informality and they suggest that 'formalizing this informality' will go a long way in revitalizing the scheme. Others think that emphasis should also be laid on the provision of easily accessible and affordable adult education within the immediate environment of the market space.

4.4 Analysis of Research Questions and Hypotheses Testing

Table 127: Analyzing Responses to Research Question One and Hypothesis One on Igbo Socio-cultural Characteristics and Entrepreneurial Success among Igbo Traders in Onitsha Markets

Religious/Income	African T. Religion	Christianity	Muslim	Others	Total
₦10.000 - ₦50,000	18.5%(5)	24.4%(286)	0.0%(0)	0.0%(0)	24.2(291)
₦60.000 - ₦100,000	25.9%(7)	30.5%(357)	100%(1)	50%(1)	30.5%(366)
₦110.000 - ₦150,000	25.9%(7)	16.9%(198)	0.0%(0)	0.0%(0)	17.1%(205)
₦160.000 - ₦2000,000	14.8%(4)	11.9%(139)	0.0%(0)	0.0%(0)	11.9%(143)
₦210.000 and above	14.8%(4)	16.3%(191)	0.0%(0)	0.0%(0)	16.3%(196)
Total	100%(27)	100%(1171)	100%(1)	100%(2)	100%(1201)
Chi-Square = X^2 = 7.040[a]	N= 1201	df = 12	P < 0.855		
Gender /Income	Male	Female			
₦10.000 - ₦50,000	24.1%(282)	31.0%(0)	24.2%(291)		
₦60.000 - ₦100,000	30.4%(356)	34.5%(10)	30.5%(366)		
₦110.000 - ₦150,000	17.2%(202)	10.3%(3)	17.1%(143)		
₦160.000 - ₦2000,000	11.9%(140)	10.3%(3)	11.9%(143)		
₦210.000 and above	16.4%(192)	13.8%(4)	16.3%(196)		

265

Total	100%(1172)	100%(29)	100%(1201)		
Chi-Square = X² = 1.689ᵃ	N= 1201	df = 4	P < 0.793		
Prevalent Type of Apprenticeship /Income	Kin Related	Non-Kin Related	Both		
₦10.000 - ₦50,000	27.4%(55)	23.2%(69)	23.8%(167)	24.2%(291)	
₦60.000 - ₦100,000	31.3%(63)	26.2%(78)	32.1%(225)	30.5%(366)	
₦110.000 - ₦150,000	17.9%(36)	15.4%(46)	17.5%(123)	17.1%(205)	
₦160.000 - ₦2000,000	10.4%(21)	14.8%(44)	11.1%(78)	11.9%(143)	
₦210.000 and above	12.9%(26)	20.5%(61)	15.5%(109)	16.3%(196)	
Total	100%(201)	100%(298)	100%(702)	100%(1201	
Chi-Square=X² = 11.680ᵃ	N= 1201	df = 8	P < 0.166		
Community Identification /Income	Yes	No			
₦10.000 - ₦50,000	23.6%(159)	25.1%(132)	24.2%(291)		
₦60.000 - ₦100,000	26.2%(177)	35.9%(189)	30.5%(366)		
₦110.000 - ₦150,000	15.6%(105)	19.0%(100)	17.1%(205)		
₦160.000 - ₦2000,000	14.1%(95)	9.1%(48)	11.9%(143)		
₦210.000 and above	20.6%(139)	10.8%(57)	16.3%(196)		
Total	100%(675)	100%(526)	100%(1201)		
Chi-Square=X² =34.825ᵃ	N= 1201	df = 4	P < 0.000		
Age category /Income	10-13years	14-17years	18-21years	22-25years	35 and above
₦10.000 - ₦50,000	28.3%(13)	25.2%(157)	22.2%(115)	38.5%(5)	100%(1)
₦60.000 - ₦100,000	37.0%(17)	31.3%(195)	29.2%(151)	29.2%(151)	0.0%(0)
₦110.000 - ₦150,000	21.7%(10)	16.5%(103)	17.6%(91)	7.7%(1)	0.0%(0)
₦160.000 - ₦2000,000	8.7%(4)	11.7%(73)	12.2%(63)	23.1%(3)	0.0%(0)
₦210.000 and above	4.3%(2)	15.2%(95)	18.9%(98)	7.7%(1)	0.0%(0)
Total	100%(46)	100%(623)	100%(518)	100%(13)	100%(1201)
	3.9%	51.9%	43.1%	1.1%	
Chi-Square=X² =17.410ᵃ	N= 1201	df = 16	P < 0.360		

Source: Computation from Field Survey, 2021

The Igbo socio-cultural characteristics comprise religious affiliation, gender, prevalent type of apprenticeship, communities' identification and age. With respect to religious affiliation, the majority of the respondents who earn between ₦60,000.00 - ₦100,000.00 representing 30.5% of the responses indicated that there is a relationship between religious affiliation and the income earned. 24.2% of the respondents that earn between ₦10,000.00 - ₦50,000.00 indicated that there is a relationship between religious affiliation and the income earned. 17.1% of the respondents that earned between ₦110,000.00 - ₦150,000.00 indicated that there is a relationship between religious affiliation and income earned. 16.3% of the respondents that earned between ₦210,000.00 and above indicated that there is a relationship between religious affiliation and income earned while 11.9% of the respondents that earned between ₦160,000.00 - ₦200,000.00 indicated that there is a relationship between religious affiliation and income earned. Few people representing 11.9% of the respondents indicated that there is a relationship between religious affiliation and income earned.

With respect to gender, the majority of the respondents who earn between ₦60,000.00 - ₦100,000.00 representing 30.5%(366) of the responses indicated that there is a relationship between gender and the income earned. 24.2%(291) of the respondents that earn between ₦10,000.00 - ₦50,000.00 indicated that there is a relationship between gender and income earned. 17.5%(123) of the respondents that earned between ₦110,000.00 - ₦150,000.00 indicated that there is a relationship between gender and the income earned. 16.3% of the respondents that earned between ₦210,000.00 and above indicated that there is a relationship between gender and income earned while 16.3%(196) of the respondents that earned between ₦210.000 and above indicated that there is a relationship between gender and income earned while 11.9%(143) of the respondents that earned between ₦160,000.00 - ₦200,000.00 indicated that there is a relationship between gender and income earned. With respect to the prevalent type of apprenticeship, respondents who earn between ₦60,000.00 - ₦100,000.00 representing 30.5%(366) of the responses indicated that there is a relationship between the type of apprenticeship and income earned. 24.2%(291) of the respondents that earn between ₦10,000.00 - ₦50,000.00 indicated that there is a relationship between the type of apprenticeship and income earned. 17.5%(123) of the respondents that earned between ₦110,000.00 - ₦150,000.00 indicated that there is a relationship between the type of apprenticeship and income earned. 16.3% of the respondents that earned between ₦210,000.00 and above indicated that there is a relationship between the type of apprenticeship and income earned while 16.3%(196) of the respondents that earned between ₦210.000 and above indicated that there is a relationship between the type of apprenticeship and income earned while 11.9%(143) of the respondents that earned between ₦160,000.00 - ₦200,000.00 indicated that there is a relationship between the type of apprenticeship and income earned.

As shown in Table 127, with respect to community identification and entrepreneurial success, respondents who earn between ₦10,000.00 - ₦50,000.00 representing 23.6%(159) and 25.1%(132) of the respondents said 'YES' or 'NO' indicated that there is a relationship between the type of community identification and entrepreneurial success (income earned). Respondents who earn between ₦60,000.00 - ₦100,000.00 representing 26.2%(177) and 35.9%(189) that said 'YES' or 'NO' indicated that there is a strong and positive relationship between the type of community identification and entrepreneurial success (income earned). Respondents who earn between ₦110.000 - ₦150,000 representing 15.6%(105) and 19.0%(100) that said 'YES' or 'NO' indicated that there is a relationship between the type of community identification and entrepreneurial success (income earned). Respondents who earn between ₦160.000 - ₦200,000 representing 14.1%(95) and 9.1%(48) that said 'YES' or 'NO' indicated that there is a relationship between the type of community identification and entrepreneurial success (income earned). Respondents who earn between ₦210.000 and above representing 20.6 %(139) and 10.8 %(57) that said 'YES' or 'NO' indicated that there is a relationship between the type of community identification and entrepreneurial success (income earned). In the final analysis, respondents (675) who indicated that there is a relationship between community identification and entrepreneurial success (income earned) are in the majority. With respect to age category and entrepreneurial success as proxied by income, 3.9% of the respondents aged between 10-13 years indicated that there is a relationship between age category and entrepreneurial success as proxied by income. 51.9% of the respondents aged between 14-17years indicated that there is a relationship between age category and entrepreneurial success as proxied by income. 43.1% of the respondents that aged between 18-21 years indicated that there is a relationship between age category and entrepreneurial success as proxied by income. 1.1% of the respondents that aged between 22-25 years indicated that there is a relationship between age category and entrepreneurial success as proxied by income.

4.4.1 Hypothesis One

Ha₁: There is a relationship between Igbo Socio-cultural characteristics and Entrepreneurial success among Igbo traders in Onitsha Markets.
Hypothesis one was tested using Chi-Square test statistics. From the test results, only community identification and entrepreneurial success nexus were found to be significant.

Chi-Square = $X^2 = 34.825^a$
No of samples = N= 1201
Degree of Freedom = df = 4
Probability Value = P < 0.000

The Probability value = P < 0.000 shows that the result of the chi-square test statistic is significant. The study therefore, rejects the null hypothesis and accepts the alternative by concluding that there is a strong and positive relationship between Igbo socio-cultural characteristics and entrepreneurial success among Igbo Traders in Onitsha Markets.

Table 128: Analyzing Responses to Research Question Two and Hypothesis Two on *Ndị Ọga* who participated in *Nwa Boyi* apprenticeship scheme are more likely to succeed in business than those who did not

Community Identification /Income	Yes	No	Total		
₦10.000 - ₦50,000	26.1%(238)	18.4%(53)	24.2%(291)		
₦60.000 - ₦100,000	30.6%(279)	30.2%(87)	30.5%(366)		
₦110.000 - ₦150,000	16.2%(148)	19.8%(57)	17.1%(205)		
₦160.000 - ₦2000,000	12.2%(111)	11.1%(32)	11.9%(143)		
₦210.000 and above	15.0%(137)	20.5%(59)	16.3%(196)		
Total	100%(913)	100%(288)	100%(1201)		
Chi-Square=X^2 =11.194^a	N= 1201	df = 4	P < 0.024		

Source: Computation from Field Survey, 2021

Table 128 shows *Ndị Ọga* who participated in *Nwa Boyi* apprenticeship and those that did not before venturing into business and their success level proxied by their average monthly income. 26.1% of *Ndị Ọga* who participated in *Nwa Boyi* apprenticeship before venturing into business earn between ₦10,000.00 and ₦50,000.00 as monthly income while 18.4% of *Ndị Ọga* who did not participate in *Nwa Boyi* apprenticeship before venturing into business earn between ₦10,000.00 and ₦50,000.00 as monthly income. 30.6% of *Ndị Ọga* who participated in *Nwa Boyi* apprenticeship before venturing into business earn between ₦60,000.00 and ₦100,000.00 as monthly income while 30.2% of *Ndị Ọga* who did not participate in *Nwa Boyi* apprenticeship before venturing into business earn between ₦10,000.00 and ₦50,000.00 as monthly income. 16.2% of *Ndị Ọga* who participated in *Nwa Boyi* apprenticeship before venturing into business earn between ₦110,000.00 and ₦150,000.00 as monthly income while 19.8% of *Ndị Ọga* who did not participate in *Nwa Boyi* apprenticeship before venturing into business earn between ₦110,000.00 and ₦150,000.00 as monthly income.12.2% of *Ndị Ọga* who participated in *Nwa Boyi* apprenticeship before venturing into business earn between ₦160,000.00 and ₦200,000.00 as monthly income while 11.1% of *Ndị Ọga* who did not participate in *Nwa Boyi* apprenticeship before venturing into business earn between ₦160,000.00 and ₦200,000.00 as monthly income. 15.0% of *Ndị Ọga* who participated in *Nwa Boyi apprenticeship before venturing into business earn between N210, 000.00 and above* as monthly income while 20.5 % of *Ndị Ọga* who did not participate in *Nwa Boyi* apprenticeship before venturing into business earn between ₦210,000.00 and above as monthly income. On the whole, the findings suggest that *Ndị Ọga* (913 respondents) who participated in *Nwa Boyi* apprenticeship scheme are more likely to succeed in business than those (288 respondents) who did not.

4.4.2 Hypothesis Two

Ha₂: *Ndị Ọga* who participated in the *Nwa Bọyị* apprenticeship scheme are more likely to succeed in business than those who did not.

Hypothesis two was tested using Chi-Square Tests. From the result of the chi-square results,

Chi-Square = X^2 = 11.194ᵃ
No of samples = N= 1201
Degree of Freedom = df = s4
Probability Value = P < 0.024

The Probability value = P < 0.024 shows that the result of the chi-square statistics is significant. Inspection of the results in Table 128 reveal that entrepreneurs having N60,000 to N100,000 income per month are the most successful since they scored highest with (30.6%) of those that did *bọyị*. The next 30.2% are those that were no. The results support Hypothesis Two.

The study, therefore, rejects the null hypothesis and accepts the alternative by concluding that *Ndị Ọga* who participated in *Nwa Bọyị* apprenticeship scheme succeeded more in business than those who did not.

Table 129: Analyzing Responses to Research Question Three and Hypothesis Three on *Ọga*'s Type of Business and the Length of Stay of *Nwa Bọyị*

Type of Business	Less than 2yrs	2-4yrs	4-6yrs	6-8yrs	8yrs and above	Total
Main Market, Textile	131(34.9%)	89(36.3%)	191(49.6%)	68(36.4%)	7(77.8%)	486(40.5%)
Ochanja Market, Shoe, and Provision	85(22.7%)	56(22.9%)	68(17.7%)	27(14.4%)	1(11.1%)	237(19.7%)
Bridge HeadMarket, Pharmaceuticals	51(13.6%)	38(15.5%)	49(12.9%)	41(12.9%)	0(0.0%)	179(14.9%)
Spare Parts Market, Nkpor	61(16.3%)	41(16.7%)	47(12.9%)	33(17.6%)	0(0.0%)	182(15.2%)
Building Materials Market, Ogidi/Ogbunike	47(12.5)	21(8.6%)	30(7.8%)	18(9.6%)	1(11.1%)	117(9.7%)
	375(100%)	245(100%)	385(100%)	187(100%)	9(100%)	1201(100%)
Chi-Square	X²=41.534ᵃ	N= 1201	df = 16	P < 0. 000		

Source: Computation from Field Survey, 2021

As shown in Table 129, five different businesses were investigated in five different markets (Main Market, Textile; Ọchanja Market, Shoe, and Provision; Bridge Head Market, Pharmaceuticals; Spare Parts Market, Nkpor and Building

Materials Market, Ogidi/Ogbunike) to find out if the types of businesses carried out in the various markets have a relationship with the length of stay of *Nwa Boyi*. From the results, respondents in the main market which represent the textile business scored 191(49.6%) which suggests that the ideal number of years for the textile business is 4-6yrs. Respondents from the Ọchanja market that trade on shoes and provision scored 56(22.9%) which suggests that the ideal number of years for the apprenticeship is 2-4yrs. Respondents from Bridge Head Market that represent pharmaceuticals scored 38(15.5%). It suggests that the ideal number of years for the apprentice is 2-4yrs. Respondents from the spare parts market, Nkpor scored 33(17.6%) indicating that the ideal number of years for the apprentice is 6-8yrs while respondents from the building material market, Ogidi/Ogbunike scored 47(12.5) suggesting the ideal number of years for the apprentice is less than 2yrs. From the foregoing, there is an obvious asymmetry in the responses on the type of business *Ọga* is dealing in and the length of stay of the *Nwa Boyi*. The majority of the respondents, that is about 40.5% from the main market, which represents the textile business, rank highest in indicating that there is a relationship between the type of business *Ọga* is dealing in and the length of stay of *nwa boy*. This is followed by 19.7% of respondents representing the Ọchanja Market - Shoe and Provision. Spare parts market, Nkpor ranked third with 15.2% followed by BridgeHead market - pharmaceuticals 14.9% and the Building Material market, Ogidi/Ogbunike 7.9%.

4.4.3 Hypothesis Three

Ha₃: There is a relationship between the type of business *Ọga* deals in and the length of stay of *Nwa Boyi* among Igbo Traders in Onitsha Markets.
Hypothesis three was tested using Chi-Square. From the results,

Chi-Square = X^2 = 41.5
No of samples = N= 1201
Degree of Freedom = df = 16
Probability Value = P < 0.001

The result shows that the test statistic is significant at 0.001 as indicated by the probability value. The study therefore accepts the alternative hypothesis by concluding that there is a positive and significant relationship between the type of business *Ọga* is dealing in and the length of stay of *Ụmụ Bọyị*.

Table 130: Analyzing Responses to Research Question Four and Hypothesis Four on *Ndị Ọga* with a Higher level of Education being more likely to achieve business success than those with a Lower level of Education

Higher level of Education/business success		N	Coefficient=R	Probability Value
Levels of Education	Highest level of education	1201	.169	.001
	Adult education			
	Masters			
	Further education			

Source: Computation from Field Survey, 2021

The educational level of *Ndi Oga* comprises the highest level of education, adult education, masters, and further education. The test of hypothesis was carried out using Pearson Product Moment Correlation Coefficient to ascertain the nature of the relationship between the various levels of education and business success of *Ndi Oga*. However, from the responses, it was revealed that *Ndi Oga* with a higher level of education are more likely to achieve business success than those with a lower level.

4.4.4 Hypothesis Four

Ha4: *Ndi Oga* with a Higher level of Education are more likely to achieve business success than those with Lower level of Education
Hypothesis four was tested using Pearson Product Moment Correlation Coefficient. The result reveal,

n= 1201
r = 0.169
P < 0.001

The Probability value = $P < 0.001$ shows a positive and significant relationship between a higher level of education and business success. The study therefore, accepts the alternative hypothesis by concluding that *Ndi Oga* with higher levels of education are more likely to achieve business success than those with a lower level.

Table 131: Analyzing Responses to Research Question Five and Hypothesis Five on Older apprentices being more likely to be in non-kin-related apprenticeship than Younger apprentices

Older apprentices/ younger apprentices	Kin Related	Non-Kin Related	Both	Total
Young Apprentice	19.5%(203)	52.1%(543)	28.5%(297)	100%(1043)
Older Apprentice	15.9%(25)	50.3%(79)	33.8%(53)	100%(157)
Total	19.0%(228)	51.8%(622)	29.2%(350)	100%(1200)
Chi-Square=X² =2.285ª	N= 1200	df = 2	P < 0.319	

Source: Computation from Field Survey, 2021

From Table 131, it is seen that 19.5% (203) of the younger apprentices indicated that they are in kin-related apprenticeship. 15.9% (25) of the older apprentices indicated that they are in kin-related apprenticeship. 28.5% (297) of the younger apprentices indicated that they are in both kin and non-kin related apprenticeship. 33.8% of the older apprentices indicated that they are in both kin and non-kin-related apprenticeship. The results suggest that the older apprentices are more likely to be in a non-kin-related apprenticeship than younger apprentices. This is indicated by the majority of the respondents (622). The result further revealed that non kin-related has been on the increase for a while.

4.4.5 Hypothesis Five

Ha₅: Older apprentices are more likely to be in a non-kin related apprenticeship than younger apprentices

Hypothesis five was tested using Chi-Square Tests. From the results of the Chi-Square,

Chi-Square = X^2 = 2.285ª
No of samples = N= 1200
Degree of Freedom = df = 2
Probability Value = P < 0.319

The Probability value = P < 0.319 shows that the result of the chi-square statistics is not significant. The study therefore rejects the alternative hypothesis and concludes that older apprentices are not more likely to be in a non-kin-related apprenticeship than younger apprentices.

Table 132: Analyzing Responses to Research Question Six and Hypothesis Six Younger Ndị Oga is more likely to hire female apprentices than older Ndị Oga

Younger Oga/ Older Oga	Male	Female	Total	
Younger Ogas	97.4%(338)	2.6%(9)	100%(347)	
Older Ogas	97.7%(834)	2.3%(20)	100%(854)	
Total	97.6%(1172)	2.4%(29)	100%(1201)	
Chi-Square=X² =0.066ᵃ	N= 1201	df = 1	P < 0.797	

Source: Computation from Field Survey, 2021

Table 132 reveals that 97.7% of the respondents indicated that younger Ndị Oga are more likely to hire female apprentices than older ones; 2.3%maintain the same. The result revealed that younger Ndi Oga are not more likely to hire female apprentices than older ones because they may not be able to fulfill the obligations of Nwa Boyi.

4.4.6 Hypothesis Six

Ha₆: Younger Ndi Oga are more likely to hire female apprentices than older Ndi Oga

Hypothesis six was tested using Chi-Square Tests. From the results of the Chi-Square,

Chi-Square = X² = 0.066ᵃ
No of samples = N= 1201
Degree of Freedom = df = 1
Probability Value = P < 0.797

The Probability value = P < 0. 0.797 shows that the result of the Chi-Square statistics is not significant. The study therefore, rejects the hypothesis and concludes that younger Ndi Oga are not more likely to hire female apprentices than older Ndi Oga.

Table 133: Analyzing Responses to Research Question Seven and Hypothesis Seven Availability of Adult Education enhances Entrepreneurship and Apprenticeship Skills Development among Traders in Onitsha Markets

Institutional Strategies	Observed No	Percentage	Expected No	Residuals
Adult Education Strategy	208	17.32%	240.2	-32.2
Formation of *isusu* and Cooperative	258	21.48%	240.2	17.8
Seminars workshop	235	19.57%	240.2	-5.2
Tax w Tax waivers	355	29.56%	240.2	114.8
Others	145	12.07%	240.2	-95.2
Total	1201	100.00%		
Chi-Square=X^2 =98.346a	N= 1201		df = 4	P < 0.001

Source: Computation from Field Survey, 2021

The Goodness-of-Fit Chi-Square results for Hypothesis Seven, $X^2 = 98.35$, df = 4, $p < .001$, indicate a significant difference in the number of endorsements to the five strategies (adult education (208), formation of *Isusu* and cooperatives (258), seminars and workshops (235), tax waivers (255), and others (145) for entrepreneurship and Apprenticeship skills development. Tax waiving received the highest endorsement (29.56%) followed by formation of *isusu* and cooperatives (21.48%), and seminars and workshops (19.57%). Adult education (17.32%) took the 4th and last position among the named strategies. Whereas adult education is seen as an enhancer of entrepreneurship and apprenticeship skills, it is not considered important relative to *isusu*/cooperatives and the other types of enhancers. Hypothesis Seven is supported by the results.

4.4.7 Hypothesis Seven

Ha7: Availability of adult education enhances entrepreneurship and Apprenticeship Skills Development Among Traders in Onitsha Markets Hypothesis seven was tested using Chi-Square. From the results,

Chi-Square = X^2 = 98.346a
No of samples = N= 1201
Degree of Freedom = df = 4
Probability Value = P < 0.001

The Probability value = P < 0. 0.001 shows that the result of the chi-square statistics is significant. The study therefore, accepts the alternative hypothesis by concluding that the availability of adult education enhances entrepreneurship and apprenticeship skills development among traders in Onitsha Markets.

Table 134: Analyzing Responses to Research Question Eight and Hypothesis Eight on the Relationship between Igba Boyi, Employment and Wealth Creation among Traders in Onitsha Markets

Igba Boyi Employment/Wealth Creation	N	Coefficient=R	Probability Value
Average monthly inome	1201	1	0.001
No of apprentice trained	1201	0.098	0.001

Source: Computation from Field Survey, 2021

Table 134 reveals the relationship between Igba Boyi, employment and wealth creation. The analysis reveals the nature of the relationship between Igba Boyi employment and wealth creation. The probability value shows that there is relationship between Igba Boyi, Employment and Wealth Creation.

4.4.8 Hypothesis Eight

Ha₈: There is relationship between Igba Boyi, Employment and Wealth Creation among Traders in Onitsha Markets
Hypothesis eight was tested using Pearson Correlations. From the result of the Pearson Correlations,

Q10 =R = Average monthly Income = 1
Q11 = R= Adult education = 0.98
No of samples = N= 1201
Probability Value = P < 0.001

The Probability value = $P < 0.001$ shows a positive and significant relationship between Igba Boyi, employment and wealth creation. The study therefore, accepts the alternatives by concluding that there is strong and positive relationship between Igba Boyi, Employment and Wealth Creation.

Table 135: Analyzing Responses to Research Question Nine and Hypothesis Nine on the relationship between the Acquisition of Basic Skills and Values by Umu Boyi and Entrepreneurial Success

Institutional Strategies	Observed No	Expected No	Residuals
Honesty	891	150.1	740.9
Good customer relationship	79	150.1	-71.1
Literacy	50	150.1	-100.1
Knowledge of ICT	2	150.1	-148.1
Good Negotiation	23	150.1	-127.1
Accounting skill	21	150.1	-129.1
Self-control/resilience	31	150.1	-119.1
Others	104	150.1	-46.1
Total	1201		
Chi-Square=X²=4230.294ᵃ	N= 1201	df = 7	P < 0.001

Source: Computation from Field Survey, 2021

From Table 135, basic skills and values comprise honesty, good Customer relationship, literacy, knowledge of ICT, good negotiation, accounting skills, self-control/resilience, and others. 891 respondents indicated that honesty by *Umu Boyi* has a relationship with entrepreneurial success. 79 respondents identified good customer relationship; 50 respondents chose literacy; 2 respondents indicated knowledge of ICT; 23 respondents identified good negotiation skills; 21 respondents chose accounting skills while 31 respondents indicated self-control/resilience. 104 respondents however, identified other skills acquired by Umu Boyi as having a relationship with entrepreneurial success. The overall results suggest that honesty stands out as the main value needed by *Umu Boyi* that significantly impacts on entrepreneurial success.

4.4.9 Hypothesis Nine

Ha9: There is a relationship between the Acquisition of Basic Skills and Values by *Umu Boyi* and Entrepreneurial Success
Hypothesis nine was tested using Chi-Square Tests. From the results of the chi-square,

Chi-Square = X^2 = 4230.294[a]
No of samples = N = 1201
Degree of Freedom = df = 7
Probability Value = P < 0.001

The Probability value = P < 0. 0.001 shows that the result of the chi-square statistics is significant. The study therefore accepts the alternate hypothesis by concluding that there is a positive and significant relationship between the acquisition of basic skills and value by *Umu Boyi* and entrepreneurial success.

Table 136: Analyzing Responses to Research Question Ten and Hypothesis Ten on the Emergence of Sales Girls as being likely to displace the *Igba Boyi* scheme among *Ndi Igbo* in Onitsha Markets.

	Observed No	Expected No	Residuals
Yes	157	400.3	-243.3
No	966	400.3	565.7
Don't know	78	400.3	-322.3
Total	1201		
Chi-Square=X^2=1206.716[a]	N= 1201	df = 2	P < 0.001

Source: Computation from Field Survey, 2021

As shown in Table 136, 157 respondents indicated that the emergence of sales girls will likely displace the *Igba Boyi* scheme among *Ndị Igbo* in Onitsha Markets while 966 respondents suggest otherwise. 78 respondents were undecided.

4.4.10 Hypothesis Ten

Ha10: The emergence of sales girls will likely displace the *igba boyi* scheme among *Ndị Igbo* in Onitsha Markets
Hypothesis ten was tested using Chi-Square Tests. From the results of the Chi-Square,

      Chi-Square = X^2 = 1206.716[a]
      No of samples = N= 1201
      Degree of Freedom = df = 2
      Probability Value = P < 0.001

The Probability value = P < 0. 0.001 shows that the result of the chi-square statistics is significant. The study therefore, rejects the alternative hypothesis by concluding that the emergence of salesgirls will not likely displace the *Igba Boyi* scheme among *Ndị Igbo* in Onitsha Markets.

Table 137: Analyzing Responses to Research Question Eleven and Hypothesis Eleven on the relationship between the decline in *Igba Boyi* and loss of family values among Igbo youths.

	N	Mean	Standard Deviation
Kin related	237	2.55	1.316
Non-kin-related	381	2.85	1.454
Both	583	2.57	1.363
Total	1201	2.66	1.389
ANOVA = 2314.978	df= 2	F = 2	P < 0.001

Source: Computation from Field Survey, 2021

Table 137, was used to examine the relationship between the decline in *Igba Boyi* and loss of family values among Igbo youths. As shown in the descriptive statistics, the relationship between the decline in *Igba Boyi* and loss of family values among Igbo youths has a mean of 2.55 and 2.85 respectively. The analysis of variance was used to find out if there is a significant relationship or difference between them. The result shows that the descriptive statistics did not meet the mean theoretical threshold of 3.0 which is the cut-off on a 5 point Likert scale. It, therefore, reveals that there is a relationship between the decline in *Igba Boyi* and the loss of family values among Igbo youths.

4.4.11 Hypothesis Eleven

Ha₁₁: There is a relationship between the decline in *Igba Boyi* and loss of family values among Igbo youths

Hypothesis eleven was tested using ANOVA. From the results,

ANOVA = 2314.978
No of samples = N= 1200
Degree of Freedom = df = 2
F = 5.673
Probability Value = P < 0.004

The Probability value = P < 0.004 shows that the result of the ANOVA is significant. The study therefore, accepts the alternate hypothesis by concluding that there is a significant and positive relationship between the decline in *Igba Boyi* and loss of family values among Igbo youths.

Table 138: Analyzing Responses to Research Question Twelve and Hypothesis Twelve on the interference by the Government in the relationship between *Ndị Oga* and *Umu Boyi*

	N	Mean	Std. Dev	T	df	Prob. Value
Specific regulation	1201	1.4471	0.91328	-58.926	1200	0.000
Government Agencies	1201	3.14	1.644	2.914	1200	0.004
Market Associations	1201	2.9334	1.61262	-1.431	1200	0.153
Adult Education	1201	1.8718	1.12111	-34.876	1200	0.000
Masters and Apprentices	1201	2.2240	1.16146	-23.155	1200	0.000
Further Education	1201	3.4113	1.44994	9.831	1200	0.000

Source: Computation from Field Survey, 2021

The analysis was presented in Table 138 which reveals the mean score of the responses. This is indicated by a mean of 3.14 and a standard deviation of 1.644. The result meets the theoretical mean threshold of 3.0 which is the cutoff for accepting or rejecting responses on a 5-point Likert scale and therefore suggests that the government does not interfere in the relationship between *Ndị Oga* and *Umu Boyi*.

4.4.12 Hypothesis Twelve

Ha₁₂: Government does not interfere in the relationship between *Ndị Ọga* and *Ụmụ Boyi*

Hypothesis twelve was tested using a one-sample t-test. From the result,
t = 2.914
df= 1200

Mean value = 3.14
No of samples = N= 1201
Probability Value = P < 0.004

The Probability value is positive and significant at P < 0.004. The study, therefore, accepts the alternative by concluding that the government does not interfere in the relationship between *Ndị Ọga* and *Ụmụ Boyi*.

Section Five

Discussion of Findings

Section Five
Discussion of Findings

This section focuses on the empirical expositions and findings from the concurrently mixed quantitative and qualitative analysis of data from the study-'Reinvigorating Igbo Entrepreneurial Behaviour through Enhanced Apprenticeship Scheme in Onitsha Markets'.

The findings from Table 127 and Hypothesis 1 revealed that there is a positive relationship between Igbo socio-cultural characteristics (religious affiliation, gender, prevalent type of apprenticeship, communities identification, age) and entrepreneurial success. This is in line with the views of Bandura (1977) that a distinctive social learning process begins from the family/kindred unit and invests in the entrepreneurial socialization of its members at a very young age. The postulations of Akhter & Surni (2014) are in consonance with the findings of this study that socio-cultural environment, in relation to entrepreneurship, can be seen as consisting of all the elements of the social system and culture of a people which positively or negatively affect and influence entrepreneurial emergence, behaviour and entrepreneurial development in general. Some proverbs that tend to drive home their socio-cultural beliefs are *"Akpaa na anwu, elie na ndo"*; *"Ngana kpuchie ute, aguu ekpughe ya"*, *"Onye fee eze, eze eluo ya"*. All the three point to timely hard work, perseverance and success. This is rooted in the traditions of the people given further impetus by the qualitative findings.

On the origin and reasons for '*Igba Boyi*', the study established that historically, the entrepreneurial and apprenticeship culture is mainly associated with the Igbo people of Southeastern Nigeria and it began in precolonial times before contact with the Europeans. The practice had existed long before the birth of most contemporary practitioners in the selected markets studied. It initially began as a skill acquisition enterprise specifically for the transfer, maintenance, and sustenance of inherited skills within notable Igbo families known for their expertise in certain crafts. Later, there was a shift from not just maintaining the skills within families, but to other families (whose children are willing to learn the craft, trade, or skill) within the extended families, village, and community levels. One of the many reasons is to alleviate the burdens of parents with large family sizes. These children were sent to learn and acquire some traditional skills in blacksmithing, traditional herbal skills, textile, crafts, pottery, oil palm processing, agricultural produce among so many others. The

Igba Boyi scheme is operated on the '*Igwe bu ike*' philosophy, '*Onye aghana nwanne ya*' ideology, '*Ọgọ bụ chi ọnye*', '*Nwanne dị na mba*' slogan, '*adịghị anọ-ofu ebe ekili mmanwụ*' cliché, among others. Some of these peculiar cultural characteristics have sustained the contemporary vestiges of the original traditional form of *Igba Boyi* practice among *Ndị Igbo*. These characteristics range from its capacity to adjust to modifications over time, its potentials to increase wealth for Igbo entrepreneurs, ensure expansion in private trade and industry, capacity for sustainable expansion of family business, provide the foundation for advancement in social mobility and ensure sustainable social protection *system for Ndị-Igbo*. All these principles put together remain the superstructure upon which the *Igba Boyi* scheme is operated and sustained. In terms of theorizations and conceptualization of *Igba Boyi* for better understanding of this apprenticeship scheme, this study established that *Igba Boyi* is best conceptualized as *Nkwado Ọgaranya* or *Apprenticepreneurship* - the sum of the complex exchanges and interactions between an apprentice and an entrepreneur which involves observation and imitation through modelling. This is further conceptualised as the *Igbo Entrepreneurial Incubation Scheme (IEIS)* that sets the apprentice on a new threshold of gaining the experiential knowledge of a master over a period of time towards sustainable empowerment and self-actualisation. The foregoing conceptualisation expunges the stigma surrounding apprenticeship that has served to de-incentivise many young persons from getting involved in apprenticeship. This implies that *Apprenticepreneurship* is a mutual relationship that promotes the interests of both the entrepreneur and the apprentice.

In terms of the structure, practice and management of "*igba-boyi*" scheme among Onitsha markets traders in Igboland, the master (*Ọga*) provides leadership and guidance to the apprentice and upon the arrival of an intending dependent-apprentice to the master's home/house. He takes directives from the master (*Ọga*) and sometimes from the wife of his master (Madam) and the senior '*ụmụ boyi*', relatives and children of his master (*Ọga*). Similarly, relatives of the master could also give orders which *Nwa Boyi* will obey and execute.

Away from activities in the master's home, the apprentice must report daily and punctually too to the shop where trading activities occur. These activities range from opening and cleaning the shop, sorting, dusting and arranging goods, hunting for customers (*ọsọ-ahịa*), loading and off-loading goods, to buying or going home to prepare food (brunch and lunch where/when necessary) among many other expectations. In the process of executing all these responsibilities, he learns the ropes and the nitty-gritty of the trade through observation, imitation and modelling. All of these are emblematic of Igbo custom and tradition.

The revelations from Table 128 and Hypothesis 2 show that *Ndị Oga* who participated in *Nwa Boyi* apprenticeship scheme are more likely to succeed in business than those who did not. These findings are clearly supported by the study of Onwuegbuzie (2017) that prolonged learning duration through experience has a direct relationship on the chances of a successful entrepreneurial outcome.

The findings are also in affirmation with the study of Ezenwakwelu, Egbosionu & Okwo (2019) that apprentices acquire technical and entrepreneurial skills for self-employment through formal and informal apprenticeship training systems. The study participants corroborate the results of the quantitative data when they chorused during the different sessions of FGD that those who did not go through the apprenticeship scheme are not complete traders as many of the nuances that are pivotal to business success remain shrouded in mystery for them.

Findings from Table 129 and Hypothesis 3 clearly revealed that the type of business *Ndị Ọga* are dealing in is related to the length of stay of *Ụmụ Bọyi*. Muskin (2009) maintains that prevalence of such long tenures in apprenticeship is a resource scarcity. It is not usually easy to access venture capital or start-up funds for budding entrepreneurs unless they have been able to establish trust and confidence from their master and this requires long-term training. Some particular trades are more demanding and require more time like pharmaceuticals and cosmetics; automobile spare parts.

From the qualitative results, it was equally evident that various types of apprentices were identified and they are mainly categorized into two namely: kin-related, and non-kin-related apprenticeship; though each category embodies variants which have been conceptualized with the following terms *Igba Bọyi* (live-in /residential or dependent-apprenticeship and *Onye n'amụ-ahịa* (Independent apprenticeship). The main difference between this and the former is that this apprentice does not live in his master's home, payment and non-payment for training as the non-dependent apprentice pays while the dependent apprentices do not pay; tenureship (length of stay/training) as the non-dependent apprentices spends shorter time under the tutelage of the master than the dependent apprentice. From the interviews, it was established that dependent apprentices with longer tenureship understand the trade better with a greater potential to succeed in the trade than non-dependent apprentices.

The findings from Table 130 and Hypothesis 4 revealed that *Ndị Ọga* with higher levels of education are more likely to achieve business success than those with lower levels of education. This is in affirmation with the recommendations of ILO (2012) that further training is a way of upskilling adults already at work. In the traditional Igbo entrepreneurial scheme, educational level did not matter, presently however, it has become imperative since higher levels of education definitely enhances general entrepreneurial skills and activities.

From the qualitative perspective, many traders were of the opinion that most 'early *Ndị Ọga* were not educated and the rate of illiteracy* seemed to be a contributory factor to the perceived decline in the Igbo apprenticeship scheme'. Another perspective of the study participants is that many people hold, believe, and perceive *Igba Boyi* as '*suffering and descending to a lower level after formal education*'. Hence, *Igba Boyi* is *now less appealing to the younger educated Igbo population* and their parents and as such, no one is ready to send his or her wards to *Igba Boyi*, including most of the contemporary *Ndi Oga* (masters). This finding makes education more imperative especially in modern society as the demand of work and business require formal education.

The findings from Table 131 and Hypothesis 5 reveal that the older apprentices are not more likely to be in a non-kin-related apprenticeship than younger ones. This is in affirmation with ILO (2012) that maintains that informal apprenticeship is more open than traditional apprenticeship and apprentices come from outside the family or kin group. Currently, there is a new trend in the *Igba Boyi* apprenticeship scheme which is gradually setting the stage for a complete shift in paradigm from kin-related to the prevalent non-kin-related apprenticeship. This gradual change in the practice of *Igba Boyi* is associated with a lot of factors namely: modern education, the Nigerian-Biafran war, suspicion and lack of trust, accusations and counter-accusations of theft, misappropriation of the master's (*Oga's*) business capital, and mismanagement, greed and court cases by extended family members who want to take over the business of their brothers/relatives (masters) at their demise thereby leaving the wife and children empty-handed. Others are bickering and outright conflicts between *Ndi Oga* and apprentices, among many other issues. These identified factors and more, therefore, led to a shift from the familial, consanguineal, affinal, or kin-related dependent apprenticeship to non-kin-related dependent apprenticeship. The above assertion also explains the age factor which can make older apprentices have a discretion on where to go for tutelage. This is amply demonstrated by Hanson (2005) who asserted that in Ghana, many masters/madams revealed that they engaged their apprentices through a network of family, kin, neighbours and co-workers. This further confirms the findings of this study, that the non-kin-related apprenticeship is an emerging phenomenon in West Africa.

Findings from Table 132 and Hypothesis 6 show that younger *Ndi Oga* are not more likely to hire female apprentices than older *Ndi Oga*. In understanding Why "*Igba Boyi*" and not "*Igba Geli*", the study established that *Igba Boyi* is energy-demanding, females being excluded automatically by nature, and the need for the maintenance of division of labour or gender-based division of labour and strict gender roles as structured by the Igbo society were the primary reasons for the male-centeredness of *Igba Boyi* scheme in Igbo land. Beyond all these, *Igba Boyi* is too demanding mentally and energy-wise and many women/girls may not cope with these demands and that is why they are naturally excluded in the *Igba Boyi* apprenticeship scheme in Igboland. From a critical gender analysis or from a feminist angle, the demands of the modern world have outlived any one-sided gender-based economy. The reluctance by the younger *Oga* and the older ones to engage female *Nwa Boyi* or *Nwa Geli* as the study has so aptly dubbed it, seems to perpetuate the exclusion of the women folk from a practice that has brought immense benefits to families and the larger Igbo society. This is counter productive.

Even the use of sales girls does not serve as a substitute for *Nwa Boyi* as the findings eloquently show.

Women have now upgraded and are not just sitting at home but are now joining their husbands in the markets and shops. Some of these women have the capacity to 'hire and fire' fellow women as 'sales girls'. One thing that has been established in this study is that there is absolute absence of female apprentices in the *Igba Boyi* scheme in Igbo land. There could be other dynamics or manifestations of women in these markets either as accountants, recorders, store keepers, *Oga*'s wife or girlfriend but not a 'live-in female apprentice'. Although, female presence in these selected Onitsha trading scenes/markets could be problematic as females could engage in pilfering, stealing, looting *Oga*'s warehouses and cash among so many atrocities. But many of these masters of businesses have devised techniques of reducing the negative aspects of recruiting females in the markets like taking care of their personal needs and paying them well in order to gain their trust.

Table 133 and Hypothesis 7 show the contribution of Adult education to entrepreneurship and Apprenticeship skills development among traders in Onitsha Markets. This is in line with the position of UNESCO in 2010 on the critical role of adult education in the development of any society. This finding also supports the view that adult education is the entire body of organized educational process and an integral part of a global scheme for lifelong education and learning. This is in affirmation with the National Policy on Education in 2013 for the promotion of mass literacy, adult and non-formal education. The study participants during the Interviews and Focus Group Discussions, also affirmed the necessity for further education towards improving their accounting, documentation and stock-taking skills.

The findings from Table 134 and Hypothesis 8 clearly indicate that there is a positive relationship between *Nwa Boyi*, employment and wealth creation. These findings affirm the study of Oyo & Oluwatayo (2015) who maintain that entrepreneurship can contribute to the reduction of unemployment, reduction in poverty and hunger, reduction in terrorism and criminal activities, increase in infrastructural development. The study by Hisrich et al (2007) supports these findings that entrepreneurial activity brought independence, economic and social reforms. This is also in line with the postulation by Orugun & Nafiu

(2014) that the Igbo entrepreneurial activities are the panacea for the Nigerian economic growth and development and recommended that Nigerians and the people of other developing countries of the world should emulate the Igbo entrepreneurship culture for economic development purposes. The apprenticeship scheme contributes to wealth creation and employment generation: 'lifted people out of poverty, contributed to capacity building, ensuring wealth succession and sustainability, producing informal 'professors' in trade and business.

The findings from Table 135 and Hypothesis 9 reveal that there is a positive relationship between the acquisition of basic skills and values by *Umu Boyi* and entrepreneurial success. These findings support the position of Olulu & Udeora (2015) that training apprentices enables the absorption of extensive skills and erudition in a particular trade or craft under the guidance of an expert which aims at accelerating the career of an apprentice towards developing into an accomplished tradesperson. (Collins, Brown & Newman, 1989 in Ezenwakwelu, Egbosionu & Okwo (2019) affirm the findings by positing that apprenticeship is an instructional method for teaching an acceptable way of understanding and doing tasks, solving problems, and dealing with problematic situations. *Igba Boyi* scheme is a system of training a new generational set of practitioners with a structured competency and expected basic set of skills. The revelation from the findings also support the position of ILO (2012) that apprenticeship is a training programme that combines vocational education with work-based learning for intermediate occupation skills and that are subject to externally imposed training standards, particularly for their workplace component.

The findings also support the inseparability of values to business success as it highlighted the integral nature of honesty, trustworthiness, diligence, patience and discipline.

The findings from Table 136 and Hypothesis 10 indicate that the emergence of sales girls will not likely displace the *Igba Boyi* scheme among *ndi Igbo* in Onitsha markets. Although our conceptual review is not in affirmation, it is important to note that the females received their own training by staying at home with their mothers learning the rudiments of housekeeping and going to farms with the whole family, when the need arose. The young females recently seem to be serving as *Nwa Boyi* apprentices in the feminine version known as *Igba Geli* or sales girls and this is a total change in paradigm which has brought in the perspective of *nwa geli*. According to Palmer (2007), apprenticeships are lopsided in terms of gender, where young girls are left only in their traditional roles like seamstress, cake making, hairdressing, and soap making.

Table 137 and Hypothesis 11 reveal that there is a decline in *Igba Boyi* among Igbo youths as a result of decline of family values. These revelations affirm the studies of Adeola (2021), Agu et al (2020), Igwe et al (2018) and Madichie et al (2008). Their observations are in line with the position of this study that the *Igba Boyi* apprenticeship institution seems to be in a state of flux, if not of crisis. There seems to be a precipitous descent, or decline in the *Igba Boyi* apprenticeship model. The romantic picture painted of Igbo apprenticeship is being debunked by the steady decline as this study has revealed. Nwanoruo (2004); Fajobi, Olatujoye, Amusa & Adedoyin (2017 in Ojo-Orusa & Destiny, 2019) argued that Igbo apprenticeship is facing many challenges which may eventually lead to its decline.

Table 138 and Hypothesis 12 reveal that the government does not interfere in the relationship between *Ndị Oga* and *Ụmụ Boyi*. This is corroborated by the study of Cedefop (2018) who maintained the importance of understanding the relevance and role of apprenticeships in national policies for collective skills formation, as part of human capital development strategies.

The findings are also in line with the study of Chankselians, Keep & Wilde (2017) who recommended the use of employer bodies as the best form of intermediary in regulating the apprenticeship scheme. The study of Chankselians et al (2017) further argued that the German Association of Commerce and Industry, and Denmark adopted the model via employer bodies, and have evolved organically, therefore, are more likely to survive, as well as having gained the trust of all the parties over time.

Section Six

Conclusion and Policy Recommendations

Section Six
Conclusion and Policy Recommendations

6.1 Conclusion

The age-old entrepreneurial behaviour of *Ndị Igbo* has been a subject of interest among scholars. The springboard for this widely recognised Igbo entrepreneurial behaviour is the *Igba Boyi* which has peculiar features and characteristics namely: family/community embeddedness, domesticity of the *Nwa Boyi*, settlement of *Umu Boyi* as evident in the provision of startup capital, male-centredness, pervasive informality and the notorious absence of government involvement. Igbo apprenticeship that made tens of thousands of Igbo men in Igboland is now on a steady decline. The central tenet of this study is the progressive decline of the apprenticeship scheme which, if left unchecked, will affect the legendary Igbo entrepreneurship spirit with ramifications on the people's development and overall well being. The dynamics of the Igbo apprenticeship scheme has introduced new patterns, like the non-kin-related apprentices, the emerging use of sales girls and a new generation of *Ndị Oga* that are averse to engaging *Umu Boyi*. The study reconceptualises the *Igba Boyi* model as Apprenticepreneurship or as *Nkwado Ogaranya* as a way of sustaining the values behind the Igbo spirit of enterprise. It was observed that the devaluation of family values and the new orientation of get-rich-quick mentality (*igbu ozu, ibute ike*) were implicated as some of the causative factors that have affected the state of Igbo apprenticeship.

The study revealed a skewed pattern of *Igba Boyi* where it is an exclusive, male-dominated scheme. *Igba Geli* or female apprenticeship is either totally absent, or minimally present in the markets studied in Onitsha. It was also shown that the majority of the traders in Onitsha Markets went through the tutelage of *Igba Boyi* under different masters, and this was critical to their business success.

The study noted the inactive nature of adult education and the almost unanimous desire of the traders in Onitsha Markets to have further education that is relevant to their trade. The study observed that the absence of formal agreements, lack of funds or startup capital, influence of peer pressure on *Umu Boyi* and a new disturbing work ethos have conspired to challenge the smooth running of the *Igba Boyi* scheme.

The centrality of *Igba Boyi* as progenetics or replicating oneself is seen in the ability of the apprenticeship scheme to transfer knowledge to upcoming generations which is regenerative in nature as the *Nwa Boyi is* also expected to do in the same tradition as the study has elucidated.

6.2 Policy Recommendations

Based on the findings of the study, the following recommendations are made with policy implications:

1) Need for Revival of Values: It is imperative that the old values which hitherto held sway should be revived. The Igbo philosophies of *onye aghana nwanne ya* (Be your brother's/sister's keeper) and *igwebuike* (Strength in unity) should replace the new, selfish, excessive individualism which is reminiscent of foreign values following modernisation that is dangerously creeping in. The value of honesty, hard work, industry, enterprise, patience which were hallmarks of the Igbo race.

2) Rebranding of Igbo Apprenticeship Scheme: The low sense of self esteem associated recently with *Igba Boyi* which has affected the psyche of the participants and would-be apprentices needs to be discarded. *Igba Boyi* should henceforth be characterised as Apprenticepreneurship which is *Nkwado Ogaranya*, as evident in the Igbo Entrepreneurial Incubation Scheme (IEIS). The study recommends that the communities, family, traditional rulers, town unions, age grades, churches, chambers of commerce, market leaders and all stakeholders should be involved in the mass dissemination of this new philosophy of *Igba Boyi* in Igboland.

3) Contract of Agreement: It is recommended that prior to the engagement of *Nwa Boyi*, a properly signed agreement involving all relevant parties - *Oga, Nwa Boyi* and his family, and a representative of the government should be undertaken. It is important that the pervasive informality should be guided to enhance the sustainability of the *Igba Boyi* institution. The study therefore recommends a semi-formal arrangement that allows the involvement of a neutral party, either the market union or the government, to cement the agreement.

4) Ministry of Apprenticepreneurship: This study recommends that given the pervasive nature or ubiquity of Igbo apprenticeship, its role in the life and wellbeing of many Igbo people worldwide, all Southeastern states should as a matter of priority, establish a new ministry of *Nkwado Ogaranya* or Apprenticepreneurship. This recommendation is given support by the Triple Helix Model of Apprenticepreneurship as the study has formulated.

5) Establishment of Igbo Entrepreneurial Incubation Scheme (IEIS) Centres: It is recommended that Igbo Entrepreneurial Incubation Scheme is

established through Public Private Partnership involving the academia, government and the market unions. This is to remove the deficiency in educational qualifications which has been a major setback of both apprentices and the masters. The IEIS should replace adult education centres that have been largely ignored and moribund. The content, curriculum and programmes of IEIS should be made relevant to the needs and Skill set requirements in keeping with modern trends. Therefore, commensurate adult and non-formal educational curricula can be made available by higher educational institutions for *Umu Boyi, Ndị Oga* and others who may wish to actualize their dreams towards that direction.

6) Use of New Technology: It is recommended that the modern world of trade and commerce demands proficiency in the use of new media and its technological tools for transactions. The study therefore recommends that these new technologies be embraced by traders and whatever apprehensions they have are addressed by the regulatory bodies.

7) Removing the Gender Bias in Igbo Apprenticeship: The study recommends that a more holistic and all inclusive apprenticeship scheme be adopted. This is to open up the institution to young females and utilise the hidden potentials inherent in the female folk. Not involving half of the youth population (females) in the apprenticeship scheme is a disservice to sustainable development.

8) Wealth Creation and *Igba Boyi*: It is recommended that a contributory fund for settlement of *Umu Boyi* be created and funded regularly, weekly, monthly by *Ndị Oga* over the duration of apprenticeship to enable a seamless settlement of *Umu Boyi* at the end of the tenure of apprenticeship. A reinvigoration of the apprenticeship scheme will serve to remove the jobless youth from the unemployment market, further leading to wealth creation and economic prosperity.

9) Involvement of Government in the Apprenticeship Scheme: The extant aloofness of the government in the apprenticeship scheme needs to change. The government has so far played the ostrich and shown palpable indifference to this cherished tradition of Igbo apprenticeship which has affected its continued flourishing. Governments at all levels should commit themselves to the apprenticeship scheme by provision of startup capital and certification of *Umu Boyi* who successfully complete the apprenticeship programme.

10) Involvement of International Donor Agencies and Bodies in the Igbo Apprenticeship Scheme: The study recommends that the Igbo Entrepreneurial Incubation Scheme (IEIS) that is reputed to be the largest incubation platform for apprenticeship training globally, should be supported by international donor agencies through grants, aids, soft loans, credit facilities and also exposure to international best practices and training programmes in the world of trade and commerce.

11) Apprenticepreneurship is an institutional response to the new creative economy with profound drive for innovation and digitization in trade and commerce.

6.3 Areas for Further Study

1) It is suggested that the scope of this study should be expanded to include other big markets in other Southeastern states. It is necessary to also look at other markets in other places in Nigeria where the Igbo are key players.
2) It is suggested that female apprenticeship and sales girls should attract further empirical investigation to unravel its dynamics, potentials and challenges with a view to having a holistic apprenticeship programme. It is necessary to investigate the feasibility of having *Igba Geli* on a wider scale in the markets.
3) It is pertinent to under study the role of market unions in conflict mediation and resolution among *Ndi Oga* and *Umu Boyi*. This is to address the undercurrents of conflicts bedevilling the apprenticeship scheme in Igbo land.
4) The state of infrastructure in the markets requires further studies, as it affects the Igbo apprenticeship scheme.

References

Adebisi, T. A. and Akinsooto, T. A. (2016). Women Apprenticeship: A Panacea to Unemployment among Women in Nigeria, *British Journal of Education, Society & Behavioural Science* 12(1): 1-7, 2016.

Adeola, O. (2021). Igbo Traditional Business School: An Introduction. In O. Adeola (Ed.), *Indigenous African Enterprise. Igbo Traditional Business School (I-TBS) (Advanced Series in Management)*, 26, (pp. 3 – 12). Emerald Publishing.

Adebukola, E. O., Olabode, A. O.and Chinonye, L. M. (2021). Igba-Boi: Historical Transition of the Igbo Apprenticeship Model pp. 13-25 in Adeola, Ogechi (ed.) (2021), Indigenous African Enterprise: The Igbo Traditional Business School (I-TBS). Advanced Series in Management, Volume 26: Emerald Publishing, UK.

Adeleke, A., Oyenuga, O.O. and Ogundele, OJ.K. (2003). Business Policy and Strategy. Mushin, Lagos: Concept Publications Limited

Adeola, O. (2021), The Igbo Traditional Business School (I-TBS): An Introduction in Indigenous African Entreprise: The Igbo Traditional Business School (I-TBS) ed. By Adeola, Odechi, Advanced Series in Management, Emerald Publishing, United Kingdom.

Agu, G. A. and Nwachukwu, A. N. (2020). Exploring the relevance of Igbo Traditional Business School in the development of entrepreneurial potential and Intention in Nigeria, *Small Business Research,* 27 (2): pp.223-239.

Akram, J., & Syed, R. (2017). Challenges faced by Female Entrepreneurs in managing their Work-Life Balance in Pakistan. *Asian Journal of Science and Technology,* 8(12):7192- 7196.

Aldrich, H. E. and Cliff, J. E. (2003), "The pervasive effects of family on entrepreneurship: toward a family embeddedness perspective", *Journal of Business Venturing,* 18(5):573-596.

Anggadwita, G., Ramadani, V. and Ratten, V. (2017), "Sociocultural environments and emerging economy entrepreneurship Women entrepreneurs in Indonesia", *Journal of Entrepreneurship in Emerging Economies,* 9(1): 85-96.

Anyadike, N., Emeh I.E.J. and O.F. Ukah (2012). Entrepreneurship Development and Employment Generation in Nigeria: Problems and Prospects, Ayodeyi, Ojo and Oluwatayo, Isaac B. (2015) Entrepreneurship as Drivers of Growth, Wealth Creation and Sustainable Development in Nigeria in *Socioeconomics,* 4(8):326

Akhter, Rahma and Sumi, Farhana Rahman (2014), Socio-Cultural Factors Influencing Entrepreneurial Activities: A Study on Bangladesh, *Journal of Business and Management,* 16 (9.Ver. II): 1-10.

Afigbo, A. (1981). *Ropes of Sand: Studies in Igbo history and culture.* University Press.

Agu, G. A. & Nwachukwu, A. N. (2020).Exploring the relevance of Igbo Traditional Business School in the development of entrepreneurial potential and intention in Nigeria.*Small Enterprise Research,* 27(2), 223 – 239.

Akimbode, A. (April 5, 2021). A Short History of Onitsha. https://www.thehistoryville.com/onitsha-history/

Anazodo, R.O. (2018). "Major Markets in Onitsha" Document of the ASMATA office, Modebe Avenue, Onitsha.

Anggadwita, G., Ramadani, V. & Ratten, V. (2017).Sociocultural environments and emerging economy entrepreneurship of women entrepreneurs in Indonesia.*Journal of Entrepreneurship in Emerging Economies,* 9(2), 313 – 344.

Anueyiagu, O. (2020). *Biafra: The horrors of war. The story of a child soldier.*Brown Brommel Publishers.

Amucheazi, O. & Orji, E. (2009).A critical analysis of Apprenticeship contract under Nigerian Law.*Labour Law Review,* 1 – 16.

Asobie, A. (2014, November 17). *Corruption and social vices in Nigeria.*2nd Zik Lecture Series, Awka, Anambra State, Nigeria.

Attride-Stirling, J. (2001). Thematic networks: an analytic tool for qualitative research. *Qualitative Research,* 2(3), 385–405.

Aziato, L., Dedey, F., & Clegg-Lamptey, J. A. (2014). The experience of dysmenorrhoea among Ghanaian senior high and University students: pain characteristics and effects. *Reproductive Health,* 11(58), 1–8. http://www.reproductive-health-journal.com/content/11/1/58

Bandura, A. (1977). *Social Learning Theory.* Englewood Cliffs, NJ: Prentice Hall.

Basden, J. T. (1966). *Niger Ibos*. Frank Cass.

Blau, P. M. (1964). *Exchange and power in social life*. John Wiley.

Braun, V., & Clarke, V. (2006). Using thematic analysis in psychology.*Qualitative Research in Psychology*, *3*(2), 77–101. https://doi.org/10.1191/1478088706qp063oa

Britannica, The Editors of Encyclopedia. Onitsha". Encyclopedia Britannica,8 july.1999. https://www.britannica.com/place/Onitsha-Nigeria

Carree, M. & Thurik, M. (2003).The Impact of Entrepreneurship on Economic Growth.Springer.

Cedefop (2018). Apprenticeship schemes in European countries. Luxembourg: Publication Office.

Cho, J. (2006). Validity in qualitative research revisited. *Qualitative Research*, *6*(3), 319–340. https://doi.org/10.1177/1468794106065006

Chrisman, S. (2012). Preparing for success through apprenticeship .https://www.proquest.com/openview/65e24452e2040435c61ccecfd1760d 8e/1?pq-origsite=gscholar&cbl=34845

Clarke, V., & Braun, V. (2013). Teaching thematic analysis: Overcoming challenges and developing strategies for effective learning Associate Professor in Sexuality Studies Department of Psychology Faculty of Health and the Life Sciences University of the West of England Coldharbour Lane Br. *The Psychologist*, *26*(2), 120–123.

Collins, A., Brown, J.S., & Newman, S.E. (1989). Cognitive Apprenticeship: Teaching the Crafts of Reading, Writing, and Mathematics. In L.B. Resnick (ed.), *Knowing, learning and institutional essays in honor of Robert Glaser*. Hillsdale, N.J.

Coombs, P.H. & Ahmed, M. (1974). Attacking Rural Poverty: How Non-formal Education Can Help. A Research Report for the World Bank Prepared by the International Council for Educational Development, Baltimore: Johns Hopkins University Press.

Dennen, V. P. (2004). Cognitive entrepreneurship in education practice.Research on scaffolding, modeling, Mentoring, and coaching as instructional strategies.*Handbook of Research on Educational Communications and Technology 2*, 813 – 828.

Dike, K. (1956).*Trade and politics in the Niger Delta 1830-1885*.https://www.amazon.com/Trade-Politics-Niger-Delta-1830-1885/dp/019821605X

Deniz, D. (2016). Sustainable Thinking and Environmental Awareness through Design Education.*Procedia Environmental Sciences*, *34*, 70–79.https://doi.org/10.1016/j.proenv.2016.04.008

Doing Business in Nigeria - World Bank Group,

Ejo-orusa, H. & Mpi, D. L. (2019). Reinventing the 'nwaboi' Apprenticeship system: a platform for entrepreneurship promotion in Nigeria, International Journal of Advanced Research, 8(9): 1-10

Ekesiobi, C. & Dimnwobi, S. K. (2020). Economic Assessment of the Igbo Entrepreneurship Model for Entrepreneurial Development in Nigeria: Evidence from Clusters in Anambra State, (A G D I Working Paper, WP/20/085)

Ekesiobi, C. & Dimnwobi, S. K. (2021). Economic assessment of the Igbo entrepreneurship model for entrepreneurial development in Nigeria: Evidence from clusters in Anambra State. *International Journal of Entrepreneurial Behaviour & Research*, 27(2), 416 – 433.

Eke, P. (1970). *Social exchange theory: The two traditions*. Heinemann.

Etzkowitz, H. (2008). *The Triple Helix: University-Industry–Government Innovation in Action*. Routledge.

Etzkowitz, H., & Leydesdorff, L. (2000).The dynamics of innovation: from National Systems and "Mode 2" to a Triple Helix of university–industry–government relationsResearch Policy, 29(2), 109–123. http://linkinghub.elsevier.com/retrieve/pii/S0048733399000554

Ezenwakwelu C. A., Egbosionu, N. A., Okwo, H. U. (2019), Apprenticeship training effects on entrepreneurship development in developing economies, *Academy of Entrepreneurship Journal*, 25 (1): 1-21

Farias, G., Farias, C., Krysa, I., & Harmon, J. (2020). Sustainability Mindsets for Strategic Management: Lifting the Yoke of the Neo-Classical Economic Perspective. *Sustainability*, *12*(17), 6977. https://doi.org/10.3390/su12176977

Fisher, John (2010). Systems theory and Structural Functionalism. Sage: Los Angelis

Fong, Y, Jabor, M. K. B., Zulkifli, A. H., Hashim, M. R. (2019), Challenges faced by New Entrepreneurs and Suggestions on How to Overcome Them, Advances in Social Science, Education and Humanities Research, volume 470, Proceedings of the International Conference on Student and Disable Student Development (ICoSD 2019).

Geertz, C. (1973). The interpretation of cultures: Selected essays. In *Contemporary Sociology* (Vol. 25, Issue 3). Basic Books, Inc. https://doi.org/10.2307/2077435

Gessler, M. (2019), "Concepts of apprenticeships: Strengths, weaknesses and pitfalls," in Handbook of Vocational Education and Training, McGrath et al, Eds. Switzerland: Springer Nature.

Gorgievski, M. J., Ascalon, M. E. & Stephen U. (2010), Small Business Owners' Success Criteria: A Value Approach to Personal Differences in Wach, D. 2010

Hamza, A. A (2013): Entrepreneurship Development; a publication of the National Open University of Nigeria in Ayodeyi, Ojo and Oluwatayo, Isaac B. (2015) Entrepreneurship as Drivers of Growth, Wealth Creation and Sustainable Development in Nigeria in Socioeconomics, 4(8):325-332.

Hanson, K. Vulnerability, Partnerships and the Pursuit of Survival: Urban

Livelihoods and Apprenticeship Contracts in a West African City. *GeoJournal* 62, 163–179 (2005). https://doi.org/10.1007/s10708-005-7915-1

Hisrich, R., Langan-Fox, J., & Grant, S. (2007). Entrepreneurship Research and Practice: A call to action for Psychology. *American Psychologist, 62*(6): 575-596.

Hisrich, R. D. (2005). Entrepreneurship education and research.in K. Anderseck & K. Walterscheid (Eds.), Grundungsforschung and grundungslehre, Entrepreneurship research and Entrepreneurship education: Wiesbaden, Germany: Deutsche University Press.

Ibekwe, O. [2018], ASMATA FORUM ASMATA House, Modebe Avenue, Onitsha.

Igwe, P. A., Newbery, R., Amoncar, N., White, G. R.T. and Maduchie, N. (2018), Keeping it in the Family: Exploring Igbo Ethnic Entrepreneurial Behaviour in Nigeria, *International Journal of Entrepreneurial Behaviour & Research*, 26 (1).

Igwe, P. A. & Ochinanwata, C. (2021). How to start an African informal revolution? *Journal of African Business.* (), 1 – 17.

Igwe, P. A., Madichie, N. O. & Amoncar, N. (2020). Transgenerational business legacies and intragenerational succession among the Igbos (Nigeria).*Small Enterprise Research*, 27(2), 165 – 179.

Igwe, P. A., Newberry, R., Amoncar, N., White, G. & Madichie, N. O. (2018).Keeping it in the family: Exploring Igbo ethnic entrepreneurial behaviour in Nigeria.*International Journal of Entrepreneurial Behaviour in Nigeria*, 26(1), 34 – 53.

International Labour Organisation (2011). *Improving informal apprenticeship.*ILO.

International Labour Organisation (2017). *Toolkit for quality apprenticeships volume I: Guide for policymakers.* ILO.

ILO (2012). Overview of apprenticeship systems and issues: ILO contribution to the G20 Task Force on Employment November 2012 (revised from September)

ILO (2012) Upgrading informal apprenticeship A resource guide for Africa. https://www.ilo.org/skills/pubs/WCMS_171393/lang--en/index.htm

Isichei, E. (1977). *A history of the Igbo people*. Macmillan.

Iwara, I. O. (2020). The Igbo Traditional Business School (I – TBS): A SWOT review synthesis. In O. Adeola (Ed.), *Indigenous African Enterprise. Igbo Traditional Business School (I-TBS) (Advanced Series in Management)*, 26, (pp. 39 – 55). Emerald Publishing.

Iwara, I. O., Amaeshi, K. E. & Netshandama, V. (2019). The Igba – boi apprenticeship approach: Arsenal behind growing success of Igbo entrepreneurs in Nigeria. *Ubuntu Journal of Conflict Transformation*, 8(1), 227 – 250.

Jennifer Fereday and Eimear Muir-Cochrane. (2006). Demonstrating Rigor Using Thematic Analysis : A Hybrid Approach of Inductive and Deductive Coding and Theme Development. *International Journal of Qualitative Methods*,5(1), 80–92.

Leydesdorff, L., & Etzkowitz, H. (1996). Emergence of a Triple Helix of university-industry-government relations.*Science and Public Policy*, 23(5), 279–286. https://doi.org/10.1093/spp/23.5.279

Kansikas, J., Laakonen, A., Sarpo, V. & Kontinen, J. (2012).Familiness as a resource for strategic entrepreneurship.*International Journal of Entrepreneurial Behaviour and Research*, 18(2), 141 – 158.

Kanu, C. C. (2020). The context of Igwebuike: What entrepreneurship development systems in Africa can learn from the Igbo apprenticeship system.*Journal of African Studies and Sustainable Development*, 2(1), 2640 – 2657.

Kanu, I. A. (2019). Igwebuikenomics: The Igbo apprenticeship system for wealth creation. *African Journal of Arts and Humanities*, 5(4), 56 – 70.

Kilani, A. O., Iheanacho, N. (2016). *Culture, development and religious change: The Nigerian perspective.* NYU Publisher.

Knowles, M. S. (1980). The modern practice of adult education: From pedagogy to andragogy. Cambridge: Englewood Cliffs.

Kuratko, D. (2003). Entrepreneurship Education: Emerging Trends and Challenges for the 21st Century. White Papers Series, Coleman Foundation, Chicago, IL.

Kuratko, D. F., Hornsby. J. S. & Naffzinger, D. W. (1997). An Examination of Owners' Goals in Sustaining Entrepreneurship, in Journal of Small Business Management, 35(1): 24 33.

Lancy, D. F. (2012). First, you must master pain: The nature and purpose of apprenticeship. *Anthropology of Work Review*, 33(2), 113 – 126.

Legas, H. (2015), Challenges to Entrepreneurial Success in Sub-Saharan Africa: A Comparative Perspective, *European Journal of Business and Management*, 7 (11), 23 www.iiste.org ISSN 2222-1905 (Paper) ISSN 2222-2839.

Littunen, H. (2000). Entrepreneurship and the Characteristics of the Entrepreneurial Personality in International Journal of Entrepreneurial Behaviour and Research, 6 (295-309)

Liu, W., Sidhu, A., Beacom, A. M. and Valente, T. W. (2017). Social Network Theory, in The International Encyclopedia of Media Effects. Rössler, P., Hoffner, C. A. and Zoonen, L (Ed). John Wiley & Sons, Inc.

Madichie, N. O., Gbadamosi, A. & Rwelamila, P. (2021). Entrepreneurship and the informal sector: Challenges and opportunities for African Business Development. *Journal of African Business*, (), 1 – 7.

Madichie, N. O., Nkamnebe, A. D., & Idemobi, E. I. (2008). Cultural determinants of entrepreneurial emergence in a typical Sub-Saharan African context. *Journal of Enterprising Communities: People and Places in the Global Economy*, 2(4), 285 – 299.

Mbaegbu, D. & Ekienabor (2018). The drivers of entrepreneurship among the Igbos of the Southeastern geo-political zone of Nigeria. *International Journal of Advanced Studies in Economics and Public Sector Management*, 6(1), 49 – 62.

McClelland, D. (1961). *The achieving society*. Van Nostrand Reinhold.

McGowan, P., Redeker, C. L., Cooper, S. Y. and Greenan, K. (2011). Female entrepreneurship and the management of business and domestic roles: Motivations, expectations and realities, Entrepreneurship and Regional development, 24(1-2): pp. 53-72

Mckenna, A. 2019," Onitsha market literature". Encyclopedia Britannica,1999. https://www.britannica.com/art/Onitsha-market-literature

Meagher, K. (2009). The informalization of belonging: Igbo informal enterprise and national cohesion from below. *African Development*, 34(1), 31 – 46.

Merriam-Webster (2021). *Dictionary of contemporary english*. https://www.merriam-webster.com/

Muskin J.A. (2009) Tinkering with the Tinker: Meeting Training Needs in the Informal Sector of Chad. In: Maclean R., Wilson D. (eds) International Handbook of Education for the Changing World of Work. Springer, Dordrecht. https://doi.org/10.1007/978-1-4020-5281-1_16

Mycostoma, [2021],Onitsha Main Market- The largest Market in West Africa. https://mycostoma.com/about-onitsha-market/

Nkamnebe A. D. and Ezemba, E. N. (2021), Entrepreneurship Incubation among the Nigerian Igbo in Adeola, Ogechi (ed.) (2021), Indigenous African Enterprise: The Igbo Traditional Business School (I-TBS). Advanced Series in Management, Vol. 26, pp. 27-38 Emerald Publishing, UK.

Nabavi, R. T. (2012) Bandura's Social Learning Theory and Social Cognitive Learning Theory: University of Science and Culture

Nnabuife, E., Okeke, T. C. and Ndubuisi. P. U. (2018). Doing Business in Nigeria: Implications for Africa's Industrialization, UNIZIK Journal Of Business, 1 (1): 59-70.

Nyeneokpon, E.E (2012): How Entrepreneurship can serve as a Handy Tool for Poverty Alleviation in Nigeria in Ojo and Oluwatayo (2015) Entrepreneurship as drivers of growth, wealth creation and sustainable development in Nigeria, *Socioeconomica* 4(8): 325-332.

Nnonyelu, N. and Onyeizugbe, C. (2020), Reimagining Igbo Apprenticeship: Bringing it up to Speed with Contemporary Realities. EJBMR, *European Journal of Business and Management Research*, 5 (3).

North, D. C. (1990), "Institutions, Institutional Change, and Economic Performance", Cambridge University Press. United Kingdom.

National Bureau of Statistics. (2021). Labour force statistics: Unemployment and underemployment report (Q4 2020).

Ndoro, T. T., Louw, L. & Kanyangale, M. (2019). Practises in operating a small business in a host community: A social capital perspective of Chinese immigrant entrepreneurship within the South African business context.

International Journal of Entrepreneurship and Small Business, 36(1 – 2), 148 – 163.

Neuwirth, R. (2017). Igbo apprenticeship system that governs Alaba International Market is the largest business incubator platform in the world.

Nkamnebe, A. D. & Ezemba, E. N. (2021). Entrepreneurship incubation among the Nigerian Igbos: The Igba - boi indigenous model. In O. Adeola (Ed.), *Indigenous African Enterprise. Igbo Traditional Business School (I-TBS) (Advanced Series in Management)*, 26, (pp. 27 – 38). Emerald Publishing.

Nnoli, O. (1978). *Ethnic politics in Nigeria.*Fourth Dimension Publishers.

Nnonyelu, N. Au. & Onyeizugbe, C. U. (2020). Reimagining Igbo apprenticeship: Brining it up to speed with contemporary realities. *European Journal of Business and Management Research*, 5(3), 1 – 9.

Nnonyelu, N. Au. (2018). Beyond Rhetorics: Unlocking the potentials of African industrialisation. *UNIZIK Journal of Business*, 1(2), 17 – 30.

Nwachukwu, C. C. (1990). *The practise of entrepreneurship in Nigeria.*Africana – FEP Publishers.

Nwanoruo, C. C. (2004). Towards the improvement of informal apprenticeship scheme for self-reliance in Nigeria. 9(1): https://www.ajol.info//index.php/joten/article/view/35661

Nwobashi, H. N. and Elechi, F. A. (2019). The Ease of Doing Business Report and Security Challenges in Nigeria: Engaging the Narratives, *Journal Of Humanities And Social Science*, 24 (12):

Obinze, S. [2020], Location and Features of Onitsha Markets-Head Bridge Market Onitsha, Oral Interview.

Obunike, C. C. (2016). Induction strategies of Igbo entrepreneurs and microbusiness success: A study of household equipment line, main market, Onitsha, Nigeria. *Economics and Business Review*, (), 43 – 65.

Olakunle, O., Iseolorunkanmi, J. & Segun, O. (2016). Indigene – settler relationship in Nigeria: A case study of the Igbo community in Lagos. *Afro Asian Journal of Social Sciences*, 7(3).

Olulu, R. M. & Udeorah, S. A. (2018).Contract of apprenticeship and Employment generation in Nigeria.*International Journal of Scientific Research in Education*, 11(3), 335 – 344.

Okechukwu, N. [2021]," History of Onitsha", Oral Narration

Okeke, G.U. [2018]" History of Onitsha markets" ASMATA FORUM, ASMATA House.

Okeke, T. C., and Osang, P. A. (2021).Decline of the Potency of Igbo Apprenticeship Scheme in Anambra State, Nigeria.*International Journal of Research and Innovation in Social Science* 5(9): p. 129

Onyima, J. K. C., Nzewi, H. N. & Chiekezie, O. M. (2013). Effects of apprenticeship on social capital on new business creation process of 'immigrant' entrepreneurs. *Review of Public Administration and Management*, 2(3), 1 – 11.

Oregun, J. J. & Nafiu, A. T. (2014).An exploratory study of Igbo entrepreneurial activity and business success in Nigeria as the panacea for economic growth and development.*International Journal of Development and Technology Research*, 3(9).

Oyewunmi, A. E., Oyewunmi, A. O. & Moses, C. I. (2021). *Igba Boyi*: Historical Transitions of the Igbo Apprenticeship Model. In O. Adeola (Ed.), *Indigenous African Enterprise. Igbo Traditional Business School (I-TBS) (Advanced Series in Management)*, 26, (pp. 13 – 25). Emerald Publishing.

Onwuegbuzie, A. J., & Leech, N. L. (2007). *Validity and Qualitative Research: An Oxymoron ?*233–249. https://doi.org/10.1007/s11135-006-9000-3

Obunike, C. (2016). Induction Strategy of Igbo Entrepreneurs and Micro-Business Success: A Study of Household Equipment Line, Main Market Onitsha, Nigeria, ACTA Univ. Sapientiae, *Economics and Business*, 4 (2016) 43–65

Ojo and Oluwatayo (2015) Entrepreneurship as drivers of growth, wealth creation and sustainable development in Nigeria, *Socioeconomica*, 4(8): 325-332.

Olulu, R. M. and Udeora, S. A.F (2018), "Contract of apprenticeship and employment generation in Nigeria", *International Journal of Scientific Research in Education*, 11(3): 335-344.

Onwuegbuzie, H. (2017). Learning from the Past: Entrepreneurship through Apprenticeship for More Successful Outcomes,*Advances in Economics and Business* 5(5): 280-287.

Onyima, J. K.C., Nzewi, H. N. & Chiekezie, O.M. (2013). Effects of apprenticeship and social capital on new business creation process of „immigrant" entrepreneurs. Review of Public Administration and Management, 2(3); 1-11

Orugun, J. J. and Nafiu, A. T. (2014). An Exploratory Study of Igbo Entrepreneurial Activity And Business Success In Nigeria As The Panacea For Economic Growth And Development, International Journal of Scientific & Technology Research, 3(9):158-165.

Oyewunmi. A. E, Oyewunmi, O. A. and Moses, C. L. (2021). Igba-Boi: Historical Transitions of the Igbo Apprenticeship Model in Adeola, Ogechi (ed.) (2021), Indigenous African Enterprise: The Igbo Traditional Business School (I-TBS). *Advanced Series in Management*, (26):13-25 Emerald Publishing, UK.

Ozurumba, I. G., Echem, C. C. G., Okengwu, M. C., Ugwuoke, A. C., Umofia, I. E. and Ifeanacho, V. A. (2021). Entrepreneurship and Adult Education: A Panacea for Economic Emancipation and Development in Nigeria, Journal of Engineering and Applied Science, 16 (7): 245-251.

Palma, P. J., Cunha, M. P. and Lopes, M. P. (2009).Entrepreneurial Behaviour, Nova School of Business and Economics.

Palmer R. (2007). Skills for work?From skills development to decent livelihoods in Ghana's rural informal economy. International Journal of Educational Development, 27(4):397-420https://www.sciencedirect.com/science /article/abs/pii/S0738059306001222

Peil, M. (2012).The Apprenticeship System in Accra.Cambridge University Press.https://www.cambridge.org/core/journals/africa/article/abs/appren ticeship-system-in-accra/73A9F74E4F2DD1B221653312CD0FA114

Ratten, V. (2014). Encouraging collaborative entrepreneurship in developing countries: The current challenges and a research agenda. *Journal of Entrepreneurship in Emerging Economies*, 6(3), 298 – 308.

Saviano, M., Barile, S., Farioli, F., & Orecchini, F. (2019). Strengthening the science–policy–industry interface for progressing toward sustainability: a systems thinking view. *Sustainability Science*, *14*(6), 1549–1564.https://doi.org/10.1007/s11625-019-00668-x

Schalk, R., Wallis, P., Crowston, C., Lemercier, C. (2016). Failure Or Flexibility? Exits From Apprenticeship Training in Pre-Modern Europe. Economic History Working Papers No: 252/2016. http://eprints.lse.ac.uk/68609/1/ WP252.pdf

Schumpeter, J (1993). The Theory of Economic Development: A Study of Entrepreneurial Profit, Capital, Credit and Economic Cycle, Berlin: Duncker & Humbolt.

Susser, B. (1992). Approaches to the Study of Politics. New York: Macmillan

Teddlie Charles & Tashakkori Abbas (2003). *Handbook of mixed methods in social and behavioural research*. Sage.

Teddlie Charles & Tashakkori Abbas. (2009). *Foundations of* Mixed method research*: integrating quantitative and qualitative approaches in the social and behavioural sciences*. Sage Publications.

Udu, A. A. (2015). Apprenticeship orientation and performance of micro businesses in Ebonyi state, Nigeria. *International Journal of Business and Management Review*, 3(12), 1 – 11.

Ugboaja, P. C., Chinedum, O., Ejem, A. E., Ukpere, W. I. and Onyemaechi, O. (2013). Role of Trade Associations on Entrepreneurial Development in Nigeria's Road Transport Industry *Journal of Social Sciences*, 37(1):45-53.

UNICEF, (2017).Education. https://www.unicef.org/nigeria/education.

Vaismoradi, M., D, P., Ms, N., Bs, N., Turunen, H., D, P., Bondas, T., & D, P. (2013). Content analysis and thematic analysis: Implications for conducting a qualitative descriptive study. *Nursing and Health Sciences*, *15*, 398–405. https://doi.org/10.1111/nhs.12048

Wach, Dominika (2010). Defining and Measuring Entrepreneurship Success in Entrepreneurship: A Psychological Approach (Lukes and Laguna) ed., Chapter 6, pp. 89-102.

Williams, D. W., Zorn, M. L., Russell Crook, T., and Combs, J. G. (2013). "Passing the Torch: Factors Influencing Transgenerational Intent in Family Firms, *Family Relations*, and 62(3): 415–428.

World Economic Forum (2016).*Europe's hidden entrepreneurs: Entrepreneurial employee activity and competitiveness in Europe.*

Yliopisto, J. (n.d.). What Is ......Thematic Analysis ? *Health Education Research,* 21(4), 508–517.

Appendices

Appendix 1: Showing the Names of the Research Assistants

S/N	Name
1.	Agu Alex Kelechi
2.	Anaduaka Ifunanya
3.	Anigbogu Onyinye Scholastica
4.	Arinze Modilim
5.	Chidi Augustine Kenneth
6.	Ekechukwu Nmesoma Blessing
7.	Ezenwafor Chidiogo
8.	Ezepue Onyedika Paul
9.	Henry Okeke
10.	Kalu Chijioke
11.	Mmadubuobi Lucy
12.	Muojekwu Hilary
13.	Muvukor, Adoniram Ufuoma
14.	Nchedo Ezenwegbu
15.	Nwafor Uzoamaka
16.	Nwankwo Ogechukwu
17.	Nweke Kenneth
18.	Nwobu Ikenna Patrick
19.	Nworah Chiamaka Jacinta
20.	Nwozugba Kennedy Onyebuchi
21.	Obidigwe Smart
22.	Oguegbe Maureen Uchechukwu
23.	Okafor Chukwudumebi
24.	Okafor obumneme
25.	Okeke Chidimma
26.	Onyeka Obinweze
27.	Onyima Ogochukwu
28.	Orajekwe Jerry
29.	Orizu Tochukwu
30.	Tochukwu Kingsley
31.	Igwebuike Sylvester
32.	Okenwa Cynthia

33.	Ogoma Nwammadu
34.	Favour Okereke
35.	Ifeoma Ilonna
36.	Michael Ejiofor
37.	Anthony Anyamele
38.	Chizoba Okafor
39.	Andy Nwachukwu
40.	Obiora Nwanna
41.	Cecilia Uwezuoke
42.	Ephraim Chetanna
43.	Beatrice Ofor
44.	Edward Sunday
45.	Perpetua Orazulume
46.	Eunice Precious Okeke
47.	Ifeoma Mbadugha
48.	Obinna Chukwueloka
49.	PaulMary Ifeacho
50.	Simon Obele

Appendix 2: Questionnaire for Ndi Oga (Masters)

Instruction: Kindly go through the questions and tick [√] or fill-in where appropriate.

Sociodemographic Characteristics

1. Please indicate your gender   (1) Male [ ]. (2) Female [ ].
2. What is your marital status? (1) Single [   ]. (2)   Married   [   ]. (3) Divorced [ ]. (4) Widowed [ ].
3. What is your age at your last birthday? ....
b. Which of the following age groups does the respondent belong to? (1) 10 – 19 years (2) 20 – 29 years (3) 30 – 39 years (4) 40 – 49 years (5) 50 – 59 years (6) 60 – 69 years (7) 70 years and above
4. What is your religious affiliation? (1) African traditional religion [ ]. (2) Christianity [ ]. (3) Muslim [ ]. (4) Others [   ].
b. If others, please specify here ....
5. What are you trading on? ....
6. Highest level of education? (1) No formal education [   ]. (2) FSLC [   ]. (3) SSCE [   ]. (4) OND/HND [ ]. (5) Bachelors Degree [   ]. (6) Postgraduate Degrees [ ]
7. State of origin...
8. Local Government of origin..
9. Market location of your business (1) Main Market [   ]. (2) Ochanja Market [   ]. (3) Bridge Head Market [   ]. (4) Spare Parts Market,

Nkpor [   ]. (5) Building Materials Market, Ogidi/Ogbunike []. (6) Others (Please specify) ....

10. Kindly indicate your average monthly income (1) 10,000.00 - 50,000.00 [ ]. (2) 60,000.00 - 100,000.00 [ ]. (3) 110,000.00 - 150,000.00 [   ]. (4) 160,000.00 - 200,000.00 [ ]. (5) 210,000 and above [ ].

11. Number of apprentices you have trained in this business presently ..

b. If none, why? ....

12. Do you have apprentices under you that pay to learn your trade (*Imu Ahia*)? (1) yes []. (2) no [].

b. If yes, are these apprentices different from *Umu Boyi*? (1) yes [   ]. (2) no [ ].

c. If yes, given reasons for your answer..

d. Do you prefer an apprentice that has come to learn a trade (*Imu Ahia*) to *Nwa Boyi*? (1) Surely [].   (2) Maybe [ ]. (3) Don't Know [ ]. (4) Not Surely [ ].

13. Were you ever a boyi to someone? (1) yes [   ]. (2) no [   ].

b. If yes, was it kin-related? (1) yes [   ]. (2) no [   ].

c. How long did you stay before you were settled (in years)? ....

14. Preferred age for apprenticeship? ....

15. Preferred gender for apprenticeship? (1) Male []. (2) Female [ ].

16. Prevalent type of apprenticeship? (1) Kin related [ ]. (2) Non kin related [ ]. (3) Both [ ].

b. What type of apprenticeship are you practicing now? (1) Kin related []. (2) Non kin related []. (3) No boyi for now [ ]. (4) Sales girls [   ].   (5) Apprentices [ ].

17. Are communities identified with particular types of trade? (1) Yes []. (2) No [   ].
Instruction: Kindly go through the questions and tick [√] or fill-in where appropriate.

18. How does the "*Igba Boyi*"(apprenticeship scheme) become a widely accepted entrepreneurial behaviour among the Ndigbo of South-East, Nigeria? (1) Modification over time [ ]. (2) Increase in wealth for entrepreneurs [ ]. (3) Expansion in trade and industry [ ]. (4) Expansion in family business [ ]. (5) Advancement in social mobility [ ]. (6) Sustainable social protection system []. (7) All of the above [ ].

19. Which of these is the most important cultural characteristic/behaviour that drives Entrepreneurial disposition of Ndigbo? (1) Igwebuike philosophy []. (2) Onye aghana nwanne ye []. (3) Extended family system [ ]. (4) Ogo bu chi onye [ ]. (5) Nwa di na mba [ ]. (6) Aku luo uno [ ]. (7) Mgbo olu labour strategy [ ]. (8) Itu mgbele finance support scheme [ ]. (9) All of the above [ ]. (10) Others [ ].

b. If others, specify ....

20. Who is the main focal person during apprenticeship negotiation and placement process (1) Biological father [   ]. (2) Biological mother [ ].

(3) Biological brothers [ ]. (4) Biological sisters [ ]. (5) Kinsmen [   ].
(6) Family friends [   ].

21. If their parents are dead, who becomes the main focal person? (1) Biological brothers []. (2) Biological sisters [ ]. (3) Uncle []. (4) Kinsmen [ ]. (5) Family friends [ ].

22. Is there any Apprenticeship agreement between "nwa boi" and his master during the placement process? (1) Yes [   ]. (2) No [ ].
b. If "Yes", what is the form of the agreement? (1) Written agreement [ ]. (2) Oral agreement [   ]. (3) Both written and oral agreement [ ] (4) Court/Legal agreement [ ] (5) Oath taking [ ] (6) All of the above [ ] (7) Others [ ]
c. If others, please specify ....

23. What is the most common provision of the agreement among the ndigbo apprenticeship (*Igba Boyi*) scheme in Onitsha Market (1) Duration of the apprenticeship []. (2) Apprenticeship code of conduct [   ]. (3) Settlement procedures [ ]. (4) Sanctions of erring trainers and trainees [ ]. (5) All of the above [ ]. (6) Others [ ]
b. If others, please specify..

24. Is there a probation period before the agreement is signed? (1) yes [ ]. (2) no [ ].
b. If yes, how many months? ....

25. What category of Igbo people are more involved with the apprenticeship scheme? (1) The wealthy [   ]. (2) The poor and indigent [   ]. (3) Both [ ]. (4) All Igbo indigenous people [ ].
26. Preferred type of apprenticeship? (1) Kin related [ ]. (2) Non kin related [ ]. (3) Both [ ].

27. Which age category do you consider ideal for *Igba Boyi*? (1) 10 – 13 years []. (2) 14 – 17 years [ ]. (3) 18 – 21 years [ ]. (4) 22 – 25 years [ ]. (5) 35 years and above [ ].

28. What number of years do you consider adequate for mastering the trade? (1) Less than 2 years []. (2) 2 - 4 years [   ]. (3) 4 - 6 years []. (4) 6 - 8 years []. (5) 8 years and above [   ].

29. Are there specific trades that require longer periods of *Igba Boyi*? (1) Yes [   ]. (2) No [   ].
b. If "Yes", indicate the trade
....

30. Preferred gender for apprenticeship? (1) Male []. (2) Female [   ].
B.What are the reason(s) for the preference? ....

31. Is *Igba Boyi* for women trade specific? (1) Yes [ ]. (2) No [ ].
b.If "Yes", list the trade where females are mostly involved
....

32. Are you willing to enlist the services of umu nwanyi and umu nwoke as apprentices? (1) Yes [ ]. (2) No [   ].
b. State reasons for your answer ....

33. Do you prefer the services of the sales girls to *Nwa Boyi*? (1) Yes []. (2) No
[].
b. If "Yes", state your reasons for your choice ....

34. What are the basic skills and knowledge needed by apprentices (*Umu Boyi*)
(Tick as many as you like) (1) Honesty [ ]. (2) Good customer relationship [
]. (3) Literacy [ ]. (4) Knowledge of ICT [ ]. (5) Good negotiation skills [ ].
(6) Accounting skills [ ]. (7)
Self-control/resilience [ ]. (8) Others [ ]
b. If others, please specify ....

35. What are the benefits of the apprenticeship scheme to the trainee (*Nwa
Boyi*)? (Tick as many as you like) (1) Learning of skills and/or trade [   ].
(2) Raising capital [   ]. (3) Building business contacts []. (4) All of the
above [   ]. (5) No benefits [ ]. (5) Others [ ]
b. If others, please specify...

36. What are the benefits to the masters (*Ndi Ọga*) (Tick as many as are
applicable) (1) It renders help [   ]. (2) Ensures continuity of the
enterprise/Growth of the business [   ]. (3) Giving back to the community
[]. (4) Satisfaction from helping a relation []. (5) No benefits [ ]. (6) Others
[ ]
b. If others, please specify...

37. What is the most common challenge encountered by *Umu Boyi* (apprentices)
(1) Breach of apprenticeship agreement [   ]. (2) Maltreatment by *Ndi Ọga*,
nwunye *Ọga*, umu *Ọga*, umunne *Ọga* or older boyi, others [ ]. (3) Non-
settlement of *Nwa Boyi* after the agreed years [ ]. (4) Accusing *Umu Boyi*
falsely and unjustly [ ]. (5) Quest for Materialism (Igbu ozu/Ibute ike/Ibute
nku) [   ]. (6) Weakening of traditional kinship ties/belief system [ ]. (7)
Others [ ]
b. If others, please specify ....

38. Workshops/Seminars are organized by government agencies to improve
entrepreneurial knowledge and improve skills for apprentices.
a. Always
b. Sometimes
c. Don't know
d. Rarely
e. Never

39. Which of these Institutional strategies can best enhance entrepreneurship
and apprenticeship among Igbo Traders?
a. Adult education strategy
b. Formation of Isusu and cooperatives
c. Seminars and workshops
d. Tax waivers
e. (Please specify)..

40. Specific regulations provided by local and state governments guide the
relationship between the master (*Ọga*) and the apprentice (*Nwa Boyi*).

a. Largely true
b. True
c. I don't know
d. Maybe
e. Not true at all

41. Government agencies do not monitor the relationship between the masters (*Ndi Ọga*) and apprentices (*Umu Boyi*).
    a. Largely true
    b. True
    c. I don't know
    d. Maybe
    e. Not true at all

42. To what extent do the market associations intervene in the relationship between master (*Ọga*) and apprentice (*Nwa Boyi*)?
    a. Great extent
    b. Large extent
    c. Don't know
    d. Rarely
    e. Not all

43. Adult Education programmes are organized by the State Government for the masters (*Ndi Ọga*) and apprentices (*Umu Boyi*).
    a. Largely true
    b. True
    c. Don't know
    d. Rarely
    e. Never

44. How often do the masters (*Ndi Ọga*) and apprentices (*Umu Boyi*) make use of Adult Education facilities?
    a. Very often
    b. Often
    c. I don't know
    d. Rarely
    e. Never

45. Further education is necessary in my daily business transaction
    a. Very necessary
    b. Necessary
    c. I don't know
    d. Maybe
    e. Not needed

46. Apprenticeship as a strategy of entrepreneurship is on the decline
    a. True
    b. False
    c. Don't know

47. Which of these statements best describes the state of apprenticeship among Igboentrepreneurs
    a. Still strong and ever expanding
    b. Declining very fast and will soon be completely supplanted
    c. It is becoming weak but cannot ever die completely
    d. Don't know

Appendix 3 Questionnaire for Umu Boyi (Apprentices)

Instruction: Kindly go through the questions and tick [√] or fill-in where appropriate.
Sociodemographic Characteristics

1. Please indicate your gender. (1) Male []. (2) Female [   ].
2. What is your marital status? (1) Single []. (2) Married [   ]. (3) Divorced [ ]. (4) Widowed [   ].
3. What is your age at your last birthday?...
    b. Which of the following age groups does the respondent belong to? (1) 10 – 19 years (2) 20 – 29 years (3) 30 – 39 years (4) 40 – 49 years (5) 50 – 59 years (6) 60 – 69 years (7) 70 years and above
    4. What is your religious affiliation? (1) African traditional religion [   ]. (2) Christianity   [   ]. (3) Muslim [   ]. (d) Others [   ].
    b. If others, please specify...
5. What trade are you learning? ....
    6. Highest level of education? (1) No formal education [   ]. (2) FSLC []. (3) SSCE []. (4) OND/HND [   ]. (5) Bachelors Degree [   ]. (6) Postgraduate Degrees []
7. State of origin...........................
8. Local Government Area of origin.......................................
9. Local Government Area where your business activity is located (1) Onitsha North [   ]. (2) Onitsha South   [ ].(3) Idemili North [   ]. (4) Oyi [   ].
10. Market location where you are learning your trade (1) Main Market [   ]. (2) Ochanja Market [   ]. (3) Bridge Head Market [   ]. (4) Spare Parts Market, Nkpor []. (5) Building Materials Market, Ogidi/Ogbunike [].
    (6) Others [ ].
    b. If others, please specify.....................................
11. Kindly indicate your average monthly income (1) Less than 3,000 [ ]. (2) 4,000.00 - 6,000.00 [ ]. (3) 7,000.00 - 10,000.00 [   ]. (4) No income (5) Above 10,000 [   ].
12. Preferred age for apprenticeship.....................................
13. Prevalent type of apprenticeship? (1) Kin related [   ]. (2) Non kin related [   ]. (3) Both [   ].
14. Are communities identified with particular types of trade? (1) Yes

[   ]. (2) No [   ].

Instruction: Kindly go through the questions and tick [√] or fill-in where appropriate.

15. How does the "*Igba Boyi*"(apprenticeship scheme) become a widely accepted entrepreneurial behaviour among the Ndigbo of south-east Nigeria? (1) Modification over time [   ]. (2) Increase in wealth for entrepreneurs []. (3) Expansion in trade and industry [ ]. (4) Expansion in family business [ ]. (5) Advancement in social mobility [ ].   (6) Sustainable social protection system [ ]. (7) Others [   ].
    b. If others, specify ....

16. Which of these is the most important cultural characteristic/behaviour that drives entrepreneurial disposition of Ndigbo? (1) Igwebuike philosophy [ ]. (2) Onye aghana nwanne ye [ ]. (3) Extended family system [ ]. (4) Ogo bu chi onye [ ]. (5) Nwa di na mba [ ]. (6) Aku luo uno [ ]. (7) Mgbo olu labour strategy [ ]. (8) Itu mgbele finance support scheme [ ]. (9) All of the above [ ].

17. Who is the main focal person during apprenticeship negotiation and placement process (1) Biological father [   ]. (2) Biological mother [   ]. (3) Biological brothers [   ]. (4) Biological sisters [ ].   (5) Kinsmen [   ]. (6) Family friends

18. If their parents are dead, who becomes the main focal person? (1) Biological brothers [ ]. (2) Biological sisters [ ]. (3) Uncle [   ].   (4) Kinsmen [   ]. (5) Family friends [   ].

19. Is there any apprenticeship agreement between "nwa boi" and his master during the placement process? (1) Yes [   ]. (2) No [   ].
    b. If "Yes", what is the form of the agreement? (1) Written agreement [   ]. (2) Oral agreement [   ]. (3) Both written and oral agreement [ ] (4) Court/Legal agreement [ ] (5) Oath taking [ ] (6) All of the above [ ] (7) Others [ ]
    c. If others, please specify..

20. s there a probation period before the agreement is signed? (1) Yes [   ]. (2) No [   ].
b. If yes, how many months?...

21.What are the common provisions of the agreement among the ndi igbo apprenticeship (*Igba Boyi*) scheme in Onitsha Market (1) Duration of the apprenticeship [   ]. (2) Apprenticeship code of conduct [   ].   (3) Settlement procedures [   ]. (4) Sanctions of erring trainers and trainees [   ]. (5) All of the above [   ]. (6) Others [ ]
    b. If others, please specify...

22. What category of Igbo people are more involved with the apprenticeship scheme? (1) The wealthy [   ]. (2) The poor and indigent [   ]. (3) All Igbo indigenous people [ ]. (4) Both [ ].

23. Preferred type of apprenticeship? (1) Kin related [   ].   (2)   Non   kin related [   ]. (3) Both [   ].

24. Do you have any kin relationship to your *Ọga*? (1) Yes [   ]. (2) No [   ]. (3) Don't know [   ].

25. Which age category do you consider ideal for *Igba Boyi*? (1) 10 – 13 years []. (2) 14 – 17 years [   ]. (3) 18 – 21 years [   ]. (4) 22 – 25 years [   ]. (5) 26 years and above [   ].

26. What number of years do you consider adequate for mastering the trade? (1) Less than 2 years [   ].   (2) 2 - 4 years [   ]. (3) 4 - 6 years []. (4) 6 - 8 years [   ]. (5) 8 years and above [ ].

27. What should be the ideal number of years for *Nwa Boyi* to stay before settlement? ....

28. Are there specific trades that require longer periods of *Igba Boyi*? (1) Yes [   ]. (2) No [   ].
b. If "Yes", indicate the trade ....

29. Do you know anyone who is currently paying to learn a trade? (1) Yes [   ]. (2) No [   ].

30. Is that person different from *Nwa Boyi*? (1) Yes [   ]. (2) No [   ].
b. If yes, give your reasons ....

31. What are the basic skills and knowledge needed by apprentices (*Umu Boyi*) (Tick as many as you like) (1) Honesty [   ].   (2)   Good   customer relationship []. (3) Literacy [   ]. (4) Knowledge of ICT [   ]. (5) Good negotiation skills [   ]. (6) Accounting skills [ ]. (7) Self-control/resilience []. (8) Others [ ].
b. If others, please specify...

32. What are the benefits of the apprenticeship scheme to the trainee (*Nwa Boyi*)? (Tick as many as you like) (1) Learning of skills and/or trade [   ]. (2) Raising capital [   ]. (3) Building business contacts [ ].   (4)   All   of   the above [ ]. (5) No benefits [   ]. (5) Others [ ]
b. If others, please specify...

33. What are the benefits to the masters (*Ndi Ọga*) (Tick as many as are applicable) (1) It renders help [   ]. (2) Ensures continuity of the enterprise/Growth of the business [   ]. (3) Giving back to the community []. (4) Satisfaction from helping a relation []. (5) No benefits [ ]. (6) Others [ ]
b. If others, please specify...

34. What are the common challenges encountered by *Umu Boyi* (apprentices) (1) Breach of apprenticeship agreement [   ]. (2) Maltreatment by *Ndi Ọga*, nwunye *Ọga*, umu *Ọga*, umunne *Ọga* or older boyi, others [   ]. (3) Non-settlement of *Nwa Boyi* after the agreed years [   ]. (4) Accusing *Umu Boyi* falsely and unjustly [   ].   (5)   Quest   for materialism (Igbu ozu/Ibute ike/Ibute nku) [   ].   (6)   Weakening   of traditional kinship ties/belief system [ ]. (7) All of the above [   ]. (8) Others [ ].

b. If others, please specify ....

35. Workshops/Seminars are organized by government agencies to improve entrepreneurial knowledge and improve skills for apprentices.
    a. Always
    b.Sometimes
    c.Don't know
    d.Rarely
    e. Never

36. Which of these institutional strategies can best enhance entrepreneurship and apprenticeship among Igbo traders?
    a. Adult education strategy
    b. Formation of Isusu and cooperatives
    c. Seminars and workshops
    d. Tax waivers
    e. Others (Please specify) ....

37. Specific regulations provided by local and state governments guide the relationship between the master (*Oga*) and the apprentice (*Nwa Boyi*).
    a. Largely true
    b.True
    c. I don't know
    d. Maybe
    e. Not true at all

38. Government agencies do not monitor the relationship between the masters (*Ndi Oga*) and apprentices (*Umu Boyi*).
    a. Largely true
    b.True
    c. I don't know
    d. Maybe
    e. Not true at all

39. To what extent do the market associations intervene in the relationship between master (*Oga*) and apprentice (*Nwa Boyi*)?
    a. Great extent
    b. Large extent
    c.Don't know
    d.Rarely
    e. Not all

40. Adult Education programmes are organized by the State Government for the masters (*Ndi Oga*) and apprentices (*Umu Boyi*).
    a. Largely true
    b.True
    c. Don't know
    d. Rarely
    e. Never

41. How often do the masters (*Ndi Ọga*) and apprentices (*Umu Boyi*) make use of Adult Education facilities?
    a. Very often
    b. Often
    c. I don't know
    d. Rarely
    e. Never

42. Further education is necessary in my daily business transaction
    a. Very necessary
    b. Necessary
    c. I don't know
    d. Maybe
    e. Not needed

43. Apprenticeship as a strategy of entrepreneurship is on the decline
    a. True
    b. False
    c. Don't know

44. Which of these statements best describes the state of apprenticeship among Igboentrepreneurs
    a. Still strong and ever expanding
    b. Declining very fast and will soon be completely supplanted
    c. It is becoming weak but cannot ever die completely
    d. Don't know

Appendix 4: In-depth Interview

Introduction

Good morning/afternoon/evening. My name is .... (Moderator; ask other research team members to introduce themselves). We are conducting a study in Onitsha market and it is focused on 'Apprenticeship and Entrepreneurship in Igbo land'. In this wise, we need to ask you a few questions and we also need you to answer them honestly to the best of your knowledge. Your responses will be strictly kept confidential and only for this survey.

- Interviewers to introduce themselves
- Why we are here, purpose of research
- Expectations from participants
- Confidentiality/anonymity
- Use of results
- Permission to use audio/ video tape

Section A: Socio-Demographic Characteristics of the Key Informant

1. Place of Residence)
2. Sex:
3. Age:
4. Actual age as at last birthday
5. Marital status
6. Form of (for ever-married respondents) Monogamous/Polygynous
7. Family Settings (Nuclear/Extended)
8. Ethnic Group
9. Religion
10 Type of business
11 Highest level of education
12. State of origin
13. Local Government of Origin
14. Length of Stay in the business
15. Length of stay in the market
16. Position/Status in the market Union

S/N	Questions	Probes
1.	Courtesies/Introduction	Tell me about yourself. Short history of how you started.
2.1.	Can we learn from you the reasons for *"Igba Boyi"* in the Igbo culture?	• Why do Ndi Igbo place so much value on apprenticeship? • Connections to an ancestral culture • An act of willingness or compulsion • If it is connected to one's success or failure in business • Is there a punishment for not taking on an apprentice? • Igbo world view of "Onye fe eze, eze eluo ya"

3. 2.	How is the *"Igba Boyi"* managed in Igbo culture?	• Are there specific criteria to meet before taking on an apprentice? • Terms of agreement • What happens when agreement is fulfilled and when it fails? • What are the contents of the curriculum? • Are there limits to what the apprentice should learn? • Is there a structure that stipulates what the apprentice learns at each point? • Is the process different when it involves a female?
3.	What are the peculiar nuances (business slangs) applied by apprentices (*Umu Boyi*) and masters (*Ndi Ọga*) in their daily business transactions?	• List them and please explain each • What are their business significance? • In what instances are they used? • What are the benefits of the coded language?
4.4.	What influence is exerted by institutions in sustaining agreements and the learning process between the apprentice and the boss?	• Influence of family and clan, including spouse and children • Influence of community leadership • Influence of the market association and union • Influence of ex-apprentices under same master • Influence of religion and spirituality • Getting the government to pay part of the settlement fund in settlement of the apprentice • Constant reminder of the settlement time of the apprentice by the government

5. 5.	What are the failures and successes of the discussed institutions?	• The need to improve or the need to wipe away completely • Are there more institutions to carry along? • Are present institutions too informal or too formal? • What are the consequences for formality and informality?
6.6.	What specific issues are contained in the way the apprenticeship system is structured?	• What are the issues? • Are there suggestions to make it better, that is to be made more formal, if they think it is too informal or otherwise
7.7.	Give practical instances where the "*Igba Boyi*" system has contributed to developing the economy.	• What lessons are there that the government can take? • Are there tribes with similar systems? • Will the system be beneficial to Anambra's economy? • Will the system be beneficial to the South East? • How can the system be advanced into something national, and what roles can they play?
8. 8.	Why "*Igba Boyi*" and not "Igba Girl"?	• The traditional significance of the male in the context as against the female • Are there verifiable cases of women getting involved in apprenticeship? • Are women involved in leadership positions in the market? • Plans for the female gender

9. 9.	Are Onitsha Market traders involved in online business?	• Are they involved in drop-shipping (*Igba oso afia* online) • As vendors or owners
10.	Which social media outlets do you prefer and why?	• Instagram, why • Facebook, why • WhatsApp, why • Twitter, why • YouTube, why
11.	What are the challenges and dynamics of online businesses?	• Do you accept digital banking? • Do you accept PoS? • Do you accept money transfers? • If no, why not?
12.	What are the challenges facing the "*Igba Boyi*" system?	• Challenges from the Nwa $Boyi$/ Oga (commitment, faithfulness) • Challenges from family and community institutions • Challenges from market institutions • Challenges from the government and the wider economy
13.	What plans can help surmount these challenges?	• Personal efforts • Family efforts • Community efforts • Union efforts • Government efforts, etc.

14.	How does the apprenticeship scheme contribute to wealth creation and employment generation?	• What do you intend to do after settlement? • Do you intend to have apprentices?
15.	How can the apprenticeship system be improved?	• Funding of the apprentices • Payment of stipends/allowances to apprentices • Adult education related to Business Management

Appendix 5: Focus Group Discussion (FGD) Guide for Chamber of Commerce

Introduction

Good morning/afternoon/evening. We are/My name is...........................
.... (Moderator; ask other research team members to introduce themselves). We are conducting a study in Onitsha market and it is focused on 'Apprenticeship and Entrepreneurship in Igbo land'. In this wise, we need to ask you a few questions and we also need you to answer them honestly to the best of your knowledge. Your responses will be strictly kept confidential and only for this survey.

- Interviewers to introduce themselves
- Why we are here, purpose of research
- Expectations from participants
- Confidentiality/anonymity
- Use of results
- Permission to use audio/ video tape

Identification

Specific Venue for FGD	
Name of Moderator(s)	
Date of FGD	

Time FGD Started	
Time FGD Ended	
Language of Discussion	English................................... Others (Specify)...........................

Idi Setting/Environment:

Give general description of:
The venue:

    Sitting arrangement:
    Weather condition:
    Level of response:
    Give other useful information:

Information about the Study Area
- Name of the Local Government Area
- Locality/community of FGD
- Name of the market
- Name of FGD group

Section A: Socio-Demographic Characteristics of Fgd Participants

1. Place of Residence)
2. Sex:
3. Age:
4. Actual age as at last birthday
5. Marital status
6. Form of marriage (for ever-married respondents) - Monogamous/Polygynous
7. Family Settings (Nuclear/Extended)
8. Ethnic Group
9. Religion
10. Type of business
11. Highest level of education
12. State of origin
13. Local Government of Origin
14. Length of Stay in the business

15. Length of stay in the market
16. Position/Status in the market Union

Questions	Probes
History	Narrate the history of the chamber of commerce? Under what act was it established What is its organizational structure?
Purpose/Activities	What are the mandates of the chamber of commerce? What are your mission and vision for apprenticeship, entrepreneurship and Onitsha markets? Do you have mandate clash between you and other related MDAs? How does this mandate clash affect your activities in Onitsha markets?
What are your perceptions/views about apprenticeship/entrepreneurial behaviours in Onithsa markets?	Discuss your opinions on the historical trajectory of apprenticeship in Onitsha markets and in Igbo land. What do you think has changed in the culture of apprenticeship today?

Relationship with the markets/traders	Are there any programs, financial, advisory assistance from the chamber of commerce and industry to the umu-boyi, ndi-*Ọga* and market unions? Are there synergy between the unions, market leaders and chamber of commerce? How often do you organize awareness/sensitization seminars/workshops? What are your programs for entrpeneurs/apprentice?
Challenges	Discuss the challenges confronting the chamber of commerce in relation to Onitsha markets. What are your operational challenges? How do you cope with these challenges?
Solutions	What do you think should be done to improve Igba-boyi and izu-afia/itu-mgbere in Onitsha markets/Igbo land? How can the chamber of commerce contribute in re-invigorating the apprenticeship culture in Onitsha markets? Do you think informality or formality should be maintained in agreement initiations?

Appendix 6: Focus Group Discussion (FGD) Guide for Market Leaders

Introduction

Good morning/afternoon/evening. We are/My name is
(Moderator; ask other research team members to introduce themselves). We are
conducting a study in Onitsha market and it is focused on 'Apprenticeship and
Entrepreneurship in Igbo land'. In this wise, we need to ask you a few questions
and we also need you to answer them honestly to the best of your knowledge.
Your responses will be strictly kept confidential and only for this survey.

- •Interviewers to introduce themselves
- •Why we are here, purpose of research
- •Expectations from participants
- •Confidentiality/anonymity
- •Use of results
- •Permission to use audio/ video tape

Identification

Specific Venue for FGD	
Name of Moderator(s)	
Date of FGD	
Time FGD Started	
Time FGD Ended	
Language of Discussion	English..................................... Others (Specify)............................

Idi Setting/Environment:
Give general description of:
The venue:
Sitting arrangement:
Weather condition:
Level of response:

Give other useful information:

Information about the Study Area

- Name of the Local Government Area
- Locality/community of FGD
- Name of the market
- Name of FGD group

Section A: Socio-Demographic Characteristics of Fgd Participants

1. Place of Residence)
2. Sex:
3. Age:
4. Actual age as at last birthday
5. Marital status
6. Form of marriage (for ever-married respondents) - Monogamous/Polygynous
7. Family Settings (Nuclear/Extended)
8. Ethnic Group
9. Religion
10. Type of business
11. Highest level of education
12. State of origin
13. Local Government of Origin
14. Length of Stay in the business
15. Length of stay in the market
16. Position/Status in the market Union

Section B: History and purpose of the market Unions

Questions	Probes
What are your perceptions/views about apprenticeship/entrepreneurial behaviours in Onitsha markets?	Discuss your opinions on the historical trajectory of apprenticeship (Igba-boyi) in Onitsha markets and in Igbo land. What do you think has changed in the culture of apprenticeship today?

Narrate the history of the market Unions in Onitsha markets here	What was the first Onitsha market? When was it formed? When was the first market union formed? What was the initial name and what is the current name? Who were the founders of the market Union? What is the organizational structure of the market union? Is every line in the market represented in the leadership of the market union or what is the level of decentralization of leadership in Onitsha markets? How many market unions are in this market and why? What is the criterion for admission or what makes one a member of the Union? Is membership compulsory for all traders? Are there those that are exempted? How are the market leaders selected/appointed/elected? Do you have women as market leaders?

Purpose of the market Unions	Narrate the purpose of the market Unions Why was it formed? Itemize the objectives of the market Unions What are the activities of the market unions? Does the union contribute to development projects in the market? What are the social responsibilities and welfare programs of the market unions?
Funding market Unions in Onitsha	How are the market unions funded? How are the market unions maintained? Do you collect market tolls, taxes and fines? Does the government also collect tolls, taxes and fines from ndi-*Ọga*/*Umu Boyi*/customers? How are the market tolls managed, used and for what purposes? Do you collect security/utility (toilet/electricity/water) tolls from umu-boyi/ndi-*Ọga* and what is it used for?

Regulations of the market Union	What are the market rules and regulations that must be adhered to by umu-boyi/ndi-*Oga* in every shop?
	Are the market unions regulated internally or externally?
	Who are the regulators?
	What is the content of the regulation?
	Under which act are the market unions registered/formed?-CAC, CAMA, etc.
	What are the functions or contributions of the chamber of commerce to the market unions?
	Do you have constitution/bye laws?
	How is the constitution drafted and who drafts it?
	How sovereign is the constitution?
	What are the various dos and don'ts of the market?
	Are defaulters punished and what are the kinds of punishment?

Conflict and hazard management in the market	What is the conflict management procedure? How are interpersonal conflicts among traders managed? How is inter-union conflicts managed? Narrate the major Onitsha market hazards (market fires/theft/floods) and how it affected the market, traders (umu-boyi and ndi-*Ọga*). How do you manage market touts to avoid mal-handling of umu-boyi/ndi-*Ọga* and customers? Do you have rules against mal-handling of customers by umu-boyi/ndi-*Ọga* and market touts? What are the acceptable contents of a typical agreement between *Oga* and nwa-boyi? Which is preferred/practiced agreement pattern –formality and informality?

Membership and welfare of the members of the market union	Who is a member of the union?
	Are umu-boyi members of the market union?
	Do you have a welfare scheme operated by the union for your members? How is the welfare scheme run?
	Are families of dead/sick umu-boyi/*Ndi Oga* visited by the market leaders and what qualifies one to be visited? How much is given and what entitles one to receive such?
	Is it the responsibility of umu-boyi/*Ndi Oga* to clean up the market or do you pay cleaners to do that and how often do you clean up the market and in what days?
	Why do you pray on certain day of the week and is it compulsory for all umu-boyi/ndi-*Oga*? Is there a fine for umu-boyi/ndi-*Oga* for abstinence from market cleaning?

Apprenticeship regulations and principles	Do you have associations for umu-boyi? Does the union play a role in managing the misunderstandings between Ndi-*Oga* and Umu-boyi? Does the union supervise or oversight the activities of ndi-*Oga* on umu-boy? How much interference can you make during a fracas between ndi-*Oga* and umu-boyi? Narrate any typical incidence of misunderstanding between nwa-boyi and *Oga*. How was it resolved?
Solutions	What do you think should be done to improve Igba-boyi and izu-afia/itu-mgbere in Onitsha markets/Igbo land?

Appendix 7: Focus Group Discussion (FGD) Guide for Ndi-*Oga*

Introduction

Good morning/afternoon/evening. My name is
.... (Moderator; ask other research team members to introduce themselves). We are conducting a study in Onitsha market and it is focused on 'Apprenticeship and Entrepreneurship in Igbo land'. In this wise, we need to ask you a few questions and we also need you to answer them honestly to the best of your knowledge. Your responses will be strictly kept confidential and only for this survey.

- Interviewers to introduce themselves
- Why we are here, purpose of research
- Expectations from participants
- Confidentiality/anonymity
- Use of results
- Permission to use audio/ video tape

Identification

Specific Venue for FGD	
Name of Moderator(s)	
Date of FGD	
Time FGD Started	
Time FGD Ended	
Language of Discussion	English................................. Others (Specify)...........................

Idi Setting/Environment:
Give general description of:
The venue:
Sitting arrangement:
Weather condition:
Level of response:
Give other useful information:

Information about the Study Area
- Name of the Local Government Area
- Locality/community of FGD
- Name of the market
- Name of FGD group

Section A: Socio-Demographic Characteristics of Fgd Participants

1. Place of Residence)
2. Sex:
3. Age:
4. Actual age as at last birthday
5. Marital status
6. Form of marriage (for ever-married respondents)
   Monogamous/Polygynous
7. Family Settings (Nuclear/Extended)

8.Ethnic Group
9.Religion
10.Type of business
11.Highest level of education
12.State of origin
13.Local Government of Origin
14.Length of Stay in the business
15.Length of stay in the market
16.Position/Status in the market Union

Questions	Probes
What are your perceptions/views about apprenticeship/entrepreneurial behaviours in Onitsha markets?	Discuss your opinions on the historical trajectory of apprenticeship (Igba-boyi) in Onitsha markets and in Igbo land. What do you think has changed in the culture of apprenticeship today?
Concept clarifications	Why Igba-boyi and not *Umu-ahia?* Why Igba-boyi and not igba girl?

Recruitment and hiring	What are the recruitment processes for umu-boyi?
	Do you consider" umu-boyi" who are not related to you?
	Has there been any situation that warranted a sack of umu-boyi and what was the resultant effect?
	So far, were all "umu-boyi" that served you or you settled, doing well?
	Taking umu-boyi, do you see it as a lift from poverty eradication campaign in society?
Security/guarantee	Do you have any bond(s) to sign before taking "nwa-boyi?
	What is the content of the bond?
	Is there any collateral?
	Why does ndi-*Oga* keep umu-boyi at home to live with you instead of coming from elsewhere? Which of these practices is prevalently practiced among Ndi-*Oga* in Onitsha markets?
What are the peculiar nuances (business slangs) applied by apprentices (*Umu Boyi*) and masters (N*di Oga*) in their daily business transactions?	List them and please explain each
	What are their business significance?
	In what instances are they used?
	What are the benefits of the coded language?

What is an ideal duration for Iba-boti?	How long does it take for an average nwa-boyi to complete his training? What are the exceptions?
What trading/business areas are preferred in Onitsha markets?	What are the prominent areas/trades attractive to umu-boyi in Onitsha markets and what trades are less attractive to umu-boyi?
Challenges in managing umu-boyi	What are the major challenges of managing umu-boyi in Onitsha markets? Narrate one of your grueling experience with nwa-boyi How did you manage the conflicting experience with nwa-boyi?
Solutions	What do you think should be done to improve Igba-boyi and izu-afia/itu-mgbere in Onitsha markets/Igbo land?

Appendix 8: Focus Group Discussion (FGD) Guide for *Umu Boyi*

Introduction

Good morning/afternoon/evening. We are/my name is.. (Moderator; ask other research team members to introduce themselves). We are conducting a study in Onitsha market and it is focused on 'Apprenticeship and Entrepreneurship in Igbo land'. In this wise, we need to ask you a few questions and we also need you to answer them honestly to the best of your knowledge. Your responses will be strictly kept confidential and only for this survey.

• Interviewers to introduce themselves
• Why we are here, purpose of research
• Expectations from participants
• Confidentiality/anonymity

- Use of results
- Permission to use audio/ video tape

Identification

Specific Venue for FGD	
Name of Moderator(s)	
Date of FGD	
Time FGD Started	
Time FGD Ended	
Language of Discussion	English................................. Others (Specify)...........................

Idi Setting/Environment:

Give general description of:
The venue:
Sitting arrangement:
Weather condition:
Level of response:
Give other useful information:

Information about the Study Area

- Name of the Local Government Area
- Locality/community of FGD
- Name of the market
- Name of FGD group

Section A: Socio-Demographic Characteristics of Fgd Participants

1. Place of Residence)
2. Sex:
3. Age:

4. Actual age as at last birthday
5. Marital status
6. Form of marriage (for ever-married respondents)
   Monogamous/Polygynous
7. Family Settings (Nuclear/Extended)
8. Ethnic Group
9. Religion
10. Type of business
11. Highest level of education
12. State of origin
13. Local Government of Origin
14. Length of Stay in the business
15. Length of stay in the market
16. Position/Status in the market Union

Questions	Probes
What are your perceptions/views about apprenticeship/entrepreneurial behaviours in Onithsa markets?	Discuss your opinions. What do you thing has changed in the culture of apprenticeship today? What do you think should be done to improve Igba-boyi and izu-afia/itu-mgbere in Onitsha markets/Igbo land?
Do you have associations for junior umu-boyi?	When was it formed? How often do you meet? Do you consider yourself too young to engage in nwa-boyi activities?

What are the basic existing regulations for junior umu-boyi by ndi-*Ọga*/market leaders?	What are the rules you must adhere to while undergoing training under an *Oga*? Do you live with *Oga*? Do you combine your training with home chores? How often do you do this and how does it affect your training? Living with *Oga* and staying outside *Oga*'s home, which do you prefer and why?
What is the nature a typical agreement between umu-boyi and ndi-*Ọga*?	Is it oral or written? Who are the main negotiators? What are the rules and regulations set by a typical *Ọga* in Onitsha markets? What is the average length of stay for various trades by ndi-*Ọga* to umu-boi? What is the relationship with *Oga*'s wife/kids/relatives and how does it affect your training?
What are the peculiar nuances (business slangs) applied by apprentices (*Umu Boyi*) in their daily business transactions?	What are the coded/business slangs when a customer is there? What are the business slangs when your *Oga* is present and you don't want him understand what is going on? What are the coded languages/slangs used by umu-boyi while trying to convince a customer/during interactions/trading?

Do you have personal savings/funds?	Narrate how you get your savings-from *Oga* or from apiriko, theft? How and where do you save your money? Do you save with older apprentice in *Oga*'s shop? What are the challenges or implications of being found with money by *Oga*?
Leisure	How often do you go home to your people? Do you have to take permission from *Oga* before doing so? Do you as nwa-boyi go clubbing/ or hang out in relaxation centres? How do you fund your leisure? Do you have a girlfriend and is it allowed by *Oga*/madam? How do these leisure activities affect your nwa-boyi training?

Appendix 9: Key Informant Interview Guide

Introduction

Good morning/afternoon/evening. My name is
.... (Moderator; ask other research team members to introduce themselves). We are conducting a study in Onitsha market and it is focused on 'Apprenticeship and Entrepreneurship in Igbo land'. In this wise, we need to ask you a few questions and we also need you to answer them honestly to the best of your knowledge. Your responses will be strictly kept confidential and only for this survey.

- Interviewers to introduce themselves
- Why we are here, purpose of research
- Expectations from participants
- Confidentiality/anonymity
- Use of results
- Permission to use audio/ video tape

Section A: Socio-Demographic Characteristics of the Key Informant

1. Place of Residence)
2. Sex:

3.Age:

4. Actual age as at last birthday

5.Marital status

6.Form of marriage (for ever-married respondents) -
 Monogamous/Polygynous

7.Family Settings (Nuclear/Extended)

8.Ethnic Group

9.Religion

10.Type of business

11.Highest level of education

12.State of origin

13.Local Government of Origin

14.Length of Stay in the business

15.Length of stay in the market

16.Position/Status in the market Union

S/N	Questions	Probes
1.	Courtesies/Introduction	Tell me about yourself. Short history of how you started.
2.1.	Can we learn from you the reasons for *"Igba Boyi"* in the Igbo culture?	• Why do *Ndị Igbo* place so much value on apprenticeship? • Connections to an ancestral culture • An act of willingness or compulsion • If it is connected to one's success or failure in business • Is there a punishment for not taking on an apprentice? • Igbo world view of "Onye fe eze, eze eluo ya"

3. 2.	How is the "*Igba Boyi*" managed in Igbo culture?	• Are there specific criteria to meet before taking on an apprentice? • Terms of agreement • What happens when agreement is fulfilled and when it fails? • What are the contents of the curriculum? • Are there limits to what the apprentice should learn? • Is there a structure that stipulates what the apprentice learns at each point? • Is the process different when it involves a female?
3.	What are the peculiar nuances (business slangs) applied by apprentices (*Umu Boyi*) and masters (*Ndi Oga*) in their daily business transactions?	• List them and please explain each • What are their business significance? • In what instances are they used? • What are the benefits of the coded language?
4.4.	What influence is exerted by institutions in sustaining agreements and the learning process between the apprentice and the boss?	• Influence of family and clan, including spouse and children • Influence of community leadership • Influence of the market association and union • Influence of ex-apprentices under same master • Influence of religion and spirituality • Getting the government to pay part of the settlement fund in settlement of the apprentice • Constant reminder of the settlement time of the apprentice by the government

5. 5.	What are the failures and successes of the discussed institutions?	• The need to improve or the need to wipe away completely • Are there more institutions to carry along? • Are present institutions too informal or too formal? • What are the consequences for formality and informality?
6.6.	What specific issues are contained in the way the apprenticeship system is structured?	• What are the issues? • Are there suggestions to make it better, that is to be made more formal, if they think it is too informal or otherwise
7.7.	Give practical instances where the "*Igba Boyi*" system has contributed to developing the economy.	• What lessons are there that the government can take? • Are there tribes with similar systems? • Will the system be beneficial to Anambra's economy? • Will the system be beneficial to the South East? • How can the system be advanced into something national, and what roles can they play?
8. 8.	Why "*Igba Boyi*" and not "Igba Girl"?	• The traditional significance of the male in the context as against the female • Are there verifiable cases of women getting involved in apprenticeship? • Are women involved in leadership positions in the market? • Plans for the female gender

9. 9.	Are Onitsha Market traders involved in online business?	• Are they involved in drop-shipping (*Igba oso afia* online) • As vendors or owners
10.	Which social media outlets do you prefer and why?	•Instagram, why •Facebook, why •WhatsApp, why •Twitter, why •YouTube, why
11.	What are the challenges and dynamics of online businesses?	• Do you accept digital banking? • Do you accept PoS? • Do you accept money transfers? • If no, why not?
12.	What are the challenges facing the "*Igba Boyi*" system?	• Challenges from the *Nwa Boyi*/ *Ọga* (commitment, faithfulness) • Challenges from family and community institutions • Challenges from market institutions • Challenges from the government and the wider economy
13.	What plans can help surmount these challenges?	• Personal efforts • Family efforts • Community efforts • Union efforts • Government efforts, etc.

14.	How does the apprenticeship scheme contribute to wealth creation and employment generation?	• What do you intend to do after settlement? • Do you intend to have apprentices?
15.	How can the apprenticeship system be improved?	• Funding of the apprentices • Payment of stipends/allowances to apprentices • Adult education related to Business Management

Index

www.ingramcontent.com/pod-product-compliance
Lightning Source LLC
Chambersburg PA
CBHW042110220326

41598CB00071BA/7325